OKLAHOMA

The History of an American State

OKLAHOMA

The History of an American State

ELLEN SUE BLAKEY

Contributing Author
RITA GEIGER

CLAIRMONT PRESS
Selma, Alabama

THE AUTHOR

Ellen Sue Blakey is a writer and published author formerly from Tulsa. She has researched and written pictorial histories for several publishers. Mrs. Blakey has also written two published state histories. She was educated in the public schools of Oklahoma and the University of Tulsa.

CONTRIBUTING AUTHOR

Rita Geiger is the Director of Social Studies and Foreign Languages for the Norman Public Schools. She has taught in the Little Rock and Tulsa Public Schools and served as the Social Studies Specialist at the Oklahoma Department of Education prior to moving to Norman. She received a B.A. in history from the University of Arkansas and a M.Ed. in secondary administration from the University of Oklahoma.

SPECIAL CONSULTANT

Dr. Duane Kendall Hale, teacher, historian, former Project Development Specialist, American Indian Institute, University of Oklahoma.

CONTRIBUTOR

James Carl Fugate, teacher, historian, writer.

Editor in Chief: Ralph Holmes

Supervising Editor: Kathleen Conway

Associate Editor: Billie Holmes

Picture Research: Robin McDonald

Design: Robin McDonald

Maps: Carolyn Higginbotham

ISBN 1-56733-056-8   Examination Copy   Printed in U.S.A.

TO THE STUDENTS

HOW CAN A STATE THAT IS SO YOUNG HAVE such a strong sense of history? After all, Oklahoma only became a state at the beginning of the twentieth century. There are still people alive who remember those events, and the stories are still fresh in the memories of families. At the same time, the geographical area that includes Oklahoma is one of the oldest places on the continent. Compared to our ancient mountains—worn away with age and time—the Rocky Mountains are still young.

There is another emotion that is part of our heritage and that is hope—the promise of life. Oklahoma represented one of the last geographical frontiers—where individuals could create themselves anew.

For the native peoples who wandered the vast prairies, this region provided food, clothing, and shelter. The land might sometimes be harsh and dry, visited by tornadoes, drought, and periodic floods, but it teemed with plant and animal life. The displaced Indians saw it as a chance to start anew, hoping that this time the white men would honor their treaties. Some hoped the territory would become an Indian state. The white settlers saw it as a place of opportunity, where they could start fresh, begin families, grow fortunes. Black settlers saw it as a place to grow and rallied for a black state. The very diversity of hopes that surrounded it brought it an energy that few other states could match.

Youth and age—hope and opportunity—a land of both harshness and beauty, poverty and wealth—it is all part of the fabric of what it means to be an Oklahoman.

*Above: The Oklahoma State Museum of History at Oklahoma City. **Front cover:** This sculpture is part of the statehood monument in Guthrie and represents the joining of the Oklahoma and Indian territories. It has been superimposed on a beautiful Oklahoma sunset. **Page i:** An exhibit at the Oklahoma State Museum of History. **Page ii-iii:** A painting by George Catlin entitled* Comanche Village, Women Dressing Robes and Drying Meat *(1834-1835). **Page iv:** This sculpture of a cowboy on a bucking bronco stands in front of south steps of the State Capitol. **Back cover:** As Long as the Waters Flow, by Allan Houser, stands in front of the south steps of the State Capitol.*

CONTENTS

Top: Fort Washita at dusk. ***Above:*** *A Cherokee craftsman is making stone arrowheads at Tsa-La-Gi, the Cherokee Heritage Center at Tahlequah.*

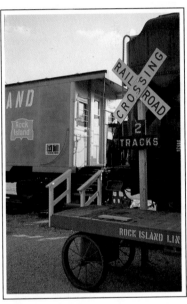

Top: *A small family farm in south-west Oklahoma in Grady County. Red rock outcroppings can be seen in the background.* ***Above:*** *The El Reno Rock Island Depot now houses a local museum.*

OKLAHOMA: WHERE VARIED LANDS AND PEOPLE MEET

IN OKLAHOMA, distinct geographies from the north, south, east, and west come together. Oklahoma's geography ranges from high plateaus to tallgrass prairies to forests to swamps. Because of this variety, the state supports many kinds of food crops and animals. From its earliest history, the state's geography has influenced the way its people have lived and worked.

The earliest inhabitants of the Great Plains were Native Americans. When the Europeans came, six or seven tribes lived in what would become Oklahoma. Initial contact between Europeans and Indians was peaceful and both groups benefited. The Indians, however, had no immunity to the diseases that the Europeans brought, and thousands died.

Oklahoma's first history was of the Indians who wandered the vast prairies of the region. Much of their history has been passed down from generation to generation orally. Native American heritage is an important part of the state's history. This young dancer at the Anadarko Indian Exposition carries on one of his tribe's traditions.

CHAPTER ONE

THE GEOGRAPHY OF OKLAHOMA

Oklahoma! Where the wind comes sweeping o'er the plain....
— from the musical *Oklahoma* by Rodgers & Hammerstein

GEOGRAPHY is the study of the physical features of the earth. But it is more than that, for it is also concerned with how the **environment** (surroundings) affects humans. Geography shapes the way people live: the jobs they do, the food they eat, the clothes they wear, and more.

Geography is also concerned with how people affect their surroundings. As people have expanded across the land, they have cleared forests; dammed rivers; introduced new species of insects, plants, and animals; and destroyed some native plants and animals. All these actions have had an impact on the land we call Oklahoma.

As people expanded across the prairie, the environment was changing. The native tall grasses (opposite page) have given way to wheat fields (below) in what was once open prairies.

LOCATION

Oklahoma's environment is affected by its location on the earth's surface. Oklahoma lies in the middle of the United States, in the middle of the land that separates the East from the West, the North from the South. Its geographical location is defined by its latitude and longitude. **Latitude** is the distance north or south of the equator; **longitude** is the distance east or west of the prime meridian, which is the arbitrary starting point at Greenwich, England. The latitude of Oklahoma's northern boundary (border) is the 37th parallel. The southern border angles southeast to 33° 35' north latitude. The western boundary of the state (excluding the Panhandle) is the 100th meridian. Most of the eastern boundary lies at 94° 29' west longitude.

The state is almost rectangular except for the *Panhandle,* the long extension of land that forms the northwest border of the state. The westernmost point of the Panhandle is at 103° west longitude. Old-timers claimed the state looked like a pot or pan, with the narrow western strip being the handle. Today, the state is sometimes referred to as the nation's largest meat cleaver.

About 1,224 square miles of Oklahoma are covered by water and over 10 million acres are covered by forest. Most of the state is part of a giant oval grassland that extends from Canada to Mexico. Known as the *Great Plains* (and, for many years, the "Great American Desert"), it

OKLAHOMA AND THE UNITED STATES

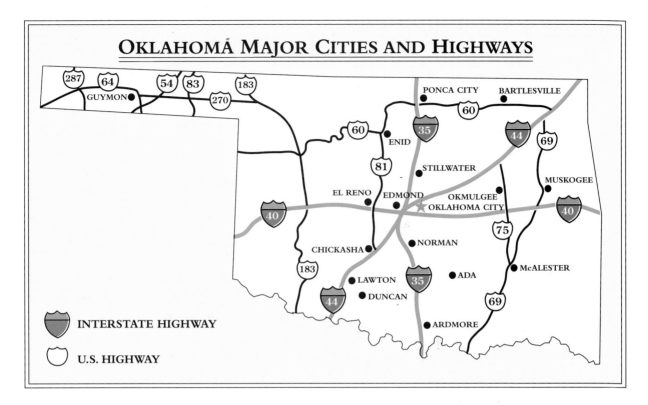

OKLAHOMA MAJOR CITIES AND HIGHWAYS

INTERSTATE HIGHWAY

U.S. HIGHWAY

acts as a barrier between the species of the eastern and western forest regions. Oklahoma City lies almost in the center of the state. It is about 450 miles north of the Gulf of Mexico and 950 miles south of Canada. It is an equal distance from both coasts—1,350 miles from San Francisco on the West Coast and from New York City on the East Coast.

The state is bordered on the west by Texas and New Mexico, on the north by Kansas and Colorado, on the east by Arkansas and Missouri, and on the south by Texas. Much of the southern border follows the Red River.

Oklahoma covers almost 70,000 square miles. It is 220 miles from the northern to the southern border and 400 miles from the eastern to the western border. This makes it the 20th largest state in total land area, larger than any of the states east of the Mississippi River except Minnesota. All six New England states combined (Maine, New Hampshire, Vermont, Massachusetts, Rhode Island, and Connecticut) are not as big as Oklahoma. It is even larger than many important countries of the world, including the Netherlands, Austria, Greece, Iceland, and England.

Do You Remember?

1. How do we measure geographical location?
2. What nickname was given to the Great Plains?
3. What states border Oklahoma on the north, south, east, and west?

REGIONS OF THE STATE

Our planet has been shaped by a number of forces. Those forces have affected the state's **topography** (physical features such as mountains or plateaus). Violent upheavals took place in Earth's crust. At one point, the ground split open and formed a basin (a deep sunken area) in what is now Oklahoma. This is now known as the Anadarko Basin. The Arbuckle and Wichita mountains rose up on either side. In between the two, deserts and shallow seas formed. In the Anadarko Basin, living things died, decayed, were compressed, and changed. This natural process resulted in the oil, gas, and coal deposits found in the state.

Additional upheavals, changes in the climate, volcanic eruptions, and **erosion** (the process of wearing away) of the ancient mountains created different regions. Oklahoma's **elevation** (its height above sea level) decreases from west to east. Today, the highest point in the state is Black Mesa (4,973 feet), which is located in the high, flat plain of the Panhandle. The lowest point—only 289 feet above sea level—is actually a mountain region along the Little River in the southeastern corner of the state.

Even early nomadic tribes viewed what is now Oklahoma as two different regions. Travelers headed west first encountered a rich land with fast-flowing streams, wooded areas, and plentiful game. But half-

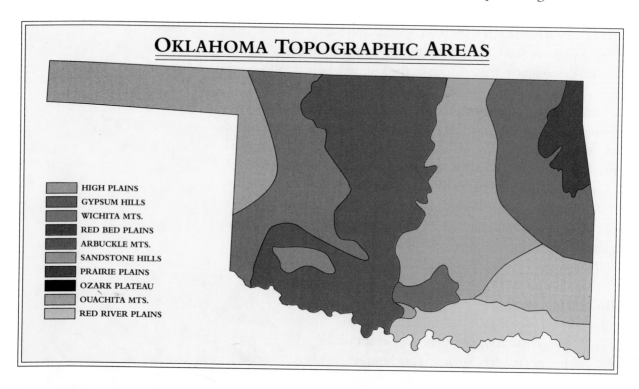

OKLAHOMA TOPOGRAPHIC AREAS

- HIGH PLAINS
- GYPSUM HILLS
- WICHITA MTS.
- RED BED PLAINS
- ARBUCKLE MTS.
- SANDSTONE HILLS
- PRAIRIE PLAINS
- OZARK PLATEAU
- OUACHITA MTS.
- RED RIVER PLAINS

way across, they encountered the Cross Timbers, a dense thicket of post oak and blackjack oak trees with wild grapevine and other underbrush. It was said a rider could not go through without getting scalped by tree limbs.

On the opposite side of the Cross Timbers, the Great Plains began. This was a land of open prairies and plains, with slow-moving streams and tall grasses that formed a thick sod. Buffalo, antelope, and prairie dogs ruled the arid (dry) and open spaces.

Today, scientists break Oklahoma into ten different geographic regions (areas where plants and wildlife are generally similar).

With a mountain being defined as any elevation over 2,000 feet, Oklahoma claims Cavanal Hill, near Poteau, as the "world's highest hill" with an elevation of 1,999 feet.

OZARK PLATEAU

The northeast corner of the state is part of the Ozark Plateau, which has many rich prairies as well as wooded areas. (A **plateau** is a high area with some level areas.) It includes the beautiful Boston Mountains and the Cookson Hills. Forests of post oak, blackjack oak, sycamore, sumac, cottonwood, and hickory cover the hills. White-tailed deer roam the creek and river bottoms. At one time, there were bear

Left: The Ozark Plateau, located in the northeast corner of the state, has many rich prairies and wooded areas. This scenic view is in Cherokee County. **Opposite page:** *The Prairie Plains once supported many cattle. Today the Prairie Plains region is Oklahoma's agricultural showplace.*

and smaller game—raccoon, opossum, skunk, beaver. Woodpeckers, passenger pigeons, and turkeys were once thick.

Prehistoric Indian tribes camped along the river bluffs in the caves and lived on the plentiful game, nuts, berries, and persimmons. When the eastern part of the state became the property of the Five Civilized Tribes, the rough landscape of the Cookson Hills was a favorite hideout for outlaws.

Miami is on the Ozark Plateau. The Illinois River, one of the last free-flowing rivers (without dams or channels) flows through the region. It is a popular stream for canoe and float trips, and conservation measures have done much to preserve it.

PRAIRIE PLAINS

To the west of the Ozark Plateau, the land forms the Prairie Plains. The prairie once supported many cattle, but civilization has changed it completely. Before barbed wire was available, Osage orange trees were planted as a living fence. They grew and harbored many types of birds and small animals.

Today the area is Oklahoma's agricultural showplace. The Arkansas River flows through the rich grassland. In the region's rich soil, farmers grow everything from strawberries to tomatoes.

Tulsa, the cultural center of the state, is in the Prairie Plains. In the smaller cities, towns, southern magnolia trees and azaleas grow next to tall northern pines.

The Prairie Plains once supported many cattle. Today the Prairie Plains region is now Oklahoma's agricultural showplace.

The Ouachita Mountains in the southeastern part of the state are a beautiful range of low mountains covered with a variety of hardwood and pine trees.

OUACHITA MOUNTAINS

The Ouachita Mountains region in the southeast is the roughest land in the state. The Ouachitas are a beautiful range of low mountains covered with shortleaf and loblolly pines, sweet gum, sycamore, pecan, and walnut trees. They are especially pretty in the fall along scenic Talimena Drive when the trees begin to turn different colors. The Ouachitas are actually part of a mountainous range in southwestern Arkansas. Several nearly parallel ridges run almost east and west. The major ridges include Winding Stair Mountains, Kiamichi Mountains, San Bois Mountains, Jack Fork, Buffalo, and Blue Bouncer.

In this region is the tallest peak in the state: Rich Mountain, which rises 2,900 feet above the plain. The largest publicly owned forest area in the state, the Ouachita National Forest, is here also. In the deep recesses of the forests, there are swamplike areas with palm-leaf-fan plants and tall trees covered with Spanish moss. The largest living tree in Oklahoma is east of Broken Bow in McCurtain County. This bald cypress tree is over 120 feet tall and has a circumference of over 43 feet; it may be 2,000 years old.

Like the Ozark Plateau, deer, bear, and mountain lion once roamed the area. Today, cattle and hogs graze on the hills, and the valleys are filled with farms. Atoka is one of the area's few towns.

RED RIVER PLAINS

Along the Red River below the Ouachita Mountains are the Red River Plains. Very low in elevation, the region has very rich soil. Indian tribes lived along the river banks, clearing land to grow corn, melons, squash, and pumpkins. Several tribes had permanent villages.

This area was once covered by ancient seas. Instead of rock or stone, the hills were covered with the fossils of tiny sea creatures. Sunfish and speckled catfish—some as tall as a man—swam in the rivers and streams. Largemouth, smallmouth, spotted, and white bass are native. Today, catfish—channel, blue, and flathead—still abound.

The state is on the Continental Central Flyway for migratory birds. In the fall, flocks of ducks and geese fly over making their way south. In the spring, they make their way back again. The Red River, like other streams, harbors mallards, herons, gulls, and coots. The Tishomingo National Wildlife Refuge provides resting areas for the migratory birds.

Marietta, Hugo, Durant, and Idabel are all in the Red River Plains.

Lake Texoma was formed by a dam on the Red River. Since the river is the boundary between Oklahoma and Texas, part of the lake is in each state, thus the name Texoma.

Above: Tulsa, the state's second largest city, is located in an oil-rich area along the Arkansas River in the northeastern part of the state. With the completion of the Arkansas River Navigation System, Tulsa is the nation's westernmost inland water port. The major portion of the Tulsa metropolitan area falls in the Prairie Plains, but with the eastern expansion many Tulsans live in the Sandstone Hills region. Opposite page: Turner Falls, located on Honey Creek, tumbles 77 feet into a natural swimming pool.

SANDSTONE HILLS

West of the Prairie Plains are the Sandstone Hills through which the Cross Timbers ran. Deer, bear, and mountain lion lived in the thicket, along with raccoon, skunk, opossum, and many smaller mammals.

Some of the most important oil fields in the world have been found in this area. Like most of Oklahoma, the Sandstone Hills region is still a **rural** (country) area, with small farms and ranches. Today, cedars and pines for the Christmas tree market are grown in some areas. Sapulpa, Wewoka, and McAlester are part of this region.

ARBUCKLE MOUNTAINS

The Arbuckles lie south of the Sandstone Hills and north of the Red River Plains. They are part of the oldest-known mountain system and are sometimes called one of the three "geological windows into our past." (The other two are the Grand Canyon and the Black Hills of South Dakota.) Limestone layers that once laid flat under the surface have faulted (tilted) and folded (turned sideways or at angles) and are now exposed. The rich limestone soil is one of the most fertile in the state, and it is good cattle country.

The Washita River, the principal western tributary of the Red River, forms a narrow canyon through the Arbuckle Mountains. On Honey Creek, the tallest waterfall in the state—Turner Falls (77 feet high)—tumbles into a natural swimming pool. Turner Falls Park is the oldest park in Oklahoma and one of the state's major tourist attractions. Indian tribes set up a popular spa at Sulphur Springs even before white settlers moved in. Ardmore is near the Arbuckles.

The orange-red, shale-and-clay soil of the Red Bed Plains is good grazing and farm land. Wheat grows well here and wheat fields such as this one in Logan County are a familiar sight in the region.

RED BED PLAINS

In the middle of the state, running north to south, are the Red Bed Plains. The land is slightly rolling, and cottonwoods, cedars, and willows grow along the streams. It is the beginning of the prairie lands, with tall waving grasses and thick roots that hold the soil. Some of today's "weeds" were originally native to the prairies and open lands. It was these grasses that fed large grazing animals such as the bison and whose seeds provided food for smaller animals such as prairie dogs. In the spring and summer, wildflowers abounded. Today, you can see

them in parks and recreation areas, along nature trails, beside county roads, and in highway wildflower plots.

The Great Salt Plains in Alfalfa County is a forty-square-mile basin with sand saturated by salt water. It was formed about 270 million years ago when a former sea dried up and became desert. Barium sulfate combined with quartz sand grains to form the rare "rose rocks." In some places, gypsum and salt in the soil are so concentrated that selenite crystals form. It is the only area in the world where these hourglass crystals are found. Golden eagles and bald eagles winter in the Great Salt Plains National Wildlife Refuge.

The orange-red, shale-and-clay soil is good grazing and farm land. In the northern part of the region, wheat grows well; in the southern part, cotton grows best.

Oklahoma City, the state capital, is in the Red Bed Plains area.

Mount Scott (2,464 feet high) can be seen on the right in this panoramic view of the Wichita Mountains. The Wichita Mountains are some of the oldest on this planet.

WICHITA MOUNTAINS

The Wichita Mountains are in the middle of the southern part of the Red Bed Plains. Formed when ancient lavaflows were pushed up, they may have been among the first mountains to rise out of the waters that covered the entire planet. As they eroded, large masses of granite were exposed. The best known peak is Mount Scott (2,464 feet high), named by Captain Randolph Marcy in 1852. The nearby Quartz Mountains mark the valley of the north fork of the Red River.

The Wichita Forest Reserve covers about 240,000 acres. One half of the reserve is commercial forest and produces products for industry. The Wichita Mountain Wildlife Refuge near Lawton has large herds of buffalo, elk, and longhorn cattle. Lawton and the Fort Sill army base have created a growing urban region.

GYPSUM HILLS

West of the Red Bed Plains is the Gypsum Hills, broken lines of hills running somewhat north to south. Rich land for raising crops or grazing cattle threads between the formations. The gypsum buttes west of Orienta were nicknamed the "Glass Mountains" because the gypsum reflected so much light.

The springs and caves along the bluffs once made it a favorite spot of the Indians. Woodward and Clinton are both in this area.

The "Glass Mountains," located in the Gypsum Hills west of Orienta, got their nickname because the gypsum reflected so much light.

HIGH PLAINS

The High Plains consists of the Panhandle and land along the western border. The Black Mesa area in this region was formed between 1 and 2 million years ago when a volcano erupted in what is now northwest New Mexico. It spewed out a snakelike stream of lava 70 feet thick that hardened into basalt and formed the top of the mesa. The softer soil around the mesa eventually eroded after long years of exposure to wind and water.

Because the area is very dry, only a few hardy grasses and grains can be grown here. Mesquite and cedar do grow in this area. The pronghorn antelope, the fastest of all American mammals, is found in the upper Panhandle. Guymon is one of the few towns on the High Plains.

The Black Mesa, in the northwest corner of the Panhandle, is the highest point in Oklahoma at 4,973 feet.

Do You Remember?
1. Name the ten geographic regions of the state.
2. Which mountains may have been the first to rise out of the seas that covered the earth?
3. How was Black Mesa formed?

UNDERGROUND WONDERS

For people who are fascinated by caves, Oklahoma is a wonderland with its more than 800 caves. Alabaster Cave (opposite page) is the state's largest cave and the world's largest alabaster cave with one room that is over 80 feet high. Outlaw Belle Starr (above) was said to have hidden out in Robbers Cave in northern Latimer County.

Oklahoma has about eight hundred caves. There are limestone caves in the eastern part of the state and gypsum caves in the west. Caves are also found on the plateaus and along rock ledges above rivers and streams. Many of these caves were used as shelters by prehistoric people. Rock-ledge caves in the northeast along Saline Creek were temporary homes for small bands of hunters as early as 7,500 years ago (or about 5500 B.C.). In the Panhandle, caves near the Cimarron River were inhabited 4,000 years ago. Many artifacts have been found in the shallow Basketmaker Caves in the rough canyons of Cimarron County. People lived in caves in the Osage Hills not far from present-day Tulsa 3,000 years ago. Because these shelters are protected from the elements, they often still bear wall paintings by their early inhabitants.

Wild Woman Cave, northwest of Springer and Ardmore in the Arbuckles, is the state's largest cave. Alabaster Caverns, also known as Bat Caves, is located in Alabaster Caverns State Park in Woodward County. It is the world's largest alabaster cave, with one room that is over 80 feet high. Cottonwoods Cave in the hills near Tahlequah is about one mile long. Nearby in the Cookson Hills is Crystal Cave. Robbers Cave in northern Latimer County takes its name from Civil War legends. Deserters from both the Union and the Confederate armies supposedly used the caves in this semiwilderness area as hideouts. Outlaw Belle Starr was said to have hidden out there.

Caves are also a rich biological resource. The life-forms within the cave create their own *ecosystem*. In an ecosystem, a threat to any one life-form endangers all life-forms. As more people explore caves, the delicate balance of the cave ecosystem is disturbed. For example, enlarging or changing the opening of a bat cave can change the air currents and air temperature. This can be uncomfortable for the bats. If they leave, the other life-forms in the cave may die.

In 1988, the Oklahoma chapter of the Nature Conservancy purchased Twin Cave near Jay in Delaware County. It is a maternity cave for the gray bat, which is now protected under the Endangered Species Act. The limestone aquatic cave is a half-mile long and contains a room about 80 feet by 160 feet and 30 feet high. The Conservancy also set up the state's first cavefish preserve in Twin Cave. The endangered Ozark cavefish is a small eyeless fish about 1.5 inches long. About one hundred live in the cave.

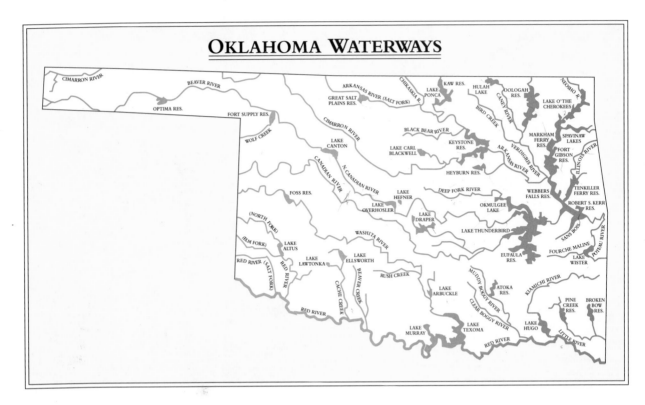

OKLAHOMA WATERWAYS

The Poteau River (opposite page, above) and the Cimarron River (opposite page, below) are both tributaries of the Arkansas River. The Poteau is the only river in the state that flows northward.

WATERWAYS

Water and waterways are crucial to development. But few of the five hundred rivers and creeks in Oklahoma provide reliable year-round travel. Spring flooding has always alternated with summer **drought** (a long period without rainfall).

Conditions were made worse because water in some streams was so salty it was undrinkable. About 3,600 tons of salt from natural sources flow into the Red River each year. Water in the Cimarron and Salt Fork rivers is so salty that cattle will not drink it.

RIVERS

Oklahoma's main rivers are the Arkansas, the Canadian, and the Red, all of which have many **tributaries** (streams or rivers that flow into larger rivers). Some are fed by springs from underground water sources.

Most Oklahoma rivers are so shallow that early travelers described them as "a mile wide but only six inches deep." Indians and French traders used canoes and **pirogues** (hollowed-out logs) to travel up the rivers. Later explorers and settlers used keelboats and flatboats to haul in troops and supplies and haul out pelts. But steamers and paddle-wheelers, boats big enough to handle passengers and supplies for settlements, had more difficulty. They snagged on driftwood, went aground

on shifting sandbars, and could not make the snakelike turns in the rivers. Paddlewheelers traveled up the Red and the Arkansas rivers usually as far as Fort Gibson, but the trip could take months because of floods and drought.

The principal eastern river is the Arkansas River, which begins in the Rocky Mountains of Colorado. Its chief tributaries are the Cimarron and Canadian from the west; the Verdigris, Grand, and Illinois from the north and northeast; and the Poteau from the south. The Poteau is the only river in the state that flows north. The Grand, Verdigris, and Arkansas rivers join at the edge of the Ozarks. This area is known as the Three Forks and was one of the first places in the state to be settled.

The Red River begins in the High Plains of New Mexico, flows east across the Texas Panhandle, and forms part of the border between Texas and Oklahoma. Sometimes the channel of the river shifts when sandbars and debris build up. In 1895, Texas filed a court case against the United States to determine which of two branches on the upper course of the Red River was the main channel. After six years and fifty volumes of testimony, the U.S. Supreme Court held that the south branch, known as Prairie Dog Town Fork, was the true main channel and thus the true southern border of the territory. This area now includes Jackson, Harmon, Greer, and part of Beckham counties.

Lake Murray is one of the many man-made lakes in the state. Oklahoma has no natural lakes, but it does have more man-made lakes than any other state.

LAKES

Although many states have natural lakes, Oklahoma has none. It does have more man-made lakes than any other state. There are 29 major federal reservoirs, ranging from 890 to 102,500 acres. There are another 1,777 smaller lakes of at least ten acres. Because there are so many lakes, the state actually has 2,000 more miles of shoreline than the Atlantic and the Gulf coasts combined.

These lakes, and the dams that created them, provide hydroelectric power, navigation, irrigation, recreation, flood control, and drinking water for nearby cities and towns. The largest is Eufaula Lake, which covers 102,500 acres and is the fifteenth largest man-made lake in the United States. It has 600 miles of shoreline and twenty park areas, including Fountainhead Resort. Lake Texoma, famous for its striped bass fishing, is the principal lake in the south-central part of the state. It is 57 miles long east to west. There are over fifty-five recreational areas at Lake Texoma with 93,000 acres for public hunting.

Grand Lake of the Cherokees is in the far northeastern corner of the state. It is the first in a chain of reservoirs along the Neosho-Grand River. It covers 59,000 acres and has 1,300 miles of shoreline. Fort Gibson Lake and Dam is on the Neosho-Grand River about five miles northeast of Fort Gibson. The area is considered one of the best retirement areas in the United States because of the mild climate, beautiful surroundings, recreational facilities, and closeness to Tulsa.

Do You Remember?

1. Name Oklahoma's three main rivers.
2. What caused the border dispute between Oklahoma and Texas in the 1890s?
3. Give three reasons why dams are built.

CLIMATE

Climate is the average weather of a region over a period of time. Weather changes constantly, but the climate of a place stays much the same from decade to decade. Climate controls what is grown, what kinds of houses are built, what kinds of clothes are worn, even what types of sports are played. Oklahoma's climate is temperate—generally pleasant and sunny—and supports a wide variety of **flora** (plants) and **fauna** (animals).

The average year-round temperature is about 60°F (Fahrenheit). That makes Oklahoma a good place to grow crops, to enjoy the outdoors, and to conduct any business that needs good weather. But temperatures and rainfall vary greatly, depending upon the area. This is because Oklahoma is truly a crossroads on the continent. It is on the northern edge of what is sometimes referred to as "the Sunbelt." But unlike many Sunbelt states, it has four distinct seasons. The cold winds of northern Canada often come south to meet the warm winds from the Gulf of Mexico. The dry air coming from the Rockies often clashes with the moist air drifting over from western Mississippi. Will Rogers once said about Oklahoma, "If you don't like the weather, just wait a minute, it'll change." He was right.

Generally, Oklahoma receives between 26 and 40 inches of rain annually. But the western part of the state has had as little as 7 inches of rain in a year (although it averages 18), and the eastern part has recorded as much as 119 inches (but averages 56). The extremes create trouble for the farmers. Too little rain and too high temperatures burn up crops; sudden drops in temperature freeze tender spring plants.

During the summer (May through early September), the temperature ranges from 80°-100°F. Winter drops temperatures to 20°-30°F. This means that temperatures can vary as much as 80 degrees in a year. And the changes are not just seasonal. There can be a drop in temperature of 30 degrees in a matter of hours.

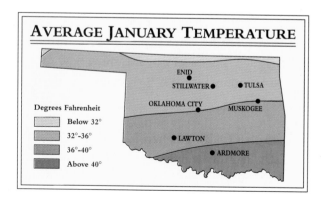

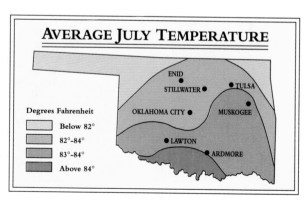

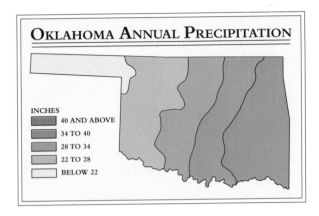

OKLAHOMA ANNUAL PRECIPITATION

INCHES
- 40 AND ABOVE
- 34 TO 40
- 28 TO 34
- 22 TO 28
- BELOW 22

July and August are the two hottest months in Oklahoma. It is not uncommon for summer temperatures to stay in the 90s and 100s in August. The hottest temperature ever recorded in the state was 120°F on July 26, 1934, at Tishomingo. Altus and Alva also have reached temperatures of 120°F.

January is the coldest month. The state's coldest temperature on record was -20°F, recorded February 13, 1905, at Vinita and again on January 18, 1930, at Watts. Below-zero cold often turns rain into sleet that covers everything with ice. On the western side of the state, snow is rare; the eastern side may see one or two snows during a winter.

TORNADOES

Tornadoes usually occur when different kinds of weather meet, such as the clash of low-pressure and high-pressure systems or the clash of dry air from the western Rockies and moist air from the East. Tornado winds blow counterclockwise and can reach speeds of up to 500 miles an hour—the highest winds of any natural weather. Most tornadoes occur from March through June, but they can occur as late as September. When the funnel-shaped storm drops from the clouds, it damages or destroys almost everything in its path. It can demolish buildings or drive pieces of straw through telephone poles.

The Great Plains has sometimes been called "tornado alley." Kansas, Oklahoma, and Texas are particularly well known for tornadoes. Oklahoma City was hit by twenty-six tornadoes between 1951 and 1980—more than any other city. For many years, the only warning was the heavy cloud buildups. People who lived in rural areas often relied on their animals, which seemed to have a sixth sense about approaching storms. Today, almost every town has a siren that warns of an approaching storm. The most sophisticated storm-warning system in the United States is the National Severe Storms Laboratory in Norman. The system uses very sensitive Doppler radar to follow storms. Doppler can detect mesacyclones, small storms that often precede tornadoes by about twenty minutes. The radar can also show how strong the wind is within the storm and which way it is rotating.

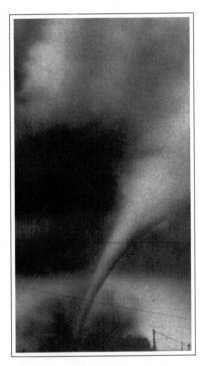

Many tornadoes strike Oklahoma each year. Oklahoma City was hit by twenty-six tornadoes between 1951 and 1980—more than any other city.

Do You Remember?
1. What type of climate does Oklahoma have?
2. Which part of the state has the largest average annual rainfall?
3. What is the coldest month?

HOW GEOGRAPHY AFFECTED DEVELOPMENT

Geography greatly influenced the history and development of the people of Oklahoma. The lack of rainfall and the extreme hot and cold temperatures made it impossible to grow many of the crops found in the southeastern United States or along either coast. This limited agricultural growth at first. But the grassy plains were perfect for grazing, and settlers turned the areas into cattle ranches that supported America's growing love for beef.

There were no large river "highways" in Oklahoma. This lack of a natural transportation system helped create independent communities that often knew little and cared little about other parts of the state. This **sectionalism** (an allegiance to local interests) increased after the forced resettlement of the southeastern Indian tribes, the land gifts to other Indian tribes, and the land runs on what had been Indian land.

Natural resources have had a major influence on the state's history and development. Oklahoma was one of the last areas of so-called unclaimed land, and the land itself was a prize. The rich grasslands in the central and western parts of the state were free feedlots for cattle and the basis of the state's ranches. Most of the early farmers were less prosperous because the virgin soil had to be broken and the native plants removed before crops were productive.

In the eastern regions, lumber was an early cash crop. Today, 23 percent of the state is still covered with forest. The cut timber is usually shipped out of state to be made into furniture and houses.

Rich clay deposits gave rise to a small brick industry and pottery making. The fine sands were the raw materials for a glass industry that flourished until the 1990s. Salt was recovered from the rivers and streams and was the major preservative for food.

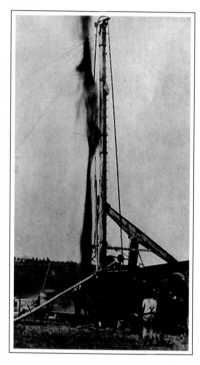

Above: The presence of oil wells such as this first well in Blackwell Field (1913), are a reminder of one of Oklahoma's most important natural resources. Left: The Cherokee harvested timber, another of the state's natural resources, in the late 1800s.

Kudzu was planted to stop erosion, but soon became an even bigger problem. The vine is poisonous to cattle and spreads rapidly, often taking over pastures.

When oil was discovered around the turn of the century, it changed the entire face of Oklahoma. Oil created new jobs—carpenters to build rigs, blacksmiths to forge machinery, haulers and handlers, petroleum geologists to search for oil, and bankers and businessmen to finance new wells. From this land that once seemed to be no bargain, an international industry was born.

HOW PEOPLE AFFECT GEOGRAPHY

Over the years, people have affected Oklahoma's geography in both good and bad ways. Conditions that almost devastated the state have led to a national conservation awareness. America's hunting grounds—the vast grassland prairies—are gone. The tallgrass prairies are gone too, covered by farms, towns, roads, and highways. In the 1920s, the natural vegetation and trees were cut down. When high winds hit the drought-stricken land in the 1930s, there was nothing to stop the topsoil from blowing away. To make matters worse, the slightest moisture created gullies and **washouts** (places where soft soils have been eroded) that can still be seen today. Much of Oklahoma's farmland became a wasteland that has taken years to rebuild.

In some rural areas, runoffs from feedlots and oil well wastes have polluted the ground water. It is now illegal to dump raw sewage into streams, once a common practice across the country.

Soil pollution has been a problem in Oklahoma. In many places, oil naturally seeped from the land. It was also often stored in open earth pits, from which it seeped back into the soil. Although such practices are no longer accepted, their effects haunt us. In a few Oklahoma towns, chemicals from old industrial dumps have leaked into basements and yards of nearby houses. Federal laws under the Environmental Protection Agency are addressing such conditions.

In most communities, garbage is hauled away and burned or buried in landfills. Burning garbage in incinerators or open dumps can create air pollution. If not properly done, buried garbage can cause offensive odors, pollute surface water, and contaminate ground water. Governments now require more sanitary landfills and better methods of disposal of toxic wastes. People recycle more glass, metals, and plastics to keep down the amount of garbage. Many retail grocers and businesses have waste disposal collection sites on or near their stores.

The low number of industrial plants has kept air pollution down in Oklahoma. The state has had the natural problem of escaping gas around the oil fields. This wasted precious resources and added to air pollution. Despite motor vehicle pollution control devices, motor ve-

hicles remain one of the biggest polluters. Pollutants from exhaust systems can be trapped near the ground during certain weather conditions. This results in ozone alerts.

Like so many others, Oklahomans hunted and trapped some species of birds and animals into extinction. The buffalo were slaughtered by buffalo hunters. Passenger pigeons whose numbers once blackened the sky are extinct. Conservation awareness has helped to return the bald eagle and the wild turkey to our land. Longhorn cattle have been reintroduced into some areas, and buffalo roam the Tallgrass Prairie Preserve. Companies that cut trees for commercial use, such as Weyerhauser, have replanting and seeding programs to replenish the cut areas of the forests.

But our flora and fauna face another problem—new species that, once introduced, take over. The South American cattle egret, which migrated north or may have been introduced with cattle shipped in from Mexico, has increased so much that it has driven many other waterfowl away from the ponds. The kudzu vine, a late introduction from the South, is poisonous to cattle. It is invasive (tending to spread), often taking over pastures and killing herds.

New species are not always beneficial. The South American cattle egret has been so prolific that it has driven many other waterfowl away from ponds.

Do You Remember?
1. How did the lack of a "natural" transportation system affect the settlement and development of Oklahoma?
2. What mineral has had the most effect upon Oklahoma?
3. What are the major causes of air pollution?

CHAPTER REVIEW

Summary

Geography has affected the development of Oklahoma. It has determined the climate and the natural resources available. It has also influenced the way the land was settled and the way people made their living. The shape of the land affected transportation routes, and the wealth of the state is largely the product of its geology and geography.

At the same time, people have affected their environment. They have lowered the quality of air and water and endangered many plants and animals. Fortunately, people have become aware of the dangers to the environment and are taking steps to do something about them.

Reviewing People, Places, and Things

Define, identify, or explain the importance of the following.

1. Anadarko Basin
2. climate
3. drought
4. elevation
5. environment
6. erosion
7. fauna
8. flora
9. Great Plains
10. latitude
11. longitude
12. pirogue
13. plateau
14. rural
15. sectionalism
16. topography
17. tornado
18. tributary
19. washout

Understanding the Facts

1. What were the Cross Timbers?
2. Which region is the state's most important agricultural area?
3. How did the depth of the state's rivers and streams affect settlement and development?
4. What is significant about Oklahoma's lakes?
5. Why is the weather so changeable in Oklahoma? What influences that change?
6. Why did sectionalism develop in the state?

Developing Critical Thinking

1. What do you think geography is, and why do you think the study of geography is important in understanding history?
2. Describe how people have influenced plant or animal life in your area.
3. What is the significance of the wilderness areas to society today?
4. Why are laws important to protect wildlife?

Using Your Skills

1. Using a globe, locate England and Oklahoma. Compare the sizes of these two areas. The lines running across the globe are called latitude lines. At what latitude is England?
2. Get a copy of an outline map of Oklahoma. With a color pencil or pen, trace the state's major rivers. Where are the longest rivers? What rivers do they flow into? How far is the southeast corner of Oklahoma from the Gulf of Mexico?
3. On a map of Oklahoma, locate the following cities: Oklahoma City, Tulsa, Muskogee, Lawton, Ardmore, Guymon. Locate the county that touches four states. (It is the only county in the United States that does.)

Special Projects

1. Collect samples of tree leaves in the area in which you live or at a nearby park. Identify the leaves with a guide book from your library. Which of these trees are native to Oklahoma?

Which have been imported from other parts of the country? Are any of these trees used by businesses in Oklahoma?

2. Research the National Severe Storms Laboratory in Norman. How does it help other parts of the country as well as Oklahoma?

3. Make a list of nature trails near your town. Visit one and give a report on it.

4. Make a chart with examples or pictures of Oklahoma's wild grasses.

Building Skills: Using Your Textbook

Making proper use of your textbook is different than reading a novel or science fiction story. Your textbook could be thought of as having two parts: the narrative, which tells the story of the state of Oklahoma, and the visual information, which makes the narrative come alive. The visual information—cartoons, illustrations, maps, charts, and captions (copy printed below or alongside illustrations)—is an important part of the study of Oklahoma.

The narrative is divided into sections by headings. The major headings are large, bold, centered, and underlined. Lower-level headings are set in boldface capital letters and boldface italics. These headings are like an outline of the chapter. They help you organize the information in the chapter. If you scan these headings before you begin to read, you may better understand the overall plan of the chapter.

Look over the terms, people, and places listed in the "Chapter Preview" before you begin reading. If you do not know the meaning of some of the terms, look them up in a dictionary. The terms appear in boldface type the first time they appear in the narrative. They are usually defined there, or you may be able to determine the meanings by the way they are used in the sentences.

Once you begin to read the chapter, read the narrative straight through without interruption. Answer the questions labeled "Do You Remember?" This will help you check your understanding of what you have read. After you have read the narrative, study the photographs and their captions and any maps and charts in the chapter. Photographs help you visualize some of the people, places, and events in the chapter. The captions may point out the important information about the photograph or provide more information about the subject or events. Maps and charts help you summarize information provided in the chapter.

Try the following activities to help you make use of these suggestions:

1. Prepare an outline of Chapter 1 using the headings in the chapter.

2. Look at the maps in the chapter. What information do the maps provide? How do they help you understand the narrative?

3. Find two captions that provide information not in the narrative. What is that information?

4. Find and list the photographs that illustrate the geographic region in which you live. Choose your favorite photograph from the list. Why did you choose that photograph?

Be sure to follow these suggestions as you read the rest of the chapters in the textbook.

Sooner Trivia

. . . The geographic center of Oklahoma is 8 miles north of Oklahoma City.

. . . During the depression of the 1930s, many families survived by operating stills in the Cookson Hills. Their "home brew" was sold in nearby Tulsa and Fort Smith.

. . . The oldest fossilized tree ever documented, the Callixylon tree, comes from the Ouachita Mountains area. Over 350 million years old, it can be seen on the campus of East Central University in Ada.

. . . The state's largest spring is the Spring of Everlasting Waters in Roman Nose Park where water flows from the red shale bluffs at 600 gallons per minute.

. . . There are more than 144 native trees in Oklahoma—more kinds of trees than grow on the continent of Europe.

CHAPTER TWO

NATIVE AMERICANS OF THE PLAINS

. . . a people who are honest without laws, who have no jails and no poorhouses.

—George Catlin, painter, 1832

THOUSANDS OF YEARS AGO, there were people in what is now Oklahoma. They left no written records, but their remains are found in many parts of the state. Because of the state's varied geography and climate, the Indian **tribes** (groups of people who share a common ancestry) were also varied—from ancient wandering hunters to woodland hunter-gatherers. Some came from the north and west while others came from the south and east. They found a land that could be both bountiful and harsh, where much of their life was spent in survival.

ORIGINS

No one knows where the Indians' **ancestors** (people from whom one is descended) came from. But many scholars believe that they came in small groups from Asia during the last ice age—perhaps as long as 20,000 years ago.

Part of the North American continent was covered by glaciers, and the sea level was three hundred feet lower. Geologists believe there were times when North America and Asia were joined in the northeastern area, along what is now the Bering Strait. That area, called *Beringia*, included the eastern tip of Siberia and much of Alaska. The warm ocean

George Catlin's paintings provide us with a view of the life of the early Plains Indians. This painting is entitled Buffalo Chase with Bows and Arrows.

CHAPTER PREVIEW

Terms: tribe, ancestor, nomad, prehistoric culture, archaeologist, artifact, atlatl, agriculture, maize, barter, totem, shaman, polygamy, jerky, pemmican

People: Paleo Indians, Archaic Indians, Plains Woodland Indians, Plains Village Indians, Caddo, Apache, Wichita, Quapaw, Tawakoni, Waco, Kaw, Tonkawa

Places: Beringia, Cooperton site, Domebo site, Kenton sites, Afton Spring

This painting depicts early Asians crossing the land bridge between Asia and Alaska during one of the Ice Ages. These Asians are thought to be the ancestors of Native Americans.

currents kept Beringia free of ice. During the long summer months, Beringia was covered with animal and plant life, which supported the **nomads** (wanderers). When the planet began to warm, glaciers melted, causing the oceans to rise. Beringia began to sink beneath the waters. Some of the nomads returned to what is now Siberia; others made their way south, following the wildlife. It probably took these early Native Americans almost 1,000 years to make their way as far south as the Rio Grande.

PREHISTORIC CULTURES

Prehistoric cultures are those groups or communities that existed before recorded (written) history. What we know about the prehistoric cultures on the North American continent (those existing before the Europeans arrived) comes from traditions and the work of scientists. **Archaeologists** are scientists who study what is left behind by ancient peoples. They carefully investigate old camping grounds, graves, and other sites where these people may have camped or lived. From **artifacts**—bits of stone, bone, pottery, tools, cave paintings, weavings, skeletons, items buried with the dead, and leftover trash—they piece together a picture of how the people lived.

The time frames given in the following sections are estimates. The cultures appear to have overlapped, often by a thousand or more years.

PALEO INDIANS

About 20,000 years ago, the climate in what is now Oklahoma was warmer and wetter. Summers were cool and moist, winters cold. There were grasslands and forests. Mammoth and camels roamed the plains as did giant bison at least 6 feet tall and weighing over 2,000 pounds. There were mammoths that stood 18 feet at the shoulder.

In 1961, in Kiowa County at what is known as the Cooperton site, the bones of a young male Columbian mammoth were found. Unusual rocks were also found there, the kind that are not natural to the area. Perhaps a small band of prehistoric hunters happened upon a young mammoth that had died of natural causes. They may have cracked the animal's bones with the rocks to get to the marrow—much as some African tribes still do with elephant bones.

Also in 1961, near Stecker, a mammoth tusk was found sticking out of a stream bank. At the site, now called the Domebo site, the skeleton of a young female Imperial mammoth, 14 feet high at the shoulder, was unearthed. Two spear points and other fragments were also found. Tests revealed that the skeleton was about 11,000 years old.

Using only stone-tipped weapons and their ingenuity, Paleo Indians killed mammoth—as in the picture—and other large animals.

Above: *The Paleo Indian projectile point was known as the Clovis point. These have been found at several sites where mammoth were killed and butchered.* **Opposite page above:** *The Folsom point appeared during the time of the Archaic Indians. How does the Folsom point differ from the Clovis point? How are they alike?* **Opposite page below:** *Woodland Indians often disguised themselves as deer while hunting. This disguise enabled them to get among the deer to kill them.*

The earliest primitive hunters are sometimes called Paleo Indians, or Old Hunters. (The word *paleo* means very old.) They lived 20,000 to 10,000 years ago, although some scientists say they may still have lived here around 5000 B.C. They were a courageous people who followed the large animals on which they depended for food and clothing. Since they had little more than spears for weapons, they had to get close to their prey. Some may have disguised themselves under animal pelts (skins). Some may have driven animals into natural traps or stampeded them over cliffs.

One of the few artifacts of these prehistoric people is the spear points they used. The *Clovis point* could kill a large animal or cause a severe wound. The spear point was made by chipping away or applying pressure to create a rough fluted (ruffled) edge. It took hours of very careful work to make a point. Too much pressure or striking could crack or break the stone, which meant that the craftsman would have to start over again. The making of such spear points is known as *flint knapping* and requires great skill even today.

ARCHAIC INDIANS

About 10,000 years ago, the large animals (mammoth, elephant, horse, and camel) died out on the Great Plains. No one knows for sure why that happened. The climate may have changed, or the Indians may have hunted the animals to extinction. In any case, deer, turkey, rabbit, raccoon, squirrel, wolf, coyote, antelope, and prairie dog began to roam the area. King of all was the bison, forerunner of today's buffalo.

The people who began to hunt across the plains had also changed. These Archaic (old) Indians had new tools and weapons. They began to craft a finer spear point—the *Folsom point*—that was smaller, with more delicate fluting, and a flat center section that could be easily attached to a shaft. One of the most important new weapons was the **atlatl**, a simple shaft or handle with weights used to throw spears or darts with more force. The hunter placed a short spear or dart in the atlatl, drew back, and then held onto the atlatl while throwing the dart or spear forward. With the atlatl, the hunter could kill from a greater distance—and have more time to escape if the spear missed.

The Archaic Indians also wove nets from plant fibers, and used them to snare small animals and to carry household goods. Strings were woven from plant roots to use with stone hooks for fishing or hanging food. The women shaped *metates* (shallow basins or bowls) out of sandstone or rock. Seeds, nuts, berries, and grains were placed in the metates and pounded with rock to crack the grains for cooking or to make flour. Grains and flours were stored in baskets made from reeds and plants.

It appears that many of these people traveled the region on a regular route, taking shelter in the natural caves, bluffs, and ledges along the rivers and living in tipis on the open grasslands.

The Kenton Sites

Near the Cimarron River in the Panhandle, the dry sheltered caves have kept the story of one native people for almost 4,000 years. The people who lived there were both hunters and gatherers. They may have been Anasazi, ancestors of the Navajo to the west. It is more likely that they traded with the Anasazi and learned many of their crafts. They ate buffalo, deer, antelope, elk, jack rabbit, cottontail, coyote, wildcat, badger, eagle, wild turkey, and even mice and rats when necessary. They gathered wild seeds and acorns. They mixed ground piñon nuts with wild plums and berries to make round flat cakes similar to a doughnut (with a hole in the middle). They knew how to start a fire with a wood drill. They dressed deer skins and made bags from prairie dog skins. They made string and cord from plant fibers and sandals of yucca leaves, some with cedar bark padding for soles. They made fancy coiled baskets, colorful mats, rugs, and cradles.

Afton points were discovered at the bottom of Afton Spring. Compare the Afton point with the earlier Clovis and Folsom points.

Afton Spring

In 1900, a group of archaeologists from the Smithsonian Institution in Washington, D.C., traveled to Afton to investigate a discovery by Dr. D. H. Harper. Dr. Harper had found 150 stone-age artifacts of flint and bone in the gravel at the bottom of the Afton Spring. There were also bushels of arrowheads, spear points, knives, and blades from later periods and the bones of mastodons with teeth as long as 18 inches. Among the items brought up from the bottom of the spring were arrowheads with points that had a distinct leaflike shape and were made from an unusual kind of flint. The Smithsonian representatives had never seen any like them. They named the arrowhead the *Afton point.* Since then, the Afton point has been found in nearby Arkansas, Missouri, and Kansas.

Do You Remember?

1. Many scholars believe that the earliest people came to America from which continent?
2. How were the first Indians able to get across the Bering Sea to North America?
3. How do we know about prehistoric cultures?
4. How did early prehistoric Indians manage to kill the giant animals in this region with only primitive weapons?

PLAINS WOODLAND INDIANS

About 7,500 years ago, small bands of woodland hunters wandered along Saline Creek, where the salt-water springs attracted white-tailed deer. They took shelter in the caves and under rock outcroppings. Many caves in the Osage Hills not far from Tulsa are decorated with painted figures on the rock walls. There are human figures and dancers playing on bone whistles. Flint from the nearby mountains provided material for weapons. From their remains and artifacts, archaeologists have determined that these people were about average height and generally in good health. Men lived to be about thirty-five; women lived slightly less.

Sometime in this period, there were two major improvements in weapons: the bow and arrow and the ax. The bow and arrow allowed the hunters to shoot prey from a long distance—and to aim more than one time without exposing themselves to danger. The bow and arrow quickly spread across the Plains and the continent. The ax was both a weapon and a tool. With it, the Indians could cut down trees to make houses. Poles were driven into the ground to form a framework, which was covered with grass thatch, cane matting, bark, or skin.

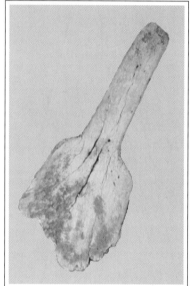

PLAINS VILLAGE INDIANS

About 2000 B.C., the once-nomadic tribes began to build villages along the river valleys. These tribes are called Plains Village Indians, and archaeologists believe they lived in the area as late as 950 A.D. Remains of their villages have been found along the Washita River (in today's Garvin and Grady counties), the North Fork of the Red River, and the Beaver River in the Panhandle.

These people adapted to whatever conditions existed and ate whatever was available—wolf, badger, coyote, raccoon, beaver, lynx, opossum, quail, rabbit, squirrel, wild turkey, duck, crow, fish, mussels, turtle, even an occasional skunk. **Agriculture** (farming) became important. Women planted small gardens with corn, beans, squash, pumpkins, and sunflowers. They tended the gardens with hoes made from stone or from bison bones fastened to wood handles. They stored grain and dried foods in underground pits.

The tribes built houses with walls and a framework of wooden posts, usually red cedar. In the High Plains and the Panhandle where there were fewer trees and grasses, similar groups built houses of sandstone slabs set on edge in the ground. Some of these groups appear to have been in the area around 1450 A.D.

Archaeologists can tell a great deal about an ancient people by the artifacts they leave behind. Archaeological digs in Oklahoma (top left) have discovered items such as the pottery (top right) and the bone tool (above).

THE MOUNDBUILDERS

About 900 A.D., a very different group moved into the east-central part of what is now Oklahoma. The Caddo may have been a branch of the Cahokian moundbuilders from the Mississippi River valley, who were originally from the Ohio River valley. Some scholars believe they were linked to Indian tribes in Mexico; others say they were descendants of the Plains Woodland Indians who adopted the customs of the southeastern moundbuilders.

The mounds of the Caddo may have been built following ancient custom or to protect against floods. At least eleven sites have been found in Oklahoma. The Williams Mound, two miles from where Fourche Maline Creek meets the Poteau River, is 5 feet high and 150 feet wide. The mound contains the earliest human burials discovered in Oklahoma. One mound contained the skeletons of 122 humans and 3 dogs.

It appears that the Caddo had one large village around which people built smaller villages. The central buildings in each village may have been used to keep track of solar events and seasons. Houses were constructed around a row of posts set upright in the ground. Small saplings or cane were set between the posts and covered with mud mixed with grass; the roof was thatched with grass.

Spiro Mounds State Archaeological Park is the most important mound-builder site in Oklahoma. The temple mound (top) was built in stages between 950 and 1250 A.D. Artifacts from Spiro Mounds include an engraved shell gorget (above center), two copper masks (above), and a large stone effigy pipe (right).

Both men and women painted themselves with red, gray, black, white, and green paints that they made from clays and ground-up rocks. Men wore flat-top or burr haircuts, although some had Mohawk-type crests or beaded forelocks. They wore breechcloths with sashes and moccasins. Unlike men from the other tribes of the area, the men were very fine craftsmen who worked in stone, shell, and copper. They carved fancy tobacco pipes of people and animals out of stone. They were great traders, and some artifacts probably came from the West Coast and Mexico.

The women wore simple fringed skirts and aprons. Even the poorer members of the clan wore jewelry, fashioning it from rope and string, pearls and seeds. Women tended the crops, the house, and the children. They grew corn and gathered wild persimmons, hickory nuts, acorns, pecans, and an edible yellow fruit known as maypop. They wove cloth and lace using rabbit hair, wild hemp, wild cotton, and nettles. They made blankets of buffalo hair, rabbit fur, and feathers.

For almost a thousand years, the Caddo were an important group on the Plains. Yet neither the Caddo nor the Plains Village Indians ever heard of the wheel, iron, or the horse. Sometime in the early 1500s, they simply disappeared.

Do You Remember?

1. Name two major improvements in tools made during the Plains period that changed hunting and shelter.
2. What Oklahoma group built mounds?

Top: *Craig Mound, a burial mound at Spiro Mounds State Archaeological Park, is actually four connected mounds built over several hundred years. It is 300 feet long, 115 feet wide, and 33 feet high. Over 725 people were buried here.*
Above: *This re-creation of a house shows Spiro building techniques.*

EARLY PLAINS INDIANS

Today, Oklahoma has more resident Indian tribes than any other state, somewhere between fifty-five and seventy, depending on how they are grouped. Thirty-seven tribes are officially recognized by the U.S. government. According to the 1990 census, there were more than 252,000 Native Americans in the state. That is about 8 percent of the state's population. Only Alaska and New Mexico list a larger percentage of their population as Native American. But in actual numbers, Oklahoma has more Indian people than any other state—more than California, Arizona, or New Mexico.

The idea of the "noble savage" pure in heart and deed was partly true. The Indians were attuned to nature because it was their only means of survival. They understood how to conserve the area's natural resources by using only what they needed. On the other hand, they were not saints, any more than were the Europeans they met. A tribe was likely to be at war with at least one other tribe at any given time. Captives or slaves resulting from tribal skirmishes were common among all tribes.

Christopher Columbus came to the New World in 1492. Explorers from other countries followed, but for the next fifty years, Spain considered itself the owner of the vast uncharted area to the north of Mexico. In 1540, Antonio de Mendoza, viceroy of Mexico, approved an expedition to find the golden cities rumored to be somewhere to the north. The next year, Francisco Vasquez de Coronado set out with 2,100 nobles, soldiers, and servants and 7,000 head of livestock in search of treasure. They wandered around the Central Plains for more than two months, trying to find any sign of civilization. They finally stumbled on a few poor tribes of Indians.

From the records of the various European explorers, it appears that perhaps only six or seven general groups of Native Americans lived in this area. Coronado identified the Apache tribe living along the Canadian River region of Texas and western Oklahoma in *rancherías* or tribal villages, "a gentle people...faithful in their friendships." Coronado's scribe Pedro de Castañada was astonished that they "neither plant nor harvest maize [but] subsist entirely on cattle [buffalo],...load their dogs like beasts of burden,...and...have no permanent residence anywhere." Although the buffalo provided their main food, shelter, and clothing, the Apache were not above eating rabbit, antelope, or prairie dog.

This Wichita lodge, painted by George Catlin, with its roof of thatched prairie grass, provided shelter from the elements. The lodge is a reminder of how Native Americans used the natural resources around them.

In the valley of the Red River near the Wichita Mountains, Coronado found the twin villages of what were probably Wichita. Their ancient legends said they had come from the north and east, perhaps south-central Missouri, but they had claimed the valley as their homeland for as long as anyone could remember. Coronado called them "truthful and honorable." When Spaniard Juan de Oñate (who later founded the colony of New Mexico) explored western Oklahoma in 1601, he too met the Wichita, calling them "fair and open." French explorer Robert Cavelier de La Salle, who explored the area in 1682, encountered the Wichita along the Canadian River and noted that they were honest, liberal, and happy.

Tradition said the Wichita were the first people west of the Mississippi to cultivate **maize** (corn). They were well-known traders and bartered dried pumpkin, maize, and other crops with hunter tribes such as the Apache. (To **barter** means to trade one item for another.) The Apache in turn bartered with the southwestern Zuni and Navajo. Thus agriculture and crafts spread across the continent.

While Coronado made his way north, Hernando de Soto made his way up from Florida and wintered near what is now Fort Smith, Arkansas. De Soto came into contact with several tribes. The Caddo had villages along the Red River in Arkansas and northeastern Texas and were principally farmers. The Quapaw were living near the Arkansas

Indian City, USA has seven re-created villages of the Plains Indians. On the opposite page is a view of the interior of a Wichita house. Pictured above is the Caddo village.

The Apache were nomads and did not build permanent structures. They built sweat lodges (foreground) and wickiups, and when they were ready to move on they abandoned them. The sweat lodge was much like today's sauna. It also had religious significance. The wickiup was a small hut built of branches. What present-day shelter would compare to the wickiup?

River and were still there when French explorers Louis Jolliet and Father Jacques Marquette came down the Arkansas River in 1673. De Soto probably also met the Tawakoni and the Waco, allied tribes who both lived along the Arkansas River. The Tawakoni lived in dome-shaped huts made from clay and reeds or in tents. In autumn, they abandoned their villages to hunt buffalo and returned in spring to sow Indian corn, beans, and other seeds. They put up tobacco in twists which they flattened between large stones.

In 1542, Spanish monks found the Kaw not far from where Coronado had found the Wichita. Originally from the north, the Kaw were a warlike people who lived mainly by hunting buffalo and growing a few small crops. French explorer Bernard de La Harpe mentioned the Kaw when he was exploring the area near present-day Haskell in 1719. He also mentioned parties of Osage, Natsoo, and Nacodoches. Coronado had met the Tonkawa in Texas. They were a fierce, warlike, nomadic tribe who were principally hunters. But La Harpe mentioned them as one of the "roving nations" in the upper Red River region.

Do You Remember?

1. Who were the first European explorers that recorded meeting the Indians?
2. Name six tribes that early European explorers encountered in the Oklahoma area.

BELIEF SYSTEMS

Although the Indians belonged to different tribes and spoke different languages, they had many common beliefs. All tribes believed in many gods and spirits that affected people on Earth. They believed that they must cleanse themselves inside and out to purify their spirits. They believed in an afterlife where brave warriors and faithful women were rewarded, where cowards and thieves were punished.

A Wichita Indian performs an Eagle Dance. An Eagle Dance, which lasted all day, was performed to lead a young man into manhood.

This burial platform at Indian City provides insight into the burial practices of the nomadic Indian tribes. The body was placed on the platform and the person's favorite items such as spears and shield were hung nearby. The platform served two purposes: it raised the body closer to the Upper World, and it kept the body away from predators.

To all Plains tribes, life was sacred. The Indians greeted the day with personal prayers of thanks for life. They prayed first to the creator-spirit and then to mother earth, from which all plants and animals received breath. If they had personal **totems** (an animal or bird whose spirit guided them), they prayed to them also.

The Indians' history and beliefs were passed down by spoken word, usually by the keepers-of-knowledge, those people whom whites called **shaman** or medicine men or medicine women. These oral tales often attributed supernatural powers and spirits to clever animals. Animals often created Earth and helped to create the human race. In the Plains Indians' legends, buffalo, coyote, and bear often played important roles.

According to traditional Indian thinking, there was no such thing as religion because the word suggested that the sacred was separate from ordinary life. To the Indians, everything had a spirit. These supernatural forces helped them to do all things well—hunt, farm, raise children, and even fight when needed. They believed that all things were tied together and part of a whole. Man was not more important than animal or plant or Earth; they were all partners and equal. Harmony existed when people lived in accord with the natural world. Even when they killed an animal, they said a prayer of respect to the animal spirit for giving its own life to help the Indians. Certain rituals were performed on special occasions (passage into adulthood, birth, death) or seasons

HOW COYOTE BROUGHT DEATH TO THE LAND

The most common of the animal spirits in all Native American tribes was Coyote, an animal that was respected for its cunning and ability to survive in all climates. Coyote often played a part in the creation of Earth. According to a Caddo legend, he was also responsible for bringing death to the land.

In ancient days, men and animals lived forever. One winter, the snow was long and famine threatened. Coyote, who liked to make trouble, began to grumble. "If the old would die," he said, "there would be plenty to eat." The Great Spirit called a meeting to prove to Coyote how bad that suggestion was. All the Indians and animals assembled at the sacred rock to discuss the matter.

Coyote pretended that he had not meant to harm anyone. If the Indian would shoot a hole in heaven with his arrows, the arrows could be joined together and the dead could move to the heavens for a time and return when there was enough food. Everyone approved, and the Great Spirit opened a door in the sacred rock and loosed death.

Before long, weeping could be heard everywhere. Night after night, the people watched the sky hoping the dead would return. But deep in his lair, Coyote sharpened his teeth. Late one night, he crept out and gnawed the arrows in two. When the Great Spirit saw what had happened, he was angry. "You must leave our midst as punishment," he said. "We were patient, hoping you would mend your ways. Now you are banished to the prairie where you will live alone forever."

And that is why the coyote sits on the prairie alone at night, yelping at the sky.

(planting, harvest) or to mark important events (beginning a hunt or war).

George Catlin, an American painter who traveled the West in the 1830s, admired the Indian way of life, their generosity, and their sense of right and wrong. "I love a people who are honest without laws, who have no jails and no poorhouses," he wrote. "I love a people who keep the Commandments without ever having read them or heard them preached, who never take the name of God in vain, and who are free from religious animosities."

Above: A Comanche lodge made of buffalo skins was painted by George Catlin. **Opposite page:** *This portrait of Wah-Chee Tee, wife of Chief Clermont (Osage), and child was painted by George Catlin in 1836.*

HOW NATIVE AMERICANS LIVED

The people of the Plains believed they dwelled along the center of Earth and lived by the cycle of the seasons. To them, life was a series of circles within circles—the tipi and the immediate family; beyond that, the extended family and the camp circle; beyond that, the tribe; and beyond that, the larger band or clan to which the particular tribe belonged and which was allied with other tribes. Thus, the Indians could travel a good distance and know that they would be able to find help and friends.

The Indian worked for the common good of the group, and the rights of others were important. A person who killed another member of the tribe was ostracized (banished or excluded from the group) if not required to forfeit her or his own life in return. The Indians held their parents and older tribal members in great esteem. The men respected

This winter tipi at Indian City is sheltered from wind and snow by the brush fence around it.

the work of their wives and loved their children, who were rarely punished. When the men received a windfall—success on the hunting ground or the battlefield—it was promptly given away or shared with the others, knowing that they too would receive in their turn. Respect for life carried over into the Indians' general moral principles. Honesty reigned above all; a liar faced dire consequences.

Marriages were permitted between related tribes. **Polygamy** (having more than one wife) was tolerated; any man could have more than one wife if he could afford the added expense. In tribes where many men had been lost in battle, this practice reduced the number of widows. The two wives shared the work and thus lightened labor. Children were a blessing. A boy would be able to care for his parents in old age; a girl was a potential source of income, for she could be bartered when she became marriageable. Babies were wrapped in cradleboards, which could be strapped to a mother's back, leaving her hands free. The board could also stand against a tree or shelter while the mother worked.

The men were warriors and hunters, and they spent their days learning how to do both well. Experienced men taught the young boys the skills of war and weaponry. They maintained camp government and saw to it that no one went hungry or cold. There were specific duties for those who held positions of importance, such as the chief, the medicine man, and the camp crier; each did his part to take care of the tribe's needs. In summer, they sought out the buffalo (the main source of food); in winter they told stories to the children, played games, and fashioned new weapons and ceremonial regalia.

The women were the keepers of the shelter. Some maintained a fixed shelter of mud and grass, bark, or poles. Almost all tribes used a tipi when moving. The tipi was usually 14-15 feet in diameter, large enough to house an average family. A woman could set it up in as little as 15 minutes and strip it down in as little as 3 minutes. In winter, a brush fence around the tipi sheltered it from wind and snow. In summer, the sides were rolled up to catch breezes.

The Apache appear to have relied on animals, mainly buffalo, for food. But in most tribes, women also tended small gardens. It was a woman's duty to keep her household well clothed and fed. In spring, she planted her garden; in summer, she gathered wild roots and berries. Autumn was the busy season; she cleaned the hides brought in from the hunt, prepared **jerky** (dried meat) and **pemmican** (dried meat mixed with berries and fat) for the winter, and dried late fruits and vegetables. In winter, she sewed new clothes and moccasins from skins, repaired the old, worked new skins, and made thread from sinew.

It was said of an industrious woman that she knew how to use everything from the buffalo except the bellow of the calf.

Young girls quickly learned these skills from the women in the family and, even at a young age, helped gather wood and prepare food. Preparing food took a good part of the day. Meats were eaten raw (particularly fresh buffalo liver and tongue), dried, roasted over open fires, or boiled in water. Corn was ground into meal for use in breads or soups. When prepared with lye made from wood ashes, the corn became *hominy*, which was cooked and then made into a soup or a drink. Pumpkins and squash were baked or dried for use in stews. Those tribes that lived in the wooded areas had more variety. Bear yielded meat as well as fat for cooking and flavoring. Deer, antelope, and elk provided meat and skins for clothing. Nuts could be eaten raw or ground into meal. Fish were baked in coals or fried; turtles were made into soup. Squirrel was fried or stewed; turkey, duck, and small birds were usually roasted. Wild honey stolen from a bee tree was a treat; but milkweed blossoms were also used as a sweetener.

The Indians believed that plants were gifts from the Great Spirit to be used for food and healing. Greens were eaten raw or cooked in soups or stews. Among the most popular were wild garlic, wild onion, milkweed, pigweed, cattails, and pokeweed. Sassafras, sumac, and honey locust were used for tonics or teas.

Many wildflowers and plants were used by medicine men and women as natural healing substances. About 170 different plants used by Native Americans have been recognized as having actual medicinal value. Digitalis, a heart medicine, is derived from the foxglove plant. Aspirin was originally developed from willow bark, which Indians boiled as a tea to stop pain. Bee balm and butterfly milkweed were commonly used for bronchial problems, colds, and sore throats. Mint was boiled and made into a drink to cure nausea. Black-eyed susan root tea was used as a healing lotion for sores and snakebite. Prickly pear was boiled to make a tea and also used as a wash to ease headaches and eye troubles. Yarrow tea cured colds. Soaproot made a good shampoo and prevented dandruff. The black powder-like spores of puff ball mushrooms were used to stop bleeding.

Many wildflowers and plants such as black-eyed susans were used as natural healing substances. Black-eyed susan root tea was used as a healing lotion for sores and snakebite.

Do You Remember?

1. Why was the buffalo so important to Indians?
2. How did children learn the skills they would need to succeed in adult life?
3. What were the Indians' principal foods?
4. Why did Indians consider plants sacred?

CHAPTER REVIEW

Paleo culture	Archaic culture	Plains Woodland culture	Plains Village culture	Mound-builder culture	Historic period begins
20,000-10,000 B.C.	10,000-2,500 B.C.	7000-1800 B.C.	2000 B.C.-1450 A.D.	900 A.D.- 1500 A.D.	1541 A.D.

At the Same Time

4000 B.C.   New stone age began in Europe

3500 B.C.   Bronze Age began in Asia and Europe

2700 B.C.   First large Egyptian pyramid was built

1400 B.C.   Iron Age began

Summary

Native Americans have lived in the Great Plains area for about 20,000 years. Before the Europeans arrived, they had developed three distinct cultures that we now call Paleo, Archaic, and Plains.

When Europeans arrived, there were only about six or seven tribes living in the area that is now Oklahoma. These tribes were traders who bartered for goods with other tribes. Mostly they lived off the land, using plants and animals of all kinds. The most important animal to the Plains Indians was the buffalo, which provided food, clothing, and shelter.

Reviewing People, Places, and Things

Define, identify, or explain the importance of the following.

1. agriculture
2. ancestor
3. archaeologist
4. Archaic Indians
5. artifact
6. atlatl
7. barter
8. jerky
9. maize
10. nomad
11. Paleo Indians
12. pemmican
13. Plains Indians
14. polygamy
15. prehistoric culture
16. shaman
17. totem
18. tribe

Understanding the Facts

1. Where is the Bering Strait? What is its importance in relation to early Native Americans?
2. How did the Old Hunter Indians live?
3. Indians did not have written languages. How were their beliefs and histories passed from one generation to the next?
4. What affect did bartering have upon the lives of Indian tribes?
5. Explain the importance of the circle to Indian life.

Developing Critical Thinking

1. How did changes in climate affect the migration of early peoples from one part of the world to another?
2. How can archaeologists tell anything about a past culture by studying bits of old tools and bones? Why is an archaeologist's work impor-

tant in understanding our culture and other cultures?

3. How did the Indians' use of natural resources for food, shelter, and clothing differ from how people use natural resources today?

Using Your Skills

1. Locate the early Plains tribes on a map of Oklahoma. Where were the tribes located when the Spanish explorers found them? When the French explorers came later? How did geography affect their location? What problems did the land cause for each tribe? What advantages did the land provide for the tribes?

2. Pretend you are an archaeologist in the year 3000 A.D. digging in an old landfill in Oklahoma. Name ten items you would be likely to find dating from 1900. Name ten items you would be likely to find from 1990. Would you know what they were or how they were used?

Special Projects

1. Because they did not speak the same language, members of different Native American tribes used sign language to communicate. Sign language is still used by people who cannot hear or who do not speak the same language. Develop a short story to present to your class; devise signs with your hands to represent the major people, places, and things described in your story.

2. Using the library, find out more information about what happened to the buffalo and what is being done to preserve it today.

Building Skills: Finding the Main Idea

When you read about a topic, don't try to remember every detail. Identifying the main idea of a paragraph will help you organize information and remember more of what you read.

The main idea of a whole paragraph is often stated in the first sentence of the paragraph, although it may also appear in the second or third sentence. The other sentences in the paragraph provide supporting details. The main idea of the following paragraph is stated in the first sentence. The other sentences in the paragraph provide the supporting details.

The early Plains Indians tribes appear to represent three of the basic language families. The Apache came from the Athapascan language family. Quapaw were Siouan. Both of these families were from the north. The Caddo, Tawakoni, Wichita, and Waco were from the Caddoan family, which came from the south and east.

What are some of the details provided by the other sentences? You are correct if you answered the names of the language groups, the names of the tribes included in each language group, and where each language group lived.

Do you think it is necessary to remember all the details in the paragraph? If not, which are most important? You can probably remember the names of the three language groups and where the tribes in each language group lived, but it would be difficult to remember which tribes belonged to each group. It is not necessary to remember all details, but try to pick out the major fact from a paragraph.

Read the last paragraph on page 46 and answer the following questions.

1. What is the main idea of the paragraph?
2. Which sentence in the paragraph states the main idea?
3. Which sentences provide supporting details?
4. What story provides an example?

Sooner Trivia

. . . Archaeologists who have reconstructed and tried the atlatl have found that a man can pierce a 4-inch target at 40 yards.

. . . In 1935, the Pocola Mining Company began digging into the Spiro Mound. People who understood the value of the buried treasures came in long touring cars at night and bargained for the best pieces.

CHAPTER THREE

THE HAND OF EUROPE

I am the first to admit that I was so eager to find land that I did not trust my own senses, so I called for Pedro Gutierrez...and asked him to watch for the light. After a few moments, he too saw it...[Sanchez] saw nothing, nor did any other member of the crew....At two hours after midnight, the Pinta fired a cannon, my prearranged signal for the sighting of land. I now believe that the light I saw earlier was a sign from God.
— Log of Christopher Columbus, October 11, 1492

THE DISCOVERY OF THE AMERICAS was led by the Vikings of Scandinavia. But the Vikings did not explore or exploit the continent. That was left to France, Holland, Portugal, Spain, and Great Britain, which competed for new trade routes that they hoped would open up the way to the Orient and result in vast riches for the winners.

With the self-confidence that was a part of European history, these nations dismissed the Native Americans as savages without religion or culture. Thus they allowed, and sometimes encouraged, the destruction of the Indians' rich cultural heritage.

Opposite page: Christopher Columbus spent many years trying to convince European monarchs to back his search for a westward water route to the Orient. Above: Queen Isabella of Spain agreed to finance Columbus's search for a water route to the Orient. Right: Columbus landing in the New World.

For centuries, France, Spain, England, and Portugal had traded with Asia. Trade routes led through the Middle East and overland to the Orient (eastern Asia), a land whose civilizations produced such treasures as Oriental silk, perfumes, drugs, gold, jewels, dyes, tea, and spices (including pepper, cinnamon, nutmeg, and cloves). The cost of such goods was high because of the dangers of transporting them back to Europe. **Middlemen** (traders who buy goods from producers and sell them to other traders or consumers) faced thieves on land, storms at sea, ships that sank, spoilage, dishonest dealers, pack animals that died, wars between countries along the way, and a host of other potential disasters. If another trader had arrived at the same destination a few weeks earlier, the trader might have a hard time selling goods and breaking even. All these factors kept costs high. Everyone—traders and the **aristocracy** (ruling class) of Europe—agreed that a shorter route was needed to bring prices down.

During the early 1400s, Prince Henry the Navigator of Portugal sent ships south along the western coast of Africa in an unsuccessful search for an eastern passage to the Indian Ocean. In 1477, the *Travels of Marco Polo* was published, leading many Europeans to believe that China's riches could be reached by ship. The riches of the East Indies, Polo said, were "something wonderful, whether in gold or precious stones, or in all manner of spicery." Ten years later, in 1488, Bartholomew Díaz rounded the southern tip of Africa at the Cape of Good Hope. Portugal now had control of the southern route. The other nations had no other way to go but west.

For years, Christopher Columbus, an Italian sea captain, had been trying to finance just such a trip. Like other experienced navigators, Columbus believed Earth was round. But he had guessed that the distance from Portugal to Japan was less than 3,000 miles. (It was really 12,000 miles.) He also believed that there was no land mass in between. He had approached the **monarchs** (kings and queens) of France, Portugal, and England to get support for a westward **expedition** (a journey for a specific purpose, such as exploration). Finally, he struck a deal with Queen Isabella and King Ferdinand of Spain, who agreed to finance the expedition.

On August 3, 1492, Columbus set sail from Palos, Spain, with three ships: the *Pinta*, the *Niña*, and the *Santa Maria*. On October 12, he landed on one of the islands of the Bahamas, which he named San Salvador. Believing he was off the coast of India, Columbus called the gentle natives *Indians*. "They do not kill or capture others and are without

THE COMING OF THE VIKINGS

The engraving (below) shows Lief Ericsson landing at Vinland in 1000 A.D. The inscription on the mountainside (left) at Heavener-Runestone State Park may have been made by survivors of the lost Viking ship in 1017.

There had been constant turmoil in Europe from the time that Rome had conquered Britain. About 750 A.D., a daring group of Norwegian warriors—the Vikings—began to raid nearby countries by sea. By 840 A.D., they controlled the Atlantic Ocean. In 874, the Vikings set up a permanent colony in Iceland, and in 986, a colony on Greenland. From there, Leif Ericsson sailed west in 1000 A.D. to a land he called *Vinland*, today's Newfoundland. Unfriendly natives sent them packing.

About eight years later, Thorfinn Karlselfni led four Viking ships to the east coast of North America to set up a colony. Something went wrong, and they decided to return to Norway. One ship reached Greenland; another made it to Ireland. A third was infested with ship worms and sank. The fourth was never heard from again.

According to legend, on board the lost craft was Karlselfni. One legend has it that the ship made its way south, sailed around Florida into the Gulf of Mexico, and then turned north into the Mississippi River. One of the tributaries of the Mississippi River is the Arkansas River, and one of its tributaries is the Poteau River. A mile from the river is Poteau Mountain (near today's Heavener). On the mountainside are eight strange figures carved on a great sandstone slab. The Choctaw Indians, who discovered the stone in 1830, considered it ancient and sacred. But no one knew what the symbols meant.

In 1967, Alf Monge, a retired Army cryptographer (one who deciphers secret codes), saw the symbols. Monge had been born in Norway, and his hobby was medieval Norse church calendars. With this special knowledge, he translated the marks: "November 11, 1012 A.D." Monge translated a stone on Terry Hill as "November 11, 1017, St. Martin's Day." A stone near Shawnee was dated November 24, 1024. If these dates are accurate, they may be the marks of the lost Viking ship.

Above: In 1519 Hernando Cortés landed in what is now Mexico and conquered the Aztec Indians.

Opposite page top: Hearing of the wealth of the Incas in Peru, Francisco Pizarro set out for the western coast of South America. In 1535 in the Andes, Pizarro defeated the Incas. During his attacks on the Incas, he captured the Inca prince Atahualpa. After the Incas paid a ransom of a roomful of gold, Pizarro had the prince baptized and then strangled. Opposite page bottom: Francisco Vasquez de Coronado set out northward from Mexico in 1540 in search of riches. His expedition finally reached the Central Plains.

out weapons," he wrote. He assured the Queen that they would make good Christian subjects and good slaves. He saw cotton, sweet potatoes, maize, tobacco, and pines from which to build ships. When he could not find gold or precious stones or pearls, he praised the land. "It is certain, Lords and Princes, that where there are such lands, there must be an infinite quantity of profitable things."

Columbus made four voyages to the western hemisphere (1492, 1493, 1498, 1502). In his later voyages, he explored the coasts of Central and South America, discovering Puerto Rico, Jamaica, and the Virgin Islands. When he died in 1506, he had not found the vast stores of gold and spices that he still believed were close at hand. What he had done was pave the way for others.

John Cabot, another Italian sea captain, sailed west under an English flag and in 1497 landed in Newfoundland. Vasco da Gama sailed around Africa in 1498. He reached India and opened the ocean trade route to the Orient. The next year, Amerigo Vespucci, an Italian navigator, sailed along the coast of South America. His journals caught the attention of a mapmaker who, in 1507, named the new land *America*.

The man who finally reached the Orient by sailing west was Ferdinand Magellan. In 1522, he sailed around the tip of South America, a long, hard, and dangerous ordeal. But the Europeans were not satisfied. They wanted a water route—popularly called the **Northwest Passage**—through the North American continent.

Do You Remember?

1. On what date did Columbus land at San Salvador? How many other voyages did he make to the western hemisphere?
2. Why did Columbus name the natives *Indians*?
3. For whom was the New World named?

THE ARRIVAL OF THE SPANIARDS

The Spaniards continued to send men to the New World. In 1519, Hernando Cortés landed in what is now Mexico. It was Cortés who would find the gold that had eluded Columbus. Within two years, Cortés had conquered the native Aztec, killed their ruler Montezuma, and won a treasure in gold and silver. In 1535, Francisco Pizarro defeated the Inca in Peru and captured the richest silver mines in the world.

Expeditions by the **conquistadores** (Spanish conquerors) to the north of Mexico were less successful. In 1528, Panfilo de Narvaez set out with a Spanish fleet to conquer Florida. They wrecked off the coast of Texas, and all were presumed dead. But four men survived: Cabeza de Vaca, Castillo Maldonado, Dorantes, and Dorantes' black slave Estabanico (Steven). For eight years, the four wandered across the Southwest trying to find Mexico's Spanish settlements. When they finally made their way into central Mexico, they babbled about "hunchback cows" (buffalo), cities with emerald-studded walls, and copper plates. The stories sounded no more fantastic than the original tales of the Aztec and Inca. Indians added to the Spaniards' tales, relaying stories about seven cities of gold.

Antonio de Mendoza, viceroy of Mexico, named Francisco Vasquez de Coronado to lead an expedition into the land north of Mexico. Coronado saw this as his chance to make a fortune. In February 1540, he set out with an **entourage** (a group of attendants and followers) of 250 nobles, 300 riders, about 70 foot-soldiers, and 1,500 Indians and servants. They also had 1,000 extra horses, 500 cows, and 5,000 sheep and hogs. The entourage included several Indian guides, one of whom was known as "The Turk." The Turk, who was probably Pawnee, constantly reinforced Coronado's hopes with tales of northern cities filled with gold and silver.

Hernando de Soto explored much of the southeastern United States. He marched through Florida, Georgia, the Carolinas, and eventually reached the Mississippi River.

No one knows the route Coronado took. But near the Cimarron River in western Cimarron County of what is now Oklahoma, there is a large sandstone boulder known as Castle Rock. The boulder lies along the most direct route south—an old trail that follows springs and watering holes. Among the names and dates carved in the rock by travelers is one that is worn and faint with age: *CORONATTO 1541.* Although the letters are formed like those in early Spanish manuscripts, the spelling is Italian. Two of Coronado's soldiers were from southern Italy, where the name was spelled in that manner.

Coronado's expedition finally reached the Central Plains. "There was not a stone, nor a bit of rising ground, nor a tree, or a shrub, nor anything to go by," he wrote. They had little water, "and often had to drink it so poor that it was more mud than water." They tried to kill buffalo, but instead lost several horses. They cooked their food over cow dung fires "because there is not any kind of wood in all these plains, away from the gullies and rivers, which are very few." Men went hunting and got lost, "wandering about the country as if they were crazy....Every night [we] took account of who was missing, fired guns, and blew trumpets, and beat drums, and built great fires, but yet some of them went off so far and wandered about so much that all this did not give them any help."

After seventy-seven days, Coronado and his exhausted men arrived at what was probably a Wichita Indian camp. "What I am sure of," Coronado wrote the emperor, trying to soften the blow, "is that there is not any gold nor any other metal in all that country, and the other things of which they had told me are nothing but little villages and in many of these they do not plant anything and do not have any houses except of skins and sticks, and they wander around with the cows."

The expedition was a financial disaster for Coronado and his **financiers** (those who provided the funds for the journey). Under torture, The Turk admitted he had lied about the gold and silver. But the Spaniards were not sure if he had simply exaggerated or had deliberately set out to lead them away from the treasures. They strangled The Turk in his sleep.

In 1541 or 1542, Friar Juan Padilla marched north to the Wichita Indian village on the Red River (Quivera, now the San Bernardo site), where almost 4,000 Indians were encamped. With Padilla were Lucas and Sebastian, two Mexican-Indian *doñados* (lay brothers who wore the friar's religious habit), and a Portuguese soldier, Andres do Campo. For a year, they worked to convert the villagers. When Padilla set out to convert the Gua (Kaw) to the east, he was ambushed and killed; Lucas and Sebastian were taken captive. They escaped almost a year

later and struck out south across what is today central Oklahoma. In their sorrow over Padilla's death, they set themselves a penance (an act of voluntary punishment): They fashioned a heavy wooden cross to carry on their backs. For five years, they wandered through the Plains carrying the cross, finally reaching Mexico. Their only companion was a dog that joined them and helped catch small game. They were the first Europeans to cross Oklahoma on foot.

Meanwhile, Hernando de Soto and his men had landed on the Florida coast and had begun traveling east. Riding donkeys and mules, they took a year to reach the Mississippi River. They had with them game chickens to stage fights when they camped as well as Andalusian hunting dogs trained to chase deer, large game animals, and Indians. They wintered near what is now Fort Smith, Arkansas. It was De Soto who claimed all the land—including most of what is now Oklahoma—for Spain. They turned back that next spring, and De Soto was later killed in an Indian battle and buried in the Mississippi River.

De Soto claimed the Mississippi River and all the land — including most of what is now Oklahoma — for Spain.

Do You Remember?

1. Who were the two explorers who conquered the Inca of Peru and the Aztec of Mexico?
2. What had the Spaniards hoped to find in the Central Plains?
3. Who claimed all the lands, including most of what is now Oklahoma, for Spain?

FRENCH TRADERS AND TRAPPERS

If Spain came searching for gold, spices, and subjects, the French came for fish and furs. French sailors crossed the Atlantic Ocean to fish in the Newfoundland Banks along the northeastern coast. When they came ashore to clean and salt down their catch, natives often wandered in to investigate and barter beaver skins for whatever the French would part with. Soon the French were taking goods especially to barter, and some took up trading furs full-time. Several years passed before Quebec was founded on the St. Lawrence River as a colony of New France (Canada) in 1608. (A **colony** is a group of people who settle in a distant land but who are still under the rule of their native land.)

*Right: In 1673 Louis Jolliet and Father Jacques Marquette, a Jesuit missionary, led an expedition down the Mississippi River as far south as the mouth of the Arkansas River. During the expedition, they stopped to preach to the Indians. **Above:** In 1682 Robert Cavelier de La Salle led an expedition down the Mississippi River from Canada. When he reached the Mississippi delta, he claimed the entire Mississippi River valley for France and called it Louisiana in honor of King Louis XIV.*

The French traders canoed up the rivers, hunting and trapping with the Indians. They did not try to conquer them but treated the natives with dignity. Many lived with the Indians and married Indian women. They did not want the Indians' lands and did not try to force the Indians into permanent villages as did the Spaniards.

The French government was eager to find the fabled Northwest Passage. The Canadian governor backed an expedition to explore the Mississippi River in 1673. He hoped that the Mississippi River would flow into the Pacific Ocean and provide a trade route to the Far East. Louis Jolliet and Father Jacques Marquette, a Jesuit missionary, led an expedition as far south as the mouth of the Arkansas River, where they encountered hostile Indians. When it became obvious that the river flowed south to the Gulf of Mexico, they turned back.

In 1682, Robert Cavelier de La Salle was given permission by King Louis XIV of France to lead an expedition to follow the Mississippi River from Canada to the Gulf of Mexico. La Salle reached the Mississippi delta in April and claimed the entire Mississippi River valley for France. The area he claimed was bordered on the east by the Appalachian Mountains and on the west by the Rocky Mountains. It stretched from the Great Lakes on the north to the Gulf of Mexico on the south. La Salle called the area *Louisiana* in honor of King Louis. "A port or two," wrote one of his companions, "would make us masters of this whole continent." If France profited, La Salle did not. On a return trip to establish a colony on the Gulf of Mexico, his men mutinied, shot him, and left his body for the wolves. But his message to build ports was heeded. In 1718, New Orleans was founded at the mouth of the Mississippi River by Jean Baptiste, Sieur de Bienville.

Jean Baptiste, Sieur de Bienville, founded New Orleans at the mouth of the Mississippi River in 1718.

The next year, Bernard de La Harpe led a French exploring party into the area near present-day Haskell. His goal was to set up trading posts among the Caddoan tribes along the Arkansas and Red rivers. In September, he met with the six principal chiefs of the Tawakoni confederacy (who were allies of the Pawnee) near the Indian village of Imaham. This was the first peace council between a European nation and Oklahoma Indians. La Harpe's visit marked the beginning of French trade activities in Oklahoma. His journal provided the first written description of lands in eastern Oklahoma.

From that time, French traders moved inland. They allied themselves with the Comanche, Wichita, Caddo, Osage, and other tribes who lived and used the hunting grounds north of the Red River. They brought brandy, guns and ammunition, metal tools, cloth and woven blankets, mirrors, and beads. In return, they packed out beaver, otter, mink, and muskrat pelts as well as buffalo hides.

One of their principal trading sites was near today's Newkirk. Known today as the Ferdinandina site, it included a large main village surrounded by a stockade of high upright posts with a dry moat around it. Archaeologists found pieces of French guns, brass with the French fleur-de-lis emblem (the symbol used on the armor of French kings), iron tools, woodworking tools, glass and porcelain beads, wedges for rail splitting, axes, hatchets and adzes of European design. About two miles northeast was a village for skinning, scraping, and tanning hides. Some blacksmithing work may have been done there as well. Ferdinandina probably served as the temporary home of three hundred traders and a depot for trade goods.

Many of the rivers, streams, and geographical points in eastern Oklahoma still carry the names given them by French traders.

Do You Remember?

1. Why were the French exploring south out of Canada?
2. What were the borders of the area called Louisiana?
3. Who held the first peace council between Europeans and Oklahoma Indians?

Above: The French developed a thriving fur trade with the Indians.
Opposite page: Fur traders often married Indian women as depicted in this painting The Trapper's Bride *by Alfred Jacob Miller, 1850.*

EUROPEAN-INDIAN CONTACT

The Native American was forever changed from the day the Spaniards set foot in North America. Europe, also, would be changed. From that moment, a new age was born—an age of exploration and exploitation (using people or objects for one's own benefit).

It was not a New World, although the Europeans called it that. It was not unpopulated, although it was less crowded than most of Europe. The people were neither simple nor ignorant nor savages, as the explorers often portrayed them. They were often physically superior in both size and stamina. They had an organized society, and their religious concepts permeated their daily activities. They understood the ecology and balance of nature far better than did the Europeans.

But neither the Spanish conquistadores nor the French traders had come to the continent to understand the natives. Their reports back to the monarchs, financiers, aristocracy, and religious authorities reflected their European ideas of who and what was important. They believed that they were the destined world leaders and rulers. The Spanish particularly believed they had been chosen by God and the church to bring all men into the Roman Catholic church. To them, the end justified the means.

FOOD

Over millions of years, the North American continent had developed different forms of plant life. Maize, beans, potatoes, and squash were unknown in Europe. Coffee and chocolate (both served as drinks by American natives) seemed strange to European taste, and neither caught on for some time.

Columbus was fascinated by the "sticks" (pipes) the natives carried with them at all times and the weed they smoked. Smoking a pipe of tobacco was an honored ritual, which many Indians considered as a time to commune with the spirits and friends. Nomadic tribes who did not grow tobacco usually bartered for it. It did not take long for the Europeans to take up smoking (or chewing) tobacco. Growing tobacco led to the later success of the English colonies in the southeastern part of North America.

ANIMALS

Perhaps the most immediate and significant change to Indian life was the introduction of the horse. When the Spaniards marched into the Plains on horseback, the natives were astounded. They had never seen an animal as large as the horse that could be tamed. They had no word for such a creature and nicknamed them "magic dogs" or "wonder dogs." The Spanish horses were descendants of the horses of Arabia and North Africa. They were strong and adaptable, able to live on small amounts of forage and grass. Coronado lost several on his trek across the Plains. Others were traded to the Indians.

The horse changed Indian life drastically. A horse could carry many times what a dog (the common beast of burden) or a woman could carry. It was swift and strong, which meant the Indians were no longer forced to stalk game on foot. They could range further in search of game, which allowed them to build more permanent villages. But it also meant that they were more likely to cross paths with enemy tribes, which opened up the opportunity for skirmishes and wars.

By the time the French traders made their way into the Plains, the Indians had become skilled horsemen and turned out well-made saddles and bridles. A man's wealth and standing within the tribe were often measured by the number of horses owned. It was even said that Apache women rode like centaurs [mythical creatures half-human, half-horse] and handled their rifles with deadly skill. The Tawakoni on the eastern side of the state traded horses to the French, while the Apache did a brisk trade with the native tribes to the southwest.

Right: Commanche Feats of Horsemanship *by George Catlin*

The demand for tobacco was so great in Europe that tobacco leaves were cured by smoke from wood fires to withstand the long ocean voyage from the New World.

When the Spaniards set out to conquer a country, they took with them everything they needed to set up an entire settlement, including domestic animals such as pigs, chickens, sheep, and goats. These animals quickly spread throughout the Plains. Some tribes, such as the southwestern Navajo, began raising sheep and goats. From their hair, the native women spun wool and wove rugs and clothing.

The Spaniards took back to Europe birds and small animals native to the North American continent. These birds and animals included the turkey, which became a fad (a temporarily popular item) among the European aristocracy.

TRADE GOODS

Indians had been trading among themselves for years to obtain food they did not raise or kill themselves; hides and furs from other animals; and beads, shells, pearls, and stones from other areas. By the time the Spaniards arrived, some tribes were already known as skillful traders. Still, the Europeans demanded such great quantities of animal skins and furs that entire tribes changed their way of life. The Abenakis tribe of Maine, for example, spent so much time catching beaver that it had to rely on the Massachusetts tribe for food supplies. The Massachusetts tribe, in turn, spent all its time producing food in exchange for the European metal tools the tribe received from the Abenakis.

There were two types of goods that transformed Indian life dramatically: metal tools and guns. Metal tools made daily chores such as cooking easier. Guns gave the Indian the power of the white man.

Europeans also gained from the trading. The many fine furs and pelts fed an increasing demand, and coat manufacturers prospered. Among the most popular items was the tall beaver hat, which almost every European gentleman wore.

RELIGION

Both the French and the Spanish made great efforts to convert the Native Americans to Christianity. The Spaniards believed that, by removing the natives from their old life, they could be brought to Christianity. In many areas of the West, they had herded the natives into new villages centered around a church. In this way, they controlled Indian activities, dress, food, and behavior.

But the Plains Indians were too independent for such a transformation. Unlike California, where the priests built a line of missions and churches up the western coast, there was only one mission established in the Central Plains: near the Wichita Indian village in Devil's Canyon in the Wichita Mountains. There were no recorded conversions.

DISEASE

No one knows how many Native Americans were living on the continent when the Europeans arrived. There were perhaps 10 million in central Mexico alone. But a century later, fewer than 1 million remained. They had fallen victim to European diseases for which they had no natural **immunity** (resistance).

To the north, one Frenchman wrote that "since the French mingle with [the Canadian Indians] and carry on trade with them, [the Indians complained that] they are dying fast and the population is thinning out." Even before the Pilgrims landed at Plymouth, Massachusetts, fishermen infected local tribes with what may have been chicken pox. The Indians "died on heapes, as they lay in their houses." To the south, it was smallpox that devastated the tribes. The Aztec were defeated by Cortez only after they had been weakened by smallpox. Once smallpox had been introduced into the Indian villages, it moved swiftly from one area to another.

Death from smallpox was terrible. In a high state of fever, victims threw themselves off cliffs or plunged knives into their hearts to rid themselves of the pangs of slow and disgusting death. Smallpox appears to have started among the Plains tribes about 1839, probably among the Pawnee. The Pawnee traded with French trappers and whiskey sellers, who probably brought the disease to North America. One trader is said to have threatened to "let the smallpox out of a bottle and destroy the Indians" if they did not do what he asked. At least one time, Indians were given blankets from people infected with smallpox in the hope that it would wipe out the tribe. Reverend Isaac McCoy, a missionary, wrote that he saw more than "three thousand carcasses cast upon the open field" as Pawnee, Otoe, Ponca, and Omaha died. The disease spread to the Osage, Kiowa, Comanche, Apache, and Choctaw. Reverend Cyrus Byington, another missionary, found himself preaching more funerals than sermons.

In time, the Native Americans acquired enough immunity to survive the European diseases. But by then, European expansion and the Indians' overwhelming population losses had reduced Native Americans to a minority in their own homeland.

Reverend Cyrus Byington, a missionary, found himself preaching more funerals than sermons as European diseases spread throughout the Native American population.

Do You Remember?

1. How did European-Indian contact change the diets of both?
2. Name some of the items traded between the Native Americans and the Europeans.
3. Why was it so easy for the Indians to get the European diseases? What happened to the Indian population as a result?

CHAPTER REVIEW

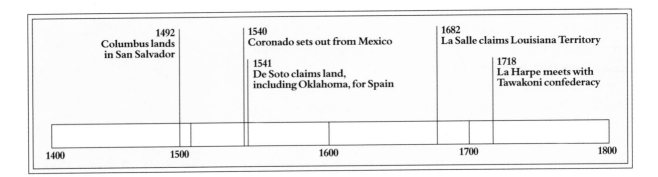

1492 Columbus lands in San Salvador	1540 Coronado sets out from Mexico	1682 La Salle claims Louisiana Territory
	1541 De Soto claims land, including Oklahoma, for Spain	1718 La Harpe meets with Tawakoni confederacy

1400   1500   1600   1700   1800

At the Same Time

1496   Jews expelled from Portugal
1500   Amerigo Vespucci discovers the Amazon River
1501   African slaves introduced into Spanish colonies
1517   Martin Luther begins the Reformation

Summary

The Spaniards and other Europeans who made their way west to the North American continent were looking for a trade route to the Orient. Columbus gave Spain its foothold in America. From the successes in Mexico and Central America, the Spanish conquistadores moved into the Plains in search of riches. They found only a hostile environment and Native Americans who had very little that Spain wanted. The Spaniards did have two things the Indians wanted very much: the horse and guns.

The French followed, moving south from Canada. They followed the waterways and brought with them valuable trade goods and weapons.

The first contacts between Europeans and Native Americans were peaceful. Exchange of food, animals, and tools benefited both groups. But poor communications, disease, and other circumstances soon made both more wary of each other. With no immunity to European diseases, millions of Native Americans died, and the lives of the tribes were changed forever.

Reviewing People, Places, and Things

Define, identify, or explain the importance of the following.

1. aristocracy
2. colony
3. Christopher Columbus
4. conquistadore
5. Francisco Vasquez de Coronado
6. Hernando de Soto
7. entourage
8. expedition
9. financier
10. immunity
11. Bernard de La Harpe
12. Robert Cavelier de La Salle
13. middleman
14. monarch
15. Northwest Passage

Understanding the Facts

1. How did the publication of Marco Polo's *Travels* affect European exploration?
2. How many voyages did Columbus actually make to the New World?
3. How did French traders and Spanish soldiers deal with the Native Americans?
4. Name some of the animals introduced to the North American continent by the Europeans.
5. What was probably the most deadly disease for the Native Americans?

Developing Critical Thinking

1. Middlemen help get goods from one place to another, from the producer to the consumer. Who are today's middlemen?
2. "Gold, glory, and gospel" are sometimes said to be three factors that attracted European exploration and settlement of the North American continent. How do you think these factors affected European voyages to the Americas?
3. How would Native American society have been affected if Europeans had never brought horses to the North American continent?

Using Your Skills

1. On a globe, locate the narrowest east-west point in the North and South American continents. Identify the two large bodies of water separated by this point. What great canal was cut through this area? When?
2. Imagine you are a leader of a Spanish expedition trying to establish a new colony on the Great Plains. Make a list of the items you think you would need.

Special Projects

1. At your local library, find a book that illustrates the great buildings constructed by the Aztec or Maya of Mexico and the mounds built in the southeastern part of the Americas by the Caddo moundbuilders. How do they compare to the Aztec or Maya?
2. Identify at least three points in Oklahoma (rivers, streams, mountains) that you think may have been named by the French. Check the library for their meaning. Why was each called by that name?

Building Skills: Finding Information

As you continue your study of the history of Oklahoma, your teacher may assign topics for you to research. In addition to looking in the card catalogue in your school media center, there are numerous reference books available. Here are the types of facts you are likely to find in some of them.

Almanac: Facts about a variety of events and dates, often in date order

Atlas: Maps and place information

Dictionary: Meanings, spellings, and pronunciations of words; origin of words

Encyclopedia: Important details about people, places, and things, usually arranged alphabetically by subject or topic

Read the following descriptions of information needed and determine in which reference source you would find the information. Some information can be found in more than one reference source or in reference sources that are not listed above.

1. The distance between Oklahoma City and Tulsa
2. The date Oklahoma became a state
3. The yearly average rainfall in Oklahoma
4. The capital of Oklahoma
5. The definition of *boomer*
6. An explanation of the Indian Wars
7. The correct pronunciation of *buffalo*
8. The location of Oklahoma's Antelope Hills
9. Another word for *liberty*
10. A map showing the counties of Oklahoma
11. A list of the major works of Angie Debo
12. A list of the Oklahoma Indian tribes
13. A biography of Will Rogers
14. Major crops grown in Oklahoma
15. The dates of the land runs

Sooner Trivia

. . . Marco Polo's *Travels* was published in 1477. Before then, the manuscript had been circulated hand-to-hand for nearly two hundred years.

. . . There are seven sites in Oklahoma with stones inscribed with what could be Norse *runes,* an early Norse form of writing. These sites are near Heavener, Poteau, Krebs, Shawnee, and Tulsa.

. . . By 1700 almost every tribe on the Southern Plains had horses.

INDIAN TERRITORY

Native Americans were forced to migrate to new lands as the westward expansion by the white settlers continued. This painting of Indians on the move, Comanche Moving Camp, Dog Fight en Route *by George Catlin, 1834-1835 depicts the nature of one such move. The Indians carried many of their belongings on a* travois *pulled by a horse.*

MANY INDIANS NOW IN OKLAHOMA came from the North and East after being displaced by the white settlers who moved inland from the eastern seacoast. Sometimes the settlers had gotten close enough to kill off the animals on which the Indians depended for food. In other cases, vastly different cultures led to trouble between whites and Indians. Often, whites coveted Indian land or the resources on their land. Treaties forced the Indians out of their homelands and reservations, continually moving them to parts of the continent the government did not want at the time.

CHAPTER FOUR

A CLASH OF CULTURES

King Philip of Spain (above) was a chief rival of Queen Elizabeth I of England (opposite page). Deeply religious, Philip hoped to spread Catholicism to the New World and prevent England, a Protestant nation, from establishing colonies there.

When our great father first came over the wide waters, he was but a little man...and he begged for a little land to light his fire on. When the white man had warmed himself before the Indians' fire and filled himself with their hominy, he became very large. With a step he bestrode the mountains, and his feet covered the plains and the valleys....Then he said, 'Get a little further, lest I tread on thee.'

— Speckled Snake, Creek Indian, 1829

THE EUROPEANS WERE DRAWN across the North American continent for different reasons. The Spaniards wanted the Indians' bodies, their souls, and their wealth. That was clear to the Indians, who were ready to fight to keep from becoming enslaved. The French wanted to take advantage of the Indians' work and knowledge of the land. But, unlike the Spanish, the French offered an acceptable trade that the Indians could take or leave. The British wanted the land upon which the Indians lived. This was a new concept to the Indians: how could anyone own the mother of all things?

COLONIAL AMERICA

The Europeans were not certain just what North America had to offer, but each country wanted to make sure it had first rights to whatever was there. The French wanted part of the growing fur trade with the Native Americans. Philip II, a devout Catholic and King of Spain in the 1550s, was determined that North America and its inhabitants would be Catholic. Queen Elizabeth I of England was just as determined that its colonies be Protestant.

CHAPTER PREVIEW

Terms: patent, indentured servant, slave, confederation, frontier, treaty, cede, boycott, repeal, monopoly, emissary, Five Civilized Tribes, livestock, light-horsemen

People: Pawnee, Comanche, Kiowa, Kiowa-Apache, Meriwether Lewis, William Clark, Captain Richard Sparks, Kichai, Shawnee, Cheyenne, Osage, Cherokee, Doublehead, Choctaw, Chickasaw, Creek, Seminole

Places: Great Spanish Trail, Louisiana Purchase, Missouri Territory

THE INFLUENCE OF FRANCE AND SPAIN

The area south of what is now Oklahoma belonged to Spain. Both Franciscan missionaries and Spanish Jesuits worked in the Southwest, but the Indians were reluctant to accept their teachings and thus European civilization. A Spanish mission was established near the Neches River, but hostile Indians forced the missionaries to leave in 1693.

In 1685, Frenchman Robert Cavelier de La Salle landed at Matagorda Bay and built a fort. La Salle did not stay, but his presence caused the Spaniards to double their efforts to build missions. The Presidio (fortress) San Augustin was built near the mouth of the Trinity River to make certain French traders knew where the line between Spain and France was drawn.

When Bernard de La Harpe traveled up the Red River in 1719, he wrote French officials in New Orleans,

There is not in the whole colony of Louisiana an establishment more useful to make than on the branch of this river not only because of the mild climate, the fertility of the land, the richness of the minerals, but also because of the possibility of trade that one might introduce with Spain and New Mexico.

Trade with the Spanish was probably the reason for one of the first trails established in the region. Tradition says that the Great Spanish Trail lay along the Red River, connecting what is now Nacogdoches, Texas, with Santa Fe and Chihuahua in Old Mexico. It crossed into today's Oklahoma somewhere close to Lake Texoma, perhaps as far west as what is now Tillman County. Then it trailed along the east and north side of the North Fork. There may have been a Spanish settlement where the Wichita Mountains rose near the North Fork at the mouth of Devil's Canyon.

French traders began making their way up the Mississippi River to explore the center of the continent and to make contact with the tribes in the area. Pierre and Paul Mallet and four companions traveled up the Missouri to the mouth of the Platte then wandered south into Comanche country. Fabre de La Bruyere, a French officer, took a company of soldiers and Canadian traders up the Arkansas River to map a direct route to Santa Fe. They started up the Canadian River but were stopped by shallow water and sand bars. In 1741-1742, the French signed a trading agreement with the Comanche at the mouth of the Little River near the present boundary between McIntosh and Hughes counties. In 1746, an agreement between the French and Caddo opened up the Arkansas River as a trade route to Santa Fe.

THE VIRGINIA COMPANY

After several unsuccessful attempts at colonization, King James I of England gave the Virginia Company a **patent** (an exclusive right) to establish colonies on the North American continent in 1606. The Virginia Company eventually established the Jamestown colony in 1607. It was the first permanent English settlement in the New World.

Many of the laborers who made the trip to America were beggars, debtors, thieves, and murderers released from prison to work in the new land. Sir Thomas Dale, governor of Jamestown, wrote the king in 1661, "If it will please his Majestie to banish hither all offenders condemned to die, it would be a readie way to furnish us with men." In 1619, the first Africans were brought to the colony to help with a shortage of labor. These may have been **indentured servants**, that is, people who agree to work for someone for a period of time (usually 4-7 years) in return for passage to the New World. At the end of that time, they would be free of debt and could do as they pleased. As the years wore on, however, Africans were treated more and more as slaves. **Slaves** had few rights and spent their entire lives in service to others.

In 1629, King Charles I gave Sir Robert Heath a patent for all the land between 31° and 36° north latitude from sea to sea. This vast territory, which the king called "Carolana," included what is today Oklahoma. England was free to move west and battle both the French trading companies and Spanish mission settlements.

PROBLEMS IN THE NORTHEAST

Several European countries established colonies in the Northeast. In 1612, Dutch traders arrived in the area of New York City. The English Pilgrims arrived at Plymouth, Massachusetts, in December 1620. A Swedish colony settled in Delaware in 1637.

From the beginning, difficulties arose between Europeans and Indians. Diseases had weakened and almost wiped out some tribes by 1616. Colonists and native Americans were at odds over land ownership and use. Through poor judgment, heavy-handed government officials created trouble. Some tribes, such as the Pequot, relocated to put distance between themselves and the New England settlers—only to quarrel with colonists or tribes in the new area.

A number of tribes tried to create **confederations** (groups united by a common cause). For example, the Iroquois Confederation—Mohawk, Oneida, Onondaga, Cayuga, and Seneca—dominated Indian matters in the Northeast. But friendships with warring groups of Europeans split many Indian tribes. For example, the Iroquois befriended the English, while the Huron and Erie supported the French.

In 1629, King Charles I gave Sir Robert Heath (above) a patent for all the land between 31° and 36° north latitude from sea to sea. King Charles called this land "Carolana." It included present-day Oklahoma.

*Right: Roger Williams landing at Rhode Island in 1636. **Below:** Samoset, a Wampanoag, greeted the Pilgrims in English, which he learned from earlier traders.*

The Wampanoag tribe had originally lived along the Atlantic Coast but were forced east of Narragansett Bay (in present-day Rhode Island) by colonists. The Narraganset tribe was menaced by a land company that claimed it held a mortgage to their land in Connecticut. The Mohegan, the Podunk, and the Nipmuck joined with these two tribes to form the Five Nations. Trouble broke out between the Indians and colonists in 1675; before the war ended in 1676, the Five Nations were almost wiped out. Their disappearance opened southern New England for settlement.

Do You Remember?

1. What country claimed the land south of what is now Oklahoma?
2. Why were Africans brought to the English colonies?
3. What was the Iroquois Confederation? Why was it formed?

THE FRENCH AND INDIAN WAR

The wars and troubles that arose on the North American continent started for two reasons: (1) European ideas of conquest and war and (2) individual exposure to freedom.

The Europeans believed that if they discovered the land, they owned it—regardless of who was on it at the time. To them, "discovery" meant the right to control trade between the Indians and the European markets. In addition, because Europeans recognized the same set of allies and enemies in America as in Europe, any war in Europe carried over to America. When one such war broke out in 1756, England and France were on opposite sides, with Spain siding with France. The Indian tribes found themselves in the middle of the turmoil, whether they wanted to be or not.

The new settlers felt a sense of freedom in North America. Many had come out of debtor's prisons or off the streets; others had spent their lives as sailors. They saw the raw land as a real opportunity: to farm, to start families, to build businesses. The European leaders were on the other side of the ocean, too far away to control the colonists. There was no stopping the people who were moving west, even farther away from the control of the European governments.

Both France and Great Britain wanted control of the Ohio and Mississippi river valleys. France built forts at key points, especially at river junctions. The British built settlements. In 1754, a twenty-two-year-old military officer named George Washington led a small band of Virginia militia into the Ohio country to drive out the French. Washington and his Virginians were defeated, but the clash marked the beginning of the French and Indian War in America.

The French encouraged the Cherokee and Creek in the South to attack the settlements along the **frontier** (a region just beyond or at the edge of settled areas). For the next six years, battles waged back and forth, usually favoring the Indians. In 1761, militia from Virginia and the Carolinas, as well as Chickasaw and Catawba Indians, marched into the Cherokee homelands. They defeated the Cherokee, destroyed their towns, and drove them further into the mountains. Pontiac, chief of the Ottawa, led the tribes of the Great Lakes area into war against

One of the French-built forts captured by the British during the War of 1812 was Fort Duquesne at present-day Pittsburgh. Two British soldiers captured a man leaving the fort and using information given by their prisoner were able to capture the fort without firing a shot.

Pontiac, chief of the Ottawa, addressing a tribal council. Pontiac was an ally of the French during the French and Indian War. He led attacks on British outposts in the Great Lakes area. When the French made peace with the English, Pontiac continued the struggle and finally concluded his own treaty with the English.

the British in May 1763. Although the Indians captured a number of forts, they could not drive the British back across the mountains.

Meanwhile, in Europe, seven years of war involving Great Britain and France finally ended with the defeat of France. In 1763, the Treaty of Paris was signed. A **treaty** is a formal agreement between two or more nations. France **ceded** (surrendered) Canada and all lands east of the Mississippi River to Great Britain. Spain, which had sided with France, lost Florida to Great Britain. To repay Spain, France gave the Louisiana Territory to Spain. The treaty opened the door to the West for the British.

The Native Americans had little idea of the real consequences of this European treaty. The Shawnee, for one, demanded to know how the French could give away something that was not theirs to give.

On November 10, 1763, the governors of the southern colonies and a group representing the Chickasaw, Choctaw, Creek, and Cherokee tribes signed a treaty at the Congress of Augusta (Georgia). This treaty was important because it directly affected tribes that would later be moved to Oklahoma. Among other issues, the terms of the treaty called for the Indians to give up land. The Creek gave up about 2.5 million acres in Georgia. The Catawba were left with a small reservation in South Carolina. In return, the British promised not to "settle upon or disturb the Indians in the Grounds or Lands to the Westward of the lines herein before described."

THE FIRST INDIAN MIGRATIONS

When the French and Indian War ended in 1763, the French and their Indian allies migrated west of the Mississippi River, hoping to find a place to settle. St. Louis became a major trading center for Indians, French, and Spaniards. The migration caused a chain reaction. As one tribe moved into another tribe's territory, the new tribe was either allowed to settle in or the old tribe moved on.

Shortly after 1763, the French found the Pawnee along the lower Arkansas and Missouri rivers. They may originally have come from southern Mexico near the Yucatan peninsula. Driven out by flood, they crossed two mountain ranges and settled in the northern Great Plains. They knew the southern Plains area, probably from hunting there. The Spaniards used them for guides.

The Comanche had come from the Rocky Mountain area, although some say they were related to the Aztec of Mexico. They had obtained horses and moved to the North Platte River area in what is now Wyoming about 1700. But they clashed with the Sioux and moved to south Texas. By the mid-1700s, the Comanche were hunting and scouting between the Platte and Red rivers. They were excellent hunters, very good at sign language, and excellent horse thieves and horse trainers. Neither the French nor Spanish traders trusted them, and both stayed away from the Texas Panhandle because of them.

The Kiowa may have originally come from western Montana in the Yellowstone and Missouri rivers area. In 1790, they joined with the Comanche. Colonel Henry Dodge described them as "tall and erect, with an easy graceful gait, long hair reaching often to the ground, with a fine Roman outline of head." They were skilled metalworkers long before the Navajo in the southwest learned to work with metal. Captain Randolph Marcy once spotted Kiowa in the distance because their silver bridles and ornaments flashed in the sun.

The Kiowa-Apache, sometimes called Prairie Apache, may originally have been a branch of the Apache in the Rocky Mountain region but were probably related to the Kiowa. They roamed the Great Plains moving south, joining the Kiowa for safety sometime early in the 1700s.

Pescolechaco was a Pawnee chief. The Pawnee may originally have come from southern Mexico near the Yucatan peninsula. Driven out by flood, they crossed two mountain ranges and settled in the northern Great Plains.

Do You Remember?
1. What treaty drastically changed the land in North America claimed by European nations?
2. What were the terms of the Congress of Augusta?
3. Name three of the Indian tribes that migrated into the Great Plains in the late 1700s.

AN AMERICAN REVOLUTION

After the 1760s, Great Britain controlled much of the trade on North America's eastern coast, but it was saddled with many war debts. It also needed to keep peace with Native Americans and bring the American colonies under better control. In 1765, the British Parliament (legislature) passed the Stamp Act, which was a thinly disguised tax. The tax money raised was to be used to defend the American colonies. The colonists, however, said it was a violation of their rights. "No taxation without representation" became a common cry. People began to **boycott** (refuse to buy) goods from Britain.

As a result of the uproar, Parliament **repealed** (canceled) the Stamp Act in 1766; but in 1767, Parliament imposed another tax to raise money to pay the salaries of colonial governors and judges. After much opposition from colonists, all the taxes were repealed in 1770—except for the tax on tea. In December 1773, Massachusetts patriots (colonists who resisted the tighter controls by the British) dumped 340 chests of tea into Boston harbor to protest the East India Company's **monopoly**

Patriots at the Boston Tea Party in December 1773 crudely disguised themselves as Indians. In fact they were farmers, merchants, artisans, and apprentices.

(exclusive control over the buying or selling of a particular product) of the tea trade. Tensions continued to increase between Great Britain and its colonies until war—the Revolutionary War—broke out April 19, 1775. On July 4, 1776, the Continental Congress approved the Declaration of Independence.

Both sides asked the Indians to remain neutral during the Revolutionary War. But some tribes saw it as a way to regain some of their lands. The Cherokee and Creek attacked the western frontiers of Virginia, North and South Carolina, and Georgia. Troops from those colonies entered the Indian lands and destroyed thirty-six Cherokee towns. In 1777, the Cherokee signed the Treaty of Long Island, ceding all their lands east of the Blue Ridge Mountains. The Cherokee and the Creek never really recovered from the losses they suffered in the war. As a matter of fact, the "Trail of Tears" had its roots in the American Revolution.

The American colonists received support from France in 1778 and from Spain in 1779. With their help, the colonists were able to defeat the British. Great Britain surrendered in October 1781; with the signing of the Treaty of Paris in 1783, the Revolutionary War formally ended. In 1787, the first formal written constitution was adopted for the United States of America.

Lord Cornwallis, commander of British troops, surrendered to George Washington at Yorktown, Virginia, on October 19, 1781.

THE LOUISIANA PURCHASE

When the war ended, the continent had a new political power, and it represented those who were eager to move west. The key, however, was the Mississippi River, a solid boundary beyond which the young nation could not expand. The French had given the territory of Louisiana to Spain in the Treaty of 1763. In 1795, a treaty was finally completed allowing U.S. citizens free passage down the Mississippi River, but the treaty was limited to only three years. By 1800, the treaty had lapsed, and President Thomas Jefferson and the young government were trying to negotiate a new one. Then they heard about a secret treaty that Spain and France had signed: Spain gave the Louisiana Territory back to France in exchange for land in Italy.

Jefferson acted quickly. He sent **emissaries** (government agents) to French leader Napoleon Bonaparte with a question: Would he sell New Orleans, and at what price? Jefferson probably knew that Bonaparte needed money due to setbacks in Haiti. If Bonaparte was surprised by such an offer from this fledgling country, he surprised them in turn. He would sell New Orleans *and* all of Louisiana Territory (827,987 square miles) for 80 million francs (about $15 million). The deal was closed in 1803. The United States doubled its area for about four cents an acre.

President Thomas Jefferson asked French leader Napoleon Bonaparte (above) if he would sell New Orleans to the United States. Napoleon offered to sell not only New Orleans, but all of Louisiana Territory (right) for about $15 million.

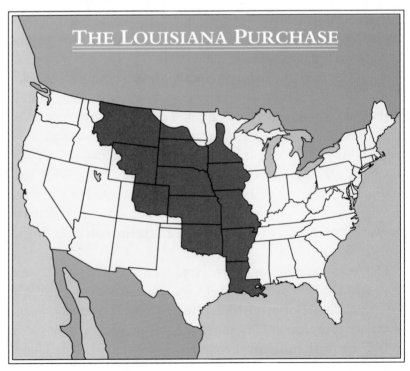

THE LOUISIANA PURCHASE

About all anyone knew about the Louisiana Territory was that it lay between the Mississippi River and the Rocky Mountains. Almost immediately, Jefferson hired Meriwether Lewis and William Clark to explore the new territory and establish peaceful relations with the Indian tribes living there. What he really hoped they would find was a way to reach the Pacific Coast, a path that would open the way for American expansion. Lewis and Clark set out from St. Louis in 1804. It would take over two years for them to cross the Rockies, reach the mouth of the Columbia River in the northwest, and return.

About this time, the vast area was divided into territories, even though only a portion of the boundaries were known. The area that would become Oklahoma was part of Indiana Territory until 1805; then it became part of Missouri Territory.

THE SPARKS EXPEDITION

A second government expedition was dispatched in 1804. Captain Richard Sparks was sent by Jefferson's secretary of war to explore the Red River. Sparks left Natchitoches, Louisiana, in June with twenty-four men in two flat-bottomed boats and a number of pirogues. Their destination was the Twin Villages on the upper Red River, where they planned to pick up horses and travel across land until they reached the headwaters of the Red River. There they hoped to join with Zebulon Pike, who had turned south after exploring the Rocky Mountains.

Texas still belonged to the Spanish, and the Red River was the border of Spanish territory. The Spanish were uneasy about this upstart little country; who knew what they might try next. What would stop them from taking over Spain's claims in North America? They watched warily from the south as the Sparks expedition made its way upriver.

The expedition halted when it ran into a large log jam in the river channel. While they were trying to clear it, Caddo Indians warned them that the Spanish were following the expedition. When Sparks reached the southeast corner of what is now Oklahoma, his party stopped to camp. Suddenly, Spanish soldiers burst from the timber on the Texas side and rode full-speed into the American camp. They offered Sparks two options: turn back or be arrested. He turned back.

President Thomas Jefferson was responsible for acquiring Louisiana Territory for the United States.

Do You Remember?
1. What was one issue that led to the American Revolution?
2. How were the Indians affected by the colonists winning the war?
3. When was the Louisiana Purchase made?
4. Who were the first men commissioned by the U.S. government to explore the territory included in the Louisiana Purchase?

Chief Le Soldat du Chene of the Osage (1804). The Osage were skilled hunters and a proud and independent people whose culture centered around the buffalo and animals of the plains and woodlands.

THE SECOND INDIAN MIGRATIONS

Shortly after 1800, four more tribes arrived in what is now Oklahoma, pushed westward by the press of settlers and the white man's treaties.

The Kichai moved to Oklahoma to live near the Wichita about 1800. They had previously lived along the upper Trinity River in Texas and the upper waters of the Red River in what is now Louisiana.

The Shawnee probably lived on the Ohio River in prehistoric times and migrated to the Southeast to avoid the Iroquois. The British found them living in what is now South Carolina and Georgia. In the late 1600s, part of the tribe moved north while another group moved to the valley of the Cumberland River in Tennessee. About 1730, the Tennessee Shawnee migrated north of the Ohio River, finally joining the main band in Pennsylvania about 1750. Around 1800, a group known as the Absentee Shawnee settled along the Canadian River near the mouth of Little River (near today's Idabel).

The Cheyenne were originally Algonquin from the Minnesota and Wisconsin region. There they had been farmers and makers of pottery

Kish-Kal-Wah, a Shawnee chief.
The Shawnee probably lived on the
Ohio River in prehistoric times and
migrated to the Southeast to avoid
the Iroquois.

and lived in permanent villages. They had been wandering the Great Plains for many years. When they came into contact with the Plains Indians, they quickly adopted the horse and the Plains ceremonies; many of their own customs and legends were lost. They were allied with the Arapaho and the Suhtai, who eventually became bands of the tribe. The Cheyenne and Arapaho were always friendly and often acted as intermediaries (go-betweens) for traders and tribes. By 1821, they were reported living in permanent villages of earth lodges along the Arkansas River.

The Osage may have lived in Virginia and the Carolinas before they migrated down the Ohio River and across the Mississippi. They were skilled hunters and a proud and independent people whose culture centered around the buffalo and animals of the Plains and woodlands. They did not chose to adopt the white man's ways and refused to learn English. Both the Spanish and the French reported that they were often at war with neighboring tribes.

The Osage had allied themselves with the French-Creole Chouteau family, who had made their way up the Mississippi River in the 1760s

THREE FORKS TRADERS

*Above: Trader Auguste Pierre Chouteau, Jr., who spoke most Indian languages and several European languages. **Opposite page top:** The stockade and blockhouse of a re-created early nineteenth-century fort and trading post at the Museum of the Great Plains at Lawton.*
***Opposite page below left:** The interior of the same trading post.*
***Opposite page below right:** A museum interpreter dressed as an early nineteenth century trader.*

The Three Forks area is located where the Grand, Verdigris, and Arkansas rivers join, at the western edge of the Ozarks. It became the great jumping-off place into the unexplored western frontier. It was also a way-station on the route south from St. Louis to Santa Fe and Mexico. Expeditions made one last stop for supplies, fresh horses, pack mules, and guides before striking out across the unknown prairie.

There were usually a dozen trappers or guides coming, going, or just waiting. Men came upriver by steamboat to unload equipment and supplies. They came downriver in pirogues, canoes, and flatboats loaded with goods for southern and western markets. Osage were likely to drop in any time, bringing furs, fowl, tallow, wild honey, bear oil, forest products, buffalo robes, and the latest tales of bickering and battle. In exchange, they returned to their camp with beads, blankets, knives, foodstuffs, trinkets, and cloth. Auguste Pierre Chouteau, Jr., spoke most Indian and several European languages, so there was never a problem communicating.

Other traders and trappers were attracted to the area. Charles Bougie opened a store in 1804. Nathaniel Pryor, who had been with Lewis and Clark, established his trading post and home about two miles above the mouth of the Verdigris. Pryor also brought in high-bred Kentucky horses. Tom Slover, a trapper, moved his family to a plot near the Neosho River. James Bogy built a trading post near the mouth of the Verdigris in 1806. John Campbell operated a salt works nearby. Joseph Revoir operated a place called "The Saline" on Grand River in partnership with Chouteau. Someone built a ferry and charged a fee to haul people, animals, and goods across the river.

and built a profitable fur trade with the help of the Osage. Chouteau's trading headquarters was the beginning of the city of St. Louis ("Chouteau's town," the Osage called it). In 1802, when the Chouteaus lost their trading monopoly, they moved south to the Three Forks area. Half of the Osage tribe moved with them.

In 1808, the federal government forced the Missouri Osage to cede all their lands in Arkansas and Missouri and move west into Kansas. They moved west into Kansas. At about the same time, the Arkansas Cherokee were settled along the border. There was no way to avoid trouble between these two old enemies.

The Osage and Cherokee were not the only tribes that did not get along, however. The chain reaction of people moving west—settlers and Indians—crowded more Indian tribes into the Great Plains. There were more people hunting fewer animals, and competition and fighting grew.

The creation of Missouri Territory in 1813 made matters worse. Veterans of the Revolutionary War and the War of 1812 were given "land script," documents that allowed them to purchase and settle land wherever they wished. Some moved west to settle; others sold the paper to land speculators. Few thought about the Indians' rights to the land.

THE FIVE CIVILIZED TRIBES

In the Southeast, the Cherokee, Choctaw, Chickasaw, Creek, and Seminole tribes had intermarried with settlers and traders. As they came into contact with more and more settlers, they began to adopt the white man's culture, and people called them the **Five Civilized Tribes**. However, these tribes too would soon be moved to Indian Territory.

THE CHEROKEE

The Cherokee may have originally come from the upper Ohio River but were driven south by the Iroquois. As early as 1690, the South Carolinians had headed an expedition into their lands in search of gold. About 1700, they were introduced to firearms, and they became a tribe to be reckoned with.

During the French and Indian War, they allowed the British to build forts on their land. But the relationship soured when whites killed and scalped Cherokee warriors who were returning from helping the British fight the Shawnee. As settlers pushed west in the 1760s, the Cherokee were driven from Virginia to Tennessee and the Carolinas. Old Tassel, the Cherokee chieftain, remarked, "The truth is, if we had not lands, we should have fewer enemies."

A Cherokee women preparing food in front of a traditional mid-sixteenth-century Cherokee house at Tsa-La-Gi, the Cherokee Heritage Center at Tahlequah.

There was so much trouble with settlers that in 1786 the Cherokee ceded large parts of their lands in Kentucky, Tennessee, and North Carolina. The Treaty of Hopewell outlined the Cherokee boundaries and prohibited white settlers from trespassing on Indian land. Then the government added,

The hatchet shall be forever buried....The utmost good faith shall always be observed towards the Indians; their land and property shall never be taken from them without their consent; and in their property, rights, and liberty, they shall never be invaded or disturbed, unless in just and lawful wars.

The settlers, however, paid little attention to the treaties. The Indians, who believed that their word was their bond, found themselves at a disadvantage: If they did not fight those who stole their **livestock** (cattle and hogs) and trampled their fields, they lost their possessions. If they fought for their rights on their own land, the government could say they had broken the treaty. They could not win.

Because the tribe had lost so much within such a short time, they were destitute (reduced to poverty). "I consider the business of hunting has already become insufficient to furnish clothing and subsistence

Some Cherokee were quick to pick up much of the culture of the white settlers. Compare this stately three-story home of Cherokee leader James Vann built in 1804 with the mid-sixteenth-century dwelling on the opposite page.

to the Indians," Thomas Jefferson wrote. "The promotion of agriculture, therefore, and household manufacture, are essential in their preservation, and I am disposed to aid and encourage it." Adopting a *civilization policy*, the U.S. government gave the Cherokee farming implements, household goods, and a $1,000 annual payment in goods. Jefferson had not ended his speech with that idea, however. He had added another sentence that was key: "This will enable them to live on much smaller portions of land."

A number of the Cherokee had made the long trek into the Plains for game for many years. When their homes were destroyed by whites about 1794, they began to think about moving west permanently. In 1805, while negotiating a treaty for the Cherokee, Doublehead, a Chickamauga chief, made a secret arrangement with U.S. commissioners. While selling off part of the Cherokee tribal lands, Doublehead kept a valuable piece of land for himself. It was his undoing. When the tribe discovered it, he was marked for death. The killing was done according to tribal law with the consent of the chiefs and a specially appointed committee, commanded by Major John Ridge.

The group known as the Arkansas Cherokee (and later the "Old Settlers") moved west of the Mississippi to the St. Francis River in what is now Arkansas sometime around 1808. The main body of the Cherokee (the Eastern Cherokee) remained in Georgia. The European culture had had a major influence on the tribe. Some families maintained

Selocta was a Creek warrior who became General Andrew Jackson's guide and adviser. In the winter of 1825-1826, Selocta was forced to move west.

a simple Indian life deep in the mountains. Others had intermarried with families of Irish, German, English, Welsh, and Scottish descent. Many of these Eastern Cherokee were planters and traders who imported goods from England and Europe. By 1800, there were Indian families in the South who ate on English china, walked on fine Turkish rugs, and sat on imported furniture. They had black slaves and large herds of cattle. They sang the songs of the "black-coats," the Moravian and Presbyterian missionaries, and adopted the white man's God.

CHOCTAW

The Choctaw had originally lived along the Mobile and Alabama rivers in southern Alabama. In the 1700s, they were divided into several factions, some siding with the British and others with the French. French influence was strong since many Frenchmen had married into the tribe. Like other southeastern tribes, they traveled west to the Plains region to hunt and often wound up fighting with the Plains bands.

The Choctaw followed the teachings of the missionaries and school teachers. They learned to read and write. They had **lighthorsemen** (Indian policemen) to act as sheriff, judge, and jury. The men herded cattle and the women raised cotton and wove it into cloth. But they were growing more cramped.

In 1765, the British authorities at Mobile negotiated a treaty with the Chickasaw and Choctaw that set the eastern boundary lines and

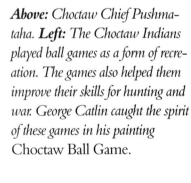

Above: Choctaw Chief Pushmataha. **Left:** *The Choctaw Indians played ball games as a form of recreation. The games also helped them improve their skills for hunting and war. George Catlin caught the spirit of these games in his painting* Choctaw Ball Game.

determined trading relations for the two groups. When the Choctaw signed the Hopewell Treaty in 1786, it was the first treaty between the tribe and the United States. It defined the boundaries of their hunting lands, set up trade relations, and established trading posts.

CHICKASAW

The Chickasaw may originally have been part of the Choctaw tribe. When de Soto camped near the Chickasaw villages (probably near the Tombigbee River) in 1540, he and his men treated the Indians with contempt. As they were getting ready to move west, De Soto demanded that the Chickasaw send him two hundred men to serve as bearers. The Chickasaw had had enough. They attacked the camp and scattered the men and their animals.

The British made contact with the Chickasaw in 1700. When the tribe allied itself with the British, it severed close ties with the Choctaw, who favored the French.

CREEK

The Creek were made up of twelve separate tribal groups. They originally claimed the land from the Savannah River south to the St. Johns River, including the islands along the Atlantic Coast, west to Apalachee Bay, and from this north to the Appalachian Highlands. When De Soto came upon their village in 1540, they were wearing European clothes and shoes, probably obtained from earlier expeditions or shipwrecks.

After the Yemassee War in 1715, they moved to the Chattahoochee and Flint rivers. Although they intermarried with both the Scots and the French, they remained loyal to Great Britain during the Revolutionary War.

SEMINOLE

The Seminole left the Creek settlements around 1750 to move into what was then a neutral zone along the present Florida-Georgia border. There were perhaps 25,000 at the time. But Florida kept changing hands—from Spanish to British and back again. Each time, the Seminole lost more warriors in the battles. By 1763, with less than 300 people left, they fled deep into the Everglades in southern Florida. Over the years, black slaves running away from Spanish owners joined them, created their own villages, and sometimes intermarried.

Do You Remember?
1. Name the Five Civilized Tribes.
2. What was the U.S. government's "civilization policy"?

Above: *Yaha-Hajo, a Seminole chief. The Seminole left the Creek settlements around 1750 to move along the present Florida-Georgia border.* **Opposite page:** *Yoholo Micco, a Creek chief. The Creek were made up of twelve separate tribal groups.*

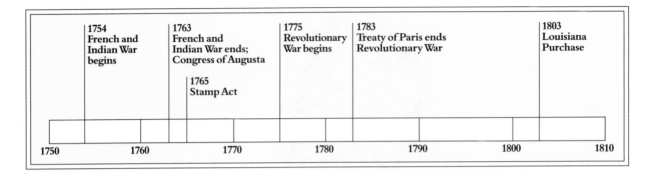

1754 French and Indian War begins

1763 French and Indian War ends; Congress of Augusta

1765 Stamp Act

1775 Revolutionary War begins

1783 Treaty of Paris ends Revolutionary War

1803 Louisiana Purchase

1750 — 1760 — 1770 — 1780 — 1790 — 1800 — 1810

At the Same Time

1718   New Orleans founded by French

1752   Benjamin Franklin invented the lightning rod

1769   Father Junipero Serra founded San Diego, the first Spanish mission in California

1781   Articles of Confederation ratified

1787   Congress passed Northwest Ordinance

Summary

Events in Europe had a major impact on the North American continent and the Indian tribes. The competition to control trade in America became a battle among three great European powers: Great Britain, France, and Spain. Indians often signed treaties with one group only to find former allies on the other side. This caused long-lasting bitterness.

When the colonies broke away from Britain, the Indians had one more country—the United States —with which to deal. When the young country purchased the Louisiana Territory, it opened up a vast unexplored land. Settlers spread out quickly, pushing native tribes from their homelands. In a chain reaction, the Indians moved, joined other tribes, and pushed even further across the continent.

Thus the first major migration into the Great Plains was not European but Native American. The Great Plains area had been a communal (common) hunting ground for centuries; only a few tribes lived along its edges or its principal rivers. The migrations meant more people were dependent on the same food sources as before. It also brought tribes that had been distant enemies closer to each other and opened the door for tribal wars.

Reviewing People, Places, and Things

Define, identify, or explain the importance of the following.

1. boycott
2. cede
3. confederation
4. emissary
5. Five Civilized Tribes
6. frontier
7. indentured servant
8. lighthorsemen
9. livestock
10. monopoly
11. patent
12. repeal
13. slave
14. treaty

Understanding the Facts

1. What countries fought over control of North America?

2. Give two reasons for the conflicts that arose in North America in the early 1700s.

3. Why did the Indians get involved in the colonists' Revolutionary War?

4. What had President Thomas Jefferson hoped to buy before Napoleon offered him the Louisiana Territory?

Developing Critical Thinking

1. What do you think the American colonists meant when they opposed British policies by saying "no taxation without representation"?
2. Do you think the American Revolution against British rule could have been avoided?
3. In the 1790s, the federal government adopted a "civilization policy" toward Native Americans. The Cherokee, for example, were given farming implements, various household goods, and an annual payment in goods.
   a. How did this help the Cherokee?
   b. How did it hurt the Cherokee?

Using Your Skills

1. In 1629, Sir Robert Heath was given all North American lands between 31° and 36° north latitude from the Atlantic to Pacific oceans. Using a modern map of the United States, determine what states today lie entirely or in part within that area.
2. At your library, find a reference book that contains illustrations of flags or banners carried during the American Revolution. One popular American flag of that period included the warning, "Don't tread [step] on Me" written beneath a coiled snake. Suppose the Great Plains tribes had been able to unite to fight for their own Indian Territory. Design a flag for them.

Special Projects

1. Research and compile illustrations of the weapons used by the early Indians.
2. Research how Indians built a tipi and the significance of the construction. Construct a small tipi and provide a written outline of the important elements.

Building Skills: Understanding Timelines

Keeping track of all the events you read about can be difficult. Timelines can help you remember events in the order they happened. Although a timeline can show events over a short period of time, most often they cover a period of years. Making a timeline is a useful way to organize the events that took place during a certain period of time. Sometimes it is impossible to include all events in a timeline; only the most important ones can be included. These important events then provide reference points for other events that occurred during the same period.

In your textbook, timelines appear in the Chapter Review section of the chapter, where they help you remember the events in the order they occurred during the chapter. They also help you place other events within the time frame of those on the timeline. You may want to expand these timelines and add other events to help you in your study of the chapter.

Look at the timeline for this chapter. It covers a period of about fifty years. On a separate sheet of paper, expand the timeline to include the events listed under "At the Same Time." Include at least two other events you read about in the chapter that were not included on the timeline.

Try This: Make a timeline of your life or one of your older relatives (mother, father, grandmother, grandfather, aunt, uncle). Start the timeline with the year you (or they) were born; then write in the present year. Show at least eight events in the order they occurred.

Sooner Trivia

. . . In 1806, Zebulon Pike briefly traveled along the Red River. In a report, he described that part of Oklahoma that he did see as similar to the "sandy deserts of Africa."

. . . The Sparks expedition was probably a reconnaissance mission although those orders were never spelled out.

CHAPTER FIVE

TRAILS OF TEARS

Brother! My voice is become weak....I have lost it mourning over the desolation and injuries of my people....I am a shadow....My people are scattered and gone, when I shout, I heard my voice in the depths of the forest, but no answering voice comes back to me—all is silent around me!

—Colonel Cobb, Choctaw chief

AS SETTLERS PUSHED WESTWARD in greater numbers, they pushed northeastern tribes into Ohio and Indiana. Those tribes, in turn, pushed other tribes further west into the Great Plains. Clashes among the Native Americans and between the Native Americans and settlers grew more frequent.

These conflicts eventually reached Congress and the Supreme Court and led to the Indian Removal Act. The tribes in the eastern United States were forced to give up their lands, their homes, and their rights. The indignities were made worse by the methods by which the Indians were removed from their homes. Over a ten-year period, 60,000 Indians were marched west—most reluctantly or forcibly. Every tribe, the Indian oral histories say, had its own trail of tears. Some were better documented than others.

This mural of the Cherokee Trail of Tears, painted by Elizabeth James in 1939, can be seen at the Oklahoma State Museum of History. The central figures are the family and servant of Chief John Ross.

As more and more Indians migrated to the Great Plains, troubles among the tribes increased. There were conflicts over hunting and trapping. Horses and livestock were stolen. In some cases, old enemies settled too close to one another. Trappers and traders sometimes encouraged the fighting between tribes. Conflict between the Osage and the Arkansas Cherokee was close to open war.

The government could no longer ignore the troubles. On December 25, 1817, Major William Bradford and a company of men from St. Louis arrived at Belle Point on the Arkansas River to build Fort Smith. It was hoped that those at the outpost would be able to settle the troubles among the Indian tribes, but it took them two years to get the Cherokee and the Osage to sit down for **negotiations** (the process of coming to terms over differences). In the resulting treaty, the Osage gave 7 million acres of their claims in Indian Territory (what is now Oklahoma) back to the government. The treaty, however, did not end the fighting between the two tribes.

In 1819, Congress created Arkansas Territory, which included present-day Arkansas and Oklahoma. In 1820, the territorial government created Miller County, one of three Arkansas counties west of Fort Smith. This county included a large area of what is today southeastern Oklahoma. Miller Courthouse was named the county seat, and a formal county government organized. The next year, new boundaries were drawn, and some land that was part of Miller County was given to the Choctaw. The white settlers who were already there were so furious they burned down the courthouse and destroyed most of the records.

Meanwhile, the Osage and Arkansas Cherokee were still battling. In August 1822, Colonel Matthew Arbuckle held a council of Arkansas Cherokee and Osage chiefs at Fort Smith. Governor Miller of Arkansas also attended. They all signed the Treaty of Fort Smith, which called for peace among the tribes. However, in 1823, Osage warriors attacked a small party of white hunters from Arkansas, killing a prominent (widely known) Arkansas citizen. People in the territory were outraged. They demanded a fort closer to the Indian problems.

Above: On December 25, 1817, Major William Bradford and a company of men from St. Louis arrived at Belle Point on the Arkansas River to build Fort Smith. You can see the foundations of the fort in the photograph. *Left:* Fort Gibson was re-created on its original site.

Colonel Matthew Arbuckle (above) held a council for Arkansas Cherokee and Osage chiefs at Fort Smith in 1822, where the Treaty of Fort Smith was signed.

In March 1824, Colonel Arbuckle moved his men up the Verdigris River to build a fort in the Three Forks area. Building supplies on the frontier were scarce, so the men hauled with them the doors, windows, and floors originally used at Fort Smith. Fort Gibson was the first U.S. military post in the territory. As soon as Arbuckle had the men working on Fort Gibson, he set up Fort Towson near the Red River to guard the Spanish border. Fort Towson served as the main U.S. Army post among the Choctaw.

A treaty with the Arkansas Cherokee in 1828 called for them to give up their land in Arkansas for 7 million acres in Indian Territory (the same land that had belonged to the Osage). The government then turned around and gave that land to the Creek, causing even more trouble. The Cherokee and the Creek fought over the land until 1833, and the Osage refused to stop hunting on it.

It took so long to settle the Indian problems on the frontier that President Andrew Jackson appointed a commission to travel to Indian Territory and straighten out matters. The three-man commission consisted of Montford Stokes, former South Carolina governor; Henry Ellsworth, a military leader; and John W. Schermmerhorn, a minister and politician. Traveling with the Commission were several writers, including Washington Irving, who were along to write details about this new country and the Indians.

In October 1832, Ellsworth and the writers set out from Fort Gibson with a detachment of infantry. They planned to travel into the center of the Territory (what is now Wagoner, Tulsa, Pawnee, Payne, Oklahoma, and Cleveland counties). Irving wrote of his adventures in *A Tour on the Prairies*. He was much taken with the wild ponies that covered the prairies. His reports of the Indians were less kind.

In the summer of 1833, trouble broke out between the Kiowa and the Osage on Otter Creek. In the Battle of Cutthroat Gap, the Osage wiped out the Kiowa. Meanwhile, in the western part of the state, the Comanche and their allies were making travel hazardous for Texas settlers and for traders on their way to Santa Fe.

Something needed to be done, and General Henry Leavenworth decided to make a show of force to see if he could strike a treaty with the Indians. George Catlin, an artist, accompanied the troops. Unfortunately, Leavenworth's timing was poor, for it was the middle of summer. Within two days, half his company—men and horses both—came down with a "bilious fever"; the other half suffered in the heat. General Leavenworth fell from his horse while chasing a buffalo calf, was badly injured, and died. Colonel Henry Dodge had to take over the expedition.

Near the Wichita Mountains, Dodge met a Comanche party. At first, it looked as if the two opposing armies might begin a war. But the Indians led Dodge and his men to their camp, which consisted of almost 800 tipis. From there, they all marched onto a Wichita village of about 200 lodges. When the Comanche chief arrived with a group of Kiowa, the official talks began. On July 25, 1834, Dodge presented the tribal chiefs with rifles and pistols; and the Indian leaders agreed to go east to meet with the government officers in the future. Dodge returned to Fort Gibson, satisfied that he had made friends of the Plains Indians. He left 150 men buried on the prairies.

While Dodge had been busy negotiating, George Catlin had wandered about the prairie villages, sketching, and taking notes. He watched the Comanche catching wild ponies with lassos, sketched women and warriors, and made notes on their daily habits. Catlin's paintings and notes about the Indians preserved their history.

This portrait of George Catlin was painted by William Fiske. Catlin was the "photographer" of his day, painting the scenes as he had seen them. He was a prolific painter of early frontier life.

Do You Remember?
1. Where was the first fort in Indian Territory?
2. What popular American writer of the times wrote *A Tour on the Prairies*?
3. The military expedition that Catlin accompanied is sometimes called the Leavenworth expedition and sometimes the Dodge expedition. Why?

INDIAN TRIBES AND TREATIES

A number of treaties were drawn up between the federal government and the Indian tribes. Unfortunately, most went sour. In some cases, neither the Indians nor the government was honest. The treaties that affected the Five Civilized Tribes in the Southeast are particularly important because they set up the early boundaries of Indian Territory. Between 1786 and 1825, the southern tribes signed thirty treaties, each time losing a little more of their **ancestral lands** (lands that had belonged to their families, tribes, or ancestors).

EARLY TREATIES WITH THE CHOCTAW

In 1820, the Choctaw signed the Treaty of Doak's Stand. In exchange for the southwestern part of their country, they received a piece of land somewhere between the Red, Arkansas, and Canadian rivers. Unfortunately, part of the land was already occupied by white settlers, and another part was owned by Mexico. Obviously, this was not acceptable to the Choctaw.

Creek Chief William McIntosh was a hero during the War of 1812, achieving the rank of brigadier general in the U.S. Army.

George W. Harkins, a district chief of the Choctaw Nation, tried to explain how his people felt. The Mississippi lawmakers had a right to govern their people, he wrote, but that did not qualify them to become lawmakers to the Choctaw. "Although your ancestors won freedom on the fields of danger and glory, our ancestors owned it as their birthright, and we have had to purchase it from you as the vilest slaves buy their freedom." He knew there would be no peace until they had found another home. The matter was not settled until 1830. That year, the Choctaw signed the Treaty at Dancing Rabbit Creek. In it, they gave up all their lands in Mississippi. The treaty also read, "No Territory or State shall ever have a right to pass laws for the People and their descendants; and...no part of the land granted them shall ever be embraced in any Territory or State."

EARLY TREATIES WITH THE CREEK

The Creek were busy taking care of their farms in 1802 when General James Wilkinson rode in to council. President Jefferson had appointed Wilkinson to deal with the Indians. He was not, however, a tactful man; he accused them of murders and thefts. Tuckabatchee Harjo, one of the Creek leaders, agreed that there had been murders— by both sides.

Wilkinson indicated that the state of Georgia would wipe the slate clean—if the Creek would simply give the state their lands. Because it was planting time, they were eager to settle. They struck a deal: the Creek would sell one prime area for $3,000 a year plus $1,000 in salaries for their chiefs, $10,000 in goods, and $15,000 in cash to pay off the debts claimed by traders.

Georgia and its white settlers continued to push for more land. Disgusted, William McIntosh, chief of the Lower Creek, engineered a law in 1811 forbidding the sale of any more tribal land under penalty of death. An unsuccessful campaign to keep whites out of their territory ended with the Creek losing the Battle of Horseshoe Bend. The resulting treaty forced them to give up half of their land, over 20 million acres.

McIntosh knew it was only a matter of time before whites took over all of their land. In 1824, he gave in and sold 5 million acres for $450,000. In 1825, McIntosh told the chiefs and warriors: "The white man is growing. He wants our lands; he will buy them now. By and by he will take them; and the little band of our people, poor and despised, will be left to wander without homes and be beaten like dogs." The majority did not believe him. So McIntosh, thirteen lesser chiefs, and fifty warriors signed a document trading all Creek lands in Georgia

for land beyond the Mississippi. He received $25,000 for signing. It was his own death warrant, carried out in the tribal manner. More than 170 Creek gathered outside his home in the dark. McIntosh defended himself like a warrior until, pierced by many bullets, he fell and was stabbed through the heart with a knife.

In 1827, Chilly McIntosh, the old chief's son, bought a steamboat and loaded it with eight hundred of his father's followers. They headed up the Arkansas River, to the Oklahoma territory. By 1830, three thousand were living in what is now Wagoner County. Most had little or nothing. Bands of Osage and Delaware had robbed them of their livestock. The supplies that the government had promised—seed for planting, tools with which to plant—were delayed for months.

A few days after the Creek were defeated at Horseshoe Bend, Chief William Weatherford (above) rode into General Andrew Jackson's camp and surrendered.

Do You Remember?
1. Why were the treaties affecting the Five Civilized Tribes important?
2. What was decided at Dancing Rabbit Creek in 1830?
3. Who was the leader of the Lower Creek in the early 1800s?

THE INDIAN REMOVAL ACT

In 1824, President James Monroe, in his last message as president, recommended that all Native Americans east of the Mississippi River be removed to the West. Four years later, when he became president, Andrew Jackson began to act on that recommendation.

Various southern states had passed laws outlawing tribal governments and making the Indians subject to state laws, a clear violation of federal treaties. Jackson's agents delivered a message to the southern tribes: "Their father" [the president] was providing a country large enough for them all, and they should remove to it. "There their white brethren will not trouble them, they will have no claim to the land, and they can live upon it, they and all their children, as long as the grass grows or waters run, in peace and plenty." The agents added, "Where [you] are now, [your] father cannot prevent [you] from being subject to the laws of the state."

In 1828, the Arkansas Cherokee signed a treaty and received 7 million acres in northeastern Indian Territory. Part of this was "a perpetual outlet west," a strip of land that allowed them to travel freely to the buffalo hunting grounds. (This area would later be called the Cherokee Outlet.) They moved to northeastern Oklahoma the next year.

Those Indians still living in the South did not want to leave. One Choctaw leader wrote his agent, "The red people are of the opinion that, in a few years, the Americans will also wish to possess the land west of the Mississippi....We have no wish to sell our country and remove to one that is not fertile and good, wherever it is situated."

Jackson would have none of their rhetoric (talk) and responded by proposing the **Indian Removal Act**. Congress was in an uproar. Edward Everett, one of the senators from Vermont, was aghast:

This 1942 painting of the Trail of Tears, by Robert Lindneux, depicts the Indians difficult trip to the West.

Ten or fifteen thousand families, to be rooted up, and carried a...thousand miles into the wilderness! There is not such a thing in the annals of mankind....To remove them against their will, by thousands, to a distant and different country, where they must lead a new life, and form other habits, and encounter the perils and hardships of a wilderness....They are not barbarians; they are essentially a civilized people....They are planters and farmers, they are tradespeople and mechanics, they have cornfields and orchards, looms and workshops, schools and churches and orderly institutions!

But Georgia Senator Wilson Lumpkin urged Congress: "Build a fire under them. When it gets hot enough, they'll move." The Indian Removal Act passed in 1830.

CHOCTAW REMOVAL

The Choctaw were the first southeastern tribe to be removed. In the winter of 1831-1832, the Choctaw of Alabama and Mississippi were rounded up and headed west. In Memphis, French traveler Alexis de Tocqueville watched as they tried to cross the Mississippi River.

It was then the middle of the winter, and the cold was unusually severe; the snow had frozen hard upon the ground, and the river was drifting huge masses of ice. The Indians had their families with them; and they brought in their train the wounded and the sick, with children newly born, and old men upon the verge of death. They possessed neither tents nor wagons, but only their arms and some provisions....No cry, no sob, was heard amongst the assembled crowd; all were silent....The Indians had all stepped into the bark which was to carry them across, but their dogs remained upon the bank. As soon as these animals perceived that their masters were finally leaving the shore, they set up a dismal howl, and, plunging all together into the icy waters of the Mississippi, swam after the boat.

The Choctaw marched through six inches of snow. There were only two wagons for every hundred people. In the muddy roads, the wagons could make perhaps five miles a day. "There are many among us who are young, and many who are old and infirm, none of whom can walk, and they have not horses," one man wrote. "They all have implements of husbandry. How are they to be got along? And how are these people to live without them in the West?"

Andrew Jackson was born on the Carolina frontier in 1767. He won fame as an Indian fighter in the War of 1812 and later served as president of the United States. Jackson was the prime architect of the Indian Removal Act.

This painting by Valjean Hessing is a twentieth-century interpretation of the Choctaw Trail of Tears.

When a cholera epidemic struck, even a weary soldier wrote, "Death is hourly among us." No one knows for certain, but perhaps one fourth of the Choctaw died on the trail. There was one good sign. One portion of the Shawnee tribe had been moved into Missouri and Kansas about 1825. When the Choctaw claimed the area in 1831, some of the fields were already fenced and plowed.

CREEK REMOVALS

The Upper (Eastern) Creek had remained in Georgia and Alabama. In 1832, a **depression** (a severe decline in the economy) swept through the Southeast. Indian Territory offered the promise of food and a fresh start. The first of the Creek made their way west in 1828. By 1830, about 3,000 lived along the Arkansas River in Indian Territory.

There was still a large group of Creek in the Southeast who had not moved, however. In March 1832, several Creek leaders, including Opothleyahola, William McGillivray, and Benjamin Marshall, signed a new treaty giving up all their lands in Alabama. No one would be forced to go; but if they did go west, the government agreed to pay their removal expenses and their living expenses for a year. In December 1834, one band of Creek headed toward Indian Territory. Those who stayed received land allotments, but they had to live under white man's law.

The government did not live up to its promises. When a famine set in, land speculators came with food and asked the Indians to sign blank pieces of paper. Somehow those signed papers were turned into deeds,

Opothleyahola was one of several Creek chiefs who signed a treaty in March 1832, giving up all the Creek lands in Alabama.

and the families lost their homes. Their cattle were killed or stolen, crops set afire, and homes robbed. Settlers shot Indians in broad daylight as they worked in their fields. When the Creek tried to defend their homes, they were arrested. When they organized a resistance movement, settlers appealed for protection. Soldiers were sent to put down the "Creek Rebellion." The soldiers rounded up the Creek and placed them in camps. Some who refused to go were shot.

Finally in the winter of 1836, more than 14,500 Creek began the trek west. Nearly 2,500 chiefs and warriors were labeled hostile and dangerous, placed in shackles (leg irons), and forced to walk to Fort Gibson. The *Montgomery Advertiser* reported, "The spectacle was...truly melancholy. To see the remnant of a once mighty people fettered and chained together—forced to depart from the land of their fathers into a country unknown is of itself sufficient to move the stoutest heart."

Like other tribes, the Creek feared the water. They believed that if they died, they would be thrown overboard and their spirits would be left to wander. Nevertheless, about three hundred boarded steamboats for the trip down the Alabama River to the Gulf of Mexico and then to the Mississippi River. There they were placed on a condemned river boat. The rotting craft sank upriver, and all passengers were lost.

Most Creek chose to walk. Shoes wore out quickly, and they wrapped their feet in rags to keep them from bleeding. Dressed only in thin cotton clothing, they were not prepared for the bad weather. There was one wagon loaded with blankets, which were offered to Indians suffering from the cold. But the soldiers would not touch those blankets; it was said that they were contaminated with smallpox. True or not, smallpox did break out, as did malaria. Horses died from exhaustion, and wagons had to be abandoned. People stripped the bark from trees for food. Families were not even given time to bury those who died. One sympathetic captain sent soldiers ahead to prepare fires so the group would at least be warm at the end of the day.

About 15,000 Upper Creek arrived at Fort Gibson alive. As many as 6,000 may have died on the way. The Creek wrote a letter to the agents who had conducted the journey:

You have been with us many moons. You have heard the cries of our women and children....Our road has been a long one...and on it we have left the bones of our men, women, and children. When we left our homes the great General Jesup told us that we could get to our country as we wanted to....We wanted to go in peace and friendship....We were drove off like wolves...and our people's feet were bleeding....We are men....We have women and children, and why should we come like wild horses?

Another 3,500 Creek died from exposure or fever in the few months after they arrived. They were not even welcomed by their Lower Creek brothers. The old betrayal was too deep to be easily brushed aside.

CHICKASAW REMOVAL

The Chickasaw were outwitted by the trading system. Thomas Jefferson had recommended that the tribe be encouraged to purchase beyond their ability to pay. "And whenever in that situation, they will always cede lands to rid themselves of debt," he wrote. By the mid-1820s, the once-proud nation had fallen on hard times. "Their power has been broken, their warlike spirit subdued, and themselves sunk into objects of pity and commiseration," wrote William Clark, superintendent of Indian Affairs at St. Louis. The only way to save them, he felt, was to remove them to a country "where they could rest in peace, and enjoy in reality the perpetuity...the lands on which their buildings and improvements would be made."

But the Chickasaw refused to leave the land where the bones of their fathers were buried. (In 1827, Thomas McKenney, a commissioner of Indian Affairs, visited their council. He urged them to "hasten with all speed to place [the children] in a situation that will secure them against the evils that your fathers endured.") When they rode out to see the new land, they kept finding fault with each piece of land the government suggested. Levi Colbert, the Choctaw High Minko (chief), even suggested that the government purchase Mexican lands along the Sabine River for them. Three years later, in 1837, the Chickasaw signed a treaty at Doaksville (near Fort Towson). They gave up 6 million acres in the Southeast and paid the Choctaw $530,000 for part of the Choctaw land in Indian Territory.

The Chickasaw collected their personal possessions and gathered in Memphis on July 4, 1837, for the trek west. They were dressed proudly in national costume. Their black slaves walked alongside them, and they herded 7,000 ponies. But there on the east side of the Mississippi River, they balked. They had heard that a boiler had exploded in one of the steamboats, and they would not board any boat. Finally, the military leaders threatened to throw away their food if they did not get aboard. They split into two groups, some went aboard a river steamer, others traveled with the wagons.

The cross-country trek was painfully slow. Cholera killed many, as did spoiled rations bought from dishonest government contractors. When someone died, they stopped and conducted a proper burial rite.

The weary Chickasaw found no relief when they arrived. Smallpox rampaged through their camp, killing almost five hundred. When ra-

In 1827, Thomas McKenney (above), a commissioner of Indian Affairs, visited a Chickasaw council. He urged them to "hasten with all speed to place [the children] in a situation that will secure them against the evils that your fathers endured." McKenney continued his interest in Indian affairs by helping compile a four-volume History of the Indian Tribes of North America. *Many of the pictures used in this book can be found in the extensive collection of lithographs included in the set.*

Cherokee Chief John Ridge (below) believed his people had little chance of holding on to their land. He and several others signed a treaty giving up their lands for $5 million.

The map shows the **TRAILS OF TEARS** with routes for CHOCTAW, CHEROKEE, CREEK, CHICKASAW, and SEMINOLE, and the INDIAN TERRITORY CEDED OR RESERVED (DATES OF REMOVAL).

tions finally arrived, the corn was so bad even the horses would not eat it. The flour was sour, and one leader claimed that the pork was so bad that it would kill what was left of the tribe if they ate it. They were even billed $700,000 for food that never arrived. Major Ethan Allen Hitchcock was outraged and announced loudly that the Territory was "full of scandals."

Do You Remember?
1. When was the Indian Removal Act passed by Congress?
2. Which southeastern tribe was the first to be moved west?
3. When did the Chickasaw Nation finally agree to move west?

CHEROKEE REMOVAL

In 1822, the Eastern Cherokee living in North Carolina and Georgia were a thriving nation. They had their own government with a written constitution. Their capital of New Echota, Georgia, was a bustling small town with public buildings, stores, and even one or two clapboard homes. They had built roads and a flourishing trade with American and European merchants. Their sons and daughters attended the best Eastern colleges. Some were even missionaries.

In December 1827, Georgia claimed the rights to all Indian land within its borders. When gold was discovered on Cherokee lands in 1828, thousands of trespassers dug up more than $16 million in gold. The legislature passed a law forbidding any Indian to dig for gold, even if it was on his own land. When the Cherokee tried to protect their property, they were jailed, beaten, or killed. Baltimore attorney William Wirt tried to bring a false imprisonment charge against the state of Georgia, but no one from the state showed up to answer the Supreme Court. Instead, Georgia passed a law requiring any white person living in the Cherokee Nation to take an oath of allegiance to the state; those who refused, like missionaries Samuel Worcester and Elizur Butler, were imprisoned. Georgia began raffling off the Indian lands.

The Cherokee appealed to reason, to mercy, and to Washington. They were educated men, and they decided to battle the white man with his own weapons—the law and the courts. In 1831 and 1832, the U.S. Supreme Court ruled that Georgia could not remove the Cherokee from their tribal land and that such an action was illegal. President Andrew Jackson ignored the ruling, saying "[Chief Justice] John Marshall has rendered his decision, now let him enforce it."

John Ridge, a young educated Cherokee, believed that the Cherokee had little chance of keeping their land. If they could not, then they should get as much as possible for it. Ridge, Elias Boudinot, Stand Watie, and David Vann formed the Treaty Party. In March 1835, they signed a treaty exchanging the Cherokee lands for $5 million. In December, when Ridge faced his people at New Echota, he begged them to be reasonable: "An unbending iron necessity tells us we must leave [the graves of our fathers]....There is but one path of safety, one road to future existence as a Nation....Give up these lands and go over beyond the great Father of Waters." When he signed the treaty, those near him heard him remark, "I have signed my death warrant."

Suddenly, the Cherokee were beset with thieves. "The lowest classes of the white people are flogging the Cherokees with cowhides, hicko-

New Echota, in Georgia, became the permanent Cherokee capital in 1825, symbolizing the willingness of the tribe to utilize the best of the white man's government and lifestyles. In 1838, General Winfield Scott brought 7,000 men into New Echota and set up headquarters to direct the roundup and removal of the Cherokee to Indian Territory.

ries, and clubs," wrote Cherokee John Ross. "We are not safe in our houses—our people are assailed by day and night by the rabble....This barbarous treatment is not confined to men, but the women are stripped also and whipped without law or mercy."

On March 10, 1838, a petition arrived in Washington, asking Congress to protect the Cherokee. The 100-page appeal carried 15,665 signatures—every Cherokee. Congress charged that the document was a forgery. On May 10, 1838, the orders to march arrived.

It was raining that October day in 1838 when federal troops were given orders to round up the Cherokee. Men were seized in their fields or while walking along the road; women were taken from their spinning wheels. Families seated at dinner were startled by blows on the door and bayonets pointed at them. U.S. troops rounded up 18,000 men, women, and children in North Carolina and Georgia and herded them into stockades. There they waited—until the government decided enough had been brought in to move them west.

They left behind schools, governments, newspapers, and printing presses. Well-to-do Cherokee left fine-blooded race horses, rich household furnishings, immense libraries, and fine silver. In many cases, they saw their homes in flames, set on fire by the mob that followed the soldiers. Often their livestock was driven off even before the soldiers had the Indians headed in the other direction.

About 1,100 Cherokee managed to escape into the mountains of western North Carolina. Those who were coaxed out of hiding were shot. About 700 hid in the area around Quallatown; these escapees would later form the Eastern Band of Cherokee.

It was also raining on the morning the Indians were loaded into 645 wagons and started west. They had 1,400 miles to go—over the Cumberland Mountains and across the icy Ohio and Mississippi rivers. By the time they reached Illinois, winter had set in. Tribal leaders were dying off rapidly in the cold. The sick were often simply left behind. Family members and possessions disappeared in the rivers. Settlers often charged as much as 75¢ a wagon and 15¢ a horse to cross their lands. If the Cherokee had no money, their horses and livestock were taken in unfair trades.

No one knows for sure how many began the journey to Indian Territory—perhaps as many as 18,000. Almost one fourth of them died in the stockades or on the journey. "Murder is murder and somebody must answer, somebody must explain the streams of blood that flowed in Indian country in the summer of 1838," wrote Private John G. Burnett in 1890. "Somebody must explain the 4,000 silent graves that mark the trail of the Cherokees to their exile."

David Vann was a member of the group that negotiated a treaty with the government giving up Cherokee lands in the Southeast in exchange for $5 million.

SEMINOLE REMOVAL

The Seminole were the last of the Five Civilized Tribes forced into Indian Territory. American troops had destroyed the Seminole stronghold of Fort Apalachicola in 1816. Andrew Jackson (who was then General Jackson) pursued the Indians into Spanish territory, capturing St. Marks in April and Pensacola in May. Jackson's actions probably led to Spain's cession of East Florida to the United States in 1819.

The Seminole had been living in exile in the Florida swamps. They had few weapons for protection or hunting. In 1832, James Gadsden negotiated the so-called Treaty of Payne's Landing. He offered to give the Seminole $15,400, plus homespun clothing and a blanket for each person if they would move to Indian Territory. However, they would have to pay $7,000 for the slaves and property that they had been accused of stealing or destroying. To make matters worse, the Seminole would be moved to the land of the Creek—their long-standing enemies.

Above left: A portrait of Seminole Chief Osceola by Robert J. Curtis. Osceola and his warriors waged a bitter war against the removal of his tribe to Oklahoma. *Above right:* Tukosee Mathla, a Seminole chief.

The Euchee originally lived in Pennsylvania and New York. As the white settlers moved into their lands they migrated south to Georgia and later joined the Creeks as they moved west to Oklahoma.

A few leaders who had no tribal authority accepted the offer, but not Osceola. Osceola was young, a new chieftain, and brash. "I will make the white man red with blood," he told them. "I will blacken him in the sun and the rain, where the wolf shall smell of his bones and the buzzard live upon his flesh." He and his warriors vanished into the Everglades, a swamp in southern Florida. From 1835 to 1842, Osceola and his followers waged war on whites. In 1837, he was finally lured to Fort Dayton under a flag of truce. When he arrived, he was captured and thrown into the federal prison near Charleston. Malaria slowly took its toll, and he died in January 1838. The war continued until the last Seminole chief to surrender, Pascofa, was placed aboard a boat on the St. Mark's River in March 1842.

About 3,000 weak, sick, hungry, and impoverished Seminole were herded aboard steamboats and sent west. An average of four would die each day until the journey ended. It cost the U.S. government $20 million and the lives of 1,500 soldiers just to remove 3,000 Seminole.

REMOVAL OF OTHER TRIBES

The Euchee had lived in Pennsylvania and New York in the 1500s. As white settlers moved in, they migrated down the coast toward Georgia. When Chief Te-so-so refused to sign a treaty, white men kidnapped and murdered him. The tribe was forced to leave although they had signed nothing and were never paid for their lands. They came west with the Creek Nation in 1829 and 1836.

The Seneca were the largest tribe of the Iroquois Nation. In 1817, a group of Seneca moved to Ohio (where they were called "Mingo"). When the government purchased their Ohio lands, they accepted a new reserve in the northeast corner of the Indian Territory in what was the Cherokee Nation. In 1831, when they saw the land assigned to them, they protested that it was unfit for cultivation. A new treaty gave them land between the Neosho River and the Missouri boundary south of Quapaw country.

The Kickapoo were in Wisconsin in the 1660s. After the French and Indian War, they moved into Illinois, then Missouri, and finally Kansas. An agricultural people, they kept traditional bark-covered houses years after other tribes adopted cabins. They moved into the Choctaw Nation in 1839.

Do You Remember?

1. Where were most of the Eastern Cherokee located?
2. What year were the Cherokee removed?
3. Who was Osceola?

LANGUAGES OF THE INDIANS

There were at least two hundred languages spoken in North America when the Europeans arrived. Some were guttural (produced in the throat), some melodic (with a musical quality), some tonal (in which the pitch or sound of the word determines the meaning). The American Indian languages were completely different from European languages and usually involved a complex description of time, action, the thing being described, and sometimes whether it involved a real or imaginary world.

In an effort to better understand the links among the Indian tribes and to determine which tribes might be related, scholars began an in-depth study of Indian languages in 1816. In 1885, J. W. Powell completed the classification system. The system identified twelve language groups, fifty-one independent Indian languages, plus numbers of *dialects* (regional variations of a basic language).

Today, linguists (language scholars) and anthropologists (scientists who study the culture and behavior of people) know a great deal more about Indian languages. We know that related languages do not necessarily mean that the tribes are related. And some tribes whose traditions and social lives were extremely similar did not speak the same language.

The early Plains Indians tribes appear to represent three of the basic language families. The Apache came from the Athapascan language family; Quapaw were Siouan. Both of these families were from the north. The Caddo, Tawakoni, Wichita, and Waco were from the Caddoan family, which came from the south and east.

Because the Plains Indians were traders, they needed to communicate with other tribes who did not speak their language. They developed a sign language, which seems to have been understood by all the tribes. It made trading easier and enabled them to pass along the latest news. It also allowed them to easily recognize friend or foe at great distances. This sign language was already in use when La Harpe came through the Plains in the 1700s. When Colonel Henry Dodge led his dragoon of men across the area in 1834, he wrote, "While, even with an excellent field glass, I could scarcely make out that the distant speck was a horseman, the Indian by my side would tell me what the speck was saying."

Enoch Hoag, a Caddo chief. The Caddo, one of the original tribes of Oklahoma, gave their name to the Caddoan family of Indian languages.

CHAPTER REVIEW

1820 Treaty of Doak's Stand	1824 Fort Gibson built	1830 Indian Removal Act passed	1831 Choctaw removal		1836 Creek removal		1842 Seminole removal
			1832 Stokes Commission visits Indian Territory		1837 Chickasaw removal		
					1838 Cherokee removal		
1820	1825	1830		1835		1840	1845

At the Same Time

1833 Colt revolver invented

1834 Whig political party formed

1836 Texas declared itself independent

1837 Financial panic led to failure of 618 banks; John Deere produced first steel blade plow

1839 Abner Doubleday wrote the rules of baseball

Summary

As more immigrants came to America, the population grew and moved westward. The Indians had stayed ahead of the frontier for many years. But during the 1800s, the two ran headlong into each other. The federal government soon began pushing the Indians to move to Indian Territory. The Five Civilized Tribes of the Southeast—Cherokee, Choctaw, Chickasaw, Creek, and Seminole—split into factions (groups within the group) over the issue of moving. Many refused to move.

The story of the Indians' removal to Indian Territory is one of the saddest in American history. Thousands of lives were lost along the way to the new land, and thousands more died from the bitter conditions they found in the untamed territory. President John Quincy Adams would write, "We have done more harm to the Indians since our Revolution than had ever been done by the French or English Nation before....We are answerable before a higher 'Jurisdiction.' "

Reviewing People, Places, and Things

Define, identify, or explain the importance of the following.

1. ancestral lands
2. depression
3. Fort Gibson
4. Fort Smith
5. Fort Towson
6. Indian Removal Act
7. Andrew Jackson
8. William McIntosh
9. negotiations
10. Osceola

Understanding the Facts

1. Why did troubles develop among the tribes in the Great Plains?
2. What artist painted pictures of the Great Plains Indians and their lives?
3. What event caused a rift between the Upper and Lower Creek?
4. How did the trading system work against the Chickasaw?
5. What poor health conditions contributed to deaths both during and after the tribes' removal to Indian Territory?
6. What was the ruling by the U.S. Supreme Court concerning the state of Georgia's claim to all Indian land? What was President Jackson's reaction to the Court's ruling?

Developing Critical Thinking

1. List as many reasons as you can why the government wanted the Indians moved.
2. If a case were presented before the Supreme Court today, could a state not appear or respond (as Georgia did)? What might be the consequences of ignoring a Supreme Court ruling?

Using Your Skills

1. Research the early days of Fort Gibson. Draw a map of the fort showing the buildings and how they were used. Show also the location of nearby settlements, such as Three Forks, and the distance from the fort.
2. Locate a map of the United States that shows the Indian removal routes. Choose any one of the tribes and determine about how far they had to travel. If they were able to travel ten miles a day, how long would it take?

Special Projects

1. Research the military outfits and equipment used during the early days of the territorial forts. Report on your findings to the class.
2. Write a poem or short story about the Indian removal from the Indian point of view.

Building Skills: Using Primary Sources

Historians often work with primary sources. *Primary sources* are documents (such as letters, diaries, and log books) written by someone who was alive at a particular time or during a particular event. Below is a portion of George Catlin's account of his travels in the West. Read this excerpt and then answer the questions that follow.

The North American Indian in his native state is an honest, hospitable, faithful, brave, warlike, cruel, revengeful, relentless—yet honourable, contemplative, and religious being...and from the very many and decided voluntary acts of their hospitality and kindness, I feel bound to pronounce them, by nature,

a kind and hospitable people. I have been welcomed generally in their country, and treated to the best that they could give me, without any charges made for my board; they have often escorted me through their enemies' country at some hazard to their own lives, and aided me in passing mountains and rivers with my awkward baggage; and under all of these circumstances of exposure, no Indian ever betrayed me, struck me a blow, or stole from me a shilling worth of my property....[yet] there is no law in their land to punish a man for theft—locks and keys are not known in their country—commandments have never been divulged amongst them; nor can any human retribution fall upon the head of a thief, save the disgrace which attaches as a stigma [mark] to his character in the eyes of his people about him. And thus in these little communities, strange as it may seem, in the absence of all systems of jurisprudence, I have often beheld peace and happiness, and quiet, reigning supreme....I have seen rights and virtue protected and wrongs redressed; and I have seen...affection in the simplicity and contentedness of nature.

George Catlin, *Letters and Notes on the North American Indians,* Vol. 1 (Minneapolis, Minn.: Ross & Haines, Inc., 1841, reprinted 1965), pp. 8-9.

1. What did Catlin mean when he said
   a. In the absence of all systems of jurisprudence
   b. Commandments have never been divulged amongst them
2. If you had met Catlin after his travels, what questions would you have asked him?

Sooner Trivia

. . . The Osage called the Cherokee *Sah-La-Keh,* "That-Thing-on-Its-Head," referring to the calico headbands the Cherokee wore.

. . . Thomas Nuttall, an Englishman and amateur botanist, visited Indian Territory in the early 1800s cataloging hundreds of plants and species of birds, many of which carry the names he gave them.

CHAPTER SIX

LIFE IN INDIAN TERRITORY

All political power is inherent in the people, and all free governments are founded on their authority, and instituted for their benefit.
　　　　　　　　　　　　　—Constitution of the Chickasaw Nation

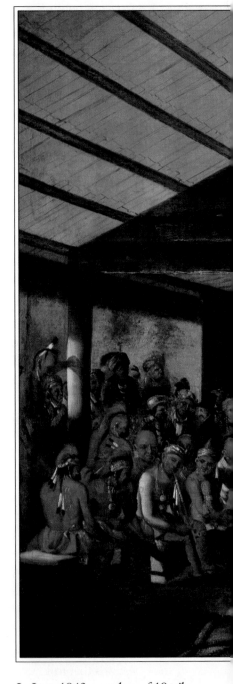

C ONDITIONS IN INDIAN TERRITORY were difficult for those tribes that were resettled there. Many of the tribes were forced to leave behind or had lost a great deal of their possessions. They had to begin new lives, often ill and without tools and shelter. Indian Territory was not part of the United States, and the tribes —particularly the Five Civilized Tribes —were considered separate nations. As soon as possible, they reorganized and set up governments.

MAINTAINING ORDER

As more Indians were removed to Indian Territory, the military became more important. To keep down trouble among the tribes and maintain some order, troops were posted at various forts in the Territory. The military operations moved as trouble broke out.

In 1834, Fort Coffee was built on the Arkansas River near Fort Smith, and Fort Holmes was built near the mouth of Little River, south of today's Holdenville. On the Washita River just north of the Red River, Fort Washita was built in 1842 to protect the Choctaw and Chickasaw from attacks by the Plains tribes to the west. Before the Civil War, it was one of the most important military posts in the area. Its first commander was Zachary Taylor, a future U.S. president.

Fort Gibson was the main stronghold of Indian Territory. Its soldiers were often called upon to monitor the roads and trails. It also served as a haven for the Indians when they were attacked by other tribes. For example, in 1845, when the Skidi Pawnee attacked the Creek near Little River, the Creek headed for Fort Gibson.

Unfortunately, the military sometimes contributed to frontier problems. It was hard for troops at the forts to know what was going on

In June 1843, members of 18 tribes attended a Grand Council at Tahlequah. Between 3,000 and 4,000 attended each session. The purpose of the Council was to renew old friendships and customs and to enact laws among the tribes.

CHAPTER PREVIEW

Terms: ferry, plantation, gristmill, missionary, denomination, temperance, regimen

People: Stand Watie, John Ross, Reverend Epaphras Chapman, John Bemo, Ottawa, Peoria, Delaware, Anadarko, Wyandot, Sequoyah

Places: Fort Washita, Tahlequah, Park Hill, Okmulgee, Nanih Wayah, Doaksville, Tishomingo, Union Mission, Dwight Mission, Tullahassee Mission

elsewhere since there was no communication system. The troops were supposed to keep peace, but it was difficult to tell who was a friend and who was an enemy because sides changed so often. Sometimes it was best to assume everyone was an enemy until proven otherwise.

CIVILIZED INDIANS IN AN UNCIVILIZED LAND

There were no established towns in Indian Territory when the southeastern Indians moved west. There was not much shelter, and the Indians had little with which to start a new life. Many had lost everything. Household goods and livestock had been stolen before they left or were lost along the way; family members and tribal leaders were dead. Reorganizing was a major undertaking.

As part of the removal treaties, most tribes had been promised tools, household goods, and foodstuffs when they arrived in the new territory. But little that was usable arrived. In some cases, Congress failed to set aside the money needed. Dishonest traders often took the Indians' goods and sold them to others. Some supplies lay for months in storehouses and on docks waiting for boats going upstream. Other goods were dumped along the river and left to ruin.

Lack of supplies caused severe problems. During the first winter, for example, the Creek Indians huddled outside the walls of Fort Gibson, dying of exposure and smallpox. They built crude shelters with the only tools they had: tomahawks, knives, and stone axes. The promised nails and hammers had not arrived. In spring, the Indians waited for the guns for hunting and the plows for tilling that they had been promised; they seldom arrived.

Those tribes that had money were charged outrageous prices by unscrupulous (dishonest) traders. When payments to the Indians were due, traders —as well as members of the tribe —often brought in "doctored" whiskey, leaving the Indians drunk and penniless.

To make matters worse, tribal members argued among themselves. Leaders who had signed the removal treaties had been killed, and the perceived betrayal split the tribes. For example, there were two factions (sides) within the Cherokee tribe. Stand Watie was chief of the followers of John Ridge and Elias Boudinot, who had been murdered; John Ross, the principal chief, controlled the government. The Creek, whom George Catlin described as the most advanced tribe "in the arts and agriculture," were split between those who had followed the McIntoshes west and those who had stayed in the South and were removed later. They banned missionaries from their lands for twenty years because they felt the missionaries had contributed to the split in the tribe.

THE FARMER-HUNTERS

Even before the move to Indian Territory, there had been two groups of Indians in most tribes—those who were small farmers and lived off the land and those who were the merchants and educated leaders.

Once in Indian Territory, those who preferred the farmer-hunter lifestyle settled in a likely spot along the river. There they cleared the underbrush and built a shelter. Sometimes two or three families would settle near each other to provide protection from the Plains tribes.

When a storm overtook Charles Latrobe and two others canoeing their way down the Arkansas River in 1832, they put in at one such settlement. Frenchman Jack, son of a Cherokee woman and a French settler, offered them shelter. Jack's wife was Cherokee, and they had several children. A black slave girl acted as interpreter.

"The dwelling-house was a substantial log building of one single apartment, in which there was the strangest mixture of European furniture and Indian apparatus and contrivances," he wrote. There were no windows; and crockery, clothes, and saddles were all stored on shelves and pegs. There were two large, low bedsteads on either side of the door. Various boxes held the family's wardrobe and other

Principal chief John Ross (above left) and Stand Watie (above), chief of the followers of John Ridge and Elias Boudinot, were rivals for lead-ership within the Cherokee Nation.

TALKING LEAVES

Native American languages were oral (spoken) languages. The Indians' history, traditions, and crafts were all passed on by stories and sign language. The Indians were very impressed when they first discovered the white man's ability to communicate without seeing or hearing the speaker.

The first person to develop a written Indian language was George Guess (or Gist), also known as Sequoyah, the son of a Cherokee woman and Nicholas Gist, a friend of George Washington. Sequoyah could not speak, read, or write English, but he was intrigued when he watched soldiers read letters from their families. Sequoyah had been crippled by a hunting accident and could not do much outdoor work. So he decided to invent a Cherokee *syllabary*, or alphabet. Instead of having individual letters, a syllabary has a group of letters that stand for whole syllables.

He probably would not have been able to complete the task, however, without the help of the missionaries. They were eager to develop written languages for the tribes because they then would be able to translate the Bible and other religious and educational materials. With the help of Presbyterian missionaries Samuel Worcester and his daughter Ann Eliza, Sequoyah began work. Several times he thought he had a system figured out, but it was not correct. Once his neighbors burned his cabin because they thought such work

Sequoyah invented the syllabary that was the basis for a written Cherokee language. The sculpture of Sequoyah (top), the interior of his cabin (above), and his portrait (opposite page) can all be seen at Sallisaw.

was not proper for a Cherokee. His wife even destroyed his papers on one occasion. Sequoyah only shrugged and started over.

Sequoyah actually developed the system some time between 1800 and 1820. The "Talking Leaves" consisted of 86 characters that represented the syllables in the Cherokee language. At first, no one believed him. To convince the tribal chiefs, Sequoyah recorded testimony in a court case. Then he had his six-year-old daughter, who had not been at the trial, read his record. The chiefs claimed it was a trick. It was several months before the tribe accepted his work. By 1828, the first Cherokee newspaper, the *Cherokee Phoenix*, was publishing text side-by-side in Cherokee and in English so that the characters could be compared to each other. Thousands of Cherokee learned to read and write using his system.

Below: A replica of the Cherokee Council House at Tahlonteeskee, the western capital of the Cherokee from 1829 to 1839. *Right:* A reconstructed Cherokee log cabin at Tahlonteeskee, circa 1830.

treasures and were also used as chairs. There were other buildings surrounding the main cabin—kitchen, smokehouse, storehouse, and a weaving shed. Cattle and horses rustled in the neighboring cane-brake; fierce-looking pigs, with bristling mane and pointed ears, ruled the forest paths. Dogs—as much wolf as dog—were numerous. There were also a "peculiar breed of ducks" and hens with "long, yellow, unsightly legs of an unusual height."

In these small clearings, the sons and daughters of trappers, traders, and Indians managed to feed and clothe their families. Tribal leaders often lived as frugally as other tribal members. When Cherokee Chief Sapulpa's daughter Sarah was born in 1836, their home consisted of three log cabins—one for cooking and two for sleeping quarters. The logs and shingles had been hand-fashioned on their own land. The floors were made from logs that they had split themselves.

THE MERCHANTS

Well-dressed Indian merchants had for years sold cotton, beef, sugar, livestock, pork, corn, dry goods, and slaves to trading firms in Augusta, Georgia; Pensacola, Florida; and Mobile, Alabama. They too lost their homes and lands in the move west. But they also lost their business connections. Now they had to develop new trading relationships.

The rivers were the only means of transporting large amounts of produce out of Indian Territory, and so the Indians had to establish themselves in towns along the Mississippi River. Chouteau (on the Canadian River), Tahlequah (near Three Forks), and Doaksville (on the Washita) became important trading centers. The Indian merchants then moved the goods down the rivers to the port of New Orleans.

One of the first improvements on the rivers were ferries. A **ferry** is a large boat designed to carry passengers, goods, or vehicles across a body of water, such as a river. The first ferries were flat barges or rafts. A rope was strung from one shore to another and used to guide the raft across. If the current was swift, it was not always easy to land where the traveler intended.

INDIAN PLANTATIONS

Tribal land was free for a citizen to use for hunting, fishing, cutting timber, or grazing livestock. Tribal members could clear land, farm, and build improvements (such as a house) as long as they did not bother their neighbors. They could sell their homes and improvements, but the land belonged to the tribe.

In the rich bottomlands, particularly along the Red River, the former Indian planters established new **plantations** (large estates or farms). They put their black slaves to work clearing fields; planting cotton, sweet potatoes, and corn; and raising horses and cattle. Robert Love, a Chickasaw, managed two plantations on the Red River with two hundred slaves. The plantations yielded about five hundred bales of cotton each fall, and Love chartered (rented) a steamship to haul the crop

One of the few remaining homes of the wealthy planters is the John Murrell Home in Tahlequah, circa 1843. Murrell was married to the niece of Chief John Ross.

Robert M. Jones (top), a wealthy half-blood Choctaw planter, had five hundred slaves, five plantations, and a fleet of river steamers that he kept constantly running between Kiamichi Landing and New Orleans. Ed Baily (above) was a slave of Robert M. Jones.

to New Orleans for sale in the open markets. Robert M. Jones, a wealthy half-blood Choctaw planter, had five hundred slaves, five plantations, and a fleet of river steamers that he kept constantly running between Kiamichi Landing and New Orleans.

The planters built houses complete with libraries and pianos to remind them of the homes they had left behind. Rose Cottage, the elegant home of Cherokee John Ross, sported a Southern-style columned porch. Robert Jones built Rose Hill shortly after he moved to the Territory in the early 1830s. It was decorated with crystal chandeliers imported from Europe and fine Oriental carpets. The planters entertained other well-to-do families regularly. Conversations centered on politics, business, literature, and government.

By 1834, George Catlin wrote that it was not uncommon to see the Creek "like the Cherokee...laying out fine farms, and building good houses...surrounded by immense fields of corn and wheat....It is no uncommon thing to see a Creek with twenty or thirty slaves at work on his plantation." When General Ethan Allen Hitchcock traveled through the territory in 1841, he was surprised at the commerce. Indian businessmen managed salt works and ran dry goods stores, trading posts, and blacksmith shops. Even women ran businesses, including boarding houses and **gristmills** (mills to grind grains).

Do You Remember?
1. Who was the first commander of Fort Washita?
2. What were the two general classes within each tribe?
3. Name three common crops grown on the Indian plantations.

GOVERNING THE PEOPLE

Those of the Five Civilized Tribes that had been relocated by this time organized formal governments as quickly as possible. They borrowed ideas from non-Indian culture when it suited them, but they tried to maintain much of their own culture. Some ideas remained at the heart of their way of life: common ownership of land, sharing tribal resources, and respect for the rights of women.

CHEROKEE GOVERNMENT
The Cherokee constitution adopted in 1839 divided the government into three branches: executive, legislative, and judicial. The seat of government was Tahlequah. The *principal chief* was the highest executive office. The executive branch also included an assistant principal chief and an executive council of five members. The Cherokee legislature

Left: The Cherokee Supreme
Court Building at Tahlequah.
Below: The seven-pointed star in
the Great Seal of the Cherokee
Nation symbolizes the seven clans of
the Cherokee and the seven characters of Sequoyah's syllabary.

consisted of a national committee and a council. The national committee had two members from each of the nine districts; the council
had three members from each district. Elections were held every two
years. To serve on the council, a person had to be a free Cherokee male
citizen over twenty-five years of age.

Law was enforced by a supreme court, a circuit court, and other
courts. Judges had to be thirty years old. In criminal cases, those accused had the right to be heard, to be told the exact nature of the accu-
sation, and to confront witnesses. The accused also had a right to a
speedy trial by jury, without having to testify against themselves.

Although the Cherokee constitution called for free exercise of religious worship, it also stated that "no person who denied the being of a
God or future state of reward and punishment" could hold office. The
drafters added: "Religion, morality and knowledge being necessary to
good government, the preservation of liberty, and the happiness of
mankind, schools and the means of education shall forever be encouraged in this Nation."

The tribe, however, was now split into three factions; the constitution did not solve their problems. There was so much violence that
some federal government officials suggested that the Cherokee would
never reconcile and should, therefore, be given separate reservations.
Legislation was introduced to Congress for that purpose, but the Cherokee were able to work out their differences. The Treaty of 1846 recognized a United Cherokee Nation and pardoned past crimes by
Cherokee members.

In 1843, the Cherokee National Council in Tahlequah authorized
the publication of *The Cherokee Advocate*, the first newspaper in the
Indian Territory. The first issue came out the following year in both

The first Creek capitol building (top) was located in Okmulgee. The name Muscogee on the Great Seal of the Creek Nation (above) is an English form of the name Muskokee, a confederacy of Ochese Creek Indians used after 1700. British agents shortened the name of the tribe to Creek, which came to be commonly applied to all Muskogee.

English and Cherokee. The newspaper's motto was "Our Rights, Our Country, Our Race."

In 1851, the Cherokee National Council opened two schools of higher education near Park Hill: the National Male Seminary and National Female Seminary. The schools were supported by tribal funds, thus making them among the first public high schools. The standard of education at the schools was so high that some called Park Hill the "Athens of the Cherokee Nation."

CREEK GOVERNMENT

The first organized seat of government for the Creek, or Muskogee, Nation was Okmulgee. The Creek council had two houses—the house of kings and the house of warriors. Each town had one representative in the house of kings who served for four years. In the house of warriors, each town had one representative plus an additional representative for every two hundred persons in the town. The principal chief had to be at least eighteen years old and council members at least twenty-two. The judicial high court consisted of five "competent, recognized citizens" at least twenty-five years old. The Muskogee Nation was divided into six districts. Each had its own judge, prosecuting attorney, and company of lighthorsemen. There was also a national interpreter. A post office opened at Three Forks in 1843 and another at Micco in 1853. The Creek government did not set up separate schools but worked with the missionaries to fund Tullahassee and Asbury mission schools.

The Creeks first settled along the rivers in the Three Forks area, not realizing how often they flooded. In 1833, the Creek Agency was actually washed away along with all its supplies, guns, and ammunition.

CHOCTAW GOVERNMENT

"All political power is inherent in the people, and all free governments are founded on their authority and established for their benefit," the Choctaw leaders wrote in their constitution. The Choctaw Nation was divided into four districts. The first seat of government was at Nanih Wayah (near today's Tuskahoma); in 1850, the capital was moved to Doaksville near the Red River.

The Choctaw legislature consisted of a senate and a house of representatives. Four senators were elected from each district and served two-year terms. A senator had to be at least thirty years old and a citizen at least one year. Members of the house of representatives were chosen each year from the counties of each district, one representative for every thousand citizens. A principal chief was the chief executive, and there were three district chiefs. The chiefs were elected for two years but were limited to two consecutive terms. Law was enforced through a supreme court, as well as circuit and county courts in each district. Each district had its own sheriff, ranger, and lighthorsemen. The constitution called for speedy and public jury trials. Excessive bail was prohibited, and the accused person had the right to be heard.

An unstrung bow with three arrows and a smoking pipe-hatchet on the Great Seal of the Choctaw Nation (above) notes the history and tradition of the Choctaw. The Choctaw Council House (left) at Nanih Wayah was the first seat of government of the Choctaw Nation.

Unlike the Cherokee, the Choctaw made no provisions concerning religion except to state that there would be no religious test for any public office. The constitution also stated that "no human authority ought in any case whatever to control or interfere with the rights of conscience in matters of religion." The constitution did provide for free speech, stating that

the printing press shall be free to every person, and no law shall ever be made to restrain the rights thereof. The free communication of opinion is one of the inviolable [secure, certain] rights of man, and every citizen may speak freely, write, and print on any subject, being responsible for the abuse of that liberty.

The *Choctaw Telegraph* was first printed in 1848 and the *Choctaw Intelligencer* in 1850.

By 1833, the Choctaw had set up schools in all districts. Several academies were opened after 1840. Spencer Academy and Fort Coffee Academy both covered manual training and agriculture for boys. There was also Armstrong Academy for boys, New Hope School for girls, and Chuahla Female Seminary at Pine Ridge.

CHICKASAW GOVERNMENT

The Chickasaw Nation organized under a written constitution in 1856 and established its national capital at Tishomingo. "All political power is inherent [inborn, fixed] in the people and all free governments are founded on their authority," the Chickasaw wrote in their constitution. Equal rights were given to all free men, and no religious test was required for public office. Several classes of citizens were excluded from voting: an "idiot or insane person" and "those convicted of any criminal violation of law against the Chickasaw Nation."

The legislature was made up of a house of representatives and a senate. There were four senatorial districts. Each district had five representatives in the house. House members were required to be at least twenty-one years of age and live in the Chickasaw Nation and the counties that they represented. The governor of the Chickasaw Nation and its senators had to be Chickasaw by birth or adoption and thirty years old. The governor was elected for two years and could serve only four years in a six-year period.

The judicial powers rested with a supreme court, district (circuit) courts, and county courts. The constitution called for a speedy public trial by an impartial jury, with no one forced to testify against himself or herself. Excessive bail or fines could not be imposed nor could cruel

The figure of the ancient Chickasaw on the Great Seal of the Chickasaw Nation symbolizes a people of great courage. The two arrows held by the warrior signify the two divisions of Chickasaw tribal society.

A governor of the Chickasaw Nation had to be Chickasaw by birth or adoption and at least thirty years of age. They served two-year terms. This photograph of former governors was taken in 1900.

or unusual punishments. All persons could seek remedy in courts of law, and no person would be imprisoned for debt.

The Chickasaw constitution was the only one that addressed issues of marriage and divorce. It outlawed polygamy (the practice of having more than one wife) and living as a couple without a proper marriage ceremony. All property that a woman owned before marriage belonged to her, even after her marriage, and could not legally be controlled by her husband. The constitution allowed for future laws that more clearly outlined the rights of the wife in relation to her separate property and any property held in common with her husband. The issue of property rights was important because many whites married into the tribe to gain access to land. Divorces were not granted except through the district court. Non-Indians who had married into the tribe or who had been officially adopted were entitled to full privileges of citizenship.

The constitution called for full support and maintenance of public schools since "a general diffusion [spreading] of knowledge [is] essential to the preservation of the rights and liberties of the people." Because of the raids by Plains tribes, the Chickasaw were not able to open a school until 1852 when Chickasaw Academy enrolled sixty children. Under Methodist supervision, Bloomfield School for girls opened with twenty-five students in 1853. Wapanucka Female Institute opened in 1852 and Colbert Institute in 1854. The Chickasaw schools were among the best Indian academies of that decade.

Do You Remember?
1. Which tribe required that office holders believe in God?
2. What was the importance of the Treaty of 1846?
3. Why were schools important to the Chickasaws?
4. Why was the issue of property rights important to the Chickasaw?

Reverend Samuel Worcester was perhaps the best known of the missionary-teachers who walked alongside their Indian friends when they were removed to the West.

Missionaries had worked among the Indians since the earliest days of European exploration. A **missionary** is one who is sent to do religious or charitable work in another territory or country. Most major **denominations** (religious groups, such as Methodists, Baptists, and Presbyterians) supported some type of mission work among Native Americans.

The missionaries made both friends and enemies. Many traders opposed their presence because the missionaries supported the **temperance** (antiliquor) movement. Those missionaries whose efforts were labors of love were recognized by the Indians as honorable people. Some missionary-teachers walked alongside their Indian friends and pupils when they were removed to the West. Perhaps the best known was Samuel Austin Worcester. Worcester had been imprisoned in Georgia because he supported the Indians in their efforts to save their lands and tribal independence.

MISSION SCHOOLS

In 1816, the American Board of Commissioners of Foreign Missions outlined a plan to establish Indian schools. The missionaries set up schools as quickly as they could get approval from the mission board, the tribal government, and the federal government. The first school in Indian Territory opened at Union Mission in 1821 with four Osage children. Union Mission was located on the Grand River in what is now Mayes County. The mission family was headed by Reverend Epaphras Chapman and included a farmer, a carpenter, a blacksmith, a doctor, and women to teach domestic skills. It was also here at Union Mission that the first press was established in Indian Territory in 1835.

Dwight Mission was moved from Arkansas to the Cherokee Nation in 1829. The log dwellings at the mission were the first built legally by white settlers in the Territory. Within a few years, there were twenty-one log houses, plus seven or eight outhouses and sheds. There was a "very pleasant yard surrounded by a rail fence and every house fenced off, and had a little yard to itself where the ladies had a few flowers, vines, and flowering shrubbery." There were perhaps three hundred cattle, and the missionary acted as "tinner, broommaker, basketmaker, and chair bottomer."

In 1843, the Creek agreed to sell the Presbyterians a small cabin for $10. The missionaries turned it into a school and called it Koweta Mission. So many pupils showed up that, three years later, they had to expand. John Bemo opened the first school for the Seminole near the

Creek Agency in 1844. Bemo, a nephew of Osceola, had come under missionary influence and was educated to work among his own people.

In 1848, the Oak Ridge School was opened by the Presbyterians on the South Canadian River not far from Edward's Post. In 1849, the Presbyterians built Tullahassee Mission across the river from Muskogee, and the Methodists built Asbury Mission close to where the North and South Canadian rivers joined. The Moravians built New Spring Place Mission in present Delaware County. The Baptists also opened a mission in Delaware County. The Presbyterians created a mission school for the Seminole in 1846, and the Methodists opened Sasakwa two years later.

Reverend Washburn at Dwight wrote to the missionary board, "A teacher should have a good knowledge of the human heart." Teachers spent twenty-four hours a day with their charges. They were expected to be mother, father, teacher, guardian, cook, doctor, nurse, gardener, laundress, and scholar—all at the same time. It was no wonder Mary C. Greenleaf, a missionary to the Chickasaw, wrote, "that there is a great lack of laborers....Those on the ground are obliged to over-work, and then their health fails."

"I wish you could see how busy I am, what constant demands there are upon all my time," Ann Eliza Worcester Robertson wrote her brother from the Tullahassee Mission. "I teach my six hours a day besides giving one evening in a week to the composition writing." She also supervised the laundry and the health care. In addition, Mrs.

This replica of a Dwight Mission cabin was built with logs from the last original building.

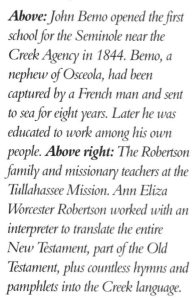

Above: John Bemo opened the first school for the Seminole near the Creek Agency in 1844. Bemo, a nephew of Osceola, had been captured by a French man and sent to sea for eight years. Later he was educated to work among his own people. Above right: The Robertson family and missionary teachers at the Tullahassee Mission. Ann Eliza Worcester Robertson worked with an interpreter to translate the entire New Testament, part of the Old Testament, plus countless hymns and pamphlets into the Creek language.

Robertson worked with an interpreter translating Creek to English to Hebrew to Greek and back again. She translated the entire New Testament, part of the Old Testament, hymns, and pamphlets.

Before teachers could be commissioned by the Board of Home Missions, they had to get four certificates: one showing that they were a member in a Presbyterian or Reformed Dutch church, a second verifying their education and ability as a teacher, a third from a physician assuring good health and strength, a fourth stating their ability to adapt to real mission work.

A single man was paid $166 a month; a single woman, $100; and a couple, $200. They were given $50 to buy clothes and equipment for the journey. Over 65 percent of the missionaries were women.

LIFE IN THE MISSION SCHOOLS

Some of the mission schools operated classes only during the day; children returned to their families in the evenings or weekends. Most missionaries, however, were convinced that the boarding school was the only way to make a real change in the children.

The schools were often frightening to the Indian children, especially those from the nomadic tribes. The children were taken away from

The Choctaw New Hope School was built in 1845.

relatives who considered them a blessing, who doted on them, and who never punished them. At the mission schools, they had to answer to stern people who spoke more of justice than of mercy. They were punished if they spoke their native language, yet they knew no other. Their Indian braids were cut off, and they were given strange, ill-fitting clothes. They ate, slept, did chores, and attended school by white man's time. Even the food tasted strange.

One Indian couple traveled 120 miles to bring their eight-year-old boy to the mission. When they left as night was coming on, the small boy began to cry. The ground was cold, he said between sobs; and he dreaded lying there until morning without a blanket. "We took him into the dormitories and explained to him the mysteries of a bedstead, with its mattress, pillows, sheets, and blankets, and [pointed] to the particular one upon which he should sleep."

At Tullahassee, Indian children arose with the school bell at daylight. They washed themselves, made their beds, and cleaned their rooms. The boys fed stock, drew water, and cut firewood. The girls worked in the dairy or helped prepare breakfast. In summer, breakfast was at six; in winter, at seven. Worship lasted until nine, with classes until noon, followed by a recreation period. Classes resumed at one. Around four in the afternoon, the children did chores for another hour or so. "Tea" was at 6:30, followed by worship and study. Bedtime was 8 p.m. On Sunday, everyone attended Sunday school, both noon and night. Monday was play day, with only a half-day of class. The lessons were endless: spelling, reading, writing, mental and practical arithmetic, algebra, geometry, English, grammar, natural philosophy, composition, and declamation (oral presentation). The girls also learned "the fine art of becoming wives, spinning, weaving, knitting, sewing, cleaning house, and milking the cows."

The strict **regimen** (system of procedures) was hard for both children and teachers. But the missionaries believed that they were winning souls. They rarely admitted that these mostly mixed-blood children had been brought to the mission schools for safety or food. In 1844, when the first school for the Seminole opened, forty children walked in the first day and wanted to eat. When they found there was no free food, fifteen left.

Do You Remember?

1. Name three religious denominations that were involved in missionary work among the Indians.
2. Where was the first mission school in Indian Territory?

SETTLING OTHER TRIBES

The U.S. government continued to resettle tribes to Indian Territory. Nineteen chiefs and leaders of the Comanche signed their first treaty with the United States at Camp Holmes on the Canadian River in August 1835. In 1846, the Penateka band of Comanche and other Texas tribes signed a treaty at Council Springs on the Brazos River. By 1858, it was reported that the Comanche were raising crops, building houses, and sending children to reservation schools. That same year, however, the Texans determined to rid the country of Comanche and Kiowa because of their continued attacks.

In 1859, the military removed the Comanche from their reservation in Texas and settled them with the Caddo along the Washita River near Fort Cobb. The Comanche lost most of their livestock and possessions in the move. They were bitter and ready to take on the white men who had taken their homeland away.

Over the years, the Quapaw had ceded their lands on the Arkansas River, only to be dogged by disaster. After floods made one reserve uninhabitable, they drifted back to their old lands along the Arkansas, starving, dying of disease, and having lost most of their possessions.

An Ottawa chief. The Ottawa were great hunters, warriors, and traders.

They were given land near the Seneca in northeastern Indian Territory, only to discover—after they had built their homes and farms—that the boundary line was wrong; they were on Seneca land. Some moved into the Choctaw Nation along the Red River area, while others went into the Creek Nation. Finally, in 1852, they were relocated on their own reserve between the Grand River and the Missouri line.

In 1857, they were joined by the Ottawa, who may have come from Canada. They were great hunters, warriors, and traders. They were driven out by the Iroquois and were taken in by the Potawatomi at Green Bay, Wisconsin. In 1833, the Potawatomi ceded all of their land on Lake Michigan for a reservation in northeastern Kansas.

The Peoria moved to the Quapaw Reservation about the same time. When the eastern Indians were moved west in 1832, the Peoria and a few Kaskaskia (once the leading tribe of the Confederacy) moved to a reservation on the Osage River in Kansas. In 1854, the Wea and Piankashaw joined them.

The Delaware were a light-complected people originally from the Northeast. Modest and trustworthy, they often acted as scouts and guides. Wherever they settled, they worked hard and built fine farms. One group moved into Indian Territory with the Western Cherokee as early as 1812. In 1859, a group known as the Absentee Delaware were granted the right to live in the Choctaw Nation.

The Anadarko had originally roamed the region of the Angelina and Neches rivers in East Texas and were listed by the French as a Louisiana tribe until 1763. They were removed from Texas in 1859.

The Wyandot, also called Huron by the French, lived east of Lake Huron near what is now Ontario, Canada. Trouble between the Iroquois and the Wyandot and wars with the French caused them to settle along the Detroit and Sandusky rivers, where they became the strongest and most powerful tribe in the area. In 1815, they were given a large part of Ohio and Michigan by treaty, but within four years the government had convinced them to sell most of it. Some migrated from Ohio in 1843 to eastern Kansas. In the 1850s, part of the tribe moved from eastern Kansas to 33,000 acres on the north side of the Seneca Reservation in Indian Territory. In 1865, the last of the Ohio tribe moved to the Quapaw country in Indian Territory.

A Delaware chief. The Delaware were modest and trustworthy. They often acted as scouts and guides.

Do You Remember?

1. Name five tribes that were moved to Indian Territory in the 1850s and 1860s.
2. What Indian tribe was known for its scouts?
3. What tribe was known as great hunters, warriors and traders?

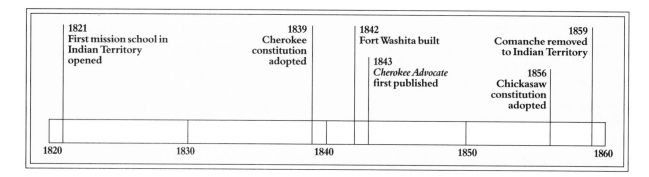

1821	1839	1842	1859
First mission school in Indian Territory opened	Cherokee constitution adopted	Fort Washita built	Comanche removed to Indian Territory
		1843 *Cherokee Advocate* first published	1856 Chickasaw constitution adopted

1820 — 1830 — 1840 — 1850 — 1860

At the Same Time

1837   Victoria became queen of Great Britain

1839   First baseball game played at Cooperstown, New York

1842   First child labor law passed in Massachusetts

1844   First telegraph message sent

1848   Gold discovered in California; the first railroad to run west out of Chicago opened

1851   Herman Melville published *Moby Dick*

Summary

Conditions in Indian Territory were difficult for those tribes that had been resettled there. They had to begin life over again, often ill and without shelter. They also had to contend with the nomadic tribes, such as the Osage, who would settle for a domestic horse or cow when buffalo or deer were not handy. The government continued to transport Indian tribes from the north and east into Indian Territory, which caused more border disputes and difficulties. As more tribes were pushed into the area, some tribes established unions with other tribes to strengthen their numbers. The transported tribes reorganized and set up governments, complete with constitutions and laws.

Both the military and the missionaries were important influences on the frontier. The military tried to bring order. They built roads and forts and they brought in a steady supply of goods. The missionaries brought white man's education and religion.

Reviewing People, Places, and Things

Define, identify, or explain the importance of the following.

1. Reverend Epaphras Chapman
2. denomination
3. Doaksville
4. ferry
5. gristmill
6. missionary
7. Okmulgee
8. plantation
9. regimen
10. Sequoyah
11. Tahlequah
12. Tishomingo
13. temperance
14. Union Mission

Understanding the Facts

1. Why did the military forts change their locations frequently?
2. Why were the goods promised to the Indians upon their arrival in Indian Territory in such short supply?
3. How did the removals disrupt business for the Indian merchants?
4. What three issues lay at the heart of all of the Indian constitutions?
5. What was the first newspaper to be published in Indian Territory?

6. What issues related to women did the Chickasaw address in their constitution?

Developing Critical Thinking

1. Park Hill, the site of the Cherokee national seminaries, was called the "Athens of the Cherokee Nation." Explain what was meant by this phrase.
2. Why were the mission schools so frightening to Indian children?
3. How did the classes at the mission schools differ from classes in schools today?

Using Your Skills

1. On a map of Oklahoma, locate the capitals of the Cherokee, Creek, Choctaw, Chickasaw, and Seminole nations.
2. In 1825, a count of the Cherokee tribe showed that there were 13,563 native citizens, 147 white men who had married into the nation, 73 white women who had married into the nation, and 1,277 African slaves. What percentage of the total population were black slaves? white women? white men?

Special Projects

1. Research and write a paper on the kinds of jobs that women held during the mid-nineteenth century.
2. Assume that you are one of the following: (a) a missionary to the Cherokee, (b) a Creek Indian living near the Texas Road, (c) a Cherokee merchant getting ready for a trip to New Orleans to sell goods, (d) an Osage Indian child enrolled in a mission school. Write a diary or a description of your activities for a week. Include the kinds of chores you would have to do, what things would be easy, what things would be hard, and why.
3. Interview an Indian chief or official. Find out how they were appointed or elected and what they hope to accomplish.

Building Skills: Finding Similarities, Differences, and Connections

One way to better understand historical events and issues is by making comparisons. *To compare* is to look for ways in which two or more things may be alike and for ways they may be different from one another.

As you study Oklahoma history, there will be many opportunities for you to make comparisons. For example, the differences among the various landform regions of the state have influenced how those regions have developed. Sometimes you might compare events within a particular time period. At other times, you might want to focus on just one issue and compare it over several time periods. It is often useful to create a chart to see the similarities and differences more clearly.

Using the information in the chapter and in other reference sources, prepare a chart comparing the minimum ages for political offices set out in the constitutions of the Five Civilized Tribes and in the U.S. Constitution or the state constitution. Why do you think the ages may be different?

Sooner Trivia

. . . One of the earliest roads in Oklahoma was a military road that connected Fort Smith to Fort Gibson near Three Forks and Fort Towson on the Oklahoma-Texas border.

. . . When Reverend Epaphras Chapman died in June 1825, he was buried in the first marked grave in what is now Oklahoma.

. . . Sarah Perkins Nicks was the first woman appointed to a U.S. government position in Oklahoma. She became a postmistress in 1832.

. . . The first printing press was brought to Fort Gibson in 1835. The first book published in Oklahoma was probably *The Child's Book.*

. . . The stone capitol building of the Chickasaw Nation at Tishomingo was finished in 1858.

. . . When Seminole slave John Coheia was given his freedom, he left and founded Wewoka.

CHANGING TIMES

The dream of the West is captured in this painting entitled Westward the Course of the Empire Takes Its Way *by Emanuel Gottlieb Leutze.*

AMERICA'S DESTINY WAS ALWAYS WEST—a land that was at least as much imagination as reality. West! A man could start a new life or strike it rich. There was enough land to start a farm or a family. It was, in the eyes of thousands of people east of the Mississippi, just a little short of heaven—a place of limitless opportunity, where a man could leave everything behind, including his name if he wished.

It was this dream that led men on, to explore the country, to start towns, businesses, and new lives. This same hunger drove the government as well, and many times pointed the way for the travelers.

CHAPTER SEVEN

WESTWARD HO!

The man must know little of the American people who supposes they can be stopped by any thing in the shape of mountains, deserts, seas, or rivers.
—Joshua Pilcher, mountain man, 1830

PEOPLE MOVED WEST for all kinds of reasons. Some thought a settlement was crowded when they could see the smoke from their neighbor's chimney. Some wanted land—a place to start their own families. Others looked for a way to make a living—a new trade or business venture. Still others were running from the law. By 1840, nearly 400,000 settlers had moved into Missouri, then considered the edge of civilization.

MANIFEST DESTINY

The mid-1800s marked a period of westward expansion in the United States. The Louisiana Purchase of 1803 had opened a vast area in the middle of the continent. In the 1830s and 1840s, Americans came to believe in "manifest destiny": their right—and duty—to extend the boundaries of the country to the Pacific Ocean. By the late 1840s, through purchase, annexation, treaty, and conquest, the United States did indeed control virtually all of the land between the two oceans.

In 1819, the U.S. government assigned Major Stephen H. Long the task of exploring the area beyond the Mississippi River. In his report, Long used the term "Great American Desert" to describe the land west of the 98th meridian. He wrote, "it is almost wholly unfit for cultivation." He added that this barren land could be considered a blessing in disguise because it could keep people from moving too far west. Long's poor impression of Oklahoma was a major reason why the federal government chose to set aside large portions of this land for the Indian tribes. Believing the land was unfit for farming, many westward-bound settlers avoided it. Most were bound for the West Coast and California.

Mule-drawn wagons were a familiar sight as more and more people headed West. The mules could be stubborn but could withstand the long, hard days.

The trickle of travelers turned into a torrent after gold was discovered at Sutter's Mill (now Sacramento), California, in 1848. When California was the destination, travelers could go by boat around Cape Horn at the tip of South America. The journey was long (usually taking six to nine months), rough, monotonous, and expensive. Those who could not afford it went overland. Transportation across the continent, however, was limited and often dangerous.

THE FIRST ROADS

The land to the southwest of Indian Territory was controlled by the Spaniards until 1821. That year, the government of Mexico lifted restrictions on trade with the United States. Traders and merchants realized that if they could be first into Santa Fe with American goods, they could make a handsome **profit** (the amount earned on a business undertaking after deducting expenses). But there were no roads through the Indian lands except for the buffalo paths and the trails Indians had made from one camp to another.

Three groups set out almost immediately for Santa Fe, determined to take advantage of the trade opportunities. On September 1, William Becknell led a party of four men and a line of pack animals from Independence, Missouri, to the Great Bend of the Arkansas, southwest across the Cimarron River, to the headwaters of the Canadian River. They reached Santa Fe on November 6, opening the first trade route. Becknell's route eventually became known as the Santa Fe Trail.

About the same time, John McKnight of St. Louis and Thomas James, a trader, headed their boats south to the Arkansas River, turned west near what is now Tulsa, and followed the Cimarron River, probably to where Guthrie is today. There they traded for Indian ponies, rode to the Canadian River, and crossed the Texas Panhandle into northern New Mexico. They reached Santa Fe on December 1.

The third group was led by Hugh Glenn, who operated a trading post on the Verdigris River. With him were Jacob Fowler, a Kentucky surveyor; Baptiste Roy, an interpreter; Paul, Fowler's black servant; and Lewis Dawson, a hunter. They left Fort Smith on September 6. Unfortunately, Dawson was wounded by a bear on November 13; they made it as far as Taos and then turned back.

A survey for the Santa Fe Trail was officially begun in 1825 and completed in 1827. It went from the western border of Missouri, southwest through Kansas to the Cimarron River, through what is now known as the Oklahoma Panhandle, then to Taos, and finally on to

Thomas James (above) and John McNight of St. Louis led one of the three groups of traders who made their way to Santa Fe after the Mexican government lifted trade restrictions with the United States. They knew that the first group to set up business in Santa Fe would make a handsome profit.

Santa Fe. The trip to Santa Fe was long and hard; but it was worth it. One party bought $30,000 in goods in Missouri and returned with $180,000 in currency and $10,000 in furs, not counting livestock.

Do You Remember?

1. What is "manifest destiny"?
2. What event in California increased the number of settlers crossing Indian Territory?
3. What were the disadvantages of traveling by boat to California?

THE FIRST TRAILS

The jumping-off places, where most people considered "civilization" to end, were Missouri (St. Louis, St. Joseph, or Independence) and Arkansas (Fort Smith). Many settlers, and later the "forty-niners" (those who headed for California to search for gold), followed the Oregon Trail: west from Independence to Kansas, onto the south bank of the Platte River, along the valley to Fort Laramie, and then into the Rockies. This route took them north of Indian Territory.

People who were headed to Indian Territory, Texas, Santa Fe, or the Southwest from St. Louis usually followed the Osage Trace, the route the Osage had taken into the Territory. From close to what is now Vinita, travelers headed south, passing between present-day Pryor and Salina toward Perryville (today's McAlester). This route extended south to Boggy Depot and later became known as the Texas Road.

Compare the Mollhausen drawing of Fort Smith, Arkansas, in 1853 (top) with the photograph of present-day Fort Smith.

The flatboats and keelboats lost favor after the invention of the steamboat. Keelboats were not only slower than steamboats, but as many as forty men were needed to move them up and down the rivers.

NAVIGATING OKLAHOMA'S RIVERS

Wherever possible, the early traders and travelers used the rivers. In the 1820s, keelboats were the most common commercial craft on Oklahoma rivers. A **keelboat** is a riverboat with a keel, a strong piece of wood or metal that runs along the bottom of the boat. The keelboats were used to ship in supplies and to transport Indians and troops. Most of the keelboats were equipped with cannon to ward off trouble.

The *Scioto* and the *Velocipede* were the first steamboats to make their way up the Arkansas River to Fort Gibson in April 1827. In May 1831, the steamboat *Enterprise*, under master Captain Hawley, made a successful trip up the Red River to the mouth of the Kiamichi, opening the Red River to commercial traffic. Only a few captains, however, were brave enough to try the shallow Oklahoma rivers. They were too unpredictable for anything except canoe or pirogue. Eventually, the rivers gave out.

Then travelers had to turn to horse, mule, wagon, oxen, or their own two feet—a dangerous undertaking. Crossing Indian Territory alone was asking to die of thirst or malaria at best or (worse) to be attacked by Indians. The Indians attacked because, by treaty, trespassers were not permitted on their land.

PACK TRAINS

Families moving westward usually joined a wagon train. Individuals joined military expeditions or pack trains. A **pack train** was a line of animals loaded with goods or supplies. Pack trains were the means of transportation people like Becknell, McKnight, and Pilcher used. They were the principal business of the area at the time. Many pack trains operated out of the Three Forks-Fort Gibson area and were run by experienced freighters (people who moved goods or cargo). These men could command as much as $125 a month in gold—a steep figure considering that a soldier stationed at one of the forts earned just $8 a month.

An average pack train had at least a dozen horses or mules. Horses were easy to manage, but mules could carry more weight and stand longer hauls. Packing a mule train required a great deal of skill if the load was to make it all the way to Santa Fe. There were no stops during the day, and the animals were tied head to tail to keep them in line.

An experienced rider or two rode in front, with several in the middle, and the rest at the end of the train. This kept the animals moving and cut down on ambushes. If there were no major rivers to cross, a pack train could make ten to fifteen miles a day.

Most of us think of horse-drawn or mule-drawn wagon trains when we think of the westward migration. But this engraving of an ox-drawn wagon indicates that the early pioneers were quite resourceful and used any type animal that was available to move their belongings and supplies across the rugged terrain.

TRAVEL GUIDES TO THE WEST

These illustrations from The Prairie Traveler *gave early pioneers advice on the appropriate preparation for the hardships they might face on the trail westward. One of the proper ways to carry a wounded or injured person on the trail is shown below. An encounter with a grizzly bear (opposite page top) might provide serious difficulty or, perhaps, food for the travelers. The diagram (opposite page below) shows how to set up a camp table and field cot. The book also included techniques for hunting, cooking, and many diagrams of items for use on the trail.*

In the mid-1800s, more than a hundred guide books on how to get to the West were written—some by men who had never been west of the Mississippi River and who gave advice that ranged from poor to deadly. Randolph Marcy's *The Prairie Traveler* was one guide book that was approved by the U.S. War Department. In his book, Marcy outlined the roads west and listed the advantages of each.

To make a safe journey, he explained, a company should have fifty to seventy men, properly armed and equipped, to herd and guard animals and to protect the company against Indians. The train should choose a captain with "good judgment, integrity of purpose, and practical experience" who would select the route, the starting and stopping points, and the campsites and would generally control the company's movements. Each company member should sign an agreement to abide by the captain's rule and to do the chores assigned to her or him.

Marcy suggested that wagons be of the simplest possible construction. The top should be strong enough to protect the contents from

149

sun and weather. Marcy suggested that mules be used where the roads were good; but if the trip was more than 1,500 miles and over rough roads, young oxen fared better and cost less. An eight-ox team cost $200, while a six-mule team cost $600.

Marcy allowed 110 days to make the journey from the Missouri River to California. He suggested the following supplies for each person: 150 pounds of flour; 25 pounds of bacon or pork; 15 pounds of coffee; 25 pounds of sugar; yeast for making bread; salt and pepper; butter boiled, skimmed, and sealed into tins; dried vegetables; citric acid to prevent scurvy; and quinine, opium, and a laxative medicine.

Then there were pots and pans, bedding, tools, and spare parts to repair the wagons. Most important were weapons—a rifle and revolver. Marcy respected the Indian as a foe. Be prepared to fight when the situation calls for it, he told travelers, and do not assume that an open and friendly hand will be returned.

Despite the warnings, freighters' wagons and prairie schooners lined up waiting for a place on the crude ferry crossing the Arkansas River on the Texas Road. In one six-week period, 1,000 wagons were counted crossing the Red River into Texas. The scars of the road are still visible where the wagons cut deep in the unturned sod.

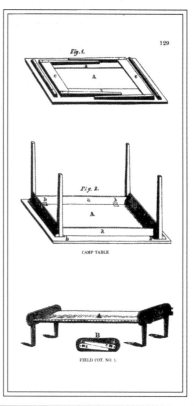

129

Fig. 1.

Fig. 2.

CAMP TABLE

FIELD COT. NO. 1.

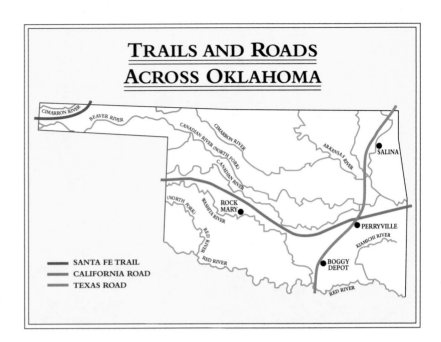

TRAILS AND ROADS ACROSS OKLAHOMA

- —————— SANTA FE TRAIL
- —————— CALIFORNIA ROAD
- —————— TEXAS ROAD

It must have taken a special spirit for a family to pack all their belongings in a small wagon and head West to a land they knew little about.

THE CALIFORNIA ROAD

Fort Smith businessmen saw the increasing numbers of settlers moving westward as an opportunity, and they approached General Matthew Arbuckle, the commander at Fort Smith. Would he support the idea of a military road from Fort Smith to Santa Fe? Gold seekers could buy supplies in Fort Smith, travel west to Santa Fe, then take the Gila Trail on to California. With Arbuckle's support, the Arkansas state legislature petitioned the federal government for a military expedition to open a wagon road from Fort Smith across Indian Territory to Santa Fe.

So many gold seekers gathered in Fort Smith to make the trip with the military expedition in the spring of 1849 that the cost of horses, mules, oxen, and food skyrocketed. Captain Randolph B. Marcy headed the group out on April 4, 1849.

The gold seekers were surprised to find a civilized Indian community (the Choctaw Agency) not far from Fort Smith. The Shawnee and Delaware tribes had built neat log cabin settlements and well-cultivated farms. The travelers bought grain, peaches, and melons from them for their trip.

Among the travelers was pretty seventeen-year-old Mary Conway, granddaughter of the Arkansas governor and cousin of President James Madison. It was rare for a young girl to accompany a military train, and the junior officers were eager to make a good impression. They had been traveling in the heat and dust for several days when they spotted the sandstone buttes rising out of the landscape. A **butte** is a hill that rises unexpectedly above the surrounding area; it has sloping sides and a flat top. As the troop neared the largest butte, someone shouted a challenge and off the young officers raced. They scrambled to the crest of the highest hill and raised the U.S. flag. Then they named the butte "Rock Mary" in the young lady's honor.

The company traveled across northern Texas arriving in Santa Fe in late June. "Marcy's Trail" became known as the California Road and was used by hundreds headed west toward the California gold fields. It was the major route across the Great Plains for the next fifty years.

In 1858, Major Enoch Steen generally followed Marcy's Trail to formally survey a road to California. The sandstone butte formation along the way would be called Steen's Buttes.

THE STAGECOACH

The stagecoach was America's first system of public transportation and traveled the West between 1850 and 1870. On September 15, 1858, a Butterfield Overland Mail stagecoach left St. Louis for San Francisco. The route west lay across Missouri to Fort Smith. Then it crossed the Indian Territory going southwest—following the trail Marcy had made popular—from Fort Gibson to Colbert's Ferry on the Red River. It was, said one traveler, "the worst road God ever built."

The coaches carried nine people inside. Others could sit on top or "ride shotgun" up front with the driver. Waterman Ormsby, a reporter

This engraving depicts the Butterfield Overland Mail stagecoach ready for its regular trip from St. Louis to San Francisco.

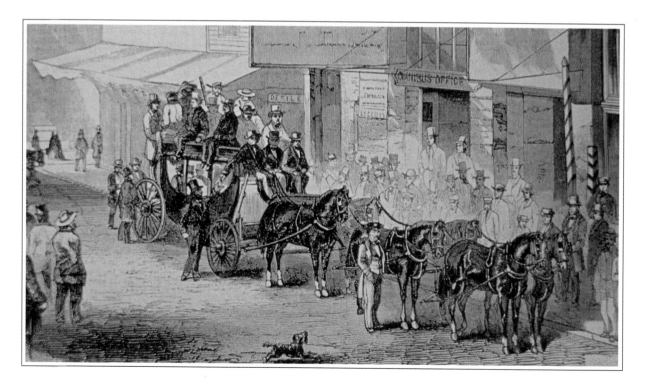

Top: A Mollhausen drawing of Camp 9 of the Pacific Railway Exploration (August 3, 1853). *Above:* A Mollhausen watercolor of Indian pictographs on a rock.

for the *New York Herald*, made the first run and worried about crossing Indian Territory. Late in the night sleep overcame fear and he dozed off. He was awakened "in the confusion of drowsiness"; at first, he thought that the driver and the mail agent had been murdered and that he had been missed because he was covered with blankets. He was afraid to move for fear the Indians would see him. But he was brought to his senses by a familiar voice urging the horses on. It was only the driver hitching up a new team at one of the relay stations.

The trip from St. Louis to San Francisco took twenty-four days—a fraction of the time needed for the fastest sea route. It was the first step in connecting the two coasts and the central part of the continent.

PLANNING A RAILROAD

To the average person in the 1850s, a **transcontinental railroad** (a railroad crossing the continent, connecting both coasts) was a major leap of faith. The longest railroad at the time—700 miles—linked Chicago and Cairo, Illinois. From the Missouri River to the Pacific was 1,600 miles—and there were two mountain chains to be crossed.

But government, railroad owners, and other business people knew that the time had come to find a way to unite the eastern and western halves of the continent. There was talk of a railroad across Indian Territory as early as 1849. In March 1853, Congress passed a bill calling for a survey to map all of the possible railroad routes to the Pacific. The War Department, under Secretary of War Jefferson Davis, would conduct the survey to determine which route was the most practical.

Lieutenant Amiel W. Whipple, a military engineer, led the group exploring a possible route along the 35th parallel—from Fort Smith to Los Angeles. The group included surveyors, topographers, geolo-

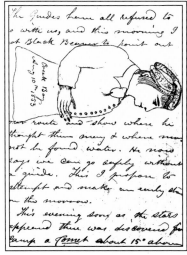

Top left: *A Mollhausen painting of an Indian on horseback.* **Top right:** *A page from Lieutenant Amiel W. Whipple's journal with a sketch of a Creek boy (August 10, 1853).* **Above right:** *A Mollhausen painting of a Choctaw man and woman.*

gists, and naturalists. With them was H. B. Mollhausen, a German artist and naturalist, who sketched the Indian Territory.

When his survey was completed, Whipple estimated that it would cost over $169 million to build the railroad along the route, compared to an estimated $96 million for a northern route. Congress dismissed it out of hand. Only later did Congress discover that a simple mathematical error had added $75 million to the true cost and thrown the route through Indian Territory out of the running.

Do You Remember?

1. Name the four major jumping-off points in the central portion of the continent for those traveling westward.
2. For what were keelboats used?
3. Why was the transcontinental railroad route across Indian Territory ruled out?

INDIAN TERRITORY IN THE 1850S

In 1854, the U.S. Congress created the territories of Kansas and Nebraska in preparation for their admission as states. Senator Robert Johnson of Arkansas proposed that Indian Territory also be considered for statehood. He recommended that it be divided into three territories: Cherokee, Muskogee (Creek and Seminole), and Chata (Choctaw and Chickasaw). He suggested that the United States survey the region, give tribal members an **allotment** (specified portion) of acres, and open the remainder for settlement to non-Indians. When all three territories had enough settlers to meet statehood requirements, they could be reunited and admitted as the state of Neosho.

The tribes opposed the plan bitterly. They had been promised that their homes would not be violated or become part of a state and that trespassers would be kept out. Johnson's bill did not pass Congress; but the seeds of an idea had been planted.

THE HARSH ENVIRONMENT

Meanwhile, Indians, military men, and missionaries struggled with daily life in the Territory. For those who had no slaves, life was difficult. The enlisted men at the forts worked hard, building barracks and roads, fighting Indians, protecting others. Military rations were meager, and they hunted and raised much of their own food. Mission life was much the same—except the mission families were also responsible for the instruction and care of the Indian children.

All were up against the Great Plains, a land that both gave and took away. They had never seen a land with so little rain and so many floods—with so much game and so little food on the table—so much sunshine and so much sickness—with so much variety in the temperature. Each time they thought they were making progress, the land struck back. The missionaries kept records for the mission boards and wrote letters to friends and family describing the hardships.

Dry winds, drought, and a plague of grasshoppers hit the Territory in the 1850s. The Irish and sweet potato crops failed in 1853, and the peach trees yielded only a few bushels. At Tullahassee Mission, the Robertsons could not gather enough pumpkin and squash to feed the mission. Nor could they afford to buy a cow because it cost too much. Even the supplies that they had ordered in the spring of 1856 had not arrived by fall because the steamboat was stranded in the Arkansas River.

Rain finally broke the drought that winter; but spring looked as bleak as the winter before. At Tullahassee, a late frost killed the peach blos-

Two Cherokee girls demonstrate the art of winnowing wheat.

soms, and the parsnip, onion, carrot, squash, cabbage, pepper, and grass seeds failed to come up. Those at the mission were lucky. Many Indians were reduced to eating the bark from the trees.

CIVILIZING THE TERRITORY

At the same time, the Indian merchants and traders had developed their connections downriver to New Orleans. When the steamboat *Arkansas Traveler* made its way into the Territory, its cargo included both necessities and luxury goods. The steamboats brought such goods as sugar, coffee, rice, candles, kettles, axes, rope, buckets, glass, bed cords, wrapping paper, indigo, soap, pepper sauce, and gunpowder. There were also saltpeter, lemon syrup, almonds, spices, and vinegar for preserving food. There were coffee mills, sieves, tongs, blacking, dyes, and tubs and trunks for household use. There were nails, hammers, scythes, shovels, and grain cradles for building and harvesting. The steamboats even brought furniture.

By 1859, Indian agents reported that there were approximately 21,000 Cherokee, including about 4,000 black slaves. Houses were being built and enlarged throughout the Territory, and the timber business was booming. Most families had a vegetable garden and a spring house to preserve milk, butter, and cheese. They were farming about 102,500 acres and had about 240,000 head of cattle, 20,000 horses and mules, 16,000 hogs, and 5,000 sheep. An acre of land yielded about 35 bushels of corn, 12 bushels of wheat, or 30 bushels of oats. Reapers, mowers, and threshing machines were changing the Indians' agricultural methods. Cattle raising had become a leading occupation.

Sequoyah's talents were not just in linguistics. He also made farm implements by hand, including these shown in the photograph.

According to the Cherokee agent, this industriousness was the result of the work of black slaves. If the tribes on the western side of the Territory had a black man and woman "who would teach them to cultivate the soil, and to properly prepare and cook their food, stock cattle given them, and a schoolmaster appointed for every district, it would tend more to civilize them than any other plan that could be adopted."

Do You Remember?

1. What did Senator Johnson of Arkansas propose for Indian Territory in 1854?
2. What conditions made Indian Territory difficult for those who chose to farm?
3. How were many of the supplies brought to Indian Territory by the late 1850s?

CHAPTER REVIEW

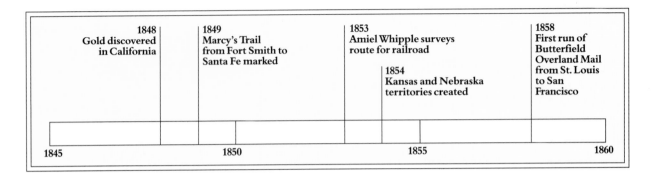

| 1845 | | 1850 | | 1855 | | 1860 |

1848
Gold discovered in California

1849
Marcy's Trail from Fort Smith to Santa Fe marked

1853
Amiel Whipple surveys route for railroad

1854
Kansas and Nebraska territories created

1858
First run of Butterfield Overland Mail from St. Louis to San Francisco

At the Same Time

1841   Cornstarch patented

1842   Sewing machine patented; first adhesive postage stamps issued

1845   Soap powder first packaged in boxes

1846   Baking soda first manufactured

1847   The rubber tire patented

1849   Safety pin patented; the first silk thread sold on spools

Summary

White settlers from the north, east, and south continued to head west in search of new lives and new lands. By 1840, nearly 400,000 settlers had moved into Missouri, which was then considered the edge of civilization. When gold was discovered in California, the race was on. The problem was how to get there.

Most chose to go overland. Transportation was limited and somewhat dangerous. Captain Randolph Marcy led gold seekers along a route that would become known as the California Road. Lieutenant Amiel Whipple surveyed the Territory for a possible transcontinental railroad route. Later, the stagecoach carried travelers to California.

Meanwhile, the Five Civilized Tribes were making every effort to overcome the removal and the hardships that met them in the new land. They built homes and farms, as well as businesses, particularly in cattle, timber, and grain.

Reviewing People, Places, and Things

Define, identify, or explain the importance of the following.

1. allotment
2. butte
3. keelboat
4. Captain Randolph B. Marcy
5. Marcy's Trail
6. pack train
7. profit
8. transcontinental railroad

Understanding the Facts

1. Explain how the mistaken beliefs about the land between the 98th meridian and the Rocky Mountains, including present-day Oklahoma, fueled westward migration.
2. Why was there little steamboat traffic on Oklahoma's rivers in the early 1800s?
3. What was the name of the first cross-continental stagecoach company?
4. What was the real value of the stagecoach?
5. Why was a transcontinental railroad so important to the United States?

Developing Critical Thinking

1. Do you believe Americans had the right to settle western lands? What assumptions did the idea of manifest destiny make about the rights of Indians and others to this land?

2. Look at the list of items under "At the Same Time." For each item, explain what effect it would have upon people living in the Indian Territory or those who wished to travel across the country. How did each of these items change daily life? How would it have affected what people took with them in a wagon train or how it was transported?

3. Spices were listed as one of the items brought upriver to the Territory on the steamboats. Why were these spices considered a necessity rather than a luxury at that time?

Using Your Skills

1. When gold was discovered in California, the *New York Herald* wrote, "All are rushing head over heels toward the El Dorado on the Pacific." Where did the phrase *El Dorado* come from, and what does it mean?

2. Using a map of Oklahoma, make a list of the modern counties that lay along the routes of the California Road and the Texas Road.

Special Projects

1. Make a list of provisions necessary for a trip by wagon train from Fort Smith, Arkansas, to Santa Fe, New Mexico. Make a list of provisions you would need for the same trip today.

2. Research scythes and grain cradles. Find out how they were made and how they were used. Prepare a short report on old agricultural tools.

Building Skills: Using Mileage Charts

When planning a trip, it is important to determine the mileage from one place to another in order to calculate how long the trip will take, how much gas will be used, and which route will be the most convenient.

Many road maps provide a mileage chart similar to the one that follows. To find the mileage between two points, identify the city that represents your starting point on either the left or the top of the chart.

Then match it to your destination city on the other side of the chart. Read across the chart to the column where your two cities intersect. The box at that point gives the number of miles between the two cities. For example, the distance from Ada to Boise City is 423 miles.

	Ada	Ardmore	Durant	Elk City	McAlester	Norman	Shawnee	Tulsa
Bartlesville	173	238	214	268	139	171	144	46
Boise City	423	428	478	265	464	360	395	393
Fort Smith	167	232	232	296	107	187	150	115
Norman	83	79	133	135	115		36	125
Oklahoma City	88	99	153	115	124	18	35	39
Tulsa	127	190	155	222	93	125	98	

Determine the mileage for each of the following trips:

1. Fort Smith to Elk City
2. Ada to Tulsa
3. Norman to Oklahoma City
4. McAlester to Bartlesville
5. Oklahoma City to Shawnee
6. Elk City to Boise City
7. Durant to Norman
8. Tulsa to Fort Smith
9. Bartlesville to Shawnee
10. Fort Smith to Ardmore

Sooner Trivia

. . . Cherokee John Rollin Ridge, who had seen his father John Ridge murdered and who was himself wanted for murder, joined a party of gold-seekers and headed to California. Although he tried his hand at panning for gold, trapping, and trading, he eventually became a journalist, author, and poet.

. . . Trying to find a shorter route to Santa Fe, travelers headed across what is now Cimarron County, a route that became known as the "Dry Route" because it was seventy miles without water—three days of traveling in the heat.

CHAPTER EIGHT

THE WHITE MAN'S WAR

The scene is silent and sad. The vulture and the wolf now have the dominion, and the dead friends and foes sleep in the same lonely graves.
— General Samuel R. Curtis, Union Army, 1862,
after the Battle of Pea Ridge

The battlefield at Pea Ridge was color blind. Blacks, Indians, and whites all lay dead when the battle ended.

I N THE 1860s, Americans found themselves facing a dilemma centered around the powers of the federal government and the powers of the states. Did the federal government have the power to dictate to the states and their citizens? Did the states have the power to override the federal government? When they could not agree, who was the final authority?

The issue that brought the debate to a head, however, was slavery. Here was an emotionally charged issue that involved social, political, ethical, moral, and legal considerations. Before it was solved, it would divide the United States and set off a war that split families and friends, set brother against brother, and killed almost an entire generation of able young men. Nowhere was the destruction worse than in Indian Territory. In the end, it broke up the Five Civilized Tribes, destroyed their governments, and cost the Indians their lands.

SETTING THE STAGE FOR WAR

In the early 1800s, tension and disagreements between the northern and southern states increased. The biggest and most serious disagreement was over slavery.

THE ISSUE OF SLAVERY

Slavery had once existed throughout the United States. But it had died out in the North because the North's economic system was different from that of the South. The small farms of the North had little need for slaves. The thousands of immigrants pouring into the United States provided plenty of cheap labor for the North's growing industrial base. Slavery was just not profitable.

Slavery might also have died out in the South if cotton had not become such an important cash crop. By 1860, cotton accounted for over 50 percent of the value of all U.S. exports. Growing cotton required a great deal of manual labor. Slaves spent endless hours in the hot sun "chopping cotton" to remove the weeds. Slave labor kept down costs so the South could compete in the world marketplace. The millions of slaves who worked the cotton fields and performed other tasks were worth over $2 billion to their owners.

In 1820, the United States had twenty-two states. Of these, eleven were **slave states** (states that permitted slavery) and eleven were **free states** (states that did not permit slavery). Until that time, all of the presidents but one had come from a slave state. In the U.S. Senate, there was an equal number of senators from slave states and free states. In the House of Representatives, however, the slave states had fewer representatives than the free states. The delicate balance would soon be upset.

In 1818, the Territory of Missouri, which had 2,000 slaves, applied for statehood. New York representative James Tallmadge added an amendment to the statehood bill requiring Missouri to abolish slavery. In the House of Representatives, the bill passed with all of the free states voting for it and all of the slave states voting against it. In the Senate, the bill was rejected. A compromise was not worked out until 1820: Missouri and Maine would enter the Union at the same time—Missouri as a slave state and Maine as a free state. A line would be drawn from Missouri's southern border across the rest of Louisiana Territory. Slavery would only be permitted south of that line. This was known as the **Missouri Compromise**.

THE GROWING ANTISLAVERY MOVEMENT

About this time, religious groups in the Northeast began to preach against slavery. Slavery became an emotional issue. Regardless of how Southerners felt personally about slavery, they began to resist the threat to their livelihood. In 1833, the American Anti-Slavery Society was formed and called for an immediate end to slavery without any thought about how that would affect the South. The Society flooded Congress with petitions, but its most lasting effect was to convince people that slavery was morally evil and that slave owners were sinners. The **abolitionists** (those who wanted to end slavery) felt morally superior and launched bitter attacks on slavery and slave owners. The abolitionists formed what came to be known as the **underground railroad.** This was a network of houses and other places used to help slaves escape to the North or Canada.

STATES' RIGHTS

In the first half of the nineteenth century, the northern states were growing so rapidly that they needed federal help to regulate immigration, finance transportation, and protect industry from inexpensive foreign imports. Only a strong federal government could provide the services the northern states desired.

The South, on the other hand, had few immigrants and few factories. It was an agricultural or rural society. Southerners had little need for federal regulations or interference. They believed in **states' rights**, the principle that the rights and responsibilities of the states should take precedence over the rights and responsibilities of the federal government. But they could see the day coming when the rapidly growing North would control Congress and tip the balance in favor of a strong central government. A united North could outlaw slavery—or push through any other issue—over the South's objections.

INCREASING TENSIONS

The slavery issue arose again and again as new territories and states were formed. The annexation of the lands taken from Mexico after the war of 1846 led to another debate over which states would be slave states and which free. Congress settled that debate by passing the

Slave market auctions were a time of fearful uncertainty and indignation for slaves.

Compromise of 1850. According to its terms, California was admitted as a free state and part of Texas was given to New Mexico. Slavery in New Mexico and Utah would be decided by **popular sovereignty** (a vote by those living in those territories). Slavery was banned in the District of Columbia, but a stronger fugitive slave law was passed requiring people in the free states to help catch runaway slaves.

In 1854, Congress passed the Kansas-Nebraska Act. Somehow a provision was put in the bill allowing the territories, which were both north of the Missouri Compromise line, to decide whether to permit slavery. Both proslavery and antislavery factions were outraged. Fighting broke out in the territory, and a new antislavery party was formed—the Republican party.

THE ELECTION OF 1860

The presidential election of 1860 brought the tensions to a head. Southern Democrats nominated John C. Breckinridge of Kentucky. Northern Democrats supported Stephen A. Douglas of Illinois. The Constitutional Union party nominated John Bell of Tennessee. The Republicans nominated Abraham Lincoln of Illinois on a platform that opposed slavery in the territories. When the votes were counted, Lincoln had won—not by a popular majority but because he won the electoral votes. All of his electoral votes were from northern states. For the first time, a candidate supported by only one section of the country had won the presidency.

Almost immediately, South Carolina voted to **secede** (break away) from the Union. Other states followed, and they soon formed a new government called the **Confederate States of America**. To the states that seceded, Lincoln's election was a denial of the Declaration of Independence. Governments derive "their just powers from the consent of the governed," their forefathers had written. As states, they had a right to be heard; if they were not, they had a right to secede. If that meant fighting for their rights and their homes, they would do so. War broke out between the North and the South in April 1861 in Charleston, South Carolina. Arkansas seceded May 6, the ninth state to join the Confederacy.

Do You Remember?
1. Give two reasons why the North was less interested in slavery than the South.
2. What were the provisions of the Missouri Compromise?
3. What president's election actually triggered the Civil War?
4. What was the first state to secede from the Union?

Abraham Lincoln's election as president in 1860 brought turmoil to the South. Many Southerners believed his election justified secession.

WAR IN THE INDIAN TERRITORY

Even before the Civil War broke out, the Five Civilized Tribes were involved. Many Indians realized that if the United States were divided, the white settlers might not be as aggressive in settling the West. Most Indians sided with the South. They still had strong family and loyalty ties to the South. Most of the crops raised by Indian farmers were sold along the lower Mississippi River and the Gulf of Mexico. Some Indian families in the eastern half of the state were wealthy slave owners. Abolishing slavery would hurt them just as it would Southern slave owners.

THE TRIBES SPLIT

Confederate President Jefferson Davis named Albert Pike, a well-known Arkansas lawyer, as Commissioner of Indian Affairs. Pike was a friend of the Indians and had represented them in legal matters before the war. He was a huge man and often wore Indian dress. Pike intended to visit each of the major tribes, hoping to enlist them on the Confederate side. He asked Robert Toombs, the Confederate Secretary of State, to send weapons to the tribes, "plain muzzle-loading rifle, large bore....Revolvers, I am aware, cannot be had, and an Indian would not pick up a musket if it lay in the road."

The Confederacy recognized that the Indians were important allies. To gain the Indians' help, the Confederacy promised to return their former homes; it also promised support, protection, and equal rights. It agreed to assume the debts they owed to the federal government and warned that the Republican party intended to open their lands to white settlers.

On the other side, the federal government had made many promises and kept few. But the federal government owed them a great deal of money from the treaties they had signed. If the Indians did not at least remain neutral, that money might never be paid. Even the Kiowa were ready to consider an alliance with the Confederacy because the Union was two years behind in paying the **annuities** (annual payments of dividends or allowances) owed them.

Cherokee leader John Ross hoped to keep the tribe neutral. Even though Ross was only one-eighth Cherokee and a slave owner, he was the leader of the traditional, full-blood "Pin" Cherokee, who had strong ties to the North. The rival group of pro-Confederate Cherokee consisted of slave-owning mixed-bloods, most from families who had favored removal to the West. They were led by Ross's longtime rival, Stand Watie. Watie had signed the first Indian removal treaty and was

Jefferson Davis, president of the Confederate States of America, named Albert Pike (above) Commissioner of Indian Affairs. Pike visited each of the major tribes in eastern and western Oklahoma to enlist their support for the Confederacy.

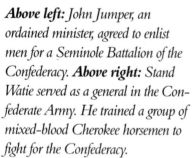

Above left: John Jumper, an ordained minister, agreed to enlist men for a Seminole Battalion of the Confederacy. Above right: Stand Watie served as a general in the Confederate Army. He trained a group of mixed-blood Cherokee horsemen to fight for the Confederacy.

the only one of the signers who had not been killed. Watie was already drilling a group of mixed-blood Cherokee horsemen to fight for the Confederacy. Ross knew that if he backed the Confederacy, he would lose the Pin's support, and Watie might gain power in the tribe.

The Upper Creek (those who had resisted removal from the East) followed wealthy Chief Opothleyahola, a traditional full-blood who was loyal to the Union. He was opposed by the Lower Creek, led by Chief Motey Kennard and the McIntosh brothers, Daniel and Chilly. The Lower Creek were eager to raise a pro-South regiment. On July 10, they signed a treaty with Pike, who told them they would only have to fight in Indian Territory. He also promised that, if they were attacked, the Confederacy would help defend them with white troops.

The Seminole were as divided as the Creek. Those who had been moved west by force wanted nothing to do with either the Union or the Confederacy. However, John Jumper, an ordained Seminole minister, agreed to enlist men for a Seminole Battalion of the Confederacy. A treaty was signed in August 1861.

By the time Pike met with them, the Chickasaw and Choctaw had already agreed to form a Confederate regiment under Indian Agent Douglas Cooper, a friend of Jefferson Davis. They were the only tribes who were not divided.

Pike also met with the tribes in the western part of the Territory—the Tonkawa, Caddo, Waco, Wichita, Delaware, and Comanche. He gave the tribes guns, ammunition, and other goods and promised that, after the war, they would receive help to build thriving communities. The western tribes signed a treaty, and some Osage, Quapaw, Seneca, and Shawnee followed suit.

Do You Remember?

1. Why did many of the tribes support the Confederacy?
2. Who was the Confederacy's Commissioner of Indian Affairs?
3. The Cherokee split into pro-Union and pro-Confederate groups. Who was the leader of each group?

THE CONFEDERACY TAKES CONTROL

In May 1861, Indian Territory was declared to be under the military control of the Confederacy. The Union pulled its troops out of the Territory and abandoned the forts. Fearing that Indian annuities would fall into Confederate hands, the federal government stopped all payments to the Indians. The Overland Mail route shifted north, and stagecoaches abandoned their southern routes. The Territory was left virtually without public transportation or mail.

Under heavy pressure from Arkansas, and lacking any federal protection, John Ross called a convention in Tahlequah in August 1861 and reluctantly recommended that the Cherokee ally themselves with the Confederacy. They signed a treaty in October. In November 1861, the Confederacy created the Department of Indian Territory. Albert Pike set up Confederate headquarters in Indian Territory at Fort Davis in Muskogee County near Bacone, across the Arkansas River from Fort Gibson. It was named for Confederate President Jefferson Davis, who had been stationed in the region as a lieutenant in the U.S. Army.

Daniel McIntosh (above), a Lower Creek, and his brother Chilly supported Chief Motey Kennard in his effort to raise a regiment to serve in the Confederate Army.

A LITTLE CIVIL WAR

Pike's rally through the Indian Territory had opened old wounds. Those Indians who supported the Union or wanted to remain neutral felt overpowered by those who favored the Confederacy.

Fearing for their lives, one group of Opothleyahola's followers packed their wagons and fled north to Kansas (a Union state). Others decided to fight and rallied around Opothleyahola. More than 3,500 men,

*Confederate Colonel James McIn-
tosh (top) led his troops against
Opothleyahola and his followers as
they made their way toward Kansas.
Confederate General Ben McCulloch
(above), who was in charge of the
Indian Territory military district, was
killed at the Battle of Pea Ridge.*

women, and children—Creek, Seminole, and a few other nearby Indians—crowded onto his plantation. As grass for the livestock and food
for the women and children gave out, Opothleyahola organized the
group and moved slowly northward toward the Kansas border.

On November 19, 1861, Confederate Colonel Douglas Cooper
attacked the group at Round Mountain, near what is now Yale. Cooper lost, but continued to harass the group. Cooper was joined by a
fresh Confederate force from Arkansas under Colonel James McIntosh.

The weather turned bitter, and food grew scarce as the group continued north. On the morning of December 26, McIntosh attacked
the tired camp. Women, children, and livestock fled in a panic. The
pro-Union Indians were already losing this Battle of Chustenahlah
when Confederate General Stand Watie and his Cherokee troops arrived to back up McIntosh. Opothleyahola's people fled into the timber, with Watie right behind, picking them off as they fled. The bodies
of the dead and wounded were left to freeze in the blizzard that hit
that night. Those who escaped trudged through the sleet and snow,
barefoot, starving, without blankets, trying to reach safety in Kansas.

The agents could hardly believe the condition of Opothleyahola's
band when they appeared outside a Union Army camp.

*When it is remembered that they were collected for the journey, with
scarcely a moment for preparation, amid the confusion and dismay of an
overwhelming defeat; that their enemies were close upon them, flushed
with victory, maddened by recent defeats, and under their well known
code of warfare would spare neither age nor sex, it may well be believed
that their preparations for the journey were wholly inadequate. It was in
the dead of winter, the ground covered with ice and snow, and the weather
most intensely cold. Without shelter, without adequate clothing, and
almost destitute of food, a famishing, freezing multitude of fugitives, they
arrived in Kansas entirely unexpectedly, and where not the slightest
preparation had been made to alleviate their sufferings or provide for their
wants. Within two months after their arrival, two hundred and forty of
the Creeks alone died, over a hundred frosted limbs were amputated
within a like period of time.*

THE BATTLE OF PEA RIDGE

General Ben McCulloch of Texas was in charge of the Indian Territory military district. His troops included one regiment each from
Texas, Louisiana, and Arkansas, plus three regiments of Indians—
Cherokee, Choctaw/Chickasaw, and Creek/Seminole. Albert Pike was
in charge of the Cherokee regiment.

Fighting in Missouri and Arkansas territories was heavy. The Confederates appeared to be winning the war in the South at the time. If McCulloch could break the Union forces in Arkansas, Confederate forces could take Missouri and virtually own the Midwest.

Union and Confederate forces clashed at Pea Ridge, Arkansas, on March 7, 1862. Ice, snow, fatigue, the late arrival of one Indian regiment, lost and delayed messages—all combined to turn the battle into chaos. McCulloch was killed in the fighting, and Pike found himself in charge of a disaster.

The loss of the battle was significant. But Pike also discovered to his dismay that the Indians had mutilated and scalped some of the Union soldiers—a common practice in Indian warfare. Newspapers picked up the story, which grew worse with each retelling. Some editors even accused Pike of getting the Indians drunk and leading them "in a carnage of savagery, scalping wounded and helpless soldiers, and committing other atrocities too horrible to mention."

Pike's reputation never recovered, and the bad press turned the tide of opinion against the Indians. Pike felt that the Confederacy abandoned Indian Territory after the battle. Hoping to save the southern part of the Territory, Pike went south to Blue River and set up Fort McCulloch, where he remained for the rest of the war.

Had the Confederacy prevailed at the Battle of Pea Ridge (above), do you think the outcome of the Civil War might have been different? Why?

THE INDIAN EXPEDITION

Opothleyahola had vowed revenge on the Confederates. In the spring of 1862, his followers joined Union brigades from Wisconsin, Ohio, Kansas, and Indiana to form the Indian Expedition to regain Indian Territory. They marched into Confederate-held territory on June 1, 1862. On July 3, they faced the Confederates at Locust Grove. When the Union brought up their heavy artillery, the Confederates fell back. The Union troops divided and headed for Tahlequah and Fort Gibson. They captured Fort Gibson and surrounded Tahlequah, capital of the Cherokee Nation. The Cherokee regiment guarding the capital deserted, and Union troops took the city without a single shot. Chief John Ross was taken into protective custody, along with the Cherokee Nation papers and treasury. Ross was sent to Philadelphia where he stayed for the rest of the war, directing tribal activities long-distance.

At that point, the Union forces probably could have taken all of Indian Territory. The military leaders were ready, but the troops were not. Fearing that they would be abandoned in Indian Territory, cut off from supplies, they revolted, arrested the commander on charges of insanity and disloyalty, and headed back to Kansas. The Confederates quickly reoccupied Fort Gibson. They burned John Ross's home at Park Hill as well as the Cherokee capitol building in Tahlequah. Stand Watie was elected principal chief of the Cherokee.

TURMOIL IN THE TERRITORY

By fall, Indian Territory was in chaos. Armed bands roamed the countryside, taking whatever they could get. Fields and farms were destroyed or deserted. With supply trains battling to get through, both Union and Confederate troops suffered, as well as the thousands who made their way to the forts, hoping for food and protection.

No one really knew what was happening. Neither the Union nor the Confederate army had a system to tell families of the death or injury of a family member. Most families had to wait for the rosters printed in the newspapers. But in the Territory, many newspapers shut down because they could not get paper.

On January 1, 1863, President Lincoln issued the **Emancipation Proclamation**, which freed the slaves in the Confederate states. It did not apply to Indian Territory, areas occupied by Union forces, or to the four slave states that had not left the Union (Delaware, Kentucky, Maryland, and Missouri). It freed slaves where Lincoln could not enforce it and left slavery intact where it could have been enforced. Southerners saw it as an attempt to start a slave insurrection.

In 1862, Cherokee Chief John Ross was taken into protective custody, along with the Cherokee Nation's papers and treasury. He was sent to Philadelphia, from which he directed tribal activities. Why was it more difficult to direct tribal activities long distance than it would be today?

In February 1863, the Cherokee called the Cowskin Prairie Council. John Ross's followers renounced the Confederate alliance and abolished slavery in the Cherokee Nation. They declared Ross chief of the Cherokee Nation and set up a temporary government until he could return. Stand Watie and his followers were declared outlaws. Now there were two Cherokee governments in Indian Territory.

Watie was having other difficulties. Union troops had captured the Confederate artillery (large weapons) at Fort Wayne in northeast Indian Territory in October. Now they pushed Watie and his men south of the Arkansas and Canadian rivers. The Union once again controlled Tahlequah and Fort Gibson. They changed the name of Fort Gibson to Fort Blunt and set up Union headquarters there.

Do You Remember?

1. Where did the Confederacy establish its headquarters in Indian Territory?
2. Why did the pro-Union Indians head toward Kansas?

THE BATTLE OF HONEY SPRINGS

In July 1863, Fort Gibson (now Fort Blunt) was under the command of Union Major General James G. Blunt. Both Blunt and Confederate Brigadier General Douglas Cooper knew that the key to victory in Indian Territory was control of Fort Gibson. It was the major link between Arkansas Territory and the furthest point inland steamboats could travel. From Fort Gibson, both land and water transportation could be controlled. Cooper intended to win it back.

At Honey Springs, about twenty-five miles south of the fort, the Confederates had a supply depot for foodstuffs. Cooper planned to wait there for reinforcements. Cooper would join his 5,000 men with Brigadier General William Cabell's 4,000 troops. Together they would march up the Texas Road and attack the Union-held fort.

Meanwhile, Union General Blunt decided not to wait for Cooper to get his reinforcements and attack. Near midnight on July 15, 1863, Blunt and his men left the fort. About five miles from Elk Creek, they met the Confederates. The battle developed quickly, and the fighting was heavy. It had been raining, and the Mexican gunpowder used by the Confederates was not very reliable even in the best of times. Damp, it became worthless. The Confederates were barely able to defend themselves. Many used their guns as clubs.

In the middle of the battle, Blunt's Union Indian regiments accidentally moved in front of the 1st Kansas Colored Infantry Regiment, which had been battling Cooper's 29th Texas Cavalry. The Indians

Union Major General James G. Blunt (above) was commander of the troops at Fort Gibson during the Civil War. The Union changed the name of Fort Gibson to Fort Blunt in part to let those reading communiques know what was happening. If the report said Fort Gibson, the fort was in Confederate hands; if it said Fort Blunt, it was in Union hands.

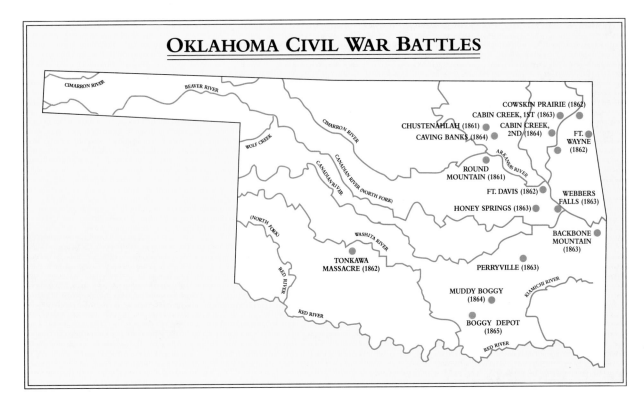

OKLAHOMA CIVIL WAR BATTLES

Map labels:

CIMARRON RIVER
BEAVER RIVER
CIMARRON RIVER
WOLF CREEK
CANADIAN RIVER
CANADIAN RIVER (NORTH FORK)
(NORTH FORK)
RED RIVER
WASHITA RIVER
RED RIVER
RED RIVER
ARKANSAS RIVER
KIAMICHI RIVER

COWSKIN PRAIRIE (1862)
CABIN CREEK, 1ST (1863)
CHUSTENAHLAH (1861)
CABIN CREEK, 2ND (1864)
CAVING BANKS (1864)
FT. WAYNE (1862)
ROUND MOUNTAIN (1861)
FT. DAVIS (1862)
WEBBERS FALLS (1863)
HONEY SPRINGS (1863)
BACKBONE MOUNTAIN (1863)
TONKAWA MASSACRE (1862)
PERRYVILLE (1863)
MUDDY BOGGY (1864)
BOGGY DEPOT (1865)

withdrew to get out of the way of the black troops, and the Texas Cavalry thought they were retreating. They charged—straight into the black infantry's line of fire. The entire front rank of the charging Texans went down. A second group smashed into the stunned survivors, then a third. With half the men down, the remainder turned and ran. Other Union units surged forward, and the Confederates retreated.

Not wanting the Union to get their supplies, the Confederates set fire to the buildings. Stacked beside the warehouse were hundreds of barrels of sorghum molasses. They broke open the barrels and dumped them, leaving the ground completely covered with sticky syrup. The Confederates then scattered south and east.

Exhausted and low on ammunition, Blunt led his men back toward the fort. Later, in his reports, he praised the black regiment, which had until that time been treated with contempt by white regiments. "They were in the hottest of the fight and opposed to Texas troops twice their number, whom they completely routed," he reported.

The Battle of Honey Springs was the largest, bloodiest, and most decisive battle in Indian Territory. But more important, the Confederates that fell defeated on the battlefield that day were black and red and white; the Union men who leaned against the trees exhausted but victorious were also black and red and white. They were all men willing to put ideals and principles—at least for once—ahead of race.

THE HOME FRONT

People and events are not always as they seem. Stand Watie is often portrayed as a ruthless warrior. The following excerpts are from letters written by Watie and his wife Sally to each other. Watie's family had been sent to Texas for safety. By April 1864, Watie was growing tired, as evidenced by this letter to his wife, which he wrote while he was camped on the Middle Boggy.

Sarah (Sally) C. Watie endured the hardships of the war alone as her husband served in the Confederate Army during the Civil War.

No propperty is safe anywhere, stealing and open robbery is of every days occurrence....Let me act as I will my conduct is always considered wrong no charity was ever shown me yet I have lived through it and I trust and hope that justice and right will be meeted out to me some day. Although these things [false accusations] have been heaped upon me and [it] would be supposed that I become hardened and would be reckless but it still hurts my feelings. I am not a murderer....I have always been opposed to killing women and children although our enemies have done it, yet I shall always protest against any acts of that kind.

Sometimes I examine myself thoroughly and I will always come to the conclusion that I am not such a bad man at last as I am looked upon....If I commit an error I do it without bad intention....I call upon my God to judge me, he knows that I love my friends and above all others my wife and children, the oppinion of the world notwithstanding.

News made its way to the families slowly in Indian Territory and elsewhere. The following excerpt is from a letter Sally Watie wrote to Stand Watie in May 1865.

We hear all kinds of rumors....Do let us know all that you know for certain if it is for the worst let us know it so we can be prepared for it....I hear that they [Union] have set a price on several of there heads and you are encluded....I do not want people to believe it for some of them would be after it....I would live on bread and water rather than to have it said you had speculated of your people I believe you have always done what you thought best for your people....if I thought you was working for nothing but to fill your pocket it would trouble me a great deal but I know it is not else it would have been filled before this time....Write all, we are all sold out I believe.

Two months after Confederate General Robert E. Lee surrendered to Union General Ulysses S. Grant at Appomattox Courthouse in Virginia, the war ended in Indian Territory as the leaders of each tribe surrendered. Winchester Colbert (above), governor of the Chickasaw Nation, surrendered on July 14, 1865.

THE BEGINNING OF THE END

Early in 1864, the Confederates tried to regain Indian Territory. They formed the First Indian Cavalry Brigade, which was made up of Cherokee, Creek, Seminole, and Osage and under the command of Brigadier General Stand Watie. A Second Indian Cavalry Brigade of Choctaw, Chickasaw, and Caddo was commanded by Colonel Tandy Walker, a prominent Choctaw leader.

Fort Smith was in Union hands, and there was traffic on the Arkansas River. In June 1864, Watie captured a steamer headed for Fort Blunt Landing. In September, at Cabin Creek, Watie captured a Union supply train on its way to Fort Gibson; there were 130 wagons with supplies worth $2.6 million. He distributed the food to needy Indian refugees.

All Stand Watie's efforts, however, could not save the Confederate cause. On April 9, 1865, Confederate General Robert E. Lee surrendered to Union General Ulysses S. Grant at Appomattox Courthouse in Virginia. The war ended in the South. Two months later, it ended in Indian Territory. On June 19, 1865, the Choctaw commanders surrendered at Doaksville. Four days later, Stand Watie surrendered. On July 14, Winchester Colbert, governor of the Chickasaw Nation, surrendered. The Civil War in Indian Territory ended not with a bang but with great sorrow.

The Union had officially lost 360,000 men in the Civil War. The Confederacy had lost another 260,000. No one counted the dead in Indian Territory.

Do You Remember?

1. What part did black troops play in the Battle at Honey Springs in 1863?
2. What tribes made up the First Indian Cavalry Brigade?
3. When did the Civil War end in Indian Territory?

THE AFTERMATH OF THE WAR

Indian Territory was devastated. Confederate, Union, and neutral Indians returned to find nothing left. Great numbers of women and children had died from disease. The countryside had been stripped of livestock, fences, and homes. Unplowed fields were now grass and weeds. In Tulsey Town, the cabin of Lewis Perryman was the only building left standing. There was no money to start over. On top of it all, there was an uneasy peace among the Nations. Families were scattered; brothers had gone against brothers.

The worst was yet to come. The Indians realized that they needed to present a united front if they were to receive any type of consideration from the federal government. They organized the Camp Napoleon Council, near Verden, adopting a compact of peace among all Indian tribes. When the Indian tribes met with government leaders at Fort Smith in the fall of 1865, they were not prepared for the Union terms. All slaves had to be freed; they had expected that. But then came the blows: They lost all rights to annuities and lands. Their treaties were void. Their tribal laws were no longer valid. Each tribe would have to negotiate a new treaty with the United States. They would have to give back a portion of their lands so the government could settle other tribes there. Even though factions in the tribes fought for the North, the federal government did not distinguish among the factions, and, instead, penalized the entire tribe.

Allen Wright, principal chief of the Choctaw Nation, was the first to use the term "Oklahoma."

Eventually four treaties—the Treaties of 1866—were signed, one with the Creek, one with the Cherokee, one with the Seminole, one with the Choctaw and Chickasaw. All of the tribes agreed to end slavery, adopt freedmen into the tribes, and allow the railroads to cross the Territory.

The Cherokee were particularly upset; their government had been pro-Union. Still, they were forced to cede 800,000 acres in Kansas and allow other tribes to settle in the Cherokee Outlet. The Southern Cherokee did not sign the treaty but finally accepted it. The Seminole had to sell all of their land to the government for 15¢ an acre. The Seminole land was in central Oklahoma, around what would become Oklahoma City. Twenty years later, this was part of the land that was said to be "unclaimed." The Creek lost more than 3 million acres, sold to the government for 30¢ an acre. The remainder was to be "forever set apart as a home" for them.

The Choctaw and Chickasaw sold the Leased District for $300,000. Their treaty was unique. In addition to tribal matters, it detailed the organization of all Indian tribes and nations living within the present boundaries of the territory. The plan was to form a territorial government to be called "Oklahoma," a term coined by Allen Wright, principal chief of the Choctaw Nation. Although this plan was never carried out, the name was widely repeated. In 1890, it would be chosen as the name for the new territory.

Do You Remember?
1. What were the Treaties of 1866?
2. What unique terms were included in the Choctaw-Chickasaw Treaty of 1866?

CHAPTER REVIEW

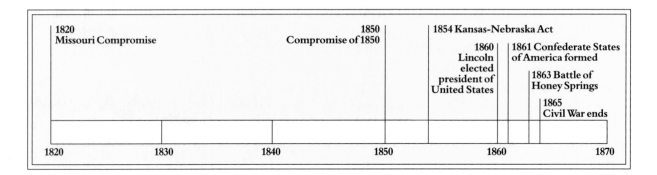

1820 Missouri Compromise		1850 Compromise of 1850	1854 Kansas-Nebraska Act		
			1860 Lincoln elected president of United States	1861 Confederate States of America formed 1863 Battle of Honey Springs 1865 Civil War ends	
1820	1830	1840	1850	1860	1870

At the Same Time

1860 Pony Express established
1862 Homestead Act signed; transcontinental railroad authorized
1863 Thanksgiving declared a national holiday
1864 Abraham Lincoln re-elected
1865 President Abraham Lincoln assassinated

Summary

The Civil War was devastating to the tribes in Indian Territory. The tribes split in their loyalties, and the old hostilities resurfaced. Of the Five Civilized Tribes, only the Chickasaw were undivided, siding with the Confederacy.

The Indians were valiant fighters; but time and again, they found themselves without supplies, ammunition, or food. Unlike the European style of warfare displayed in the major battles between the North and South, guerrilla warfare reigned in the Territory. By the time the war ended, the Indians had nothing left. Their homes, plantations, livestock—all were gone. To make matters worse, the United States forced the Five Civilized Tribes into treaties that took large amounts of their land from them. They were in worse shape than when they had arrived after the Indian removals.

Reviewing People, Places, and Things

Define, identify, or explain the importance of the following.

1. abolitionist
2. annuity
3. Compromise of 1850
4. Confederate States of America
5. Emancipation Proclamation
6. free state
7. Abraham Lincoln
8. Missouri Compromise
9. Opothleyahola
10. Pea Ridge
11. Albert Pike
12. popular sovereignty
13. secede
14. slave state
15. states' rights
16. underground railroad

Understanding the Facts

1. List the terms of the Compromise of 1850.
2. Why was the Republican party formed?
3. Why was the Emancipation Proclamation flawed?
4. What was the outcome of the Cherokee Cowskin Prairie Council?
5. Why was Fort Gibson so important to both sides during the Civil War?

Developing Critical Thinking

1. Why would it have been difficult to know how many people died in Indian Territory battles?

2. What do letters, such as those between Stand Watie and his wife Sally, show us about people? Did they change your attitude about Stand Watie from earlier in the chapter?

Using Your Skills

1. On a map of the United States, highlight using different colors: (a) the Union states, (b) the Confederate states, (c) the border states that did not secede, and (d) the territory of the Five Civilized Tribes in Indian Territory.
2. On a map of Indian Territory, mark:
   a. Fort Gibson
   b. Honey Springs depot
   c. Tahlequah
   d. Cherokee Outlet
   e. Leased District

Special Projects

1. Assume that you live near Bowling Green, Kentucky, and you are part of the underground railroad. You have been told that a black slave from a nearby farm is to be smuggled into Indian Territory where other family members live with the Creek Indians. Plan how you will get the slave into Indian Territory.
2. Prepare a report on one of the Indian leaders or other persons mentioned in this chapter. What happened to that person after the war? How did the war affect that individual? If the person died in the war, how did it affect her or his family?

Building Skills: Reaching Compromises

Americans have always had a knack for compromising between tough choices and almost impossible deadlocks between opposing points of view. The alternatives to not being able to reach a compromise can be lack of progress, indecision, and, in some cases, violent action.

America has sometimes been referred to as a "great melting pot" containing nationalities, social and political viewpoints, and religions from around the world. Certainly, the ability and willingness of Americans to reach compromises have helped our country survive and grow.

In late 1849, there were several bills before the U.S. Congress that threatened to disrupt the Union. Each side felt strongly about the issues involved and it seemed that any kind of compromise was impossible; yet compromise was eventually achieved. Do some more research on the Compromise of 1850. Make careful notes on the different views held on each of the issues. Be able to present each point of view and discuss the give-and-take that allowed people with differing opinions to reach an agreement. Did any of the compromises cause a problem? Could conflict have been avoided? Do compromises leave basic problems unresolved?

As citizens of the United States, we all must make compromises. Almost daily, we must give-and-take with our fellow citizens in order to coexist. It is important, though, that we recognize that there are some areas of our lives—our basic values—that cannot be compromised. As citizens, we realize that there are parts of our constitutional democracy that we cannot compromise. What issues are not open to compromise in our society? What types of compromises are necessary for us to be able to exist in society? Would life as we know it be possible without compromise? Are there times when compromise is just not possible? Why are respect, open-mindedness, tolerance, and patience important qualities to have when making compromises?

Sooner Trivia

. . . Samuel Cheocote, a Southern Methodist preacher, gave up preaching to command the First Creek Confederate Regiment.

. . . Cherokee Stand Watie was the only Indian general in the Confederacy.

. . . In April 1866, the U.S. Congress passed a Civil Rights Act. It granted citizenship to all persons born in the United States—except Indians.

UNIT IV
FROM TERRITORY TO STATE

THE PERIOD FOLLOWING THE CIVIL WAR was a momentous time for Indian Territory. The federal government settled more tribes in the Territory, which led to conflict among the various tribes and between the tribes and the settlers pushing westward. The Civilized Tribes in the eastern part of Oklahoma struggled to rebuild after the devastation of the war.

In the late 1800s, the federal government began to dissolve the Indian tribal governments and open Indian lands to settlement. Two territories existed side by side: Oklahoma Territory and Indian Territory. Finally, in 1907, the two territories were combined and joined the Union as the state of Oklahoma.

In the late 1800s, the federal government began to dissolve the Indian tribal governments and open Indian lands to settlement. This led to land runs to claim the land. No one expected the pandemonium that resulted. More than 100,000 people lined up for the opening of the Cherokee Outlet in 1893. The photograph below was taken as people made their run for land.

CHAPTER 9

THE OTHER INDIAN TERRITORY

We will not have the wagons which make a noise [steam engines] in the hunting ground of the buffalo. If the palefaces come farther into our land, there will be scalps of your brethren in the wigwams of the Cheyenne.
—Roman Nose, Cheyenne chief

THE END OF THE CIVIL WAR did not bring peace to the area that is now western Oklahoma. For years, Indian tribes fought with each other and with settlers. Federal troops had to be stationed at forts in the area.

As the railroads inched westward after the war, the buffalo provided meat for the railroad workers. When buffalo hides became popular, buffalo hunters slaughtered the herds and helped end the Plains Indians' way of life. Without the buffalo to provide food and clothing, the Indians were forced onto reservations and became dependent on the federal government for food and supplies.

With the buffalo gone, ranchers began to raise cattle on the Plains, often leasing the land from the Indians.

CROSSING INDIAN TERRITORY

Almost immediately after the Civil War, stagecoaches returned to Indian Territory. The Butterfield Stage carried mail and passengers from Baxter Springs, Kansas, to El Paso, Texas. In most parts of the West, accommodations ranged from poor to nonexistent. Often, there was little more than a roof and a dirt floor. Separate rooms were rare, and travelers counted themselves lucky to find a bed, particularly one free of bedbugs and lice. Hotel owners short of space rented beds by the hour or half-night.

Compared to accommodations in Arizona and New Mexico territories, those in the Territory were luxurious. Well-stocked and guarded

The Attack at Dawn *by Charles Schreyvogel depicts the Battle of the Washita where Lt. Col. George Armstrong Custer and his men attacked a Cheyenne camp.*

CHAPTER PREVIEW

Terms: Homestead Act, Pacific Railroad Act, dugout, renegade, writ of habeas corpus, nationalism, railhead, drover, arbitration

People: Black Kettle, Colonel Christopher (Kit) Carson, General Philip Sheridan, George Armstrong Custer, Quanah Parker, Ponca, Jesse Chisholm

Places: Camp Supply, Washita River, Fort Sill, East Shawnee Trail, Chisholm Trail, No Man's Land

relay stations were built ten to fifteen miles apart in Indian Territory. These were usually owned by Indian families who prided themselves on hospitality. Carriage Point near Atoka was owned by Calvin Colbert, a Chickasaw and a graduate of Vanderbilt University in Tennessee. It was spacious (large), with clean beds, plenty of food, and friendly hosts.

Steamboats made their way upriver to Fort Gibson as soon as the Civil War ended. They were the main method of transporting goods into the Territory. By 1870, twenty steamboats connected Fort Gibson to Fort Smith, Little Rock, New Orleans, Memphis, St. Louis, and Cincinnati. The steamboats brought in dry goods, groceries, hardware, machinery, and other items and took out hides, furs, and buffalo robes.

Building a railroad across Indian Territory was first suggested in 1849. A route was finally surveyed in 1854, going west from Fort Smith across the Territory to Albuquerque, New Mexico. Work on the line, however, was halted by the Civil War.

The **Homestead Act** changed everything. The act had been signed into law during the Civil War (May 20, 1862). It enabled citizens to acquire up to 160 acres of public land by occupying it for five years and paying $1.25 an acre. But there was no practical way to move west. Two months after the Homestead Act was passed, President Lincoln signed the **Pacific Railroad Act**, which authorized the construction of the first transcontinental railroad. The Union Pacific Company was to build westward over the Rockies, while the Central Pacific Company would build eastward from California across the Sierras.

In 1863, the Union Pacific struck out from Omaha going west, building track with Irish immigrant labor. The Central Pacific struck out from Sacramento, using Chinese immigrant labor. Both employed more than 12,000 men. The government paid them as much as $48,000 a mile and gave them land along the right-of-way. It was not an easy task. Indians were bitter about the "iron horse" making its way through their lands. Workers fainted in sweltering heat on the prairies and were sometimes buried when rock tunnels collapsed during blasting.

In 1865, the Southern Branch of the Union Pacific Company was organized. It would later become known as the Missouri, Kansas & Texas Railway Company—the MK&T or "Katy." The planned route was south from Junction City, Kansas, across Indian Territory to Denison, Texas.

Do You Remember?

1. Right after the Civil War, what method did most people use for travel to the West?
2. When were the Homestead and the Pacific Railroad acts enacted?
3. What minority groups were involved in building the railroads?

TROUBLE ON THE PLAINS

In 1864, the band of Cheyenne led by Chief Black Kettle was driven from Colorado after many of the Cheyenne were massacred at Sand Creek. They were given a reservation in the Cherokee Outlet between the Cimarron and Arkansas rivers. As trails cut through their lands and buffalo were killed off by white hunters, they rode further and further off their reservation in search of food. Embittered by their dealings with the military and white settlers, they retaliated (fought back) by joining the Kiowa and Comanche in raids on encroaching settlers, freighters, wagon trains, and even an occasional railroad crew.

GUARDING THE SANTA FE TRAIL

In the spring of 1865, Colonel Christopher (Kit) Carson, commanding the First Regiment of New Mexico cavalry volunteers, was ordered to set up a fort along the Santa Fe Trail. It was hoped that the fort would provide some protection for the pack trains against the Cheyenne, Kiowa, and Comanche. The troops, many of them Mexican, set up Fort Nichols in what is now the Oklahoma Panhandle. There were perhaps ten officers and three hundred soldiers at the fort. There were also ten Indian scouts, two Indian women, two Mexican women (wives of the soldiers), and two officers' wives.

Opposite page: The train waits as a herd of buffalo cross the railroad track in the painting Hold Up, *by H.N. Trotter, circa 1870.* **Above:** *Colonel Christopher "Kit" Carson was a fur trapper, guide, Indian agent, and soldier. When the Civil War broke out, he resigned as Indian agent and helped organize the First New Mexican Volunteer Infantry Regiment of the Union Army. His regiment would later guard the Santa Fe Trail.*

Indian scouts rode out each morning and returned at sunset. During the day, the enlisted men dug houses, hauled stone, laid walks, and built corrals. Timber for roof supports was cut and hauled eleven miles. The officers lived in army tents until the houses were finished. Carson lived in a tent with rolled-up sides; his bedstead was made of four short forked posts set into the ground with poles laid across them. The enlisted men slept in **dugouts,** houses that were built half in the ground, half above. The houses were made of stone and had dirt floors and sod roofs. Each had two rooms, blankets for doors, and white cloth stretched over the window frames in place of glass.

One officer's wife was twenty-year-old Marian Russell, the young bride of Lieutenant R. D. Russell. The Russells had two pieces of furniture: a folding army table and a bed made from a six-foot log that had been split in two, laid on the floor, and covered with boughs and blankets. Cooking was done in Dutch ovens in an open fireplace. The food was limited to hardtack (a hard biscuit), bacon, beans, beef, venison, flour, sugar, and coffee. Marian lamented that there was no rice, potatoes, fresh vegetables, or dried fruit.

The Indian women kept busy tanning deer hides; the Mexican women served as laundresses. But for an officer's wife, "life often was monotonous," Marian wrote. The fort was never attacked, perhaps, as the Indians said, because Carson had "strong medicine." The only time the cannon was fired was to celebrate July 4. In September, the fort was abandoned.

Lt. Col. George Armstrong Custer had fought valiantly at Bull Run during the Civil War. After the war Custer was assigned to Camp Supply under General Philip Sheridan. There he participated in Sheridan's campaign against the Plains Indians.

THE BATTLE OF THE WASHITA

Early in 1868, General Alfred Sully hastily constructed Camp Supply, a group of flimsy barracks at the mouth of Wolf Creek on the North Fork of the Canadian River. During the summer of 1868, General Philip Sheridan had warned the Cheyenne to stay on their own lands. But the Cheyenne had to hunt to feed and clothe themselves, and game (animals) paid no attention to the government's boundaries. When winter came, instead of returning to their reservation, the Cheyenne joined other tribes along the North Fork and the Washita—a common custom. Black Kettle's camp consisted of perhaps 180 lodges. Less than twelve miles away were another 400 lodges—Kiowa, Comanche, Apache, and Arapaho—with six hundred warriors and several thousand women and children. Black Kettle sent word to General Hazen at nearby Fort Cobb that his people had set up winter camp on the Washita. He asked for a promise of safety, but he did not receive it. As far as the federal government was concerned, Black Kettle's band was off the reservation illegally.

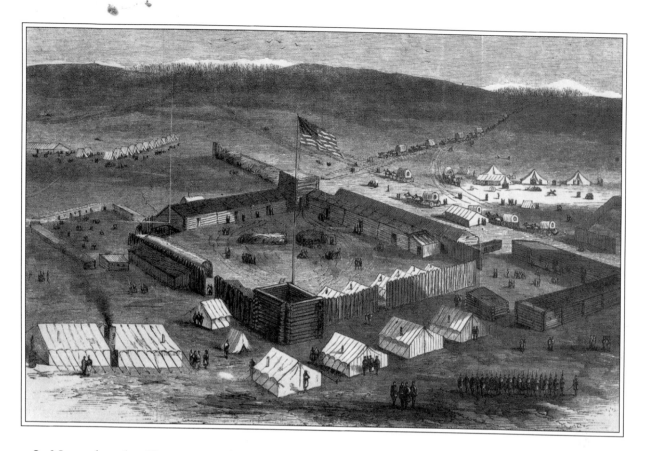

In November, the Cheyenne made a short journey to Fort Cobb, where they were welcomed as friendly Indians. As they made their way back to winter camp, General Sheridan ordered Lieutenant Colonel George Armstrong Custer to attack. The U.S. Army knew that winter was usually a quiet time for the tribes. The Indians had little grain to feed their horses, which were no match for the cavalry's grain-fed mounts. Custer's orders were to ride south from Camp Supply with eight hundred mounted soldiers of the Seventh Cavalry, forty sharpshooters, and a half-dozen Indian scouts. One of the officers was Captain Albert Barnitz, a Civil War hero, who had mixed feelings about the government's handling of the Indians. "It is certainly foolish to fight Indians with one hand, and to make presents and give them arms with the other," he wrote.

From Camp Supply, the troops marched through a heavy, crusted snow following the Indians' trail. The soldiers killed their own dogs with knives to keep them from alerting the Indian camp dogs. They reached the Indian camp in the early hours before dawn on November 27, 1868. The sentry had slipped into a lodge to warm himself, and Barnitz's men moved stealthily into the camp, holding their fire so as not to alert the Indians until the last minute. But the military band at

In 1868, Camp Supply was hastily constructed on the banks of Wolf Creek on the North Fork of the Canadian River to protect the trails and those using them.

the top of the ridge unexpectedly began to play "Garry Owen" (probably under Custer's orders), and the cheers of the men went up as "Custer and his legion came thundering down the long divide....The Indian village rang with unearthly war-whoops, the quick discharge of fire-arms, the clamorous barking of dogs, the cries of infants, and the wailing of women." More than a hundred Cheyenne men, women, and children were killed, among them Black Kettle and his wife. Fifty Indians were captured. Hundreds of Indian ponies were shot, and vital supplies destroyed. A number of Cherokee on a trade mission to the Cheyenne were also killed.

The troops did not emerge unscathed. Captain Barnitz was severely wounded. Major Joel H. Elliot and eighteen of his men were cut off from the main body of troops; all were killed. Sixteen others also died, including Captain L. M. Hamilton, the grandson of statesman Alexander Hamilton. After the shouts and gunfire aroused the nearest Indian camp, Custer ordered a retreat, taking with him saddles, rifles, ammunition, buffalo robes, and blankets. He left behind Barnitz's group without even checking to see if anyone was alive. It was the first time since the Revolutionary War that a U.S. commander had left his dead and wounded troops behind on the battlefield.

The ambush was one of the most controversial incidents of the Indian wars. The Five Civilized Tribes protested because Cherokee people had been killed. "Justice to the Indians," the delegates wrote, "requires that all the facts of this unfortunate affair should be laid before the world." Custer was reprimanded and relieved of duty for a time.

FORT SILL

In 1869, the army set up Fort Sill in the middle of the Comanche, Kiowa, and Apache reservation near present-day Lawton. Conditions at these frontier forts were terrible. Army life was dangerous because the Plains Indians were good fighters, and the troops had little experience at first with the Indian way of fighting. Pay was poor—less than $14 a month for a private. That did not attract the best men. When the men first began building Fort Sill, the daily rations consisted of unsalted meat and ten crackers each. Troops suggested they call the place "Camp Starvation."

The "Buffalo Soldiers," black troopers of the Tenth U.S. Cavalry, put up the first permanent buildings. In June 1869, twenty-five wagons with tools, hardware, civilian stonemasons, carpenters, and plasterers arrived. The post trader John Evan hauled lumber three hundred miles from Kansas to build a store at Fort Sill and another at nearby Cache Creek to handle Indian trade. A springhouse was built north of

Indian agent Lawrie Tatum, a Quaker, was sent to help with tribal affairs at the Kiowa-Comanche Indian Agency at Fort Sill. Many Indian agents were Quakers (members of the Society of Friends), who believed that kind, fair treatment of the Indians would bring about peace.

the hospital and lined with mortar. A slab stone trough was placed inside to provide a cool place for melons and fruit during the summer. Permanent quarters were finished about 1870. A road was cut to the Texas border. The men then built a race track at the fort.

Fort Sill was the largest of all the military posts west of the Mississippi. Forty or fifty men were stationed at most posts; Fort Sill had over five hundred. Over the next few years, it became a showplace. Limestone buildings faced a common square. There were lawns, gardens, a church, and a general store. Three barracks housed two companies of soldiers each. Social life could be brisk, especially if a single young girl were visiting. One young lady wrote about skating parties, music, cards, dancing, and tennis.

THE RED RIVER CAMPAIGN

Fort Sill served as the seat of the Kiowa-Comanche Indian Agency. The Indian agent sent to help with tribal affairs was Lawrie Tatum, a Quaker. Tatum worked hard to bring about justice for the Kiowa, but the Kiowa were bitter because of the broken promises of the U.S. government. During one council at Fort Sill in 1871, General William Tecumseh Sherman narrowly escaped being killed.

A replica of the trading store at Fort Sill. The post trader John Evan hauled lumber three hundred miles from Kansas to build the original store at Fort Sill and another at nearby Cache Creek.

The Kiowa continued to raid Texas settlements, killing whites, and taking livestock and captives. In 1871, Kiowa chiefs Satanta, Satank, and Big Tree were captured and sent to Texas for trial. Satank was killed on the road shortly after leaving Fort Sill. Satanta and Big Tree were pardoned two years later. Satanta was re-arrested the next year and later committed suicide in a Texas prison. Quanah Parker and his Quahada Comanche, along with a number of Kiowa, continued their raids.

In 1874, the U.S. government declared that all Indians must be living on the reservations by August. Any Indians off the reservations

Kiowa chiefs Satanta (above), Satank, and Big Tree led raids on settlements in Texas. In 1871 they were captured and sent to Texas for trial. Satanta was pardoned after two years in prison but was re-arrested the next year. Later he committed suicide in a Texas prison. Quanah Parker (right) and his Quahada Comanche, along with a number of Kiowa, continued their raids on the settlements.

would be considered **renegades** (outlaws). The Red River Campaign was undertaken to force the Comanche back to the reservations. The campaign involved more than three thousand troops from New Mexico and Indian Territory. Fourteen battles were fought before the four hundred Indian warriors finally gave up—and that was only after most of the women and children had been captured.

Quanah Parker and his Quahada Comanche surrendered in June 1875. Seventy-five Comanche and Kiowa were sentenced to prison in Florida. Chief Kicking Bird was told to identify twenty-six Kiowa to serve as prisoners of war. While he was making the difficult choice, an enemy tribesman poisoned him. These were the last of the Plains tribes to be settled on reservations in the Indian Territory.

Do You Remember?
1. Who led the U.S. troops into battle at the Battle of the Washita? Who was the Indian leader?
2. Who were the "Buffalo Soldiers"?
3. Name at least two active forts during the campaign against the Plains Indians.

RELOCATING OTHER INDIAN TRIBES

Two other tribes were settled in Indian Territory during the 1870s. During the mid-1800s, the Pawnee entered into three treaties with the federal government. With each treaty, they ceded a little more of their land until they had only a small area left in Nebraska. In 1876, they purchased their own reservation in Indian Territory just south of the Osage, bordering the Cherokee Outlet.

The Ponca were closely related to the Osage, Kansa, and Omaha. They may have been living along the Niobrara River in Nebraska as early as 1673, although they had villages in southwestern Minnesota and South Dakota's Black Hills. In 1858, they ceded all of their lands except those near the Niobrara River. The Sioux, however, were given that same land three years later and overran the Ponca, killing families and livestock. For eight years, the Ponca asked the U.S. government for help. Finally, an Indian agent arrived unannounced and unexpected in 1876 and told the Ponca to move to Indian Territory. Chief Standing Bear led his people into northeastern Oklahoma, between the Chikaskia and Arkansas rivers.

Shortly thereafter, Standing Bear's young son died. The grieving chief did not want to bury his son on foreign soil. Accompanied by thirty mounted warriors, the chief began the trek to the tribe's ancestral lands.

After the Quahada Comanche surrendered in June 1875, seventy-five Comanche and Kiowa were sentenced to prison in Florida. Chief Kicking Bird (above) was told to identify twenty-six Kiowa who would become prisoners of war. While making the difficult decision, he was poisoned by an enemy tribesman.

Some nervous settlers called on the military, and General George Crook and his troops arrested and jailed the Ponca near Omaha. When Omaha residents heard why Standing Bear was making the pilgrimage, they asked for a **writ of habeas corpus**, a court order that would release the Ponca from unlawful restraint. The government's attorneys suggested that the writ be denied on the grounds that Indians were not *persons*, as defined by the U.S. Constitution. Before a packed courtroom, the judge ruled that Standing Bear and his party were, in fact, persons and were entitled to be released to continue their journey to the burial grounds.

THE PASSING OF THE BUFFALO

While the railroads were building westward, independent hunters provided meat for the workers. "Buffalo Bill" Cody earned his nickname by killing more than 4,000 buffalo for the Union Pacific crews. Joseph W. McNeal hunted across western Kansas and northwestern Oklahoma, selling hides to railroad crews in eastern Kansas and Missouri. Buffalo meat went for 25 cents a chunk and hides for $3 to $5.

The early hunters used both meat and hides. The hides with hair made fine carriage robes. But it was not until 1871, when a new tanning process was developed in Germany, that buffalo hide could be

Some 40,000 buffalo skins piled up at Rath and Wright's in Dodge City. If the hunters were paid $3 per hide, how much money did Rath and Wright's have invested in the piles of buffalo hides in the picture?

tanned into leather. The price for hides immediately jumped. Eastern firms paid young men $50 a month to shoot and skin the buffalo and ship the hides. Several traders set up armed fortresses along the most popular trails, selling supplies, and buying hides from independent hunters. As early as 1872, the firm of Rath and Wright shipped 200,000 hides east over the Santa Fe Railroad from Dodge City.

So many hunters made their way into the Plains that the buffalo herds north of the Arkansas River were wiped out. The hunters then approached the Army officer at Fort Dodge for permission to hunt south of the Arkansas River—a clear violation of the Indian treaties. The commanding officer could not give formal permission, but he did add, "If I were a buffalo hunter, I would hunt where the buffalo are."

Thousands of buffalo were skinned on the prairies; the meat and bones were left to rot, breeding maggots and disease. The sight and stench were almost unbearable. From 1872 to 1874, the Santa Fe Railroad carried a half million buffalo hides to market. Probably six million were shipped from Dodge City between 1871 to 1887.

The last herd of buffalo was seen in 1877. The next year, the Indians held their final buffalo hunt. In 1879, the Kiowa were reduced to killing their ponies for meat to keep from starving. They had no choice but to learn to farm to stay alive. The Indian's nomadic Plains culture disappeared into history with the buffalo.

Do You Remember?

1. Name two tribes that were relocated to the Indian Territory in the 1870s.
2. How did "Buffalo Bill" Cody earn his nickname?
3. What year was the last buffalo herd seen on the open plains?

CATTLE COUNTRY

In the better restaurants in New York, Chicago, and Kansas City, American beef was the latest trend. It developed as part of a growing sense of **nationalism** (pride in one's country) and an American culinary (cooking) art. On the Plains, domestic and wild longhorn cattle had bred to create a strong meat animal. Cattle were so plentiful in Texas that a fine longhorn steer might bring $5 in Fort Worth; in Chicago or New York, that steer would bring $100. Smart businessmen knew they could make a fortune if they could find a way to get the cattle from the Midwest to the Eastern markets.

Meanwhile, the Union Pacific Railroad inched westward across Kansas Territory, creating **railheads**, towns to which farmers and

Most Americans have heard of "Buffalo Bill" Cody (above), even though many years have passed since he rode the Western plains. He earned his nickname by killing more than 4,000 buffalo to provide meat for the Union Pacific Railroad crews.

ranchers could bring their goods to be shipped. Quick to fill a need, the railroad built cattle cars to haul live cattle to the slaughterhouses in Kansas City, St. Louis, and Chicago. They also invented the first refrigerated railroad cars. Fans blew across blocks of ice placed in compartments at each end of the car. This lowered the temperature so that perishable fruits, such as strawberries, could be transported by rail. It also meant that beef could be butchered at railyard locations and shipped as carcasses, rather than as live cattle.

THE CATTLE TRAILS

From Texas to the railheads in Kansas Territory was eight hundred miles, much of it through Indian Territory. Luckily, the Texas longhorns were suited for hard travel. They had tough hoofs, could thrive on almost any kind of plant, and were known to walk sixty miles without water—something no pedigreed animal could do. A good-sized animal weighed in at 800 pounds; some were over 1,000 pounds. Their bodies were so long that their backs often swayed as they walked. Some said they were all legs and horns, but they carried a lot of meat—and they were free to anyone who could round them up. Of course, the businessmen had to find willing cowhands, strong horses, and contractors who could provide supplies along the trail.

The first cattle drive probably took place around 1866, along the East Shawnee Trail (the Texas Road) in the eastern part of the Indian lands. It entered Indian Territory east of Boggy Depot and went north just east of Fort Gibson. It crossed over into Kansas near Baxter Springs. Along this early trail were rough timbered areas where cattle could hide and deep streams that were hard to ford (cross). Spirit Spring, near what

The most famous cattle trail across Indian country was the Chisholm Trail, which roughly follows today's Highway 81. The trail was named for Jesse Chisholm (above), a Cherokee, who marked the trail to Abilene for the Texas cattlemen.

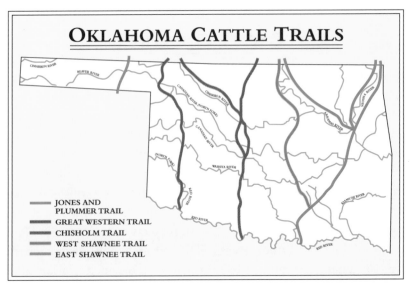

OKLAHOMA CATTLE TRAILS

JONES AND PLUMMER TRAIL
GREAT WESTERN TRAIL
CHISHOLM TRAIL
WEST SHAWNEE TRAIL
EAST SHAWNEE TRAIL

is now Afton, was so marshy that cowboys, horses, and cattle often sank in quicksand. Herders cut down trees at a nearby creekbed and made walkways to get to the spring.

The Indians bitterly protested this invasion, as did farmers in Missouri and eastern Kansas. The cattle not only ate their grass and trampled their crops, but also brought tick fever (Texas fever), which infected milk cattle. To avoid problems, the railroads extended westward and installed cattle pens at Abilene, Kansas. The trail to Abilene was—at least at first—on open land away from farms.

In 1867, the West Shawnee Trail opened from Texas to Baxter Springs and Wichita, Kansas. That same year, Jesse Chisholm blazed the most famous trail: the Chisholm Trail, which roughly follows today's Highway 81. Chisholm, a Cherokee, had been hired by Joseph McCoy to mark a route and then go south to tell Texas cattlemen about Abilene. Red Blanket, a Delaware Indian, led the first herd north across the Red River to the South Canadian River. Chisholm's trail became the main cattle highway to the north. The herds came from as far south as San Antonio, then headed north to Austin and Fort Worth before crossing the Red River. Chisholm's family, who were traders, kept supply wagons busy running from Caldwell, Kansas, to Texas and back.

The Texas longhorns were well suited for the rugged trek from ranch to railhead or market. They could thrive on almost any kind of plant and were known to walk sixty miles without water.

Much has been written about the life of the cowboy of the West. The cowboy had many responsibilities including branding the cattle (top left) and keeping watch over the cattle at night (above left). The cowboys stopped by the chuck wagon as they changed shifts.

The cattle trails were largely determined by the location of the rail-head, available water, the number of rivers to be crossed, and the number of farms and towns along the trail. **Drovers** (drivers of livestock) didn't care that they actually had no legal right to cross Indian lands or graze or water cattle on other people's land along the way.

Trails changed as grass grew scarce along the route. By the early 1870s, so many cattle had passed over the Chisholm Trail that it was twelve miles wide in some places. In the 1870s, two trails were cut through No Man's Land—the Tascosa Trail from Tascosa, Texas, and the Jones and Plummer Trail. The Western Cattle Trail crossed the Red River upstream from Doan's Crossing, ran north to Sherman Ranch on the

Cowboys "rode herd" on the cattle to guard against stampedes or attacks by Indians or rustlers.

Kansas border, and then on into Dodge City. The trail was popular because there was little timber; soon Dodge City was known as the "cow capital of the world."

Between 1866 and 1885, six million cattle crossed the Territory on their way north. By 1885, railroads sprawled across the south and west, and the long drives were no longer needed.

Do You Remember?
1. What is a railhead?
2. Who was Jesse Chisholm?
3. What Kansas city was known as "the cow capital of the world"?

GET ALONG LITTLE DOGIES

Cowboys Sam and Chester were pals. Notice the chaparejos.

Trail driving was the great cowboy experience. The herd usually had at least 2,000 head of cattle. There was one cowboy for every two hundred head and five or six solid ponies per man. They moved across the rolling, unsettled plains through all kinds of weather, constantly on the alert against *stampedes* (sudden rushes of frightened cattle) and raids. They averaged ten or twelve miles a day, and the trip could take anywhere from fifty days to five months. If the drive went too fast, the cattle lost too much weight.

It mattered little to the cattleman if the cowboy was Mexican, black, Irish, or Indian as long as he did his job and did not complain too much. It was a young man's job—hard and dusty. Through driving rain, wet snows, and hot sun, the cowboy rode while grit caked his clothes. *Chaparejos* ("chaps" or leggings), adopted from the Mexican cowboys, protected his legs from thorny brush. His handkerchief reduced the amount of dust he swallowed on the trail and doubled as a washcloth or coffee strainer. His gloves, usually fine buckskin, kept him from getting rope burns. He dreaded the sudden prairie storms that sent the herd into a frenzy, the dry riverbeds that meant parched throats, the alkaline waterholes that meant an ache in everyone's belly. At night, he sang to the cows to quiet them or, if other cowboys objected, he told stories or read tin can labels aloud. For his troubles, he was paid $15 to $25 a month.

In 1866, Iowan George Duffield purchased a herd of cattle in Texas and headed north to Kansas. His diary recorded a full share of troubles:

June 14. Last night there was a terrible storm Rain poured in torrents all night & up to 12 M today our Beeves left us in the night but for once on the whole trip we found them all together near camp at day break. all the other droves as far as I can hear are scattered to the four winds our Other Herd was all gone. We are now 25 Miles from Ark River & it is Very High we are water bound by two creeks & but Beef & Flour to eat, am not Homesick but Heart sick

19th. Good day 15 Indians come to Herd & tried to take some Beeves. Would not let them. Had a big muss One drew his Knife & I my Revolver. Made them leave but fear they have gone for others they are the Seminoles

23rd. worked all day hard in the River trying to make the Beeves swim & did not get one over. Had to go back to Prairie Sick & discouraged. Have not got the Blues but am in a Hel of a fix. Indians held High Festival over stolen Beef all night. lost 2 Beeves mired & maby more

27th My Back is Blistered badly from exposure while in the River & I with two others are Suffering very much I was attacked by a Beefe in the River & had a very narrow escape from being hurt by Diving

The chuck wagon was an important part of any cattle drive. The usual daily diet on the trail consisted of bacon, beans, biscuits, and strong coffee.

On early drives, the owner or trail driver often stopped at the nearest ranch and paid the woman of the house to bake bread for his men. But this slowed the drive, and there were few farms along the western trails. The "chuck wagon cook" became a regular part of the crew. He was considered worth his weight in salt pork. The usual daily fare on the trail consisted of bacon, beans, pan biscuits, and strong coffee. A good camp cook could turn canned peaches into a tasty cobbler, keep sourdough starter going, and mix up a hot stew. A complainer was liable to find himself mixing up the next meal.

Although the conditions were harsh in No Man's Land, cattlemen saw the potential for grazing cattle on the land and began moving into the area. In 1877, the 101 Ranch was set up and shelters were built for the ranch hands. The sod house (above) was one type of construction used for these shelters.

LIVING IN NO MAN'S LAND

When the territories of New Mexico, Kansas, and Colorado were created (1850, 1854, and 1861, respectively), two strips of land were accidentally left unclaimed. One was the Cherokee Strip, a two-mile-wide strip just south of the southern border of the Osage reservation in Kansas and north of the present boundary of Oklahoma. (The Cherokee Strip was sold to the United States by the Cherokee in 1866.) The second piece was 34 miles wide and 167 miles long, and most people assumed that it belonged to the Cherokee. It actually belonged to no one, having been given up by Texas in 1850. This area was commonly called "No Man's Land."

Among the first ranchers in No Man's Land were Juan and Vicenta Baca. They drove three thousand sheep from Las Vegas, New Mexico, to the Cimarron Valley in 1863. Several other families followed. In 1870, cattlemen who wanted the area for grazing livestock paid one of the Bacas $25,000 to move his sheep out of the area. That same year, Juan Baca took a wagon train loaded with wool to Independence, Missouri. Juan was killed in an Indian ambush on the return trip.

The cattlemen moved in, building cabins, dugouts, and shelters for the ranch hands. In 1877, the 101 Ranch and the OX Ranch were set up about ten miles apart. They had a single wire telephone system installed from Trinidad, Colorado. It connected both ranches as well as the ZH Ranch further downriver and was used to warn of cattle thieves and Indian attacks. These ranches were among the first to use barbed wire to fence in the land.

Settlers too moved into the area, many of them former Kansans who had lost their lands in prairie fires and droughts. Many families were young and able to stand up to the harsh land. They gathered currants, wild grapes, and sandhill plums for fruit and killed deer, antelope, and prairie chickens for meat. They gathered loads of buffalo bones, hauling them to Dodge City to sell for fertilizer. Another group consisted of Dunkards, German immigrants who opposed military oaths or military service on religious grounds. At least one band of outlaws, led by William Coe, hid out in an area known as Robber's Roost. From there, they led regular raids, stealing livestock in the Cherokee Outlet and herding them into New Mexico.

A few stores were opened (usually one room of a dugout) and often a post office. Mail was delivered to the post office, where settlers rode in, perhaps once a week, and dug through the mail bag to see if there was anything for them.

LEASING THE LAND

With the buffalo gone, there was no shortage of fertile grassland. It did not take long for Texas cattlemen to realize that if they wintered their cattle in the Indian Territory, the cattle would gain weight on the grasses and bring better prices at market. The colder climate would also kill the Texas ticks.

The Cherokee were the first to realize that they could make money from the grazing. They charged a "drover's tax" on animals crossing their land. In 1875, this was commonly 1 cent a head for sheep, 5 cents for cattle and horses. If they stayed too long, the fee went up. In 1879, cattlemen were charged 10 cents a head to pasture or winter the cattle, a fee that later rose to as much as $1 a head. When some cattlemen could find no land to rent or could not afford the fee, they married into the Indian tribes to gain grazing rights.

The Department of the Interior at first refused to approve leases or grazing permits and called for the War Department to clear out all the intruders. The War Department, however, knew it could not be done. It was not only impractical; it was illegal. The U.S. military had no authority in the Indian Territory.

Leasing quickly grew once the railroads moved into Indian Territory. Both the Osage and the Creek leased range lands to cattlemen from Texas and Kansas, shipping cattle out of Red Fork, Catoosa, and

Many Creek had large herds of their own on the rangeland. One, Creek Chief Pleasant Porter (above), specialized in fine horses.

Tulsa. However, many Creek ran large herds of their own on the range-land. Both Josiah and Legus Perryman and Charles Clinton had large herds of cattle, while Pleasant Porter specialized in fine horses.

On the Cheyenne-Arapaho reservation, which adjoined the Cherokee lands, conditions were desperate. Money and food promised by the government did not arrive, and the dry climate made it almost impossible to grow crops. There was no way for the Indian families to feed themselves. John Miles, the Indian agent, helped the Cheyenne-Arapaho negotiate a lease with seven cattlemen. The tribe rented three million acres for ten years at an annual fee of 2 cents an acre, or $62,000 a year. This was too much for Washington to ignore. But instead of addressing the issue, the government announced that it would not police the area, protect life or property, or enforce the lease. Unautho-

Indian agent John D. Miles (second from the left) helped the Cheyenne-Arapaho negotiate a lease with seven cattlemen. The tribe received 2 cents an acre, or $62,000 per year.

rized individuals made deals on already-leased land, with little chance of being punished.

By 1885, there was so much rivalry and trouble on the Cheyenne-Arapaho reservation that President Cleveland ordered all cattle removed. At least 210,000 head were herded to nearby ranges, which were already crowded. It was a disastrous move. The winter of 1885-1886 was extremely cold. Shortly after January 1, 1886, it began snowing. There were already eighteen inches on the ground before the blizzard hit. The wind was so cold and blowing so hard that the cattle drifted into the barbed wire fences the ranchers had put up to keep the cattle from straying. The ranch hands tried to drive the cattle back into the range, but the minute they were left alone, the cattle drifted back, piling up against the fence, where they froze to death. Those cattle that made it through the winter found little grass to eat on the overgrazed land. Ranchers estimated their losses at 80 percent. Many lost everything they had to the banks.

LIVESTOCK ASSOCIATIONS

Some dishonest cattlemen let their cattle "drift" onto Indian lands to take advantage of the good grazing. In the spring of 1883, honest ranchers who paid grazing taxes organized the Cherokee Strip Live Stock Association at Caldwell, Kansas. More than a hundred people joined. The association negotiated favorable contracts with the Cherokee, fenced the area, and subleased parts to cattlemen. The association paid the Cherokee $100,000 a year for five years; cattlemen paid 2 cents an acre rent to the association. The association fixed dates and places for roundups. It also surveyed the range, improved cattle breeds, built better shipping facilities, protected the members' property, and maintained an arbitration court. **Arbitration** is a method of settling disputes where both parties agree to abide by the decision made by an impartial third person. For the next six years, the organization maintained order in the Cherokee Outlet lands.

In 1884, the Creek and non-Indian ranchers in northeastern Oklahoma organized a similar association with Pleasant Porter as president. They divided up the Tulsa region into two districts, one on each side of the Arkansas River. Men patrolled for rustlers, gathered up strays, organized spring roundups, and checked the brands.

A Cherokee "Stripper." Early cattle ranchers in Indian Territory referred to the whole Cherokee Outlet as the Cherokee Strip.

Do You Remember?
1. Why did early settlers gather old buffalo bones?
2. What was the main reason that the Cheyenne-Arapaho opened their lands for lease?

CHAPTER REVIEW

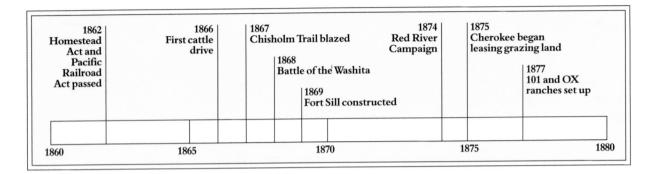

1860	1865	1870	1875	1880

1862
Homestead Act and Pacific Railroad Act passed

1866
First cattle drive

1867
Chisholm Trail blazed

1868
Battle of the Washita

1869
Fort Sill constructed

1874
Red River Campaign

1875
Cherokee began leasing grazing land

1877
101 and OX ranches set up

At the Same Time

1869 Patent granted for a moving picture projector

1872 Yellowstone authorized as first national park

1874 Barbed wire invented

1876 Alexander Graham Bell patented the telephone

1878 Thomas Edison patented the phonograph

1883 The first Wild West Show staged by Buffalo Bill Cody

1888 The first rodeo competition held in Prescott, Arizona

Summary

After the Civil War, the military was involved in a series of campaigns against the Plains Indians in the western half of Indian Territory. The Cheyenne and the Kiowa finally gave in to reservation life after several bitter battles, especially the Battle of the Washita.

As the railroads made their way west, cattlemen began to drive their herds across the Territory in order to load cattle at railheads in Kansas. The first trail drives were done without permission from the Indians. They were long and hard, but young men were eager to do the job because of the adventure. The trail drives only lasted for twenty years, ending when the territory opened and railroads expanded; but they left a legacy of rich cowboy folklore.

Cattlemen turned to leasing Indian lands, which brought a new set of problems.

Reviewing People, Places, and Things

Define, identify, or explain the importance of the following.

1. arbitration
2. Black Kettle
3. Chisholm Trail
4. George Armstrong Custer
5. drover
6. dugout
7. Fort Sill
8. Homestead Act
9. nationalism
10. No Man's Land
11. Pacific Railroad Act
12. railhead
13. renegade
14. writ of habeas corpus

Understanding the Facts

1. What two pieces of legislation led to the opening of the West?
2. What problems did the railroads face trying to build the transcontinental railroad?
3. Why was the Battle of the Washita one of the most controversial incidents of the Indian wars?
4. What was the difference between the way white hunters killed the buffalo and the way Indians did?
5. How did the refrigerated railroad car change how goods were transported?

6. What factors determined the route cattle trails took northward?
7. How did the annihilation of the buffalo affect the cattle industry in Indian Territory?
8. What was the Cherokee Strip Live Stock Association? How long did it exist? What was its purpose?

Developing Critical Thinking

1. Why were minorities hired to build the transcontinental railroads?
2. Why was the price of beef higher in the East than it was on the Plains?
3. About 1870, a Comanche chief arrived at one of the forts on the Plains to meet General Philip Sheridan. The chief had come on his own to introduce himself and to explain that some of the raids occurring were not made by members of his tribe. When he explained that he was a "good" Indian, Sheridan replied, "The only good Indian is a dead Indian."
   a. If a leader today were to make this remark, what do you suppose would be the reaction?
   b. Have attitudes changed in the last century, or have they stayed the same?

Using Your Skills

1. On a map of Indian Territory, locate
   a. the forts constructed by the military after the Civil War: Fort Nichols, Fort Cobb, Camp Supply, Fort Sill
   b. the site of the Battle of the Washita
2. On a map that shows Indian Territory, Kansas, Texas, and Arkansas,
   a. Draw the major cattle trails in one color. Carry the trails from their starting points in Texas to their destinations in Kansas.
   b. Draw the stagecoach routes in a different color. Carry them into Arkansas and Texas.
   c. Draw the major rivers in Indian Territory.
   d. Which cattle trail is the longest? Which the shortest? Which appears to be the hardest?

Special Projects

1. Many women and children were taken captive by the Plains Indians in raids on settlements. Cynthia Ann Parker, the mother of Quanah Parker, spent many years with the Indians after being captured. Research details of her story and prepare a report. Discuss her attitudes toward both white and Indian culture. Why was it difficult for her to return to white society? How did she feel about her Indian captors? What happened to her after she returned to white society? How do you think she would be treated today?
2. There were hard feelings between cattlemen and sheepherders. Part of the problem was the result of incompatibility of the two livestock. Interview a veterinarian or research livestock publications to find out why the two do not graze well on the same land.

Building Skills: Historical Maps

If you study an Oklahoma road map, it tells you about the state today. Historical maps tell facts about places at a particular time in the past. The map on page 192 shows the routes of the cattle trails that crossed Indian Territory.

1. Through what Indian lands did the various trails pass?
2. Why do you think the cattle trails were "blazed" (marked) along those particular routes?
3. Did the cattle trails pass near any settlement?

Sooner Trivia

. . . Johnny Murphy, an Irish ambulance driver, drove the first stake marking Fort Sill.

. . . The song "Home on the Range" was sung all along the cattle trails in the 1870s and 1880s. It was written by Dr. Brewster Higley while he lived in Kansas. It was printed in a local paper sometime around 1870. Higley never received any royalties or payment for his song even after it was printed. He died in Shawnee, Oklahoma, in 1911.

CHAPTER TEN

REBUILDING INDIAN TERRITORY

Our tribal government was upset by a stroke of the pen.
— John Kelly, Creek Indian

I N THE YEARS FOLLOWING THE CIVIL WAR, the Civilized Tribes made great strides in restoring the economy, tribal governments, and society of Indian Territory. Towns began to develop, and the tribes developed some of the best schools in the United States.

At the same time, the Indians had to contend with those who disregarded their territory and their rights: homeless veterans and former slaves, dishonest traders, squatters, outlaws. The federal government added to the Indians' troubles by dissolving the tribal governments in the late 1800s and breaking up tribal ownership of the land.

AGRICULTURE

In the late 1800s, the Five Civilized Tribes turned to rebuilding the land. Some Indians—most of them full-bloods—chose to live in simple cabins in remote areas far from white man's civilization. Others built model farms or ranches. A Creek citizen, for example, was allowed to occupy all the land he or she could fence and cultivate. Enterprising citizens hired whites to take care of large sections of land. Thus, **tenant farmers** became part of Indian Territory. A tenant farmer was responsible for clearing the land and growing a crop. The landowner owned any improvements (wells, fences, and so on) as well as part of

The Cherokee capitol at Tahlequah was rebuilt in 1867 after the original capitol building had been destroyed during the Civil War.

CHAPTER PREVIEW

Terms: tenant farmer, royalty, labor union, spa, boarding house, haberdashery, academy, rhetoric, arsonist, Dawes Severalty Act, Curtis Act

People: Jacob Bartles, J. J. McAlester, Alexander Posey, Judge Isaac C. Parker, Chitto Harjo

Places: Bartlesville

the crop. Most tenants were of Scotch, Irish, Scotch-Irish, and English descent; there were also a few French-Canadians. Many of these people had followed the tribes west, hoping for some land of their own.

The most common crops among the Cherokee and Creek were a mottled type of corn (probably related to today's blue corn), melons, and sweet potatoes. Choctaw and Chickasaw farmers preferred cotton, sweet potatoes, and beans. Another crop that prospered for a short while was tobacco. Cherokee leaders Elias Boudinot and Stand Watie purchased a Missouri tobacco factory in 1868 and moved it to the Cherokee Nation. They then bought tobacco from local farmers and manufactured chewing tobacco, snuff, and pipe tobacco. A clause in the Cherokee Treaty of 1866 allowed tribal citizens to manufacture and sell any product anywhere without federal taxes. The tax-free Indian tobacco products were shipped throughout the United States. Southern tobacco dealers immediately complained, and Congress soon invalidated (canceled) the tax-exempt clause. The Cherokee protested, but to no avail. The Indian tobacco industry collapsed.

One of the first businesses near any settlement was a mill. Farmers hauled their grain to the nearest mill for grinding. Nelson Carr built perhaps the first commercial mill in northern Oklahoma in 1870. A few years later, Jacob Bartles purchased it and added a store. That was the beginning of the town of Bartlesville.

Cattle, horses, and hogs were important livestock. Cattle and horses foraged on the prairies. Hogs roamed the oak woodlands until fall butchering, which was a community ritual. It was said that everything on the hog was used but the squeal. The fat was used to make soap; the feet were pickled in vinegar. Some meat was packed in crocks and preserved for winter use. Hams were covered with spices, wrapped in burlap sacks, and cured in the smokehouse. The hams could only be smoked in areas where winter was cold enough to freeze and where spring was not so warm as to spoil the meat. Such conditions existed along the Mason-Dixon line: in Virginia, Kentucky, Arkansas, Missouri, and Oklahoma.

In 1873, tribal leaders held the first International Indian Territory Agricultural Fair in Muskogee. Agricultural products, livestock, and Indian handcrafts were displayed. The rodeo held with the fair—perhaps the first organized rodeo in the United States—was the most popular event in the Territory until statehood.

Two brothers—Josiah and Legus Perryman—set up large ranches in the northeast section of the Creek land near Lochapoka (now Tulsa) around 1877. They also planted large orchards. Chauncey Owen, a white man married to a Creek woman, was the leading farmer in the area. He also owned large herds of cattle, and his fine ranch became known as the "Big House." W. E. Halsell, a young Texan, married a part-Cherokee, and they took up their land rights in the Tulsa area. As many as thirty thousand cattle with his Mashed O brand roamed the range from Vinita to Tulsa.

NATURAL RESOURCES

Steam-powered lumber mills were built in the forested areas of the Territory as early as 1868. Some Indians contracted with white businessmen to cut and log trees.

When J. J. McAlester discovered coal deposits in the Choctaw Nation in 1871, he organized the Oklahoma Mining Company. He then leased the mine to a coal company. The Choctaw Nation received a **royalty** (a payment for the right to exploit a natural resource) of 10 cents a ton. Mines were opened at Krebs, Coalgate, and Lehigh. They were worked by miners imported from Czechoslovakia, Hungary, Germany, France, Wales, Sweden, and Italy. The mines were very dangerous places to work. Because the veins of ore were thin, men often worked on their knees or lying on their backs; there was no escape if there was a cave-in or fire. Wages were $2.50 a day for a 9°-hour day—above average for the time. There was one problem: Miners wanted unions to help maintain safety standards. A **labor union** is an organization of workers formed to improve wages, benefits, and working

Once the trees in an area had been cut, it was time to move the saw mill to another wooded area—where the process started all over again as shown in the photograph "Wilder's Saw Mill on the Move."

J.J. McAlester organized the Oklahoma Mining Company after he discovered coal deposits in the Choctaw Nation in 1871.

conditions. Indian Territory laws, however, made labor unions illegal until 1889. Peter Hanraty, an immigrant from Scotland, led several strikes protesting working conditions.

Oil seeps or springs could be found throughout Indian Territory. People believed that crude oil would help those with such diseases as arthritis, rheumatism, and dropsy. The Chickasaw Nation developed several **spas** (health resorts) around the oil seeps. People from all over the Southwest came to bathe in the waters. The Choctaw Oil and Refining Company drilled the Fawcette Well sometime in the early 1880s, and another was sunk west of Atoka; but neither was impressive. The market for oil was still small; it was used mostly as a lubricant and in lamps.

Do You Remember?
1. Who were the most common tenant farmers in Indian Territory?
2. Which natural resources proved profitable for the Indian tribes?

THE GROWTH OF TOWNS

Even in remote areas, at least one trader hauled in supplies on a regular basis or opened a small store. Small towns grew up around those stores. Growing a new society required workers. The Indians sold licenses to non-Indian laborers, allowing them to work in the Territory although they could not own land. The licenses were a source of revenue for the tribes and cost between $2.50 and $5.00. Thousands of non-Indians moved into the Territory and set up small businesses. In some towns, almost all the residents were non-Indians, mixed bloods, or adopted citizens of the tribe.

Many of the larger towns had at least one bank and one drugstore. There were usually one or two lawyers, a doctor, and sometimes a dentist. A hotel was sparsely furnished and never over two stories high. **Boarding houses**, which provided a room and a place at the table, were run by enterprising women, as were bakeries. Cafes served plain fare but large portions. Barbershops were the newsstands of the day, where men came for a haircut, shave, or a hot bath.

Meat markets sold beef as well as turkey, venison, and other local game. **Haberdasheries** (stores selling clothing and small goods) carried high-button shoes, bolts of cloth, ready-made suits, hats, coats, and shirts. General stores with everything from lamp wicks to tin pans were often part of the lumber yard. Furniture stores carried parlor sets, stoves, and coffins. Livery stables and blacksmith shops mended wagons and shoed horses.

Doaksville, in the Choctaw Nation, was the principal trade center of Indian Territory, but trade flourished in many Indian towns. The Katy Railroad crossed the old Butterfield Stage route at Atoka, making it an important business center. In the Cherokee Nation, the Three Forks area continued to be a major trading center, and Bartlesville was starting to grow.

When the railroad passed through the Creek Nation in the 1870s, Eufaula became an important center. Marshall Town, where the Arkansas and Verdigris rivers met, was an active black settlement in the 1880s. In 1882, when the Frisco Railroad moved into the Creek Nation, Red Fork and Sapulpa became important cattle shipping centers.

In the Chickasaw Nation, Tishomingo served as the capital. After the railroads made their way through in the late 1880s, Ardmore, Pauls Valley, and Purcell all became important shipping centers. The railroads bypassed the small Seminole Nation. Its most important town at this time was Wewoka, the capital.

POLITE SOCIETY

When Agent Robert Owen of the Union Agency at Muskogee passed through Vinita in 1886, the town had comfortable cottages, broad streets, and respectable buildings of stone, brick, and wood. The stores were well stocked with merchandise, and there were four churches.

Below: Compare Agent Robert Owen's description of Vinita with this 1883 photograph of a house in Vinita. *Bottom:* This 1873 photograph of the F.B. Severs Cash Store in Okmulgee was typical of the general stores on the frontier.

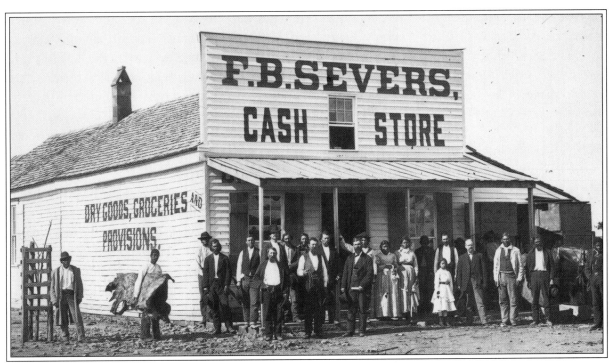

The people dress the same [as people in frontier Missouri], read the same newspapers and periodicals....They listen to the same teaching and preaching, and one of the churches happens to have an orchestra of stringed instruments. The people visit each other as they do in the adjacent States, follow the same fashions, do an equal amount of innocent and of mischievous gossiping, the boys talk base-ball and the school-girls chew gum.

Isidore Robot was the first Catholic missionary permitted to live and teach among the Choctaw. In 1876 he founded Sacred Heart Mission west of Atoka, which was attended by many young girls from wealthy Indian families.

As some urban Indian families grew prosperous, they built large homes, hired servants, and bred fine-blooded horses. They imported the latest European furniture and fashions. They entertained extravagantly with dinners and parties, and they attended theater and music programs.

For those who preferred more excitement, there were horse races at the larger ranches. Quarter horses and racehorses were known by name in the Territory, and at least one favorite horse had a Mississippi River steamboat named after it. Tulsa was not even a town when Bill Sennett pitched his tent in the Creek Nation. He brought with him a string of racehorses; all of the stores emptied of customers when he announced a race was about to begin. His races became so popular that he built a regular race track—one of the first businesses in Tulsa.

Politics was discussed at least as much in the Territory as it was in the East and South. One Indian woman recalled that everyone in Boggy Depot was a Democrat except her father, and discussions about the political issues of the day grew very heated.

Schools and churches were the basis for social life, and they were closely intertwined. The same Protestant denominations that had been active before the Civil War continued to work in the Territory after the war. Atoka had one of the first Catholic churches. Friar Michael Smythe, an Irish priest, rode the circuit from Fort Smith through the Choctaw Nation until St. Patrick's Church, a one-story wood building, was completed. Isidore Robot was the first Catholic missionary permitted to live and teach among the Choctaw. He founded Sacred Heart Mission west of Atoka in 1876.

Christmas was the biggest holiday of the year and involved the entire community. At Boggy Depot in 1880, citizens hauled in a great green tree and set it up in the little white church, its top touching the ceiling. On Christmas Eve, it was loaded with presents for every man, woman, and child in town—Indians, blacks, and whites. The festivities usually ended with firecrackers and Roman candles, since no one celebrated the Fourth of July.

Cowboys rode into town to attend the Christmas church ceremonies and especially to hear the singing and taste the special holiday

As some Indian families grew prosperous, they built large homes, such as the Peter Conser House near Heavener (left), imported the latest fashions, entertained lavishly, and attended theater and music programs. Peter Conser (above) was a district chief of the Choctaw and captain of the Choctaw lighthorsemen.

spreads. The songs the women sang at the programs could often be heard months later as cowboys gathered around campfires or tried to quiet the restless cattle.

Do You Remember?
1. Name at least three important trading centers in Indian Territory.
2. What two institutions were the basis of social life in the Territory?
3. What was the biggest holiday?

School pictures, such as this one from Wheelock Academy, were as much a part of a student's school experience in the 1800s as they are today.

EDUCATION

The crossroads nature of the Plains had exposed the Indians to many cultures. Missionaries frequently read Hebrew, Latin, and Greek; traders often spoke French, Spanish, English, and several Indian dialects. When the Five Civilized Tribes organized after they arrived, each tribe elected a commissioner of education and set aside land and funds for schools. These schools were a great source of tribal pride. Neighborhood schools usually went from kindergarten through sixth, or sometimes eighth, grade. In the Creek Nation, there were separate schools for the children of black freedmen (freed slaves) and for those with physical handicaps. The Chickasaw operated twelve neighborhood schools in 1869.

Teachers, many of them educated Indians, received $3 a month for each pupil and were expected to furnish books and supplies. The teacher might stay six weeks with each student's family or might board with one family. Teacher Minnie Rector Fitts lived with the Henry Carter family in Okmulgee County. "I learned to eat sofke, sour bread, blue dumplings, and all the other Indian dishes," she said.

The one-room schoolhouse had an immense wood stove in the center. The school directors were supposed to provide the wood, but sometimes teachers and students gathered it. Usually there was a water well near the schoolhouse with a hand pump. Privies were in back, one for boys, one for girls.

Children of non-Indian families attended missionary schools or subscription schools, where a few families collected money to hire a private teacher and rent a building. This was not always successful. In 1883, the residents of Tulsa quickly dismissed their new teacher when they discovered that he spent his spare time gambling.

The **academies** were the next level beyond the neighborhood schools and were the same as high schools. Many were for Indian girls: Henry Kendall College at Muskogee (later the University of Tulsa), Carter Seminary (for Chickasaw girls), Oklahoma Presbyterian College at Durant. These schools taught the fine arts and introduced physical education such as tennis and basketball. At Wheelock Academy, for example, students learned arithmetic, grammar, geography, natural philosophy, astronomy, botany, chemistry, geometry, and the Bible.

Best known of the Indian institutes of higher education were the Cherokee National Female Seminary at Park Hill and the National Male Seminary near Tahlequah. Some students boarded in the dormitories, while others attended day classes. When the female seminary

The Cherokee National Female Seminary at Park Hill (below) and the National Male Seminary located near Tahlequah were two of the best-known Indian institutes of higher education.

Students pose in front of Creek Seminole College at Boley. The college was established for black freedmen and their families.

was destroyed by fire, it was rebuilt in 1888 after the fashion of Eastern colleges. The main building housed classrooms, library, offices, kitchen, dining room, chapel, and dispensary (a medical office). It was the largest school ever built by a tribe.

The seminary was considered a model of education for young women aged fourteen to eighteen. They awoke to a bell at 5:30 a.m. The first-term juniors took algebra, **rhetoric** (public speaking), Latin, chemistry, and Bible. Second-term seniors studied geometry, English literature, Virgil, moral philosophy, vocal music, and drawing. They also studied needle arts, painting, and piano. There were three exercise periods and study hours. About an hour a day was spent on chores. Lights went out at 9 p.m.

The Cherokee schools were so superior that when Oklahoma became a state, anyone with a degree from a Cherokee school was automatically given two years of college credit. Many Creek and Chickasaw attended Eastern colleges and universities at the tribes' expense. They returned with degrees from Yale, Harvard, and Princeton—an accomplishment few white men on the frontier could claim.

Well-educated Indians became tribal leaders, doctors, lawyers, educators, and journalists. The Cherokee had begun printing newspapers as soon as Sequoyah developed the alphabet. By 1876, the Creek had also developed an alphabet, and *The Indian Journal* was printed in Muskogee. One of its most famous editors, and a member of the Creek Council, was Alexander Posey, son of a Scotch-Irishman and a Creek Indian woman. Posey also edited the *Eufaula Indian Journal*.

All those who practiced medicine in the Cherokee Nation were required to pass an exam in order to get a permit to practice. To make sure that standards were met, the Cherokee National Council appointed a board of medical examiners in 1873. The Choctaw passed a similar law in 1884. When the Choctaw tried to enforce the law, they found that the majority of white doctors in the Nation had never been to medical school. A few agreed to leave; but most simply moved to another part of the Territory to practice.

Do You Remember?
1. How important was education to the Five Civilized Tribes?
2. What was the difference between the Indian physicians and most white doctors before statehood?

TAMING THE TERRITORY

Each of the Five Civilized Tribes had a seat of government with an impressive capitol building for legislative, executive, and judicial affairs: the Cherokee at Tahlequah, the Choctaw at Armstrong Academy (Chahta Tamaha), the Creek at Okmulgee, the Chickasaw at Tishomingo, and the Seminole at Wewoka.

Tribal laws had been established under the Indian constitutions, and these laws were enforced by Indian lighthorsemen. Disputes were settled in courts of law modeled after U.S. courts. Under Creek law,

Taming Indian Territory was a job for the lighthorsemen. They served as the police force of their day. The photograph below is of a group of Choctaw lighthorsemen.

Many of the outlaws of this era escaped from the law into Indian Territory. A different side of these criminals can be seen in this poem (top), "Rufus Buck's Dream," written on the back of a photograph of his mother. The poem was found in Buck's cell after he was hanged at Fort Smith. Jesse James (above) often stopped at Belle Starr's station.

for example (and other tribal governments had similar laws), thieves received fifty lashes for the first offense, one hundred for the second, and death by shooting for the third. If a person injured another, that individual was fined for damages or an amount of work equal in value to the fine. The injured party received full damages. **Arsonists** (people who set fires) paid full damages and were given one hundred lashes. Murder was punishable by death. When punishment was death, the defendant was released and told to return on execution day. Not one Creek ever failed to show up for his own execution. If he had, he would have been branded a coward and denied a home in the eternal hunting grounds with his ancestors.

Liquor caused the most trouble in the Territory. Whiskey had been the "indispensable companion" of the early fur traders. But what the Indian bought was usually a mixture of strychnine, tobacco, lye soap, and red pepper. One bottle of the gut-rotting formula was traded for one buffalo robe. In the 1870s, the federal government outlawed liquor in Indian Territory; it was not, however, outlawed in the surrounding areas. Travelers carried it over the border in their high boots (thus the term *bootlegger*). Dealers in Arkansas, Missouri, and Texas set up business just far enough from the borders to be beyond the law. One daring man built a tavern on stilts in the middle of the Red River.

From the end of the Civil War until statehood, Indian Territory was plagued with a lawless element. White men were not bound by Indian laws, and Indian Territory was not under U.S. law. Criminals realized that they could, as a popular song said, "go to the Indian Territory and live outside the law."

Everyone knew the outlaw gangs at least by reputation and often as neighbors: the Doolins, the Daltons, the Jennings brothers, the Cook gang, the Turner gang, Wesley Barnett's bunch, Mose Miller's gang, the ruthless Buck gang. Some gangs were white Anglo-Saxon, others were a mixture of Indian, black, and Mexican. Most were young. Among the most notorious of the outlaws was Myra Belle Shirley, better known as Belle Starr. Tagged "The Outlaw Queen" by the tabloids of the day, Starr ran a station for outlaws at Younger's Point, where Cole Younger and Jesse James often stopped.

The comings and goings of these men and women kept the Indian lighthorsemen and the federal posses busy. Banks, mail trains, and an occasional store were common targets. A gang might rob a bank in Missouri, Kansas, or Arkansas, and race back to Indian Territory, where they were beyond the reach of state lawmen. They would then hide in remote areas—in cabins or natural rock outcrops in the western hills or in the central Cross Timbers.

Their exploits were often exaggerated by the press. They actually spent most of their time rounding up someone else's livestock. Stealing cattle and sheep was a dishonorable trade; but stealing horses was more serious. Without a horse, a man was at the mercy of the land—usually a death sentence. Thus, to call a man a "horsethief" was to indicate that he could fall no lower. The penalty was usually hanging from the nearest tree. It was just such a charge that finally sent Belle Starr to Detroit federal prison in 1884, where she served nine months.

But it was business crime that finally led to the establishment of a territorial court. Dishonest people would run up large debts then move to the Territory and refuse to pay those debts. Businessmen had no way to collect their money. In 1875, the federal government hired Judge Isaac C. Parker to be judge over the U.S. District Court for the Western District of Arkansas at Fort Smith. This district included Indian Territory. When he arrived late in the spring, no one really believed that this 6 foot tall, 200-pound ex-Congressman could tame the 74,000 square miles of territory. But Parker was determined.

He held court around the clock, closing only on Sundays and Christmas. He hired Noah Frank as Indian interpreter. He organized an army of U.S. deputy marshals, some of whom had seen both sides of the law. They were authorized to hire posses for "hunting expeditions." They armed themselves with warrants to arrest any outlaw that might happen to cross their path. They carried handcuffs, ankle chains, and leg chains to shackle prisoners to a tree if a nearby jail was lacking. Sometimes a U.S. commissioner accompanied them. The posse might be gone 2-3 months and return with 50-100 prisoners.

Federal Judge Isaac C. Parker (above) was known as the "hanging judge." In Judge Parker's courtroom at Fort Smith, wrongdoers found quick and harsh judgment.

A public gallows was built at Fort Smith to carry out the sentences of Judge Parker, who believed people should be responsible for their actions—and sentenced them accordingly.

Like most leaders at that time, Judge Parker believed that people were responsible for their actions. A public gallows was built, and thousands turned out for the hangings. Soon newspaper editors nicknamed Parker the "hanging judge." Parker sat on the bench for twenty-one years. During his tenure, he heard 13,400 cases; imposed 9,454 sentences; charged 344 defendants with offenses punishable by death; and sentenced more than 160 people to hang.

Do You Remember?

1. What were Indian police called?
2. What famous judge was known as "the hanging judge"?

A MAKESHIFT PRISON

When Congress failed to provide for a prison at Fort Smith, Judge Isaac Parker housed prisoners in the musty courthouse basement. The building had never been meant to confine men, and rumors of the horrid conditions there soon began to reach the public. In 1886, Eastern reporter Anna Dawes described the wretched conditions for a Boston newspaper. The prison had neither light nor outside ventilation. The basement was divided into two areas, each about 60 feet by 24 feet. Each area had a single sink and a coal oil barrel sawed in two for a tub. The latrine was a single bucket in a chimney closet. A bed was a wooden cot with a single blanket. There were no provisions for the sick. For exercise, the men divided themselves into squads and periodically marched up and down the room. "Into these reeking holes are crowded criminals of every age and degree," Dawes wrote. Some were awaiting trial. Some had been tried and found guilty.

If a man received a sentence of less than one year, he stayed at Fort Smith. If the sentence was longer, he was sent to Michigan. "Happy the convict whose crime is large in the Indian territory," Dawes wrote, "for worse is a single year of Fort Smith than a cycle at Detroit."

Anna Dawes's articles, combined with the efforts of the Indian Rights Association and the Quakers, finally aroused enough public anger. Congress included an appropriation (public funds set aside for a specific purpose) in the budget for a prison annex.

Judge Parker was criticized for housing prisoners in the musty courthouse basement (above).

BREAKING UP THE NATIONS

Beginning in the 1870s, the U.S. Congress took steps to dissolve the Indian nations. An 1870 U.S. Supreme Court ruling in the Cherokee tobacco case stated that the laws of Congress took precedence over any treaty. This meant that Congress no longer had to use the signed treaties as a basis for working with the Indian tribes. In 1871, Congress passed a law stating that no new treaties would be made with the tribes; tribes would now be subject to the laws of Congress.

THE DAWES ACT

In 1887, Congress passed the **Dawes Severalty Act**. Until this time, the Indian lands were owned not by individual members of the tribe but in commonality, that is, by the Indian tribe as a whole. The Dawes Act dissolved tribal ownership and gave to families and individuals specific amounts of land.

A Creek delegation meeting with the Dawes Commission at Muskogee. The Commission never tried to hide its real goals: to dissolve tribal governments and divide up Indian land.

When it was passed, the law applied only to Indians in western Oklahoma. In 1893, Congress extended the act to the Five Civilized Tribes. President Cleveland appointed the Dawes Commission to negotiate with tribal leaders. The act was supposed to correct injustices that Congress perceived in land distribution and use within the tribes. But the Commission never hid the government's real goals: to dissolve the tribal governments and to divide up the Indian land.

Chitto Harjo (above left), also known as Crazy Snake, led a group of Creek who formed a separate government in defiance of the Dawes Commission. Some of his followers, known as "Snakes," are seen in the jail at Fort Gibson in 1901 (above right).

The land involved was not wild land but vast tracts and large towns. The towns were divided into town lots, which were then sold to the highest bidders. If there were improvements (houses, businesses, fences) on those lots, the Indian owner had the right to bid on the improvements that he already owned at below-market prices.

This was a major blow to the five Indian nations. When they refused to cooperate, the Commission was not surprised. "The Indians...would never surrender by consent what they did not want to give up at all," the Dawes Commission wrote in 1903. "Some of the tribal members held passionately to their institutions from custom and patriotism, and others held with equal tenacity because of the advantages and privileges they enjoyed. It was almost worth a man's life at that time to advocate a change." Over the Indians' protests, the government gave the Dawes Commission the right to prepare tribal rolls and make land assignments to Indians without tribal approval.

The Cherokee banded together under the old Keetoowah secret society and tried to refuse the allotment system. The Creek, led by

*Right: Chickasaw freedmen are seen here filing for their allotment, which was about 40 acres of land. **Below:** Editor Alexander Posey worked with the Dawes Commission to locate those Creeks entitled to land allotments.*

Chitto Harjo (Crazy Snake), formed a separate government. They refused to cooperate and arrested and whipped those Creek who accepted allotments.

Some tribal members, such as Alexander Posey, worked on the Dawes Commission field parties, going out to find Indians who had disappeared and to soothe the "Snakes" (followers of Chitto Harjo). When Posey encountered John Kelly, a well-known Snake, he tried to explain how useless it was to hold out against the federal government. But Kelly replied that

> *The real Indian was not consulted as to allotment of lands; if he had been consulted he would never have consented to depart from the customs and traditions of his fathers. Our tribal government was upset by a stroke of the pen, because a few cried "Change," and because we were helpless.... The real Indian does not change and is steadfast in the truth. He will not be reconciled to the wrong. The government of the United States has made us solemn pledges, and without our consent has no right to break them. As for us we will keep good faith.*

Finally, Chitto Harjo was arrested and tried in federal court at Muskogee. Faced with prison, the Indian leaders gave in. In 1897, the Choctaw and Chickasaw signed the Atoka Agreement, which laid out rules for the sale of townsite lots, railroad right-of-ways, and land leases. The **Curtis Act** followed two months later, extending the allotment to the Creek and Cherokee and later the Seminole. The Curtis Act voided all leases for agricultural or grazing purposes. It provided for surveying and incorporating towns in Indian Territory. It gave townspeople the right to vote and set up free public schools. A special provision reserved minerals (oil, coal, asphalt) for the tribe as a whole;

leases were to be regulated by the Secretary of the Interior. Most important, the Curtis Act abolished the tribal courts. All people in the Territory were now subject to federal law and the laws of Arkansas.

STEALING THE LAND

The land allotments varied, depending upon the amount of land each tribe originally owned. Choctaw and Chickasaw citizens were supposed to receive about 320 acres; Cherokee, 110 acres; Creek, 160 acres; and Seminole, 120 acres. Choctaw and Chickasaw freedmen and their descendants received about 40 acres each. In some cases, however, there was not enough land left, and money was taken from the tribal coffers to pay landless Indians.

For all practical purposes, the federal government considered that the Indian Nations no longer existed. Dishonest men made certain of it. The method of alloting land to individual Indians was complex. The lands were divided into homestead and "surplus." Different laws governed each type, including when and if the land could be sold. Some land could be sold only after a specified number of years or when certain laws changed. But it was not uncommon for a land dealer to give an Indian $5 or $10 for a ninety-nine-year lease on an entire allotment or a townsite. The dealer then subleased it at a handsome profit. Pleasant Porter estimated in 1902 that almost one million acres of Creek lands were held under such leases.

Lumber companies managed to pay only a few dollars to the Choctaw for leases in the Kiamichi forest. Then they cleared the leased area of pine and hardwood and made a fortune. Wills were written that named land dealers as heirs to the estate when government restrictions expired. One Kansas firm employed a part-Choctaw to help obtain powers of attorney that gave the firm control of the allotments and the right to sell the land when restrictions were removed.

Land was also stolen from the estates of minors. The law required that professional guardians be appointed for full-blood children and orphans. It was the guardian's job to see that the lands were leased properly to provide income. Some "professional" guardians leased the land to someone for a very small sum. That person would then sublease at a handsome sum and split the profits with the guardian.

The photograph depicts the Creek Nation's election in 1897. This was the last time these proud people would vote as a separate Nation. The Curtis Act abolished tribal courts, and all people in Indian Territory were now subject to federal laws and the laws of Arkansas.

Do You Remember?

1. By what name was Chitto Harjo commonly called? For what is he known?
2. What was the purpose of the Atoka Agreement?
3. What was the purpose of the Curtis Act?

CHAPTER REVIEW

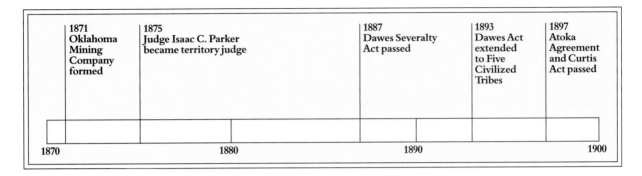

1871 Oklahoma Mining Company formed	1875 Judge Isaac C. Parker became territory judge	1887 Dawes Severalty Act passed	1893 Dawes Act extended to Five Civilized Tribes	1897 Atoka Agreement and Curtis Act passed

1870 — 1880 — 1890 — 1900

At the Same Time

1869   Wyoming passed law granting women the right to vote

1871   Great Chicago Fire

1873   The first postcard issued

1877   The first Flag Day held

1881   The American Federation of Labor organized in Pittsburgh

1891   The first electric automobile designed

1896   First modern Olympic Games held

Summary

The Indian nations made economic progress after the Civil War despite political problems. Livestock and farming operations grew; coal mining began, with European miners imported to work the mines. The Indian towns along the edges of settlement were thriving business and market centers.

Law enforcement was a problem. Indian law did not apply to non-Indians, and the lawless took advantage of that. A federal court was set up in Fort Smith, and posses and marshals roamed the area to arrest outlaws.

In the 1880s and 1890s, the U.S. government began to take steps to dissolve the tribal governments. Despite protests and lawsuits, the tribal lands were broken up, with families and individuals receiving an allotment of land. The U.S. government asserted that its laws were sovereign, and the power of the tribal governments was broken.

Reviewing People, Places, and Things

Define, identify, and explain the importance of the following.

1. academy
2. arsonist
3. boarding house
4. Curtis Act
5. Dawes Severalty Act
6. haberdashery
7. Chitto Harjo
8. labor union
9. Judge Isaac C. Parker
10. rhetoric
11. royalty
12. spa
13. tenant farmer

Understanding the Facts

1. How did tenant farmers become part of Indian Territory?
2. Name at least three towns in Indian Territory that grew up along the railroad lines.
3. What subjects were taught in the schools in Indian Territory that are rarely taught today?
4. Name at least two things that contributed to lawlessness in the Indian Territory.
5. What were the goals of the U.S. government toward the Indian tribes?
6. What three Congressional acts took away the powers of the tribal governments?

Developing Critical Thinking

1. In the Indian Nations, it was common for those sentenced to death to be turned loose and told to return on the day appointed for execution. Would this work today? Why or why not?

2. At the time covered by this chapter, the Indian tribes were not citizens of the United States. If they had been, how would some of the government's actions have violated their civil rights?

Using Your Skills

1. Using the data given in this chapter, how much did a miner earn for a normal workday? For a six-day workweek?

2. In the late 1800s, steamboats were the main means of transporting goods into and out of the Territory. Each year about 25,000 tons of goods were shipped out of Fort Gibson in Indian Territory. Steamboats averaged 300 tons a trip. How many trips were needed to handle 25,000 tons? How many trips would it take to send 20,000 tons to New Orleans if 1/3 of the goods were unloaded along the way and one boatload was usually wrecked or stranded along the way?

Special Projects

1. There are several stories about how Tulsa got its name. Research the origins of the name and its relation to Creek history.

2. Research what kinds of hardwood trees grew in the eastern forests of the Indian nations. What are grown today? How does today's timber industry differ from the timber industry a century ago? What is done today to make certain that forests are not depleted?

Building Skills: Traveling Through Time

You have the following task: For your vacation you want to visit as many of the state historic sites as you possibly can. You have two important limits on your plans: time and money. You can travel no more than 600 miles roundtrip on your vacation. Don't forget the mileage for the return trip.

If you wish, choose a partner to help you plan your trip. Use a list of the state's historic sites and an Oklahoma highway map to help you design your route. You may also wish to consult other maps. Start from the town in which you live or the town in which you attend school. If you live in Tulsa, for example, you might begin your trip as follows:

Leave Tulsa traveling north on I-169 to Bartlesville to visit Frank A. Phillips Home, 1107 South Cherokee (41 miles). Then to north end of Frank Phillips Avenue, Johnstone Park, to see replica of first commercial oil well, the Nellie Johnstone (2 miles)...

Present your vacation trip to the class by marking your route on a map. After completing your plan, consider the following questions.

1. What parts of Oklahoma history will you visit on your trip?

2. Will you see all the sites you want to see?

3. How did your starting point limit the number of sites you could include?

4. Why do you think the state chose to make the sites you visited historic sites?

5. Is there a local site that you would like to nominate as a historic site? Why do you think it would make a good site?

Sooner Trivia

. . . Wewoka, the capital of the Seminole Nation, was first settled by John Coheia (Gopher John), a former black slave.

. . . The last execution under the old Choctaw law was in 1899 near Alikchi, McCurtain County.

. . . Judge Parker's basement prison was one of only four federal prisons in the United States in the 1870s.

. . . The city of McAlester was named after J. J. McAlester, the founder of the Oklahoma Mining Company.

CHAPTER ELEVEN

BOOMERS, SOONERS, AND OKLAHOMA TERRITORY

Flooded out in Illinois—
Cinch-bugged in Kansas—
Indian Territory or bust.
    —Slogan on covered wagon bound for the Oklahoma land run

PRESSURE TO OPEN INDIAN TERRITORY to white settlement began to build in the late 1800s. Both the U.S. government and the Indian tribes fought a constant battle trying to keep out those who had no business in the Indian lands. Some well-educated Indians felt the only hope for true equality for the Indian nations was statehood, and that meant opening the Territory to white settlement.

Boomers set up camps in the Cherokee Outlet in preparation for the opening of the land run. Boomers were those who took part in the land "booms" of the late 1800s when land was opened for settlement.

David L. Payne, a pioneer guide, led a number of wagon trains of white settlers into Indian lands illegally. He also promoted the cause of the boomers in his newspaper The Oklahoma War Chief.

BOOMERS

In 1878, Elias C. Boudinot, a Cherokee lawyer who practiced in Washington, D.C., backed a bill in Congress that would create an Oklahoma Territory. He had identified 2 million acres in the High Plains (the Unassigned Lands) that had belonged to the Creek and Seminole before the Civil War. It was harsh land with little water and not good for much except grazing cattle. Boudinot wanted to open that land to settlement by whites. He saw the land as a wedge that would lead Indian Territory to statehood. But the bill was defeated. In February 1879, Boudinot published an article in the *Chicago Times* describing 14 million acres in Indian Territory that he believed were legally public domain—Greer County (then part of Texas), the Unassigned Lands, and parts of the Cheyenne-Arapaho and Comanche-Kiowa-Wichita reservations. He even included a map.

Boudinot's article set off an unexpected furor. Charles C. Carpenter, a former scout, began talking of taking whites into the Territory to homestead. With some support from the *Kansas City Times*, he gathered a small group of boomers. **Boomers** were those who took part in the land "booms" of the late 1800s, when western land was opened to settlement. Carpenter got as far as the North Canadian River before he was turned back by U.S. troops. President Rutherford Hayes warned settlers to stay out of Indian Territory, but that had little effect.

When Carpenter was threatened by the law, he backed off. But David L. Payne, a frontier guide, was more determined. In 1880, he led a column of wagons into central Indian Territory (the site of Oklahoma City). Cavalry from Fort Reno burned the settlement and forced them to return to Kansas; Payne was taken to Fort Smith for trial. From 1880 to 1884, Payne campaigned for settlement, organizing groups and leading them into the Territory, usually with a newspaper reporter along to tell the story. Each time, he was turned back by U.S. troops. The number of homesteaders who flocked to the boomer camps grew.

In June 1884, Payne moved into the Cherokee Outlet to a tent town called Rock Falls. He printed the first newspaper in the Cherokee Outlet, *The Oklahoma War Chief*, in which he called for Oklahoma lands to be opened to white settlers. His newspaper drew national attention and sympathy for his ideas. In August, the boomers were disbanded by federal troops, and the printing office was burned. Payne died a few months later. W. L. Couch, one of his trusted supporters, took up Payne's cause. In December 1884, Couch led three hundred followers to what is now Stillwater. They managed to build a few log cabins before troops from Fort Reno arrived and starved them out. The next

year, Buffalo Soldiers from the 9th and 10th Cavalry removed a group of boomers from a spot near what would become Oklahoma City.

THE TERRITORY OF CIMARRON

In 1885, the Supreme Court ruled that No Man's Land was public domain, subject to squatters' rights. A **squatter** is one who settles on unoccupied land in order to gain the title to it. A tidal wave of settlers moved across the Kansas border. Ranchers built shelters (usually sod houses or dugouts) and planted crops. Since neither federal nor Indian law applied there, it was not uncommon for a family to make improvements and then find someone at the other end of a gun barrel claiming to have been there first. Outlaws raided herds constantly, driving the livestock into Colorado or New Mexico to sell.

The settlers formed a vigilance committee and an informal claims board. In March 1887, they organized the Territory of Cimarron and established executive, legislative, and judicial branches of government. Although they sent delegates to Congress, Congress never officially recognized the Territory of Cimarron.

THE UNASSIGNED LANDS

Meanwhile, farmers were eyeing the so-called Unassigned Lands in the center of the Indian territories. In spite of protests from the Cherokee Nation, the secretary of the interior recommended that part of the Indian land be opened for settlement.

Top: Boomers being escorted back to Kansas by the Buffalo Soldiers.
Above: W.L. Couch continued Payne's cause after Payne's death.

Federal troops had a difficult time keeping order during the Oklahoma land rushes. In this photograph, a group of sooners have been arrested by soldiers and scouts from Fort Reno.

All during the Congressional session of 1889, Congress wrestled with the Indian Appropriations bill. Just before it was to adjourn, one legislator added a **rider** (an addition) to the bill calling for the Unassigned Lands to be opened for settlement. Tired and trying to wind up business, the politicians passed the bill with the rider. President Benjamin Harrison issued a proclamation formally announcing that the Unassigned Lands would open for settlement at noon on April 22, 1889.

Do You Remember?
1. Name one of the men who led would-be settlers across the borders into Indian Territory.
2. What are squatters' rights?

THE GREAT LAND GIVEAWAYS

In the late 1880s, the country was in a financial depression. Several years of drought had caused severe problems for the nation's farmers. They had formed a new political party, the People's (Populist) party, and were demanding that the money supply be increased to help them get out of debt. They also demanded lower **tariffs** (taxes on goods) and legislation to regulate banks and railroads. In addition, women were beginning to organize and demand the right to vote.

Giving away a little Indian land appeared to be a good diversion to government politicians. But no one had ever planned a land run before, and no one expected the pandemonium (wild uproar) that resulted. Anyone over twenty-one could make the run, except Indians. People could enter the Unassigned Lands from any side. On the northern border, there were at least four major starting points. The run from Caldwell and Buffalo Springs, Kansas, led south to Kingfisher. Serious racers focused on land near the Santa Fe Railroad, which led south into Guthrie, Edmond (a coal and watering spot on the rail line), and Oklahoma Station (Oklahoma City). On the eastern border, the major starting point was near the North Canadian River and the stage and wagon route, just slightly northeast of Oklahoma Station. There were a dozen spots where groups crossed on the southern border along the South Canadian River. The main one was a few miles from Purcell (a trail and rail crossing point). From the western border in the Cheyenne-Arapaho land, most would make the run just west of Kingfisher or along the North Canadian River near Darlington and Fort Reno. Land offices to register claims were set up at Guthrie and Kingfisher. The claims, subject to the Homestead Act, required each person to live on the land for five years before he or she would get a valid title.

One of the hazards of staking a claim on Indian lands was claim jumpers who took over other people's claims forcibly. This photograph of a mock lynching is entitled "Claim Jumpers Beware."

THE RACE FOR LAND

Newspapers throughout the world picked up the story: Free land! Groups formed in Chicago, Topeka, Omaha, Kansas City, and Texas to sell shares in town-site companies and colonies. Blacks in North Carolina made their way to Fort Smith to join other blacks headed to Guthrie. Rich and poor, young and old, men and women, people from all kinds of backgrounds with all kinds of skills—all headed toward the promised land. Some who couldn't wait for the official start of the run slipped past the troops guarding the borders of the Unassigned Lands and hid in the riverbeds and ravines. When they were caught, the names of these **sooners** were recorded, and they were marched back across the line. But not all of them were caught.

Easter Sunday, April 21, 1889, the day before the run, was one big celebration. In the border towns, there was not even space to pitch a tent. A preacher gave a sermon calling for tolerance the next day. Newspapermen swarmed over the area. Soldiers and deputy marshals patrolled the train depots, keeping out anyone who tried to get off early.

On April 22 at two minutes to twelve, Captain D. F. Stiles, of the 10th Infantry and provost marshal of the new Territory, raised his telescope and looked across the empty green prairie of waving grass. Then the bugle sounded. Everything disappeared in a cloud of dust and an incredible wave of sound as thousands of people, horses, wagons, cattle, buggies, surreys, and even bicycles lunged forward across the line.

Top: Huge crowds gathered for the election of the first mayor of Guthrie. *Above:* The land rush offered new opportunities for craftsmen who wanted to be a part of the push westward. Pictured here is the first blacksmith to set up business in Guthrie.

The first train to pull out of Purcell on the Santa Fe Railroad carried surveyors for the Seminole Townsite and Improvement Company. They planned to lay out both Oklahoma and Edmond stations. "Fifteen minutes after twelve, the men of the Seminole Land and Town Company were dragging steel chains up the street on a run, the red and white barber poles and the transits were in place all over the prairie, and neat little rows of stakes stretched out in regular lines to mark where they hoped the town might be," one reporter wrote. "At twenty minutes after twelve over forty tents were in position, and the land around them marked out by wooden pegs."

One journalist called the run "one of the most noteworthy events of Western civilization." It was also a time of colossal disappointment. Men on swift horses found men on foot already staking claims. "Nine-tenths of these people made settlement upon the land illegally," a reporter noted. "The other tenth would have done so had there been any desirable land left to settle upon. This...will cause a great deal of land litigation in the future."

GUTHRIE

Men who had expected to lay out the town of Guthrie were shocked when they stepped off the train, ran across the prairie, and discovered the town already laid out and dotted with white tents. A reporter running with the crowd asked one man how he had managed to pitch his tent so quickly. The man explained that he was a U.S. deputy marshal

who had helped lay out the town. Legal or not, the marshal and fifty other deputies had already staked their claims to choice sites.

By late afternoon, Guthrie was a city of 10,000 people. "In some respects the recent settlement of Oklahoma was the most remarkable thing of the present century," a reporter wrote. "Unlike Rome, the city of Guthrie was built in a day....Never before in the history of the West has so large a number of people been concentrated in one place in so short a time."

By evening, saloons and gambling establishments were running full blast. Lawyers and real estate speculators had signs posted above neat tents. In one tent, Frank Greer was setting type for the first edition of the town's first newspaper. The next day, three men with only $8.31 among them opened the doors of the Bank of Guthrie. They stored the bank's money in a pot-bellied stove.

For the next three days, so many people and animals were running around that red dust "rose in clouds and hovered above the feverish city until the air was like fog at sunrise," wrote one writer for *Harper's Weekly*. The railway station was jammed, but the trains were not running on schedule. The post office could not handle the mail. The lines at the land office were a mile long. Worst of all, the federal government had not provided for any kind of temporary or territorial government. There was no official law in the territory. Guthrie citizens decided that Kansas state law and the Wichita town ordinances would have to do until proper laws could be written.

Frank Greer set type for the first edition of Guthrie's first newspaper.

Top: Albert Maywood at his first home (a dugout) in Oklahoma City. *Above:* The C.A. McNabb, Flour and Feed store was the first business to open in Oklahoma City.

OKLAHOMA CITY

The scene was repeated at Oklahoma Station. There the town had been laid out not by one advance group but by two. Many choice lots were already claimed by government and railroad workers who had started the run illegally from the railroad depot.

The Reverend James Murray and a Mr. Kincaid, who represented the Oklahoma Colony (the Kansas boomers), may have been the first legal claimants. Their horse and buggy made the fifteen miles from the border in just over an hour. When the first train from the south reached the depot at 2:05, 2,500 people "scattered like a stampeded herd over the prairie, driving in their little stakes, and changing their minds about it and driving them in again at some other point." For every lot, there were usually at least three claimants. If people left their lots to get a drink of water or to try to get their baggage at the railway station, others would claim their lots.

The real work began the next day. When the different land companies refused to re-adjust their plans, a committee of citizens was chosen to decide the rightful claimant to each piece of property. It took over a week to make a preliminary judgment. The crowd became so angry at times that the committee had to call for a military guard.

Events at Kingfisher, Edmond, and Norman were much the same. It was difficult to make an official count, but about 60,000 people made the run. Many were from the North, which was significant since so many of those living in Indian Territory had southern backgrounds. Some of the boomers were farmers from Kansas and Nebraska, who brought with them livestock, supplies, seed, and good farming and livestock practices.

Nearly a thousand blacks made the run. Not long after the run, Edward McCabe, a black who had served as state auditor in Kansas, purchased 160 acres about eleven miles east of Guthrie. He called it Langston in honor of a black U.S. congressman from Virginia. He began the *Langston Herald* to promote the town and sent men into the South to attract black settlers. McCabe and many others hoped to establish an all-black state.

This photograph shows how Oklahoma City looked on May 2, 1889, only two weeks old.

Do You Remember?
1. Who were the sooners?
2. How did people acquire land in the land runs?
3. From what general area of the United States did many of those who made the run come?

Washington officials handed out Oklahoma territorial offices as political favors, which angered Oklahomans. George Steele (top) of Indiana was appointed governor. The supreme court justices were Abraham J. Seay (above) of Missouri, Edward Green of Illinois, and John Clark of Wisconsin.

THE TERRITORY OF OKLAHOMA

The runs presented at least as many problems as they solved. The lands had been forcibly taken from the Indians, causing bitterness and eroding morale among the tribes. The settlers' disputes over land ownership tied up the courts for years. The activity in the new towns was little short of chaotic (very disorganized) as people nailed together shelters, opened new businesses, and tried to start homesteading. The lack of official government added to the chaos.

Congress did add a federal court in Muskogee. It also placed the southern parts of the Choctaw and Chickasaw nations under the jurisdiction of the federal court in Paris, Texas. With the court seven hundred miles away, the territory was virtually wide open for outlaws. People were arrested for minor offenses, and then the government was charged fees and mileage for transporting them to Texas. The one case tried in the Texas court—a murder at Wild Horse Lake—was dismissed even though the witnesses were mysteriously murdered. There was such a national uproar over the affair that Congress realized it had to do something. On May 2, 1890, President Benjamin Harrison signed the **Organic Act**. There were several major parts to the law:

- It created Oklahoma Territory, combining most of western Indian Territory and the so-called Territory of Cimarron (No Man's Land). It provided for a territorial governor and a supreme court of three judges, all appointed by the president. A legislative assembly was set up with a house (twenty-six members) and a council (thirteen members), plus a delegate to Congress elected by the people.
- Seven counties were established. First known by letters, they were later named Canadian, Cleveland, Kingfisher, Logan, Oklahoma, Payne, and Beaver (in the Panhandle). Guthrie was named the capital.
- Until a code of laws could be adopted, the territory would operate under the laws of Nebraska.
- Indian reservations in the western part of Indian Territory would automatically become part of Oklahoma Territory as soon as they opened to white settlement.

It also ordered the federal government to determine whether the north or south fork of the Red River was the southern boundary. A territorial university was to be located at Norman because Cleveland County gave $10,000 to build the school and citizens donated forty

Left: One of the few Oklahomans appointed to a position in Oklahoma Territory was Horace Speed of Guthrie, who served as U.S. district attorney. *Below:* Warren Lurty of West Virginia served as U.S. marshal.

acres. The state's land-grant institution, Oklahoma Agricultural and Mechanical College (A&M), was to be set up in Stillwater on land donated by the federal government. Its purpose was to work with farmers and ranchers to improve agricultural and livestock skills. A third school, the territorial **normal school** (teacher training institution) was to be set up at Edmond.

Washington officials handed out territorial offices in return for political favors, which angered Oklahomans. George W. Steele, a Republican from Indiana, was appointed territorial governor. The supreme court justices were Edward B. Green of Illinois, Abraham J. Seay of Missouri, and John Clark of Wisconsin. The secretary of Oklahoma Territory was Robert Martin from El Reno; the U.S. district attorney was Horace Speed of Guthrie; and the U.S. marshal was Warren Lurty of West Virginia.

When elections were held in August for the territorial legislature, fourteen of the twenty-six house seats went to Republicans, eight to Democrats, and four to Populists. In the council, six seats went to Republicans, five to Democrats, and two to Populists. David A. Harney was elected Oklahoma Territory's delegate to Congress.

The first bill introduced in the legislature authorized the governor to contract with a neighboring state or territory to house criminals. A territorial library was set up, and land was earmarked for the Wichita Mountain National Forest and for Fort Sill.

Governor Steele provided a system of public schools, allotting $50,000 for salaries, books, and supplies. Two sections in each township were set aside for public education. The income from leasing these lands helped to finance the school system.

THE CHEROKEE (JEROME) COMMISSION

The next step was to convince the Indians on western reservations to cede their surplus lands. A three-man Cherokee Commission (later known as the Jerome Commission) was appointed in 1889. The commission offered to purchase the lands in the Cherokee Outlet from the Cherokee tribe for $1.25 an acre. The Cherokee had been offered $3.00 an acre by a cattle syndicate, but the federal government refused to approve the sale and the Cherokee refused to sell the land to the government. In February 1890, the attorney general issued an opinion stating that grazing on the lands of the Cherokee Outlet was not in the public interest. President Harrison ordered all cattle be removed, which deprived the Indians of income from the land. Three years later, the Cherokee sold the land to the government for $1.40 an acre.

Meanwhile, the commission convinced the Sac and Fox, Iowa, Shawnee, and Potawatomi to sell their surplus lands—about 870,000 acres. This parcel was opened for settlement on September 22, 1891. The towns of Chandler and Tecumseh were laid out by government surveyors. Although there were only about six thousand claims available, more than twenty thousand people made the run.

When over 4 million acres of former Cheyenne-Arapaho reservation lands were opened for settlement on April 19, 1892, about twenty-five thousand persons made the run. A large number of Mennonites settled in the dry western country.

A homesteader in Dewey County shortly after the excess lands of the Cheyenne Arapaho Reservation were opened for settlement in 1892.

BANKING AND FINANCE

In 1893, a financial panic swept the nation. Banks closed in record numbers when large numbers of people tried to withdraw their money in a short period (called a *run*). T. M. Richardson at the First National Bank of Oklahoma City kept his bank open for twelve hours one day while he gave depositors their money; he had nothing left for the next day. He called Joseph McNeal of Guthrie National Bank for help. McNeal managed to find $5,000 in $1 bills. To make sure everyone heard about the big ship-

A view of Oklahoma City in 1893. The First National Bank of Oklahoma City is on the left.

ment of cash, McNeal sent a telegram asking for armed guards to escort the shipment coming in by train the next morning. Richardson begged depositors to be patient while he counted and deposited such a large sum. The crowd decided that the bank must be solvent and slowly left. The bank was saved.

In spring 1907, cash was scarce and western banks found it almost impossible to get adequate supplies of cash from major East Coast banks. Depositors feared they would lose their savings and began withdrawing their money. Nine banks in Okmulgee County closed for a day while the bankers met in Muskogee. They knew they could not stay closed for more than a day without trouble; a run on the banks would be disaster. Each bank managed to get a small amount of cash, but not enough to do business. They finally hit upon the idea of issuing scrip in place of cash. Anyone who came in to cash a check would receive some dollars, but mainly a cashier's check (a bank IOU). When the banks opened the next day, merchants brought in all available cash to deposit and pledged to do business in the bank scrip. Businesses asked out-of-town creditors to hold bills until the crisis was over. One irate depositor appeared in front of Citizens National Bank with a rifle. He informed anyone who would listen that he was going to get his money in cash. But he wandered off without doing anything. Farmers, who were especially suspicious, quickly spent the scrip to make sure it was good. That only increased local business and helped ease the problem.

In 1893, the city of Enid (top) was one of the four places where land offices were set up for settlers to register and pay for their claims. The train (above), loaded with people, awaits the signal for the opening of the Cherokee Outlet on September 16, 1893.

OPENING THE CHEROKEE OUTLET

Many of the settlers who had taken part in the early land runs were now destitute. Their crops had withered or were eaten by pests, and many were forced to borrow money to survive. The financial difficulties of the 1880s carried over into the 1890s. Then, in June 1893, the stock market crashed. By the end of the year, 600 banks, 74 railroads, and more than 15,000 businesses had shut down.

It was no wonder then that more than 100,000 people lined up for the opening of the Cherokee Outlet on September 16, 1893. There were almost 6½ million acres up for grabs—about 40,000 homesteads. Once a settler staked a claim, he or she would pay $2.50 an acre in the east, $1.25 in the west. Land offices were set up at Perry, Enid, Woodward, and Alva.

The race was to begin at noon; but someone at Arkansas City fired a pistol eleven minutes early, and nothing could stop the crowd. At Hennessey, a gun went off five minutes early. A reporter for *Frank Leslie's Weekly* wrote,

> *Confusion reigned everywhere....Horsemen were unseated, wagons overthrown, and pedestrians prostrated in the mad rush to be off. The cries of angered men, mingled with the neighing of panic-stricken horses, the shouts of the racers, the clatter of hoofs, the rattling of wagons, and the shrieking of locomotives, combined in a roar like that of a tornado.*

In some areas, sooners had set prairie fires to slow down the racers. Fred Sutton rode through one such fire, blistering his face, burning off his hair, and badly burning his horse. He was run off the first claim

he wanted. His horse was killed trying to jump a ravine. After staking a second claim, Sutton ran back to Perry. The former spot on the prairie now had 20,000 residents. **Entrepreneurs** (those who take the risk and start new businesses) were taking advantage of the situation. One man was selling malt tonic for $1 a bottle and ice at 10 cents a pound. One man with a railroad car of watermelons was doing a brisk business, selling them at $1 each.

*Top: The surveyors and lawyers were ready for the land rushes. The sign on this office stresses the major interest of the firm. **Above:** When a crowd gathers, entrepreneurs find a way to make money. The crowd lined up outside the land office in Enid provides a captive market for the "hawkers" selling food.*

Do You Remember?

1. Who appointed territorial governors?
2. Who was the first territorial governor?
3. How were schools to be financed?

THE EARLY DAYS OF THE TERRITORY

The turmoil in Oklahoma Territory was reflected in the territorial government. Governor Steele returned to Indiana in 1891. Robert Martin, secretary of the territory, filled in until February 1892. Abraham Seay, an associate justice of the territorial supreme court, served a year as governor before he was replaced by William Renfrow, the only Democratic territorial governor. Renfrow, who was from Norman, recommended that Indian Territory and Oklahoma Territory be combined into one state. He backed legislation to open the Colored Agricultural and Normal School at Langston and Northwest Normal School at Alva as well as a territorial "insane asylum" at Norman.

In December 1891, a territory-wide convention was held in Oklahoma City. Delegates urged Congress to grant Oklahoma Territory immediate statehood. A bill was introduced in Congress the following January, but Congress took no action due to the problem of Indian Territory and the issue of single or double statehood. More important, there was no real tax base upon which a new state could support itself.

THE PASSING OF THE FRONTIER

In 1893, Frederick Jackson Turner, a historian at the University of Wisconsin, announced that the "American frontier" was closed. Turner claimed that there were four stages of frontier—first the traders moved in, then ranchers, miners, and farmers. Frontier conditions, he claimed, decreased dependence on a distant government (such as England or Washington), created a new nationality and a new mixed race, and made people strong and practical. Now, he said, the frontier—and the first period of American history—had ended.

Certainly the territories were becoming more organized. In 1895, Congress provided for developing a volunteer militia—the Oklahoma National Guard. Laws were passed to regulate game and bird hunting so that no more species would be destroyed. That same year, on May 23, a second part of the Kickapoo lands was opened to settlement. Almost half those filing claims were on the land before the legal time. Another 4,000 homesteads were opened in Greer County in 1896 when the U.S. Supreme Court settled a long dispute with Texas, fixing the southern border as the South Fork of the Red River.

The hopes of territorial blacks had been high when Green Currin of Kingfisher was elected to the House in 1890 and D. J. Wallace of Guthrie in 1893. But neither was re-elected. Edward McCabe, founder of Langston, was appointed secretary of the Republican Territorial

Top: *Territorial Governor William Renfrow favored combining Indian Territory and Oklahoma Territory into one state.* ***Above:*** *The hopes of territorial blacks were high when Green Currin of Kingfisher was elected to the House in 1890.*

League in 1894 and was named deputy territorial auditor in 1897—
the first black to hold a major political office in the West. But the year
before, in 1896, the U.S. Supreme Court had opened the way for **segregation** (the separation of the races) and separate-but-equal public
facilities. In *Plessy v. Ferguson*, the Court ruled that state-imposed racial
segregation in public facilities was not unreasonable and did not vio-
late the equal protection clause of the Fourteenth Amendment. That
ruling gave territorial legislators the wedge needed to work toward a
series of **Jim Crow laws**—laws limiting the rights of black citizens.
Clearly the frontier was changing.

POLITICAL PROGRESS

Cassius M. Barnes of Guthrie was appointed territorial governor in
1897. The long drought that had reigned over the Plains for a decade
broke in 1896. But there was still so little cash in 1900 that Governor
Barnes pushed through the Free Homes Bill, canceling back payments
owed for homesteads taken in prior land runs.

In 1901, Governor Barnes was replaced by William M. Jenkins. In
trying to clean up questionable leasing practices, Jenkins made political foes, who charged that he had secretly profited from a government
contract. President Theodore Roosevelt removed Jenkins after only
six months, although there was no proof of wrongdoing. He was
cleared of the charges two years later.

*Top: The Colored Agricultural and
Normal School is now Langston
University.* ***Above:*** *Edward R.
McCabe was the founder of the city
of Langston.*

Thomas B. Ferguson (top) was appointed territorial governor by President Theodore Roosevelt. Frank Frantz was the last territorial governor. He was a former Indian agent to the Osage. Frantz is seen (above) with two Osage.

President Roosevelt offered the position of territorial governor to Thompson B. Ferguson, a former Methodist minister and schoolteacher and then the owner of a newspaper called the *Watonga Republican*. Ferguson's wife, Eula, actually accepted the appointment for him knowing that he could not then refuse it. Ferguson was a good choice. He was tall, handsome, and admired by Oklahomans. He believed in principles and fair play.

Ferguson made government appointments based on merit. He acquired Fort Supply, the old military fort, to house the mentally ill. While he increased the funding for education, he recommended that both rural schools and higher education institutions be consolidated. But he opposed statehood with Indian Territory. He felt it would turn Oklahoma into a southern state, which he considered a step backward.

In 1901, Congress ruled that all Indians in Indian Territory were citizens of the United States. It was not an honor they wanted. At best, it was second-class citizenship with limited rights. They were not allowed to vote, serve as jurors, or hold civil offices. They could not carry firearms, and it was a misdemeanor for anyone to provide them with weapons or ammunition.

THE LAST LAND DISTRIBUTION

The courts were still filled with land-run cases in 1901 when the surplus lands of the Kiowa-Comanche and the Wichita-Caddo reservations were opened. About 13,000 quarter-sections of land (3½ million acres) were available, for which nearly 170,000 persons registered. Instead of a run, a **lottery** (drawing) was held. Numbers were drawn at random, and only 125 winners could file claims each day. The filing lines were long, sometimes lasting three to four days.

In 1904 and 1906, lands of the Ponca, Kaw, Osage and Otoe, and Missouri were distributed among the citizens of those tribes. In 1906, the last land distribution for white settlement was held, involving 480,000 acres in the Big Pasture area of the Kiowa-Comanche and Wichita-Caddo reservations. Registration was held at Fort Sill. So many people showed up that the military organized people in groups of 100. Many were European immigrants who had originally settled in Texas.

Nearby Lawton was laid out with neat streets, but all the buildings were tents. Every other tent seemed to be occupied by a firm of locators, real estate men, or land lawyers. The lines at the land office were long. Each time a section of land was claimed, it was marked off on a large map that could be seen through the window. Some people used opera glasses to see whether the land they wanted had been taken as they waited in line.

In 1906, Frank Frantz of Enid became the last territorial governor. A former Indian agent to the Osage, Frantz spoke of honest politics. "The lesson of the present day is progress with honor," he said in his inauguration. "The spirit in the very air is for fair play." Through his efforts, the railroads were forced to lower freight rates, and he saved the school fund $200 million. Frantz could honestly say that almost no public land capable of cultivation was left in the Oklahoma Territory except in the Panhandle.

In 1901, the reserve lands of the Kiowa-Comanche Reservation were opened for settlement. The lottery for this land was held in El Reno.

Do You Remember?
1. Why did Congress decide not to act on statehood for Oklahoma Territory in 1891?
2. How did the the separate-but-equal concept that led to segregation of blacks and whites come about?
3. What was different about the Ponca and Osage land distributions?

CHAPTER REVIEW

1880	1887	1889		1906
David Payne leads group of settlers into Indian Territory	Territory of Cimarron organized	Unassigned Lands opened for white settlement		Last Oklahoma land distribution
		1890 Territory of Oklahoma created		
		1893 Cherokee Outlet opened for white settlement		
1880		1890	1900	1910

At the Same Time

1890   Sherman Antitrust Act passed; Battle of Wounded Knee in South Dakota

1891   The zipper patented

1894   Hershey invented the chocolate bar

1897   Campbell's introduced canned soups

1898   U.S. and Spain go to war over Cuba

1903   First Ford Model A sold for $850; Orville Wright made first machine-driven flight

Summary

Although the Indian Nations and tribes had been promised their own lands "forever," Congress decided to open part of the Indian lands to white settlement. A land run was organized; and thousands made the run, hoping for free land. The cities of Guthrie and Oklahoma City literally sprang up in one day. Unfortunately, the newly opened lands were without official law and order for a year.

There were now two distinct territories side by side, with very little in common. Most citizens in Oklahoma Territory were newcomers, with a wide variety of backgrounds and nationalities. They had a government and a governor appointed by the president, and they voted largely Republican. To the east was Indian Territory, which had been in existence from before the Civil War and whose allegiances and culture were more southern and Democrat. It had been under Indian Nations government since the Civil War. It was old, wise, rooted in ancient traditions—and it looked to the past for guidance. There was bound to be a clash.

Reviewing People, Places, and Things

Define, identify, or explain the importance of the following.

1. boomer
2. entrepreneur
3. Guthrie
4. Jim Crow law
5. lottery
6. normal school
7. Organic Act
8. rider
9. segregation
10. sooner
11. squatter
12. George W. Steele
13. tariff

Understanding the Facts

1. What were vigilance committees and why were they necessary?
2. How did the opening of Indian Territory actually get through Congress?
3. What national conditions helped to create interest in the land runs?
4. When was the first land run? What area did it open for white settlement?

5. What was the purpose of the Cherokee (Jerome) Commission?
6. What was the dispute over Greer County?

Developing Critical Thinking
1. What effect did the Homestead Act of 1862 have on the territory that became Oklahoma Territory? What effect did it have on Indian Territory?
2. Territorial Governor Thompson Ferguson remarked: "I believe an appointed or elected official should never use his public office to enhance his private fortune." Do you agree? Has there been any recent case in the news of corruption in government office?

Using Your Skills
1. On a map of Oklahoma, outline and shade in the area that was included in the first land run.
2. Suppose you were a boomer taking part in the Cherokee Outlet land run in 1893. If you staked a claim to 640 acres, how much would you have to pay if that land were in the eastern part of the territory? What would you pay if the land were in the western part?

Special Projects
1. Assume you are a television or radio reporter covering one of the Oklahoma land runs. Prepare a five-minute report for the evening broadcast. Interview a boomer (a classmate) who is making the run.
2. Research *Plessy v. Ferguson* (1896). What was the original case about? In what state did it originate? What was the outcome? How did *Plessy v. Ferguson* affect state laws?

Building Skills: Recognizing Propaganda
The use of propaganda to persuade people to make certain decisions has been part of political life since political parties were organized. These same techniques are used in advertising and in our daily lives.

Here are some basic techniques:

Bandwagon: You have probably used this technique if you have ever said to your parents, "But everybody else is going." You hope your parents will think it is all right since other parents are allowing their sons and daughters to go.

Testimonial: With this technique, a well-known person—an athlete, for example—describes how great a particular brand (of motor oil, sport shoe, drink, and so on) is. When an influential person is shown with another person or thing, it is an attempt to transfer honor and respect from one individual to another. Think of all the television commercials that try to transfer the good feeling about an athlete to a particular product. Has this ever influenced your decision about buying a product?

Repetition: Watch television one evening and you'll see that many short commercials are repeated several times during a particular show. Advertisers use repetition to drive home a particular message.

Cause-effect relationship: A misleading cause-and-effect relationship is often used to persuade. "Twenty students in the class who used 'computer X' to write their Oklahoma history report got an A." Would this statement persuade you to buy computer X? Why or why not?

Write an ad for a newspaper or television station for a product or political candidate using one or more of the above techniques.

Sooner Trivia
. . . High above the crowd on a wooden platform, William S. Prettyman, a Kansas photographer, recorded the Cherokee Outlet land run for posterity. The photographers on the ground could see nothing but the dust.

. . . The first Oklahoma City newspaper was published before there was a city. It was printed in Wichita, Kansas, on December 29, 1888.

. . . When the citizens of Guthrie elected Colonel D. B. Dyer as mayor in 1889, he took office in a circus tent labeled "City Hall."

CHAPTER TWELVE

FROM TERRITORIES TO STATEHOOD

The signs of the times are pointing to better things.
—Reverend C. W. Kerr, pastor,
First Presbyterian Church, Tulsa, 1905

THE PERIOD BETWEEN 1890 AND 1907 was a bustling and exciting time in the two territories. Small towns, businesses, and industries were growing as statehood approached and agriculture flourished.

The big question was whether Oklahoma would enter the Union as one state or two. A new spirit of political and social reform was sweeping the country, and many of the issues concerning social and working conditions would be dealt with in the new state's constitution.

But it was what lay beneath the land—the Indians' hidden wealth—that would change the two territories and the entire country.

THE RAILROADS AND THE TOWNS

The railroads were permitted by federal law to lay out townsites along their routes, about five to ten miles apart. The route and the towns it passed through were sometimes determined by geography or land ownership but just as often by which towns would give the railroad "bonus" money. A railroad almost guaranteed growth, and any town that was bypassed was certain to find its pocketbook hurt. The Santa Fe Railway originally planned to go through the little town of Cross, missing Ponca City entirely. Furious, Ponca City town leaders applied

A locomotive at McCurtain, 1906. A railroad almost guaranteed growth, and any town that was bypassed was certain to find its pocketbook hurt.

After the breakup of tribal governments, the railroads began to build further into Indian Territory. The arrival of the first train in Tishomingo in 1902 made travel and movement of goods to and from Indian Territory much easier and faster.

political pressure, and the Santa Fe agreed to stop at Ponca City. The Frisco (St. Louis-San Francisco) Railroad arrived in Oklahoma City in 1897, linking Tulsa, Kansas City, and St. Louis. Within two years, Oklahoma City's population doubled, and brick and stone commercial buildings replaced its wooden structures.

With the breakup of the tribal governments and the distribution of tribal lands, the railroads began to build further into Indian Territory. The Frisco Railroad moved into the Creek Nation almost as soon as the nation was dissolved in 1899. Rails for the Oklahoma and Southern Railway were laid from Sapulpa to Denison, Texas.

Sapulpa was the end of the Frisco Railroad and a cattle shipping point. In 1902, the Frisco Railroad made Sapulpa its division headquarters, giving the little town an advantage in the race for civilization. An electric light franchise was approved, and the town began construction on a new waterworks system. By 1903, there were a number of new businesses including a meat packing house, an ice plant, a wagon factory, a bottling works, and a brick plant.

Tulsa was Sapulpa's rival across the Arkansas River. Town leaders tried to get the Frisco Railroad to move its headquarters from Sapulpa to Tulsa, but Tulsa did not have a reliable water supply. The town's leaders also learned that the Katy Railroad did not plan to stop at Tulsa on its route from Muskogee to Pawhuska. Tulsa's Commercial Club offered the railroad a bonus of $12,000 and right-of-way land if it would stop in Tulsa. The ploy (gamble) worked.

Interurbans (short railroads or electric trolleys that ran within a region) first appeared in Oklahoma City in 1902. The success of the Metropolitan Railway Company brought other interurbans—to Guthrie and El Reno in Oklahoma Territory and to McAlester and Muskogee in Indian Territory.

AGRICULTURE

An Oklahoma couple and their family pose in front of their sod house, known as a "Soddie."

The major agricultural products in early Oklahoma were wheat, corn, and cotton. The Indians had been producing and selling wheat since the 1880s. Settlers who moved into Oklahoma Territory planted wheat and corn as soon as they could break ground.

The year 1896 was a turning point. The long drought in the Plains broke, and there was plenty of fall and winter rain. In the Cherokee Outlet, farmers got 42 bushels of corn to the acre. By 1897, the wheat yield was 18 bushels an acre, and the year's crop was more than 11.7 million bushels. The average price rose to 76¢ a bushel, up 28¢ from two years earlier. By 1899, Oklahoma was producing more than 20 million bushels of wheat. The town of Garber opened a grain elevator; but there was so much wheat and so few places to store it that some people stored it in their houses. Grain trader John Kroutil, who had arrived in Yukon in 1890, began grinding flour to sell to stores, and his brand name "Yukon's Best" became known all over the Southwest.

Cotton had been an important part of the Indian nations' economies, and an entire class of white tenant farmers had sprung up with

A farm family is seen here baling hay in the 1890s. Although hay was not a cash crop, it was important as food for farm animals.

Indian landlords. Minnie West, a young black woman and former slave, stuffed a handful of cottonseed in her apron pocket as she prepared to leave Georgia to make the land run in 1889. Her first efforts in Payne County near Stillwater resulted in a crop good enough for even the cotton specialists at the agricultural college to notice. It was not long before Oklahoma Territory settlers realized that they could earn more money growing cotton than growing wheat or corn.

There were two problems with cotton. First, cotton farmers tended to plant only cotton, eventually depleting the soil's nutrients. The land then had to be "rested" until it could become productive again. Second, the Mexican boll weevil arrived in Oklahoma around the turn of the century. The **boll weevil** is an insect that attacks the boll of the cotton plant where the fibers are formed. The weevil destroyed cotton crops until farmers learned how to poison it.

Do You Remember?
1. Why would a town give a railroad bonus money?
2. What was an interurban?
3. What were the three most important agricultural products in early Oklahoma?

UNDERGROUND WEALTH

Below the soil of the territories lay riches—coal, oil, and lead—mainly in Indian Territory.

KING COAL

Coal was being mined around McAlester in the 1870s. Later, strip mines were opened in the Cherokee Nation near Dawson. (A **strip mine** is an open mine where the top layers of soil are removed to expose the shallow veins of, usually, coal.) By 1889, there were two thousand miners working underground mines at Krebs, Coalgate, Lehigh, Alderson, and other small towns.

In 1896, a law gave mineral rights to the mining companies, thus cutting off the royalties the Indians received. Later, under the Atoka Agreement and the Curtis Act of 1898, coal and asphalt rights were reserved for the tribes, with the royalties earmarked for education. By the turn of the century, thirty-nine mining companies, most owned by railroad companies, were operating in the Indian nations. Over one

Many of the miners for the area's coal mines, such as this one near Wilburton in Indian Territory (1902), came from Pennsylvania and the East Coast, as well as Wales, Great Britain, and Italy. Mining communities were real "melting pots."

Just ten years after the first commercial oil well was completed, wells such as this one near Madill, shown in a 1907 photograph, dotted the Oklahoma countryside.

hundred mines were producing 3 million tons of coal a year. The largest was Osage Coal and Mining Company, owned by the Katy Railroad.

Oklahoma had the most dangerous mines in the world. For each 1 million tons of coal produced, British mines claimed an average of 6.46 lives, Pennsylvania mines claimed 7 lives, but Indian Territory mines claimed 13.1 men. In 1891, Congress passed an act establishing safety regulations for Territory mines. But those regulations were not yet in place when an explosion ripped through Osage Coal and Mining Company Mine No. 11 at Krebs on January 7, 1892. In the state's worst mining disaster, 87 men were killed and 150 injured.

Many of the miners who had come to Oklahoma from the East were familiar with labor unions. Unions were illegal in Indian Territory, but that did not mean that they did not operate or try to organize. When the coal companies reduced wages 25 percent in 1894, miners went out on strike. About one thousand of the Lehigh and Coalgate miners marched on a strip mine operated by Williamson Brothers, which was still operating. Fifty women marched in front carrying banners. More than a hundred miners marched behind with shotguns and rifles. Behind them came the Coalgate band, and behind them hundreds of men and boys with clubs and other makeshift weapons. Outnumbered, Williamson suspended operations.

In 1898, the first collective union was formed in the state. In 1903, the Twin Territorial Federation of Labor formed to unite mine workers in both territories to push for reforms. In 1907, more than 7,000 workers organized into the United Mine Workers of America.

BLACK GOLD

In 1901, Charles Gould, a young geologist at the University of Oklahoma, joined the U.S. Geological Survey Team. They traveled across the state in a covered wagon, making a record of its geological formations and natural resources. Gould mapped gypsum, salt plains, and water resources along the way, occasionally noting where he thought oil might be located.

The first commercial well was completed in April 1897 by the Cudahy Oil Co. The Nellie Johnstone No. 1 well struck oil on the south bank of the Caney River near Bartlesville. Then in January 1901, the Spindletop well came in near Beaumont, Texas. People flocked to the Texas oil fields. It did not take long for them to start looking north into Indian Territory. By April, a well had been dug on land belonging to Sue A. Davis Bland, the half-Creek wife of Dr. John C. W. Bland. The well site was near Red Fork, just across the Arkansas River from Tulsa. The Sue Bland No. 1 turned into a gusher on June 24, 1901.

The driller telegraphed the news to the drilling contractor in Joplin, and telegraphers for two hundred miles picked up the news and flashed it through the territories and three other states. By morning, the roads to Red Fork were jammed and special trains were running from Oklahoma City to "the oil fields." Although the well produced only 5-10 barrels a day, the area filled with oil men and workers.

On November 22, 1905, Robert Galbreath and Frank Chesley brought in the Ida E. Glenn No. 1 well just southeast of Sapulpa. The Glenn Pool field became one of the most prolific fields in the Territory, the world's richest small oil field, and the most important oil field in the world at that time.

The oil fields attracted hundreds of oil field supply and support firms—haulers, blacksmiths, carpenters, machine toolers, and equipment manufacturers. Every nearby town was filled with khaki-clad, high-booted men directing heavy wagons pulled by teams of ten or twenty mules or horses. "Everyone has oil fever," one woman wrote. "Gushers are flowing thousands of barrels of black gold daily [and] a well can be drilled easily almost any place."

The Texas Company (Texaco, Inc.) and Gulf Refining Company built pipelines from their Texas refineries to the Glenn Pool field in 1906. At one point, 3,000 laborers were at work with pick and shovel breaking ground for Gulf's 413-mile-long line. When Gulf reached the field in November, 127 wells had been drilled. Of those, 107 had struck oil and 12 had struck gas; only 11 were dry. Galbreath alone had more than 35,000 barrels of oil in steel tanks and 20,000 in wooden tanks, not counting earthen pits.

This oil field near Bartlesville (1905), like many others throughout the state, attracted hundreds of oil men — investors, speculators, wildcatters, drillers, teamsters. Nearby towns would fill with khaki-clad, high-booted men directing heavy wagons pulled by teams of ten or twenty mules or horses. Everyone had "oil fever."

The lead and zinc mines were less glamorous than the gushing oil fields, but they supported an industry important to Oklahoma's economy. Lead and zinc mining contributed $2.3 million to the state's economy in 1908. The mine in the photograph was located near Miami.

Tulsa became the most rapidly growing city in the United States. Oil operators and workers in the fields were arriving by the hundreds. Every train brought new families, and housing was in short supply. The Frisco Depot had to be expanded. The Commercial Club's earlier bonus payment, which brought the Katy Railroad to Tulsa, had worked so well that the Club tried it again. This time the Club offered the Midland Valley Railroad $16,000 if it would come through Tulsa. Tulsa also built its first interurban rail line.

LADY LEAD

Peoria Indian families had mined lead in northeastern Oklahoma as early as 1893. Near what is now Peoria, men dug the shafts, 50 to 75 feet deep, then brought the rock to the surface by horse or hand pulleys. Women and girls broke up the rock, freeing the lead or washing it in sieves. Unlike coal mines, lead and zinc mines were often cavernous (cavelike). Before modern equipment was available, mules lived underground in the mines, hauling ore cars in the tunnels.

Mines opened in the Lincolnville area in 1897. Miners from the Joplin district moved in. The four men most responsible for developing the Tri-State District were James Robinson, Charles Harvey, Alfred Coleman, and George Coleman. They formed the Commerce Mining and Royalty Company, which lent its name to the new town of Commerce.

When tribal restrictions were removed, the Emma Gordon Mining Company was organized. The mine included 30,000 feet of tunnels and six shafts. When the miners told Joplin experts how rich the Emma Gordon ore was, the experts laughed and called them liars. When the miners reworked the tailings (leftover waste) from the mine, they found it contained 20 percent mineral (compared to only 4 percent in some Missouri-Kansas mines).

The Oklahoma, Kansas & Missouri Inter-Urban Railway Co. built spur lines to the lead and zinc mines in Ottawa County in order to ship the minerals to the smelters. The lead and zinc mines in the Tri-State District were less glamorous than the gushing oil fields, but they supported a thriving industry. In 1908, the governor reported that lead and zinc contributed $2.3 million to the Oklahoma economy.

Do You Remember?

1. What is a strip mine?
2. Where was the first commercial oil well drilled in Indian Territory?
3. How did lead and zinc mines differ from coal mines?

THE STATE OF SEQUOYAH

In July 1905, there was a call for a convention to draft a constitution for a separate Indian state. (A **constitution** sets out the rules under which a government will operate.) Several men realized that the convention provided an opportunity to become involved in state politics. Among them were Charles N. Haskell and William H. Murray. Haskell was a non-Indian businessman from Muskogee. Murray was the tribal attorney for the Chickasaw.

They convinced Creek Chief Pleasant Porter to call for the convention and made certain that principal chiefs W. C. Rogers (Cherokee), Porter (Creek), and Green McCurtain (Choctaw) were listed as the organizers. Haskell pledged to push through an Indian state; but, if that failed, the Indians had to agree to support single statehood.

William H. Murray (above), a tribal attorney for the Chickasaw, was known as "Alfalfa Bill." Murray and others convinced Creek Chief Pleasant Porter (left) to call for a convention to draft a constitution for a separate Indian state.

Delegates to the Sequoyah convention elected five vice presidents, one to represent each tribe. Charles N. Haskell (top), a non-Indian from Muskogee, was elected as the Creek representative. Cherokee Principal Chief W. C. Rogers (above) was chosen to represent his people.

Delegates to the convention were chosen from district conventions, which ensured that both whites and Indians were involved. There were 182 delegates to the convention, which opened August 21, 1905, in Muskogee; seven districts were not represented. Pleasant Porter was elected president of the convention. Vice presidents were elected representing each of the five nations: W. C. Rogers (Cherokee), Green McCurtain (Choctaw), John F. Brown (Seminole), Charles N. Haskell (Creek), and William H. Murray (Chickasaw). Alexander Posey was named secretary of the convention. William Wirt Hastings, a well-known Cherokee lawyer, was chairman of the committee to draft the constitution. These men, all of whom were at least financially comfortable if not wealthy, would shape what would become Oklahoma.

The Indian state was to be called Sequoyah, after George Guess who had invented the Cherokee alphabet. It would have forty-eight counties, with Fort Gibson as the capital. The constitution called for three branches of government (executive, legislative, and judicial) with a system of checks and balances. It also contained a bill of rights that outlined citizens' basic rights "to life, liberty, the pursuit of happiness, and the enjoyment of the gains of their industry." It called for separation of church and state, the right to trial by jury, freedom of speech, and the right to bear arms. It outlawed slavery. When the people of Indian Territory voted on the constitution, it carried by a wide margin.

The convention was important historically for at least three reasons:

- It was the first time that both white and Indian citizens had worked together toward a common goal.
- It set into print perhaps the most progressive quasi-government document of its day.
- It gave the Democrats a focus. They now had a platform and a clear idea of what the people wanted and would support.

The Sequoyah delegates arrived in Washington, D.C., in the spring of 1906, constitution in hand. But it was far too late. A bill to admit the state of Sequoyah had been shelved in the House of Representatives three months earlier; a later bill in the Senate had met the same fate. Congress and the president had already decided to create one state.

STATE OF OKLAHOMA

By the turn of the century, it was no longer a matter of *whether* the citizens of Oklahoma and Indian territories would become U.S. citizens; it was a question of whether they would live in one state formed by combining the two territories or in two separate states. When President Theodore Roosevelt toured the territories in 1905, he made it plain that he intended there be only one state.

There were plenty of reasons given for admitting the territories as one state: It would cost the citizens less to govern themselves. The borders were geographically easier to follow. The manufacturing and agricultural operations would complement each other. There were just as many reasons against single statehood: The older, more resource-rich Indian Territory would end up supporting the still undeveloped Oklahoma Territory. The cultures and interests of the two territories were vastly different. Whites from Oklahoma Territory would dominate all offices. The real issues were political. Republicans controlled Oklahoma Territory; Indian Territory favored the Democratic party. Both parties feared losing control if the territories entered as one state, but they also feared that the other party would gain national power (Congressional seats) if the territories became two states.

The Hamilton Statehood Bill was signed into law June 16, 1906, as the Oklahoma Enabling Act. It called for the people in the two territories to write a constitution and take steps toward statehood. It required that the constitution:

- organize a government much like that of the other states
- provide religious liberty
- prohibit polygamy
- guarantee all races and colors the right to vote
- prohibit liquor in the Indian Territory and Osage Nation for twenty-one years
- set up a system of free public schools
- set up Guthrie as the state capital until 1913.

Delegates to the constitutional convention would be elected by the people. The territories were divided into 112 districts; 55 delegates would come from Indian Territory, 55 from Oklahoma Territory, and 2 from the Osage Nation.

Do You Remember?
1. What was the state of Sequoyah?
2. Name two reasons why single statehood was considered a good idea and two reasons why double statehood was considered a good idea.
3. When was the Oklahoma Enabling Act signed into law? What was its purpose?

Green McCurtain (top), principal chief of the Choctaw, and John F. Brown (above), a Seminole chief, both supported the unsuccessful movement for a separate Indian state.

The Oklahoma Enabling Act, signed into law in 1906, called for the Indian and Oklahoma territories to write a constitution and take steps toward statehood. There were 112 delegates to the convention (photograph above)—55 delegates each from Indian and Oklahoma territories and two from the Osage Nation.

STRUCTURING A NEW GOVERNMENT

The election for delegates to the constitutional convention was heated. Many citizens were still angry that so many territorial offices had gone to Republicans who had never lived in the territory. The Republicans found themselves constantly squabbling, trying to decide what issues they should address. Democrats, on the other hand, were well organized and supported most of the issues that had been part of the Sequoyah constitution. Even the Democrats were surprised at the outcome of the election. Out of the 112 seats, the Democrats took 99, the Republicans only 12, and the 1 Independent decided to throw in with the Democrats.

William Murray was elected president of the convention. Peter Hanraty, labor leader from Indian Territory, was vice president. Charles Haskell was majority leader, and Henry Johnston of Perry was Democratic caucus chairman. Henry Asp, Guthrie attorney, was leader of the Republican minority. There were thirty-eight farmer/ranchers, twenty-nine lawyers, fourteen merchants, and eight ministers, as well as a handful of doctors, bankers, newspaper editors, and teachers, and one college student. There were no blacks or women.

The convention opened in Guthrie on November 20, 1906. William Murray's opening speech hit heavily on the racial issue, calling for separate schools, separate waiting rooms, and separate facilities in state institutions. His speech received wild applause. The convention ended its work in July 1907, having taken only a break for Christmas. The new constitution drew heavily on the Sequoyah constitution.

The constitution laid out the basic structure of state government. Because so many offices in Oklahoma Territory had been filled by political appointees, the delegates insisted that almost every state official be chosen by popular election. The constitution set up a **bicameral** (two-house) legislature: the house of representatives and the senate. The **governor** would be head of the executive branch and responsible for administering the state's laws. The judicial branch consisted of a supreme court and various local and appeals courts.

The constitution included two procedures that were found in few other state constitutions. Citizens could propose and vote on a law without it going through the state legislature. They also had the right to demand that an act of the legislature be subject to a statewide **referendum** (a vote of the people on a law before it can be put into effect).

THE PROGRESSIVE MOVEMENT

In the early 1900s, the **progressive movement** spread across the country. Progressives believed that government was best equipped to correct the ills of society. They usually focused on three areas. First, progressives wanted government to fight poverty and improve the living conditions of its citizens. Second, they wanted to break up large corporations and regulate business. Third, they wanted voters to have more influence in government. The constitution of Oklahoma reflected many of these concerns. More than any other state constitution, it attempted to put political power in the hands of the people and to break down the advantage possessed by corporations.

Education

The constitution called for free public schools—schools that were not affiliated with any religious group and schools where the instruction was taught in English. All children between eight and sixteen were required to attend. It provided for separate schools for whites and blacks and schools for the deaf and blind.

Prohibition

The issue of **prohibition** (forbidding by law the making or selling of alcoholic beverages) was an especially sensitive one in the territories. Oklahoma Territory was "wet" and proud of it. Indian Territory was "dry," although there were plenty of places where liquor could be purchased. Many distilleries and taverns operated just over the border from Indian Territory.

Oklahoma's Anti-Saloon League was organized in Oklahoma Territory in 1899. Mrs. Margaret Olive Rhodes of Guthrie organized the first Women's Christian Temperance Union (WCTU). Maude Thomas of Beaver, publisher of the *Territorial Advocate*, refused to print liquor advertisements and wrote numerous editorials in favor of prohibition. But it was Carrie Nation who drew the most national attention. She campaigned throughout Kansas and Oklahoma, tearing down saloons, breaking mirrors, smashing bottles with her famous hatchet. In 1905, Carrie Nation moved into Guthrie for a time to support the prohibitionist movement and print her paper, *The Hatchet*. That same year, she made an unsuccessful attempt to clean up Tulsa.

Not everyone favored prohibition. Many settlers were immigrants from European countries where alcohol was a part of the culture. The Citizens League stressed abstinence (voluntary choosing not to drink). To avoid making the decision themselves, the constitutional convention delegates submitted the prohibition issue to a referendum.

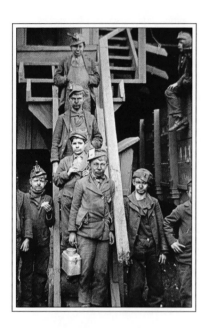

Working conditions were often poor during the early days of industrial growth. Children often worked in mines and were paid as little as 25 cents per day for a 10-12 hour day.

Labor Rights

Working conditions were poor during the early days of industrial growth. Ten-year-old children often worked in factories and mines and were paid as little as 25 cents per day. The average job was often hazardous and involved working 10-12 hours a day.

The constitution was one of the first and most thorough documents protecting the worker. Most of the labor code was written by Peter Hanraty, president of the Twin Territorial Federation of Labor, who served as chairman of the Labor and Arbitration Committee. It called for laws to protect the health and safety of employees in factories, mines, and on railroads. The chief mine inspector was required to have eight years of actual experience as a miner. It recognized that employees should have the right to recover damages for injuries on the job. The eight-hour day was accepted as the standard in all public works projects and in the mines. Convict labor was prohibited. Children under fifteen could not be employed in any hazardous occupation. Boys under sixteen and women and girls could not be employed underground in the mines.

The Oklahoma constitution was one of the first and most thorough documents protecting workers. Most of the labor code was written by Peter Hanraty (above), president of the Twin Territorial Federation of Labor.

Suffrage

The fight for woman **suffrage** (the right to vote) began in 1890 with the first territorial legislature. Women were given the right to vote in school matters—but not in other elections. The issue came up again in the Oklahoma territorial legislature in 1892, 1897, and 1899.

When the state constitution was written, citizens over twenty-one who had lived in the state a year were allowed to vote. When qualifications for electors were read, Peter Hanraty moved that the word *male* be stricken from the description. The fight was on.

But it was women's right to vote in school elections that may have cost them the vote in general elections. A school election in Guthrie in April 1907 brought out 751 black women and only 7 white women. This was a red flag to all southern Democrats who feared that allowing women to vote would turn the issues in favor of the black vote.

The only other people who could not vote in general elections were felons, paupers, lunatics, and idiots.

Black Rights

After the Civil War, many blacks had gone into government and business, attended colleges, and moved into professions. But as people moved closer together and settled in towns, fear and misunderstanding grew. Some growing towns found ways to avoid selling land or renting houses to blacks, thus creating segregated communities.

The influence of such groups as the **Ku Klux Klan** (KKK) grew. The KKK had been formed in Tennessee after the Civil War to keep blacks from exercising their new-found rights. Klan members were called on to preserve the family, help the needy, uphold law and order, and protect the peace. But the Klan had a darker side: they blamed society's problems on immigrants, blacks, Catholics, Jews, and other groups with different ideas or backgrounds. The influence of the KKK was strong even before statehood, and many political leaders had strong ties to the KKK.

Democrats were gaining strength in the territories, and Republicans—who had been long associated with Southern blacks—began to abandon black voters in hopes of gaining more white votes in the state elections. In the Third Congressional District of Indian Territory, the Republican party called for separate schools, separate coaches [railroad cars], and separate [railroad] waiting rooms. They went on record as opposing blacks "on any elective tickets" and pledged to prevent their nominations. Blacks were incensed.

The constitution could not deny blacks the right to vote, but delegates could (and did) require separate educational systems.

Business Issues

From 1895 to 1905, more than 3,000 U.S. firms were gobbled up by competitors in **mergers** (unions of two or more businesses). Large business corporations appeared. A **corporation** is a company that is formed by a group of investors and that has a life of its own. Some of these corporations abused their power, both nationally and in the territories. Railroads throughout the territories were so powerful they sometimes ignored paying property taxes. Some companies bribed the territorial legislature to get favorable treatment. About the same time, prices for goods began to rise. Between 1897 and 1909, industrial prices rose by 35 percent, food jumped 36 percent, and fuel costs 53 percent. The progressives claimed that the increased prices were due to the lack of competition. Business people insisted it was the result of increased costs—higher wages, higher costs of shipping and other services.

The new constitution required that all corporations receive a **charter** (official permission to operate) from the state. They could not contribute to or influence political campaigns. They could not own stock in competing firms. Their records, books, and files were subject to state inquiry.

All corporations, including public service corporations (utilities), were to be regulated by a state corporation commission. Railroads were defined as public highways and thus subject to the commission. Al-

Robert L. Owen, a part-Cherokee from Muskogee who had served with the Bureau of Indian Affairs in Indian Territory, was elected as one of the state's first two senators.

though this was an appointed commission in most states, in Oklahoma, commission members were elected.

Consumer, Health, and Social Issues

Another major issue was product safety. Upton Sinclair's novel *The Jungle* focused national attention on the unsanitary conditions in the meat industry. But similar conditions existed in the territories. A chemist who tested milk in Muskogee, for example, found it laced with a half-dozen dangerous drugs, chalk, saltpeter, boric acid, and bacteria-infested water.

The constitution called for a board of health, board of dentistry, board of pharmacy, and a pure food commission. A department of charities and corrections was set up to deal with orphans, mental patients, and prison inmates.

Do You Remember?

1. Why did the Democrats win so many seats for the constitutional convention?
2. List three provisions of the constitution affecting labor.
3. Why did progressives want to regulate big business?

RATIFICATION

Not everyone was happy with the new constitution. Republicans criticized it because of the heavy taxation and regulation of business. Residents of eastern Oklahoma were upset because the new state was to assume the debts of Oklahoma Territory but not the debts of Indian Territory. Citizens in Woods County filed suit because their county had been chopped into smaller counties. Black citizens were angry, and near-riots broke out in some towns. Even President Theodore Roosevelt was upset when he read it and called it "not fit for publication." He refused to approve it unless some items were changed. William Murray called the convention back into session to make those alterations.

On September 17, 1907, the first election for the state of Oklahoma was held. The new constitution passed overwhelmingly, and the entire Democratic slate was elected. Charles N. Haskell was elected the first governor. The state's two U.S. senators were Robert L. Owen, a part-Cherokee from Muskogee and Thomas P. Gore, a prominent Lawton attorney. With no opposition, Kate Barnard was named commissioner of charities and corrections. She was one of the first women in the nation to be elected to a state office.

The prohibition clause passed 130,361 to 112,258, making Oklahoma the fourth state to "go dry."

Thomas P. Gore, a prominent Lawton lawyer, was elected as one of Oklahoma's first two senators.

TWO FACES OF STATEHOOD

On November 16, 1907, Oklahoma joined the Union as the forty-sixth state. It had an official population of 1,414,177—more than any other territory at the time of statehood. The capital city of Guthrie staged a mock marriage of Mr. Oklahoma Territory and Miss Indian Territory on the steps of the courthouse. There were fireworks and barbecues. Indian Territory towns where there were many white settlers also joined in the celebrations. In Okmulgee, for example, merchants decorated store fronts, and there was an official parade with ladies dressed in red, white, and blue.

There were few celebrations among the Indians, however. A letter from Mary L. Herrod, a Creek Indian, appeared in the *Okmulgee Democrat* the day before statehood:

As Friday the 15th of November will be the last day of the Indian Territory, and after that we will be no longer a nation, some of us feel that it is a very solemn and important crisis in the history of the Indians....Now I've lived to see the last step taken, and the Indian does not count any more even in his own territory....I shall never write another letter. I cannot date my letters 'Indian Territory', and I shall not write.

BLACK'S
ENILE BAND
OWATA OKLA.

The Carnegie Library in Guthrie (above) was the site of the swearing in of Charles N. Haskell, the first governor of Oklahoma. The photograph on the right captured scenes from that first inaugural on Statehood Day.

Kate Barnard was a "crusader." She convinced legislators to authorize a mental hospital in Enid, a reformatory near Pauls Valley, an orphanage at Pryor, and state prisons at McAlester and Granite.

ONE STEP FORWARD, TWO STEPS BACK

On December 2, 1907, the Oklahoma state legislature held its first meeting at Guthrie. Lieutenant Governor George Bellamy presided. The first law addressed by the legislature called for segregating passengers on railway cars and in waiting rooms. Blacks and members of the Socialist party were outraged, and local riots broke out. In the black community of Taft, citizens burned down the railroad station.

The first legislature also addressed issues involving taxes on businesses and personal income, the regulation of banks, and protection for depositors against losses from bank failures. It established a board to solve labor disputes and created the nation's first statewide system of publicly financed employment agencies. It authorized a college of mining and metallurgy. Then it declared Labor Day a state holiday.

Oklahomans participated in a national election for the first time in November 1908. Republican William Howard Taft was elected president, although Oklahoma's electoral votes went to Democrat William Jennings Bryan. The Democrats won in the state, but the margin of victory was less than in previous elections. More blacks were voting, and they voted Republican.

In 1910, the Democrats in the legislature decided to slow Republican gains by cutting off the black vote. The bill sent to Oklahoma voters provided that to be registered to vote a person had to prove that he could read and write parts of the state constitution and was a descendant of persons who were eligible to vote on January 1, 1866. This was commonly called the **grandfather clause**. Although the law did not specifically mention blacks, it virtually denied blacks the right to vote.

During this period, Kate Barnard was one of the most active people in the state. She forced Oklahoma County officials to hire female nurses to care for women patients in local hospitals. She toured county and city jails. She investigated the mental hospital in Norman, where, she wrote, "Hell has reigned for twenty years undisturbed." She was able to influence legislators in the second session to authorize a mental hospital at Enid, a reformatory near Pauls Valley, an orphanage at Pryor, a school for delinquent girls at Wynnewood, and state prisons at McAlester and Granite.

MOVING A CAPITAL

Lawmakers had originally named Guthrie the capital until 1913, at which time a new capital could be chosen. As the cities began to grow, Guthrie became a Republican stronghold and Oklahoma City

SETTING HEALTH STANDARDS

In 1890, the Oklahoma Territory created a public health service and regulated the practice of medicine. There were few hospitals. Most early physicians traveled from place to place to care for the sick. Dr. Elizabeth Borden was one of the pioneer doctors, traveling in her buggy across the prairies of Oklahoma Territory.

During its first session in 1890, the Oklahoma Territory legislature created a public health service and regulated the practice of medicine, pharmacy, and dentistry. Traveling dentists crossed the territory. Most physicians in the territory were "riding" doctors—trained for a few weeks with another riding doctor. A doctor was usually called to make the long trip to a settler's home only when there was little hope left. This was a labor of love, for the doctor was lucky to be paid with a chicken or a bushel of turnips or potatoes.

One of the first trained physicians in Oklahoma Territory was Dr. John B. Quinton, a black surgeon who had been a colonel in the New York brigade during the Civil War. Most of Guthrie had never seen a trained doctor, but they knew he was a doctor because he wore the doctor's traditional Prince Albert coat. He set up his office in a three-room log house, which he divided with wooden screens to create a reception room and a treatment room.

But Quinton was more than an ordinary doctor. He had been known during the war for his ability to treat bullet wounds. It was said that he could study the angle a bullet had entered the body, determine its path, and find it with incredible accuracy and minimum surgery—rare in the days before x-rays. He had also gained a reputation for saving limbs from wounds and infections. In those days, most severe wounds developed gangrene. He used green tree moss and molds to combat the infection—treatments he had learned from his African grandmother. Quinton did a great deal to improve medicine in the territory. He worked with the midwives and the Indian medicine men to teach them about antiseptics and germs.

*Above: Governor Charles N. Haskell's first office in Oklahoma City was located in the Lee-Huckins Hotel. He is seen here in the hallway of the hotel signing authorizations for a class of Oklahoma University graduates. **Opposite page, above:** A scene from the inauguration of Oklahoma's second governor, Lee Cruce of Ardmore. **Opposite page, below:** Cruce, a lawyer and banker, tried to consolidate public institutions to save money.*

Democrat. Democrats, hoping to weaken Republican power, passed a bill allowing any town to petition to be named the capital. This was easy to justify since Guthrie still had not provided the promised capitol building.

In June 1910, Governor Haskell called a special election to determine which city would become the capital. The site of the state capital was important to businesses, railroads, and stage lines because it created jobs and brought income into the area. The election was heated. Granite offered a granite mountain as a capitol site. Oklahoma City was expanding rapidly, supported by oil money from the eastern side of the state. It guaranteed a half-million-dollar building free.

Governor Haskell, who openly campaigned for Oklahoma City, packed his bags and the necessary legal items even before the official results were in. After the election, citizens awoke to find Oklahoma City the new state capital and the governor already in offices in the Lee-Huckins Hotel. Secretary of State Bill Cross joined Haskell, but the state supreme court and other state officials remained in Guthrie. Guthrie officials put up a legal battle, and the election was ruled invalid because the ballot had not been worded correctly. Haskell called a special session of the legislature and pushed through a bill making Oklahoma City the state capital. The court battles wore on.

Haskell had made so many people angry that he lost the gubernatorial election in 1910 to Lee Cruce, a Democrat lawyer and banker from Ardmore. Cruce's efforts to consolidate public institutions to save money made him enemies in the legislature. Democrats tried to redraw the state into eight congressional districts, which would have strengthened their political position. Cruce felt this gerrymandering (redrawing boundaries to help a particular group) was unfair and vetoed the bill. Legislative leaders struck back by calling for his impeachment. He escaped that impeachment by a single vote, although some members of his administration were forced to resign.

The issue of the state capital was still on many people's minds. Another petition was circulated for the November 5, 1912, general election. Ballot boxes were guarded to make sure the election was honest. Finally the vote came in: 86,549 in favor of Guthrie, 103,106 for Oklahoma City. The state supreme court and the U.S. Supreme Court upheld the decision.

Do You Remember?
1. Who was the first governor of Oklahoma?
2. What two major cities vied for the capital of the new state?
3. What is gerrymandering?

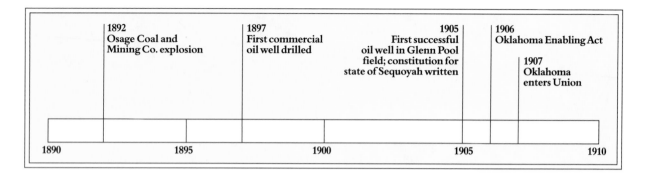

| 1892 Osage Coal and Mining Co. explosion | 1897 First commercial oil well drilled | 1905 First successful oil well in Glenn Pool field; constitution for state of Sequoyah written | 1906 Oklahoma Enabling Act 1907 Oklahoma enters Union |

1890　　　　1895　　　　1900　　　　1905　　　　1910

At the Same Time

1906　San Francisco earthquake

1908　General Motors Corp. formed; Ford brings out Model T

1910　The National Association for the Advancement of Colored People (NAACP) founded by W. E. B. Du Bois

Summary

The Oklahoma lands had turned golden—from rolling acres of wheat in the western Oklahoma Territory to the lead, zinc, and oil buried beneath the eastern Indian Territory. As statehood approached, the Indians pushed for a separate Indian state. The federal government, however, had decided that there would be one state. The constitution produced in 1906 reflected many of the concerns of the progressive movement sweeping the country.

Reviewing People, Places, and Things

Define, identify, or explain the importance of the following.

1. Kate Barnard
2. bicameral
3. boll weevil
4. charter
5. constitution
6. corporation
7. Glenn Pool
8. governor
9. grandfather clause
10. Charles N. Haskell
11. interurban
12. Ku Klux Klan
13. merger
14. progressive movement
15. prohibition
16. referendum
17. strip mine
18. suffrage

Understanding the Facts

1. What agricultural crop produced the best return per acre?
2. What were the three most important minerals in the state?
3. Who owned most of the mining companies operating in the Cherokee Nation?
4. What was the first well in the Glenn Pool field? In what year did it come in?
5. What was the real importance of the documents created for the proposed state of Sequoyah?
6. What is a bill of rights?

Developing Critical Thinking

1. Workers in the mines quickly joined the unions; workers in the oil fields did not. Can you think of any reasons why there was a difference?
2. The first state to give women total suffrage was Wyoming in 1892. That was followed by Colo-

rado (1893), Kansas (1894), Utah (1896), and Idaho (1896). Why do you suppose women first received the right to vote in frontier states?

3. Would the U.S. government be allowed to set up special laws to govern a particular group of citizens today? Are there such laws?

Using Your Skills

1. The following prices were typical for groceries in 1900. How much is each item per pound? What is the current unit price of each of these items?

   Holland's Special coffee (2 pounds): 30¢
   sugar (19 pounds): $1.00
   flour (50 pounds): $1.10
   navy beans (25 pounds): $1.00
   bacon (4 pounds): 64¢
   ham (5 pounds): 50¢

2. On a map of Oklahoma, locate the following.
   a. The site of the first commercial oil well
   b. The site of the Glenn Pool field

Special Projects

1. Assume you are a coal miner in Oklahoma in 1894. Write several paragraphs describing work conditions in the coal mine, wages, living conditions in the company towns, and any feelings about the Lehigh/Coalgate strike.

2. Today, a parent company that owns many other companies is called *diversified*. Often, the other companies may not seem to have any relation to their parent company, other than common ownership. Choose one of the following companies (or some other diversified company) and find out what other companies they own or who they are owned by: (a) Pepsico, (b) Walt Disney, (c) General Foods, (d) Phillip Morris.

Building Skills: Researching Topics

Researching topics is just one part of historians' work. Historians are much like detectives looking for clues and possible solutions to questions or mys-

teries. The historian knows that a library is often a researcher's best friend.

During the year, you will be given assignments that make it necessary to find information in a library. When you visit a library for research, there are specific places to look for information. Your key aids in the library are the card catalogue (either paper or electronic) and the *Reader's Guide to Periodic Literature*.

Visit your school library or media center and find information on the following subjects:

- Women's Christian Temperance Union movement in Oklahoma
- prison reform in Oklahoma
- United Mine Workers labor union

All these topics have to do with the progressive era. For each of these topics, find one reference in each of the following types of sources: encyclopedia, periodical, biographical or historical dictionary, and general history book.

Once you locate your sources, list the name of the book or periodical, making sure to include all the information for a bibliography: the title of each book or article, date of publication, publisher, and author. This list will help you find the information again if necessary. After completing this task, think about these questions:

- Are there sources in your library that emphasize Oklahoma history or give information on the state? Does your library have an "Oklahoma Collection"?
- In which of the categories above was it most difficult to locate the information you needed? Why do you think it was difficult?

Sooner Trivia

. . . The 1907 state constitution had 45,000 words—ten times more than the U.S. Constitution.

. . . The names of the early lead and zinc mines were as colorful as the mines were dreary: Queen City, Old Chief, King Jack, Frosty Morning, Lucky Strike, Buckeye.

UNIT V

OKLAHOMA IN THE TWENTIETH CENTURY

TO MANY, THE TURN OF THE CENTURY was a fresh start, a bright new morning. Oklahoma was a new land with fresh hope for people from all across the country. Here people from north, south, east, and west came together to form a new society. They were determined to overcome the social injustices they had left behind and to create a new progressive era. Although there were some wealthy citizens, and a few who moved into the area represented a moneyed class, most of these people were young, idealistic, and poor. They brought the idealism of youth, and they found themselves facing the age-old problems that plague mankind—the struggle to tame the land and manage the climate, and even greater—the struggle to tame man himself.

This photograph of a picnic in Sulphur typifies the feelings of many at the turn of the century: a fresh start, a bright new day, and hope for a people from all across the country.

CHAPTER THIRTEEN

OKLAHOMA AT THE TURN OF THE CENTURY

Tulsa is the recognized Oil Capital of the World.

—*Tulsa Spirit*, May 1916

O IL FEVER drew people to Oklahoma. If people were any kind of risk-takers or entrepreneurs, they recognized that opportunity lay just beneath their feet. Many made their fortunes in the Oklahoma oil fields of the early 1900s. In spite of the wealth in the state, there were problems. Blacks fought discrimination and attempts to disfranchise them. Farmers, and tenant farmers in particular, had been hard hit by crop failures and many were deep in debt. The state responded to the call to serve in World War I and made valuable contributions to the war effort.

OIL CAPITAL OF THE WORLD

The state was alive with men hunting for black gold. First came the men looking for telltale signs—a rise or dip in the earth or an oil seepage. Then came those who made the deals and sealed the leases. Right behind them came the rigbuilders and pipefitters, drillers and roustabouts. Well after well went down. In some areas, the rigs were only a few feet from each other.

THE OIL MEN

The Glenn Pool field was the first major oil field in Oklahoma, but it was not the last. These fields produced the millionaires who would support the state's growth. Robert F. Galbreath brought in the first well in Glenn Pool in 1905, then drilled 126 more wells there; only one was dry. When bankers would not make loans to Harry F. Sinclair even after his success, he organized the Exchange National Bank in downtown Tulsa, the first "oil man's bank." Red Fork and Glenn Pool also brought fame and fortune to W. F. Roeser, who spread his money across Tulsa. Charles Colcord invested in Oklahoma City real estate and organized the Commercial National Bank of Oklahoma City. Charles Page's philanthropy became legendary in his home community of Sand Springs. J. Paul Getty's father make his first money in the Bartlesville area; his son would later make his in the Muskogee area. Getty would

A panoramic view of the Healdton oil field. About one half of all the oil used by the Allies in World War I came from this field.

Terms: wildcatter, disfranchise, ordinance, speculator, absentee owner, coalition, worker's compensation, impeachment, neutral, draft, dissent, quarantine, armistice

People: Harry F. Sinclair, W. F. Roeser, Charles Colcord, Charles Page, J. Paul Getty, Frank A. and L. E. Phillips, Joshua S. Cosden, E. W. Marland, Alex R. Preston, Tom Slick, Cyrus Avery, Robert L. Williams, Woodrow Wilson

Places: Drumright, Cushing, Healdton, Camp Doniphan

Opposite page above: An oil rig at the Cushing-Drumright field topples into the Cimarron River.
Opposite page below: Frank Phillips (left), one of the founders of Phillips 66 Oil Company, with Oklahoma aviator Wiley Post.

become one of the richest men in the world. Frank A. and L. E. Phillips drilled eighty-three wells in the Bartlesville area; only the first two were dry. They would create Phillips 66 Oil Company, which became the backbone of the Bartlesville community. Joshua S. Cosden began makeshift refinery operations not far from Bigheart near Bartlesville. By 1916, the Cosden Refinery on the west side of the Arkansas River was the largest independent refinery in the world. E. W. Marland of Pennsylvania was one of the first men to believe in and practice petroleum geology. He struck oil in 1922, opening the rich Ponca field. He was one of the most colorful of the oil characters. But he was also one of the most fair to his workers, beginning such benefits as profit-sharing plans and free medical care.

There was so much activity in Oklahoma that *The Oil & Gas Journal*—the "Oil Man's Bible"—moved from Texas to Tulsa. Although Sapulpa and Sand Springs were closer to the oil fields, Tulsa was where all the oil men met. Tulsa had 126 companies of people in oil. And the place to gather the best information was the Hotel Tulsa. Harry Sinclair commuted to the hotel daily from Independence. The lobby was filled with men doing business, day and night. Leases and wells were bought and sold on a handshake.

Wildcatter Alex R. Preston brought in the discovery (first) well of the Preston Pool near Okmulgee in August 1909. (A **wildcatter** is a person who drills for oil in a doubtful or untapped area.) By 1910, the Preston Pool had nineteen gushers. Okmulgee County oil production was running 18,000 barrels a day, with new pools at Tiger Flats and Bartlett.

CUSHING-DRUMRIGHT AND HEALDTON FIELDS

In March 1912, Tom Slick's fourth well came in. Slick tried to keep it quiet; but when he hired all the buggies in Cushing and put guards around the well, people knew something had happened. Drumright sprang up overnight. The field was twelve miles east of Cushing; but wire services and newsmen named it the Cushing field. Wild gushers darkened the sky, and streams of wasted oil flowed down creeks and ravines. People even drilled in the Cimarron River. When the river drillers were denied access across nearby land, they built boardwalks from rig to rig to move people and equipment.

The freight road to Cushing was so crowded a second road had to be laid out just for automobiles. Some car owners ran a taxi service to and from Cushing, charging $1.50 each way.

In 1913, the Cushing-Drumright field was producing over 25,000 barrels a day. Total production was already over 9 million barrels of oil,

RIG IN THE RIVER FALLING
ELECTRIC STUDIO

representing nearly $10 million. Still, the price of oil kept going up; by August, it was $1.03 a barrel. More small settlements sprang up in the field: Shamrock, Ragtown, Tiger Town, Oilton. The names of the active companies were a who's who of the industry: Sinclair, Tidal, Prairie, Texas, Cosden, Magnolia, Gulf, Pure Oil, Deep Rock, Gypsy, Standard, Cities Service.

People slept on the derricks. Tents sheltered entire families or companies. The Blue Goose tent restaurant cleared its tables at night and rented them to sleepers. Cushing grocers delivered tent to tent. Syrian-Lebanese peddlers walked through the fields, carrying cases of thread, fabrics, and clothing. As soon as they could afford a tent or store, they set up retail establishments. The first was John Saffa, followed by Massad Brothers.

In the Cushing field, much as in other oil fields, natural gas was piped into the open air and burned as waste. Precious oil leaked from earthen pits, polluting the soil and ground water. It was not only wasteful, it was dangerous. In August 1914, the field went up in flames. The fire

The lack of paved roads made it difficult to transport equipment into the oil fields. In the rain, roads turned into a sea of mud.

destroyed two 55,000-barrel tanks, five 16,000-barrel tanks, and several gas wells; nearly 200,000 barrels of oil were in flames at one time. As a result of the fire, enforcement of conservation laws and regulation of natural gas lines were transferred from the mine inspector to the state corporation commission.

When Wirt Franklin discovered the Healdton field twenty-five miles west of Ardmore in 1913-1914, it was a poor man's dream. The oil was shallow, and the cost of drilling low. Thousands descended on the field. The night lit up with wells flaring off the cheap natural gas. Earthen pits held the oil while wooden and steel tanks went up.

By 1915, the state was awash in oil. Pipelines could not handle the flow; millions of barrels had to be placed in storage. The output of the Cushing-Drumright and Healdton fields broke the market. Prices tumbled. In March 1915, Healdton oil dropped to 30¢ a barrel and Cushing oil to 40¢.

The oil and gas glut led many companies to find other ways to use their product. The family-owned Bartlett Development Co., for example, had plenty of gas but no buyers. The company piped the gas to Sapulpa, built a refinery there, and then used the gas in the Bartlett-Collins glass plant and in a brick plant. It also built the Bartlett addition to house workers and personnel.

BUILDING ROADS

The first automobiles appeared in Oklahoma shortly after the turn of the century. In 1906, the Ford Motor Co. opened a plant in Oklahoma City. Automobiles even replaced a few horses in Tulsa's police force in 1909. The roads, however, were unpaved, and the heavy oil field equipment churned them into cardboard in dry weather. In the rain, the roads turned into a sea of mud. In spring, it was almost impossible to get five miles from Tulsa. Cars sank past their hubcaps into the mire. The demand for better roads increased.

Oklahoma established the State Highway Department in 1911. Sidney Suggs, an editor from Ardmore, was named director. Counties were given permission to establish county road taxes, and townships could levy taxes for road building. In 1912, Cyrus Avery of Tulsa convinced Governor Lee Cruce to declare a holiday "to pull Oklahoma out of the mud." Avery, who served as chairman of the Tulsa County Board of Commissioners, then persuaded the *Tulsa World* to help raise $25,000 for state roads. They began by improving the road from Sand Springs to Tulsa with a cinder surface then laying oil on top.

In 1915, a highway act set up a state tax that would be divided among counties that would match it. The state commissioner was given the

The first automobiles appeared in Oklahoma shortly after the turn of the century. Even Geronimo could not resist taking a ride in this early car with some friends.

The coming of the automobile brought an increased demand for better roads. A State Highway Department was established in 1911 to oversee the building of roads throughout the state.

power to condemn property in order to get the land needed for roads. The fee for motor licenses was increased—to $10-$30 for newer cars, $4 for cars three years old and older.

One of the first all-weather roads built in Oklahoma connected Oklahoma City and Norman in 1917. The twenty-mile trip had often taken a half-day by horse and buggy; now it could be made by automobile in little more than an hour. Paved roads had a major effect upon small-scale farming. A farmer could now haul produce in a truck to the nearest market town without having to pay the high price for a short-haul on the railroad. Farm-to-market roads were built and graded all across the state.

Trying to travel across the country was another matter. The United States did not have highways, national roads, or a national highway system before 1900. Cyrus Avery was one of the early organizers of trail associations, which traveled around the country, often in caravans, marking trails and roads to simplify automobile travel. Their efforts were the forerunner of today's highway signage. Cyrus Avery would become a power in the national association of state highway officials.

Do You Remember?

1. Who was responsible for opening the Cushing-Drumright field?
2. What caused oil prices to drop in 1915?
3. Why were roads troublesome in Oklahoma?

PROBLEMS AND PROGRESS
FOR BLACK OKLAHOMANS

A grandfather clause was included in legislation passed by the first Oklahoma legislature. That clause basically **disfranchised** (took the right to vote away from) black voters. A number of state election officials were charged, tried, convicted, and sentenced to prison for trying to enforce that clause. When those officials were pardoned, the decision was appealed to the U.S. Supreme Court. In *Guinn v. United States*, the Court declared that Oklahoma's grandfather clause violated the Fifteenth Amendment to the U.S. Constitution. The Oklahoma Election Board then tried to keep blacks from voting by setting a two-week registration period for voters not already eligible.

Oklahoma blacks also suffered under *de facto* (actual, if not legal) segregation. In Oklahoma City, for example, blacks made up about 10 percent of the population. Most lived in three generally segregated neighborhoods, all near the railroad tracks or the river on generally undesirable lands. Jobs were plentiful and, as blacks' wages increased,

After the Civil War, Indians were required to treat their slaves as citizens and provide them land. From 1875 to 1910, twenty-six black towns were established in Oklahoma. The town council of Boley (one of the twenty-six) is shown in this photograph.

Roscoe Dunjee (above), publisher of The Black Dispatch, *encouraged William Floyd, a black shoemaker, to purchase a house in an all-white neighborhood in Oklahoma City to test the city ordinance that had effectively segregated everything.*

they began to buy houses in previously all-white neighborhoods. The Oklahoma City Board of Commissioners enacted an **ordinance** (a law passed by city government) making it illegal for a person to move into a block on which 75 percent of the buildings were occupied by people of a different race. This ordinance effectively prevented blacks from moving into white neighborhoods and legally segregated everything from churches to dance halls.

Roscoe Dunjee, publisher of *The Black Dispatch*, and William Floyd, a black shoemaker, tested the law. Floyd purchased a house in an all-white block and tried to move in four times. Each time, he was arrested and jailed. Each time, Dunjee paid his bond and encouraged him to try again. When the case finally reached court, a federal judge ruled that such ordinances were unconstitutional and Floyd had the right to move into his property.

Despite the laws, blacks were generally better off in Oklahoma than in the South. Compared to Texas, for example, in Oklahoma more black children were in school, fewer were illiterate, and the average value of a black-owned farm was double that of one in Texas. By 1910, the state had a black population of 137,612—8 percent of the total population. About 18 percent were enrolled as members of the Indian tribes. There was a large population of blacks near Muskogee and other strong communities at Ferguson (near Watonga) and Foreman (on the Arkansas border). In Okfuskee County, 40 percent of the population was black, with new groups in Logan and Kingfisher counties. Near Tulsa, an area called Greenwood was becoming an important black community. Blacks owned their own land and their own businesses. Many worked for the wealthy white oil families at good wages.

THE PLIGHT OF OKLAHOMA'S FARMERS

In the midst of all the wealth in the state, there were many who were less fortunate. In the United States, one person out of eight lived in poverty. The average wage was 22¢ an hour. Oklahoma had more than its share of the poor, and their existence was grim.

The tenant system, unpredictable weather, and difficult farming conditions had combined to create a "working poor." In Oklahoma, the railroads and **speculators** (those who buy items—in this case, land—hoping it will increase in value and earn them a profit) had managed to acquire large amounts of the best properties, while the poor struggled with what was left. Neither tenant farmers nor **absentee owners** (property owners who do not live on or actively manage property) were inclined to make improvements to the land. If the land

came less productive, many tenants moved on. Those who owned land often borrowed heavily to carry them through rough periods. One observer remarked that the farmers "were worse fed, worse clothed, worse housed, more illiterate than the Chicago packing house [workers] Upton Sinclair described in his *The Jungle*." The Socialist party offered these people hope when they thought there was none left.

In the United States, the Socialist party supported public ownership of property (such as banks and railroads) and the right of society to make all economic decisions. Many of the issues socialists supported were also championed by the progressive movement; in fact, in Oklahoma the socialists *were* the progressive movement. Democrats often adopted their issues in order to gain votes.

Oscar Ameringer, a labor journalist, and Patrick S. Nagle, a radical lawyer, both started Socialist newspapers and were active in organizing unions and political **coalitions** (alliances). In the 1912 presidential election, the Socialist candidate for president got over 16 percent of the state vote.

A Socialist party encampment. The Socialist party offered hope to the poor in the state. It was such a strong third party in Oklahoma that both Republicans and Democrats had to take the party into account when developing their own strategies.

THE ELECTION OF 1914

In 1914, the candidates for governor included Democrat Robert L. Williams, Al Jennings (a former outlaw), Republican John Fields, and Socialist Fred Holt. Williams, who was from Oklahoma City, was elected. The Socialists captured 21 percent of the vote and won 6 of the 142 seats in the state legislature (a first) and more than a hundred local and county offices. This had a significant impact upon the laws passed during the 1915 legislative session.

A **worker's compensation** law was enacted, which provided government insurance for accidental death or injury in the workplace. The

GREEN CORN REBELLION

Patrick Nagle, a radical lawyer, helped found the Oklahoma Renters' Union and started The Oklahoma Tenant Farmer, *considered the best newspaper on agrarian reform.*

One group of Oklahomans who opposed the draft were the tenant farmers along the North Canadian River. If the men were drafted, their families would be destitute. They joined with other poor farmers from the South, a few blacks, and a small number of Snake Indians to form the Working Class Union (WCU). In August 1917, the WCU decided to march on Washington in protest. There were some in the group who, perhaps deliberately, encouraged their plans. A few men from the WCU did manage to burn a bridge or two and a few barns.

It was just the excuse the state's "solid citizens" needed to go after those they viewed as dissenters and Socialists. Republicans saw it as a way to split the Socialists and the Democrats and break their power before the coming election. So many men were rounded up that local jails overflowed. Four hundred people were shipped to the state penitentiary because there was no other place to put them. A few escaped into the Winding Stair Mountains or into nearby states. The so-called rebels were tried at Ardmore. About thirty were convicted on a variety of charges and sentenced to prison in the Kansas State Penitentiary.

Despite the fact that the Socialist party had not endorsed the Green Corn Rebellion, the party was blamed for it. In Chicago, the entire national executive committee of the Socialist party was tried for conspiracy. When the public in Oklahoma turned against the party, Patrick Nagle, a lawyer for the Socialists, called for them to disband.

When the farmers were sentenced to prison, they left behind women and children. Kate Richards O'Hare, a Socialist from Kansas, knew that they had no way to support themselves. Few could manage to sharecrop alone; they certainly could not get credit to tide them over through the next year. With practically no funds, O'Hare marched hundreds of wives and children 2,000 miles to Washington to picket at the White House. She brought them all safely back and earned pardons for their husbands and fathers.

work day for women was limited to nine hours. Small pension funds were set up for Confederate veterans and widows. To help farmers, a warehouse law was enacted, cotton gins were classified as public utilities (and thus licensed by the corporation commission), and a state bureau of weights and measures was set up. A law regulating impeachments was also passed. **Impeachment** is the act of charging a public official with wrongdoing while in office. Corporation Commissioner A. P. Watson was immediately impeached and convicted for accepting a fee from a corporation that had business before the commission.

Do You Remember?
1. What is an absentee owner?
2. Name at least three progressive laws passed by the 1915 state legislature.

WORLD WAR I

For forty years, Europe had been in a state of unrest. Nations jockeyed for power on the continent and in overseas trade. On July 28, 1914, a Serbian student assassinated Archduke Franz Ferdinand, heir to the throne of Austria-Hungary. Austria-Hungary declared war immediately, despite Serbian apologies. The other European nations were quickly drawn into the conflict. The *Central Powers* were led by Germany, Austria-Hungary, Turkey, and Bulgaria. The *Allied Powers* included England, France, Italy, and Russia. In August 1914, President Woodrow Wilson proclaimed that the United States would remain **neutral**, that is, it would not take sides.

In January 1917, Germany began a U-boat (submarine) war against all neutral merchant ships trading with Great Britain. Germany hoped to stop the flow of war supplies to the Allies and cripple the British economy before the United States became involved. President Wilson also discovered that Germany was pushing Mexico to declare war on the United States. On April 6, 1917, he asked Congress to declare war on Germany "to make the world safe for democracy."

The response was instantaneous. The Selective Service Act authorized a **draft** (a compulsory enrollment for military service). More than 91,000 Oklahomans, including 5,000 blacks, signed up. The state militia, already on active duty in Mexico, was rushed overseas. The National Guard was called out on July 5th. Oklahoma organized two regiments—the 179th and 180th—of eighteen companies with a hundred men each. Their symbol was a swastika, a good luck symbol of Indian country.

Camp Doniphan was set up near Fort Sill as a field artillery training base. The two camps became the "West Point of the Field Artillery," training over 60,000 soldiers. One officer who was stationed at Camp Doniphan was Captain Harry S Truman, who later became president of the United States.

Top: *Democrat Robert L. Williams was elected governor in 1914 in a race with Al Jennings (a former outlaw), Republican John Fields, and Socialist Fred Holt.* ***Above:*** *The conning tower of a World War I German U-boat rises out of the water. The U-boats were a major threat to Allied shipping.*

Oklahomans wore the uniforms of the U. S. military forces with great pride and distinction. Col. A.W. Bloor (top), commanding officer of the 142nd Infantry, credited the Choctaw code with being an important factor in the success of a major assault. Campbell Leflore (below), a Choctaw, was one of many Native Americans who served their country in World War I.

OKLAHOMANS IN THE WAR

A number of Oklahomans distinguished themselves as members of the American Expeditionary Forces. Patrick J. Hurley, an Irish miner's son from Coalgate, was the national attorney for the Choctaw Nation before entering the army. He refused a commission as a lieutenant colonel in the regular army to organize a company of engineers to build roads, bridges, and quarries. Hurley was twice cited for gallantry by General Joseph Pershing, earning the War Service Medal, Silver Star Medal, and Distinguished Service Medal.

Major Charles Fowler Hopkins, vice president and general manager of Tulsa's Pan-American Refining Company, was in charge of troop trains and railway transportation offices in southwestern France.

The 179th (Oklahoma) Brigade joined with the 180th (Texas) Brigade to form the 90th Division, Infantry. The 90th suffered severe casualties in the St. Mihiel and Meuse-Argonne operations. But it was said of the 90th that they never failed to accomplish a mission, and they never gave up a foot of ground to the enemy.

It was apparent from the battles that messages from the American Expeditionary Force in France were being decoded by the enemy. At one meeting, British military officials suggested that messages be relayed in another language to confuse the Germans. Someone recalled that the troops included a regiment of American Indians, who spoke twenty-six dialects or languages. Only four or five of those languages were written; one was Choctaw. The Oklahoma Indians attended radio school and worked out an elaborate scheme of identifying people and places by animals, birds, and other objects, all of which were then relayed in Choctaw—a double code. "There was hardly one chance in a million that the Germans would be able to translate these dialects," wrote A. W. Bloor, commanding officer of the 142nd Infantry. When a major assault surprised the enemy, Allied commanders knew that the Choctaw code worked.

THE HOME FRONT

During the war, **dissent** (disagreement or opposition) was suppressed, and people of German heritage were the object of fear and distrust. Many of German ancestry were fingerprinted, photographed, and labeled aliens (noncitizens) even though they had been pillars of the community. People with German names were snubbed; some were stoned. To prevent any suspicion of disloyalty, the German-Russian settlement at Korn changed the spelling of the town's name to Corn. When the Industrial Workers of the World (IWW) set up a Tulsa headquarters to distribute literature, opponents claimed they were trying

to paralyze the oil industry in Oklahoma, Texas, and Kansas. Its headquarters was raided; and seventeen people were run out of town.

The governor ordered the organization of a Home Guard. Each company was made up of one hundred fully armed men whose job was to maintain order, using force when necessary. They guarded government aviation property and occasionally rounded up idlers for work in war factories.

Farmers prospered during the war. Wheat was almost $3 a bushel, corn $2. Cotton was 50¢ a pound, hogs 25¢ a pound—good prices compared to pre-war days. Families grew their own "victory gardens" and endured wheatless and meatless days. The Miller Brothers at the 101 Ranch provided livestock to the government. Farmers in Woodward County grew castor beans, which were processed into an oil for airplane engines.

All the zinc from the U.S. Zinc smelter in the Tri-State District went to the war effort. Ore prices jumped from $40 a ton in 1915 to $135 a ton in 1918. Afton miners supplied lead. An oil and gas division was created in the corporation commission to inspect oil and gas fields and enforce conservation laws. Oil prices rose to 50¢ a barrel in August 1915, then to $1 in November. By March 1916, a barrel of oil was $1.55. By August 1917, oil prices had risen to $1.85, and they climbed to an astounding $2.25 in March 1918.

Children dressed in World War I military uniforms wave the British and American flags to welcome a British officer to Broken Bow.

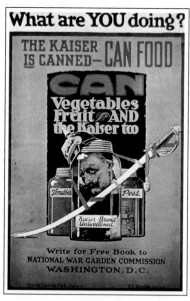

Patriotic posters like the two above stirred the emotions of citizens and enlisted their help and support for the war.

Business people who remained at home signed on as "dollar-a-year men," people who donated their time as civil servants or government officials. Alexander H. Kerr of Tulsa/Sand Springs served as an assistant to the secretary of agriculture.

With so many men volunteering or being drafted, women began working in the factories, stores, and offices. They ran streetcars and drove the first automobile canteens. They managed the American Red Cross, Liberty Bond campaigns, and food operations. Many cut their hair, shortened their skirts, and talked of voting and equal pay.

Young girls packed bandages at the Red Cross, while the older women knitted socks, caps, and mufflers. Young women entertained the young military men at proper parties and socials. Thousands of Oklahoma boys volunteered to harvest wheat, cotton, and other crops.

To raise funds for the war, the government issued Liberty Bonds. Buying bonds became patriotic, but many were pressured to do so. The Alfalfa County draft board informed young men that they could "buy a bond or fight." Tulsa opened the first War Savings Stamps Bank in the United States, selling small-denomination stamps that could eventually be turned into a savings bond.

THE END OF HOSTILITIES

There were those who said that Spanish influenza was germ warfare; no one could be sure. It moved across Europe, into the trenches of the Allies, and across the sea with the men. It spread into Arkansas early in 1918 and into Oklahoma by fall—just when a third of the state's doctors and half the nurses were in Europe. Country doctors were on call around the clock. State Health Commissioner John Duke closed churches, schools, and all gatherings of more than twelve people, including funerals. The **quarantine** (a restriction of people's movements in order to prevent the spread of a contagious disease) lasted most of October. When the quarantine was lifted, a second wave of influenza hit in November, a third in December. There were at least 125,000 cases in the state; probably 7,000 people died. It was followed in the spring of 1919 by smallpox, a deadly killer at that time.

On November 11, 1918, the German army surrendered and the two sides signed an **armistice**, a temporary stop to the fighting. A peace conference was held in France at the palace of Versailles in January 1919.

During the war, 10,064 Oklahomans died in combat, 4,154 were wounded, 502 were missing in action, and 710 died of disease (usually influenza). Some of those who came home were permanently damaged by "shell shock." Three of the fifty medals of honor awarded were given to Oklahomans.

There were the silent heroes as well—those who had worked on the home front. Miners in the little town of Picher, in the center of the Ottawa County mining district, had dug out $17 million of lead ore in 1918 alone. And it was often said that the Allies floated to victory on a sea of Oklahoma oil. In reality, the little Healdton field in southern Oklahoma supplied one half of all the oil used by the Allied Powers.

In the November 1918 election, Oklahomans elected Democrat James B. Robertson of Chandler as governor, defeating Republican Horace G. McKeever. The once-powerful Socialist party gained only 7,000 votes for its candidate, Patrick Nagle.

The efforts women made during the war did a great deal to change attitudes. In the November 1918 national election, just a week before the war ended, both the prohibition amendment (18th Amendment) and the woman suffrage amendment (19th Amendment) passed. In 1919, because of the nationwide contributions made by American Indians, all Indian veterans were given U.S. citizenship. (The rest of the Indians received U.S. citizenship by the Act of 1924.)

Do You Remember?

1. What led President Wilson to declare war on Germany in 1917?
2. How were the Allies able to get messages past German codebreakers?
3. What kinds of work did women do during World War I?

*Top: The first Red Cross Hut was built at El Reno in 1917. These canteens served traveling soldiers during the war. **Above:** James B. Robertson was elected governor in the 1918 election.*

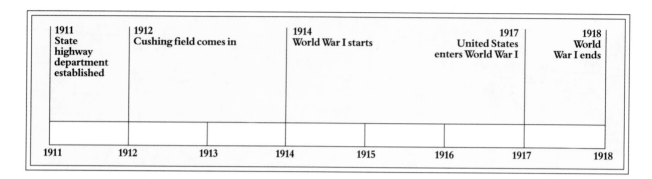

1911 State highway department established	1912 Cushing field comes in	1914 World War I starts	1917 United States enters World War I	1918 World War I ends
1911	1912	1913	1914	1915	1916	1917	1918

At the Same Time

1911 Marie Curie first woman to win Nobel Prize

1912 Girl Scouts of America formed

1913 Federal income tax authorized

1914 Panama Canal opened

1915 The British ship *Lusitania* sunk by Germans

Chapter Summary

In the years following statehood, thousands rushed to Oklahoma to see if they could make their fortune in the oil fields. So many oil fields opened and so much oil flowed that prices dropped.

At the same time, conditions for farmers and tenant farmers were among the worst in the country. The Socialists provided an alternative and gained strength in Oklahoma. At the height of their influence, one third of Oklahomans voted Socialist. World War I, patriotism, and the Green Corn Rebellion led to the party's downfall.

As World War I erupted, Oklahomans joined the crusade to "make the world safe for democracy." Wartime conditions brought farm and oil prices up. Oklahomans served bravely on the front lines, and those at home made important contributions.

Reviewing People, Places, and Things

Define, identify, or explain the importance of the following.

1. absentee owner
2. armistice
3. Cyrus Avery
4. Camp Doniphan
5. coalition
6. disfranchise
7. dissent
8. draft
9. impeachment
10. neutral
11. ordinance
12. quarantine
13. speculator
14. wildcatter
15. Robert L. Williams
16. worker's compensation

Understanding the Facts

1. Name three major oil fields in Oklahoma that were discovered between 1905 and 1915.
2. Why did the Cushing-Drumright field change conservation measures?
3. What type of treatment did Oklahoma blacks experience before World War I?
4. Who was president of the United States during World War I?
5. How were citizens of German descent treated in the United States during World War I?
6. What was a dollar-a-year man?
7. What contributions did Oklahoma and its citizens make to the war effort?

Developing Critical Thinking

1. Why did the Socialist party gain a foothold in Oklahoma?
2. What happened to the Oklahoma economy when war was declared? Why?
3. Was government action to suppress dissent during World War I justified?
4. Explain why the war helped the cause of woman's suffrage.

Using Your Skills

1. This chapter lists several price changes for oil throughout the 1910s. Locate the prices given for the following dates: August 1913, March 1915, August 1915, November 1915, March 1916, August 1917, March 1918.
   a. Calculate the amount and percentage of increase or decrease in oil prices.
   b. Prepare a line graph illustrating the change in oil prices.
2. Locate a map showing Oklahoma between 1905 and 1916. Mark the general location of the major oil fields. If the map does not already show them, trace the route of the early roads and railroads into those area. Compare this early map with a current map.

Special Projects

1. World War I spurred many technological advances: in medicine, in communications, in aviation, and in armament. Choose one of these areas and prepare a report on the advances made in the late 1910s.
2. Imagine you are one of the following: (a) a nurse in the war, (b) a woman tenant farmer, or (c) a man fighting on the front lines in France. Write a letter or poem describing your conditions.
3. Study the photographs of the posters on page 290, then create a poster that you think would have encouraged people to buy Liberty Bonds during World War I.

Building Skills: Distinguishing Fact from Opinion

A *fact* can be proven by examining it against other information or by your own observations or research. For example, "Eighteen-year-old U.S. citizens have the right to vote" is a statement of fact. This can be proven by reading the Twenty-sixth Amendment to the U.S. Constitution.

An *opinion* is something a person thinks, believes, or feels is true. For example, "A person should not be allowed to vote until she or he is twenty-one years old" is a statement of opinion. This may be the way someone feels. It may be shared by others, but it is a personal opinion.

Examine the following statements carefully, then decide which of the statements are fact and which are opinion.

1. In a democracy, workers should gain control of the government and use it to change the free enterprise system.
2. The Socialist party of the early 1900s had ties to Communism.
3. In the November 1912 election, Socialist party presidential candidate Eugene Debs received over 16 percent of the votes in Oklahoma.
4. Those who took part in the Green Corn Rebellion were planning a seditious rebellion against the federal government.
5. At least one hundred socialists were elected to local, township, and county offices in Oklahoma in 1914.

Sooner Trivia

. . . The great underground pumps used to keep the Afton lead mines dry during World War I were run so often that they pumped dry the underground stream that fed Afton Spring.

. . . Fourteen-year-old Briscoe Jones of Okmulgee built a wireless transmitting and receiving set in 1918. When the army wanted to teach soldiers wireless, they hired Briscoe as a civilian instructor. He transmitted codes to the army camps to help soldiers learn to copy messages.

CHAPTER FOURTEEN

GROWTH AND CHANGE IN OKLAHOMA

Well, this week just passed has been pretty busy in New York. It looked like my hometown of Claremore, Oklahoma, on a Saturday afternoon.
—Will Rogers, 1923

THERE WAS A SIGH OF RELIEF when Americans came home from France in June 1919. The troops were greeted with enthusiastic parades in Oklahoma City, Tulsa, Enid, and Ardmore. But few were prepared for the changes that had occurred—in the people, the communities, and the economy.

The men who came back were not the same. They had seen a whole new world, been exposed to European cultures and people. They had learned new trades and used new technology, and they had seen its effects. Black, Indian, and white had worked alongside each other. If those who had gone away to war were changed, so was the world to which they returned.

Those left behind—particularly the women—had shouldered the emotional and financial burdens of families and communities. There were now 8.5 million women in the U.S. work force. They had a new measure of independence, including the right to vote.

ECONOMIC CHANGES

A popular song of 1919 lamented "How you gonna keep 'em down on the farm after they've seen Paree [Paris]?" After the war, many young veterans were not content to return to the family farm. Many moved to cities, but there was one problem: There were few jobs.

Compare this view of Oklahoma City (1920s) with the photograph of Oklahoma City on page 235.

ECONOMIC UNREST

The wartime economy had brought a measure of prosperity to Oklahoma. Companies had expanded and purchased new equipment to meet government contracts. Now the government contracts were gone, and companies began to cut back or shut down.

Miners who had earned $6 a day during the war watched their paychecks dwindle. Unrest grew. There were labor union strikes by streetcar workers in Chickasha and Tulsa, boilermakers in Tulsa, newspaper printers in Oklahoma City and Okmulgee, telephone operators in Shawnee and Muskogee. Strikes broke out at the mines, mines closed, factories slowed down. Citizens tried to drive city officials from office.

On October 31, 1919, union coal miners called a nationwide strike. Nine thousand men in the Oklahoma coal mines joined them. In Pittsburg, Latimer, LeFlore, Haskell, and Okmulgee counties, authorities declared **martial law** (a temporary use of military rule when civilian authority breaks down). Coal supplies fell, train service decreased, and many industries shut down. The strike was not settled and martial law not lifted until December.

THE OIL INDUSTRY

The end of the war did not stop oil production. Oil could always be stored until better prices and times arrived. In fact, Waite Phillips opened the Phillipsville Pool northwest of Okmulgee in 1919, a field that would become one of the county's top producers. By 1920, however, oil prices began to drop—from $3.50 a barrel at the end of the war, to $1.75 in 1920, then to $1.00 a barrel. Oklahoma-trained petroleum workers moved on to new fields opening up around the world. But Oklahoma was not finished yet.

The Burbank field roared open in 1920 with the Bertha Hickman No. 1, brought in by E. W. Marland. The mineral rights to the land were owned by the Osage Indians, who held public auctions for additional land leases. The auctions were held annually under what became known as the "million dollar elm." All the important oil companies came to bid, and they paid handsome bonuses as well as royalties. The tribe distributed the profits to tribal members; by the mid-1920s, many Osage families were receiving $65,000 a year in royalties. Stories of the wealthy Osage made headlines around the world. One Osage woman's demand for a red car led the automobile industry to switch from providing only black cars to brightly painted cars.

Many Indians lost their entire fortunes to dishonest lawyers, guardians, and "gold diggers" of both sexes. The escapades of Katie Fixico and Jackson Barnett (two Creek oil millionaires) made headlines

around the world. In Fairfax, a group of white men devised a scheme to murder an entire family to gain access to the family's annual income of over $250,000 and another $2.5 million in other accounts. It took the FBI three years to solve the "Osage Reign of Terror," finally cracking the case before the final murder. There were actually more FBI agents in Oklahoma during that time than in New York.

On March 17, 1923, the Betsy Foster No. 1 well opened the Seminole field two miles south of Wewoka. It was followed by oil strikes at Cromwell, Earlsborough, St. Louis, and Seminole. By 1926, there were twenty-six pools and 5,000 wells. Overnight, Seminole became the center of the Greater Seminole field and went from a population of 500 to 20,000. The bank was so busy it had to stay open six days a week, unusual for those times. Every oil company and supply house was trying to get its supplies and equipment into the area. The railroad depot at Seminole was among the most active in the world. At one point, 2,000 freight cars backed up for a hundred miles in each direction. One year, Christmas mail and presents did not get unloaded until spring.

In 1928, Dr. G. E. Anderson of Indian Territory Illuminating Oil Company (later Cities Service) brought in a deep well that showed oil lay beneath Oklahoma City. During the next thirty days, Oklahoma City No. 1 produced more than 100,000 barrels of oil. By 1929, Oklahoma City was covered with big steel derricks. Oklahoma City became one of the fastest-growing cities in America.

Top: After the Betsy Foster No. 1 opened, the town of Seminole went from a population of 500 to 20,000. *Above:* Creek Jackson Barnett became an oil millionaire.

The Capitol T & R No. 1 well blew in on December 30, 1930, and once again Oklahoma City was showered with oil. The oil showers had become a common event in 1930 as well after well blew in.

In March 1930, the wild Mary Sudik well blew in south of Oklahoma City, showering the countryside with oil all the way to Norman, eleven miles south. Fire and explosions were a distinct possibility as the wind shifted and oil began to blow across Oklahoma City. No one near the well or in their homes could light a match. It took the crew eleven days to cap the Mary Sudik; during that time nearly 800,000 barrels of oil were lost.

Two months later, Gas-Slick No. 1 Sigmon barreled in, and Morgan Petroleum's No. 1 Stout Fella sprayed Oklahoma City with 60,000 barrels of oil a day, drenching residences. So much oil covered the top of the North Canadian River that the river caught fire; the fire spread five miles downriver before it could be controlled. When another field opened in east Texas, there was so much oil that prices collapsed to a low of 25¢ a barrel. Oklahoma oil men were broke again.

THE AVIATION INDUSTRY

When young pilots returned from World War I, they created jobs for themselves as barnstormers, skywriters, engineers, and builders of planes. Young daredevil pilots "stormed" the fairs and offered rides to the daring. "All rides are guaranteed to get you back in one piece," one pilot told prospective passengers. "Your money back if you get killed."

The early aviation efforts in the state centered around Tulsa because the city was so close to the oil fields and oil men understood the value of the airplane. Tulsa oilman Harold Breene managed the state's first airfield, which consisted of one hangar and one biplane. In 1919, Breene joined with W. T. Campbell to form the Curtiss-Southwest Airplane Company. They flew the nation's first commercial interstate air freight shipment from Tulsa to Kansas City.

In 1926, the first Tulsa-built airplane was proudly displayed by designer Willis C. Brown and contractor Paul Meng. The next year, Phillips Petroleum sponsored—and won—an airplane race from California to Hawaii, gaining national recognition in the process. When Tulsa had an opportunity to be included on a cross-country flight if it had an airport, forty-seven Tulsa individuals and firms put up the money, purchased land, and built a temporary terminal/waiting room/administration building—just in time for the Ford Tour plane to land.

The state's first commercial airport, Wiley Post Airport in Tulsa, was opened in 1928. Brothers Thomas and Paul Braniff organized the Tulsa-Oklahoma City Air Line. The first flight from Oklahoma City to Tulsa had three passengers and flew at less than fifty miles an hour, but it was the beginning of commercial aviation in the state. Spartan School of Aeronautics opened in 1928, with J. Paul Getty, the wealthy

oil man, as owner and president. In February 1929, several oil men formed the Southwest Air Fast Express (S.A.F.E.); by the end of the year, five other airlines were operating out of the city.

AGRICULTURE

During the war, farmers had gone into debt to buy land on which to plant more crops. After the war, farmers suffered through difficult times. Hoping to better control prices, farmers began to organize **co-operatives** (organizations owned by and operated for those using the organizations' services). Both the Oklahoma Cotton Growers Association and the Oklahoma Wheat Growers Association organized in 1920. But they could not stop the drop in prices. Cotton prices dropped first—from 34.6¢ in June 1920 to 9.4¢ in December then to 7.2¢ in April 1921. Wheat dropped from $1.42 a bushel to 85¢ a bushel.

More farmers lost their farms, and more farms were taken over by absentee owners. In September 1921, a convention was held at Shawnee. Those attending were representatives of the Farmers Union, the unions of the State Federation of Labor, and the railroad brotherhoods. They organized the Farmer-Labor Reconstruction League. The League called for state entry into private industry, a state-aid program to help the poor with home building, and free textbooks.

Mechanized farm equipment was slow to appear in Oklahoma. Oklahoma land was not level enough for some of the equipment, and such equipment was costly. Mechanized combines did cut 50 percent of the wheat in 1926. Cotton harvesting machines appeared in Oklahoma that year.

The aviation industry started to boom after World War I when young men returned from the war. Daredevil pilots, like Andrew Payne (above), stormed the skies in pursuit of fame and fortune.

The 1923 flood was the most disastrous flood ever recorded on the North Fork of the Canadian River.

One thing almost every farmer did purchase or build was a truck. Instead of having to sell to local grocers or wholesale houses, farmers could truck their produce into whatever town they chose and sell it along the highway or main roads. This became even more important as more local grocers purchased from non-local sources.

Agricultural extension agents (who worked for the agricultural university) tried to find new crops, such as soybeans, that could bring better yields per acre. But Oklahoma's erratic weather made farming a big gamble. After three days of heavy rain in May 1923, water rushed down the North Fork of the Canadian River, flooding the land all the way to Eufaula. It was the most disastrous flood ever recorded on the North Fork. Nearly all the bridges on the streams in northwestern Oklahoma were washed out, as well as many highway bridges in central Oklahoma. Crop damage was severe. More rains in east-central Oklahoma flooded the lower Arkansas River. There, 14,500 acres of bottom lands were washed out, along with bridges, culverts, highways, and livestock. In October, the Deep Fork in Okmulgee County flooded thousands of acres. One bridge was swept away, the railroad tracks were flooded, and the highway was not repaired for months.

Do You Remember?

1. What new oil pools opened in Oklahoma in the 1920s?
2. Why was Oklahoma's aviation industry centered around Tulsa?
3. What was a cooperative?

THE GREATEST RANCH OF ALL

The 101 Ranch started as a cattle ranch on 60,000 acres of Indian land in the Cherokee Strip. It became a showplace of quality livestock and agriculture and a vast manufacturing and entertainment industry.

The business panic of 1893 left George Miller with just eighty-eight old horses and a handful of cows. George and his sons Zack, Joe, and George sold the cows and then borrowed enough money to plant 5,000 acres of wheat and to buy 500 calves.

They began experimenting with crops, new equipment, and new farming methods. They raised garden crops such as tomatoes, cabbage, and melons; they created groves of nut and fruit trees. They set up a canning factory and sold peach and apple butters, jellies, cider, and vinegar. Their poultry operations were among the first to use incubators, brooders, and large poultry houses. They kept a hundred fine brood mares, stallions, and mules and a herd of about two hundred spotted ponies for the Indians. The ranch had thousands of hogs and herds of the finest cattle.

By 1926, the ranch had expanded to almost 100,000 acres in Kay, Noble, Osage, and Pawnee counties and had thirty-five miles of telephone lines. The ranch had its own electric light plant, waterworks system, power plant, and oil refinery. They operated an ice plant, machine shop, woodworking shop, laundry, cafe, meat packing plant, dairy and ice cream factory, tannery, and filling station.

One outgrowth of the ranch was the Miller Brothers 101 Ranch Real Wild West Show. The first show was in 1904, and it began touring in 1908. Bill Pickett, Lucille Mulhall, Tom Mix, Hoot Gibson, and Buck Jones were all part of the crew, along with Geronimo, the Apache chief. The show demonstrated calf roping, bronco busting, bow and arrow shooting, trick roping, and bareback riding. What made the show unusual was the participants were all people who spent the rest of their time actually working on the ranch.

The Miller Brothers may have been the first to make western movies. Their early attempts on the Oklahoma ranch were disastrous, so they began looking for somewhere with natural lighting and better weather where they could make movies more easily. They found an ideal place in southern California; they called it Hollywood. Their early westerns were hits. Before long, other film makers flocked to southern California, and a new industry was born.

Joe Miller (above), along with his father and brothers, made 101 Ranch famous. What started as a cattle ranch later spawned the Miller Brothers 101 Ranch Real Wild West Show featuring such cowboy stars as Tom Mix, Hoot Gibson, and Bill Pickett.

CULTURAL AND SOCIAL CHANGES

The period following World War I was a time of great cultural and social change.

THE TULSA RACE RIOT

Greenwood, just north of downtown Tulsa, was the "model" black community. Its population was about 15,000. Much of the land, buildings, and businesses were owned and operated by blacks. It was a thriving business community, and there were a number of black professionals. Many blacks worked in the homes of the wealthy oil men, but they bought and shopped in Greenwood. So much business was conducted in Greenwood that it became known as the "Black Wall Street of America."

Dick Rowland, a young bootblack, worked a regular spot in downtown Tulsa, and many businessmen were regular customers. No one knows what happened on May 31, 1921, when Rowland stepped into the elevator of a nearby office building. A white female elevator opera-

Billowing clouds of smoke from the Tulsa race riot in May 1921. The white mob drove the blacks toward Greenwood, setting fire to black homes and businesses as they went.

tor accused Rowland of grabbing her arm, fleeing when she screamed. Rowland insisted that he accidentally stumbled against her when the elevator lurched. Regardless, Rowland was jailed, and by morning newspapers talked of a lynching. About five hundred angry whites gathered at the jail. Blacks marched to the jail to protect him. Both crowds had guns; someone fired a shot and violence erupted.

The white mob drove the blacks back toward Greenwood, setting fire to black homes and businesses on the way. Firemen who tried to put out fires were threatened; bystanders were shot. The fighting went on for two days and nights. Planes supposedly dropped bombs, but no one knows who flew them. Finally, martial law was declared. Black men, women, and children were rounded up and taken to the Tulsa Fairgrounds, where they were treated as prisoners. Bodies of the dead were dumped in the Arkansas River; the real number of dead was never known. More than thirty-five blocks of Greenwood were leveled.

Within a few hours, city officials passed laws denying blacks the right to sell or possess weapons. All blacks were required to wear identification tags when on the street. If employed, they had to wear green job tags signed by their employers. But a more systematic approach was designed to deprive them of property ownership. A law was passed calling for all construction in the Greenwood area to be fire-resistant. Insurance companies refused to pay claims because the fire was the result of a riot. Without money to rebuild, many blacks sold out and moved. Real estate agents moved in, buying lots at rock-bottom prices.

The Colored Citizens Relief Committee demanded protection for black property owners. A test case was brought by a black law firm who claimed that the law was stealing from people who could not help themselves. The court agreed. A grand jury investigation resulted in the impeachment of the chief of police who had failed to take proper precautions for the protection of life and property during a riot.

After two days and nights of fighting, martial law was declared. Blacks were rounded up and taken to the Tulsa Fairgrounds, where they were treated as prisoners.

By 1920, the age of the car had arrived. More people wanted to own cars than wanted to own homes. This late 1920s car is being glamorized by a "flapper." Find what a flapper was. Why do you think this model was used to promote the car?

THE INFLUENCE OF THE AUTOMOBILE

By 1920, Americans had almost 2 million cars on the road. By the end of the decade, there were 23 million cars registered. More people lived in the country and commuted to city jobs. Sunday outings for the family now involved the car. When asked what most men worked for, a trade union official replied that 10 percent wanted to own their own homes and 65 percent worked to pay for their cars.

Two-lane roads were graded to the oil fields and major cities. Everyone wanted the roads, but no one wanted to pay for them. Financing measures were soundly defeated. Desperate, the state government raised the automobile license fee to $10.

When Highway 75 was completed from Canada to Mexico in 1923, it created so much traffic that counties had to launch paving programs. Tulsa, for example, claimed in 1926 "one hundred miles in every direction a surfaced road"; but the roads were nothing to brag about. Sometimes, the concrete expanded so much in the heat that it raised up off the roadbed. County engineers simply roped the section off, tied it down and waited for cold weather to pull it back in place.

The automobile and better roads meant business to even small towns. Entire new industries developed: automobile dealers, auto repair shops, garages, and gas stations. Because there was so much traffic in Okmulgee, the city installed traffic lights, but the lights were only operated during times of heavy traffic. This typical small town had six wholesale oil and gasoline stores, eight auto dealers, three auto accessory shops, twenty-one filling stations, five garages, and three tourist parks. The Sanditen brothers opened their first Oklahoma Tire and Supply (OTASCO) in Okmulgee and expanded to Henryetta, Tulsa, Shawnee, and Fort Smith during the 1920s. Many families put food on the table and children through school by pumping gas at their own small stations. Some added soda pop, bread, and a few other items to become forerunners of today's convenience stores.

POPULAR ENTERTAINMENT

Oklahomans never suffered from a lack of entertainment, even in the small towns. People entertained themselves with crossword puzzles, yo-yos, roller-skating, dance marathons, and cross-country races. They tried to get their names in the *Guinness Book of World Records* by sitting in trees or on flagpoles, chewing gum, pushing peanuts, or bobbing up and down in water.

Actors and actresses toured small towns regularly. In the oil towns, the theaters and opera houses were small but elegant. The Okmulgee Hippodrome Theatre and Opera House opened in 1921 and sported a swimming pool in the basement and a second-floor dance floor mounted on huge springs to create the feeling of dancing on a cloud.

The **myth** (a popular belief or tradition that has grown up around someone or something) of the frontier cowboy and the noble red man was growing more popular across the country. Many Oklahomans took advantage of it to make their living. Eddie Burgess, son of a Creek rancher, was a popular attraction on the rodeo circuit, known for his roping, his bright striped silk shirt, and his wide-brimmed hat. Al Jennings, former banker and reformed outlaw, was making pictures in Hollywood. Although his films always had a "crime-does-not-pay" ending, he was blackballed (ostracized) by those who felt that no "criminal" should be glorified on the screen.

Oklahoma's most famous son was Will Rogers, a modest cowboy from Claremore. Rogers moved from roping in the wild west shows, to vaudeville, and then to writing for national newspapers. He was a homespun philosopher who poked fun at the pompous and prosperous—and they loved it. "I never met a man I didn't like," he once said, and audiences felt the same toward him. Over the years, he would introduce thousands to Oklahoma, polo, and aviation.

Rogers was one of the first voices over the airwaves when KDKA in Pittsburgh, Pennsylvania, became the first regular radio station in 1920. In November 1922, Earl Hull installed a 20-watt transmitter in his

Al Jennings, a former banker and reformed outlaw, made films in Hollywood in the 1920s. He had run unsuccessfully for governor in 1914.

Above: Gene Autry, Oklahoma's Yodeling Cowboy, moved on to Hollywood where he became the first singing cowboy in motion pictures.
Right: Will Rogers, Oklahoma's most favorite son, moved from roping in wild west shows to vaudeville, and then to writing in national newspapers. His homespun philosophy poked fun at the pompous and prosperous—and they loved it.

garage in Oklahoma City and went on the air under the call letters WKY. It was only the third radio station in the nation to broadcast on a regular schedule and the first regular station west of the Mississippi. The first programs were recordings; but before long, people were lining up for the chance to play the piano or sing on the air.

In August 1923, Okmulgee Broadcasting Station officially was on the air as WPAC. It broadcast news, weather, puzzle programs for children, cultural programs, piano recitals, and services from the Okmulgee

Methodist Church. Other stations followed quickly: WNAD at the University of Oklahoma and KFRU in Bristow. Station KFRU was later moved to Tulsa and renamed KVOO, the Voice of Oklahoma.

Oklahoma radio influenced musical culture throughout the country. Otto Gray and his Oklahoma Cowboys performed on KFRU. Gray was the first singing cowboy in American show business, and his musicians were real cowboys recruited off Oklahoma ranches. Gene Autry, who had once been turned down by a group of local western singers because "he couldn't carry a note in a tin bucket," became Oklahoma's Yodeling Cowboy on KVOO. From there, he moved to Hollywood where he became the movies' first singing cowboy.

CHANGING VALUES

To many, the automobile, movie theater, and public dance halls seemed to have replaced the old-fashioned activities that had centered around home, church, school, and family. Men's stiff high collars were gone. Women cut their hair into sharp "shingles" or bobbed it with a "permanent wave." Skirts crept up to the calf, and flesh-tone stockings were in. Liquor was everywhere, and drugs were fashionable in certain parts of towns.

The people most upset by these changes were Christian **fundamentalists**. They believed that the Bible was the source of all religious authority. They believed the Genesis creation story as written in the Bible, and they believed that man was the last and highest living being created. They were troubled by new developments in science being taught in schools. Bombarded on all sides, they turned to God for answers. Growth in churches was phenomenal. Traveling preachers and evangelists held tent meetings and revivals with regularity.

The Ku Klux Klan also gained strength during this time. Its members included lawyers, business people, and church deacons. The harsh economic times, the constant upheaval, the rowdy oil camps and towns—all made Oklahoma fertile ground for the Klan. Klan members openly marched in parades and showed up in churches to donate money to widows, orphans, and injured workers. Some towns even had a Klan meeting hall.

EDUCATION

Before World War I, more men than women were teachers. Now women filled the schools—as teachers, superintendents, and board members. Many young widows began to support themselves outside the home after the war. Higher education opened opportunities for better teaching jobs, and women returned to the classrooms. A junior

Top: *Norma Smallwood of Tulsa, Miss America of 1926, getting her hair done.* ***Above:*** *The cover of the sheet music "Ku Klux Klan Blues," which was published in Muskogee.*

Senator John Golobie of Guthrie opposed a 1923 law prohibiting the inclusion of Darwin's theory of evolution in Oklahoma textbooks.

college movement emerged throughout the nation. A **junior college** is a school that offers the first two years of college work. The Oklahoma legislature converted eight of the smaller teacher training schools into junior colleges. A dozen more were created by the local school districts in smaller towns, such as Elk City and Muskogee. Classes in these junior colleges were usually staffed by high school teachers.

About this time, the theory of evolution became popular with biologists. English biologist Charles Darwin wrote *The Origin of Species* after an around-the-world voyage to study the world's fauna. Darwin believed in the process of "natural selection"—that over thousands of years animals adapted physically to a changing environment or they died out. Darwin also believed in **evolution** (the theory that man evolved, or developed, from earlier simpler life forms).

In 1923, a law was passed by the Oklahoma legislature to provide free textbooks in the public schools. It included a clause stating that no textbook that taught Darwin's theory of evolution over the Biblical theory could be purchased. When the bill was introduced, a near-riot broke out. Senator John Golobie of Guthrie cautioned, "If this legislature forbids the study of evolution in the public schools, it will make Oklahoma the laughing stock of the world." The bill did pass, and Oklahoma was the first state to prohibit the teaching of evolution in public schools. Within a few months, thirty-nine other states introduced such amendments.

When Tennessee passed such a law in 1925, the American Civil Liberties Union (ACLU) offered to defend any teacher willing to test the law. John T. Scopes, a high school biology teacher in Dayton, Tennessee, was indicted (charged with a crime) and brought to trial. The trial drew national interest. William Jennings Bryan, who had run for the presidency in 1896, 1900, and 1908, was the lawyer for the state. Clarence Darrow, who was the most famous criminal lawyer of the day, defended Scopes. The trial was heard by a judge with no jury. The judge refused to hear testimony about whether Scopes had a *right* to teach evolution. The only issue was whether Scopes had or had not taught the theory of evolution in the school. Scopes was found guilty and fined $100. On appeal, the decision was overturned by the Tennessee Supreme Court.

Do You Remember?

1. What was Oklahoma's first regular radio station?
2. What types of changes did the automobile bring to Oklahoma?
3. Why did fundamentalists object to the theory of evolution being taught in schools?

OKLAHOMA POLITICS

The year 1921 was historic for two reasons: First, Mary Alice Robertson, daughter of Oklahoma missionaries, became the first woman elected to the United States House of Representatives from Oklahoma. On June 20, 1921, she presided over the House for 30 minutes, the first woman in the country to do so. Second, partisan politics almost brought the entire state government to a halt. Democrats and Republicans could not agree on a state budget. The highway commissioner was removed from office; and a half-dozen impeachment threats were made against Governor James B. A. Robertson, Lieutenant Governor M. E. Trapp, and State Treasurer A. N. Lee Craft to get them to give in to opponents. In March, the house simply adjourned. A special session had to be called later in the spring to allocate the funds for the state government.

Mary Alice Robertson, daughter of Oklahoma missionaries, was only the second woman elected to the U.S. House of Representatives.

In 1922, John C. Walton was elected governor. True to his promises, he gave a barbecue (right) instead of an inaugural ball. Walton (below) and his wife enjoyed the festivities with fellow Oklahomans. Walton was impeached and removed from office after only ten months in office.

In 1922, John C. Walton, a Democrat and former Oklahoma City mayor, ran for governor. His platform included such "revolutionary" ideas as a state bank, a bonus for World War I veterans, and an increased tax on oil taken out of the state by foreign corporations (those not chartered in the state). Walton portrayed himself as a common man. "When I am elected governor, there will not be any inaugural ball, and there will not be a 'tea dansant.' I am going to give an old-fashioned square dance and barbecue; it will be a party for all the people, and I want you all to come." Walton won and was true to his word about the barbecue. There was also a band and other entertainment.

But Walton had made so many political promises that he could not begin to keep them. The Socialists had thought they had a friend. Suddenly, jobs promised to them went to others, and Walton no longer answered their phone calls. Klansmen showed up at the capitol building in broad daylight. The "common man" bought an expensive house in Oklahoma City's most exclusive residential district. When he tried to install political friends in important positions at both Oklahoma A&M and the University of Oklahoma, he had to call out a military escort.

When he commuted all death sentences to life imprisonment, citizens already worried about lawlessness grew restless. The Klan issued a public warning to all law violators, stating, "We stand for law and order, and its enforcement." Law officer Tom Boggous of Spelter City opposed the Klan and was killed outside a local movie house. Matters were so out of hand by June 1923 that Governor Walton mobilized the Oklahoma National Guard and declared martial law—against a group that had helped put him in office. Before summer was over, he had declared martial law in Okmulgee, Henryetta, Oklahoma City, and Tulsa. In September, he suspended the writ of habeas corpus in Tulsa and ordered the militia to collect all weapons. The press began calling for his impeachment. A grand jury was formed in Oklahoma City to investigate charges of misconduct. Walton placed the entire state under martial law and issued shoot-to-kill orders to the National Guard to prevent the grand jury from assembling.

It did not work. The Klan provided clear evidence of bribery and extortion (using one's position or power to obtaining money or other property to which one is not otherwise entitled) by Governor Walton. Walton offered to resign if the legislature would pass a law to limit Klan activity, but there were too many Klan members in the legislature for the legislature to even consider his proposal. Walton was impeached on twenty-two counts, convicted of eleven. He was ousted in November 1923 after only ten months in office.

Lieutenant Governor Martin E. Trapp replaced Walton and served until 1927. He was very interested in conservation and helped to establish the Forestry Commission, the Conservation Commission, and the Fish and Game Commission. He also supported a law that made it unlawful to wear the mask and robe of the Klan.

Trapp was succeeded by Henry S. Johnston, a Democrat from Perry. Johnston was instrumental in funding a state hospital for crippled children and increasing school aid. But he and the legislature crossed paths on changes in the highway department. When he pardoned two Klansmen from Altus and then tried to put a Klansman into an influential position, the newspapers turned against him. The presidential election of 1928 did not help. Democratic candidate Al Smith, a Roman Catholic, supported the repeal of prohibition. His Republican opponent was Herbert Hoover. When Johnston campaigned for Smith in Oklahoma, the Women's Christian Temperance Union, the Anti-Saloon League, and Protestant clergy soundly denounced him. Hoover carried the nation, and Oklahoma went Republican for the first time.

The legislature decided to impeach Johnston. They came up with thirteen charges (most of which were trivial) and finally voted to remove him for "general incompetency." Lieutenant Governor William Holloway became governor. Under his guidance, the legislature increased aid to schools, adopted a new mining code to improve health and safety conditions, and expanded the child labor code.

Top: *Lieutenant Governor Martin E. Trapp replaced John Walton as governor.* ***Above:*** *Henry S. Johnston was elected to succeed Trapp as governor, but he locked horns with the legislature, which impeached and removed him from office.*

Do You Remember?
1. Why was the 1921 legislature unusual?
2. Name at least one reason why Governor Walton was impeached.

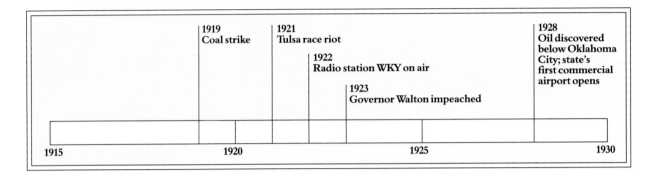

	1919 Coal strike	1921 Tulsa race riot		1928 Oil discovered below Oklahoma City; state's first commercial airport opens
		1922 Radio station WKY on air		
		1923 Governor Walton impeached		
1915	1920		1925	1930

At the Same Time

1920 Eighteenth Amendment initiating national prohibition went into effect

1922 Lincoln Memorial in Washington, D.C., dedicated

1923 Teapot Dome oil scandal resulted in the conviction of Harry F. Sinclair, owner of Mammoth Oil

1925 The first woman was elected governor of Wyoming

1927 Charles Lindbergh made first solo nonstop flight across Atlantic Ocean

1928 Walt Disney creates "Steamboat Willie," the first Mickey Mouse cartoon

Summary

The 1920s brought great economic, social, and cultural changes to both the United States and Oklahoma. Wartime demand for Oklahoma's natural resources—oil, gas, lead, zinc, and agricultural products— dropped sharply. Oklahomans again found themselves with plenty of goods and nowhere to sell them. A depression set in, compounded by bad weather and floods. New oil fields did bring hope when prices rose. The surprise field was at Oklahoma City, on the western side of the state where few wells had been discovered. Technology—automobiles, aviation, radio, movie houses—brought national influences to even the most remote households.

Reviewing People, Places, and Things

Define, identify, or explain the importance of the following.

1. cooperative
2. evolution
3. fundamentalist
4. junior college
5. martial law
6. myth
7. Will Rogers

Understanding the Facts

1. What Indian tribe became wealthy due to the discovery of oil in the early 1920s?
2. What was the first commercial airline company in Oklahoma?
3. What was truck farming?
4. What community was known as the "Black Wall Street of America"?
5. What event led to the the Tulsa race riot in 1921?
6. Name at least two ways in which small towns were affected by new roads. What kinds of businesses opened in small towns as a result?
7. Why did Oklahomans support the Republican candidate for president in 1929?

Developing Critical Thinking

1. What kinds of changes in society happened because of the war?

2. How did the concerns of the fundamentalists and the Ku Klux Klan overlap?

3. In our economy, how does overproduction of a crop or product usually affect its price?

Using Your Skills

1. On a large sheet of posterboard, paper, or chalkboard, draw a map of the downtown area of your city or town. Draw in the main civic buildings and label them by name and the date they were built.

2. Earlier in the chapter, it was noted that cotton prices dropped from 34.6¢ in June 1920 to 9.4¢ in December then to 7.2¢ in April 1921. The price of wheat dropped from $1.42 a bushel to 85¢ a bushel. What is the amount and percentage of decrease for each crop?

3. Assume you are a newspaper reporter in 1928. Research and write a story about the new Wiley Post Airport that has opened in Tulsa.

Special Projects

1. Choose one of the following topics and prepare a short, three-minute report to the class: (a) Katie Fixico, (b) Jackson Barnett, (c) the million dollar elm, (d) Osage Reign of Terror.

2. During the 1920s, many beautiful buildings were built by wealthy oil men. Find out when the civic buildings in your community or county were built. Find out who built them and when. Were any built during the 1920s? Do they have any details that would make them difficult to build today?

Building Skills: Using Road Maps

Road maps provide information about the distances between locations, types of highways, and connections to other roads. Travelers can purchase road maps at most bookstores, service stations, and convenience stores; they can sometimes be obtained free of charge from tourist bureaus, chambers of commerce, and welcome centers.

Using an Oklahoma highway map, plan a trip from your town or city to any one of the following destinations: (a) Oklahoma City, (b) Tulsa, (c) Ardmore, (d) Eufaula, or (e) Ada. Answer the following questions.

1. Which highways make up the shortest route to your destination?

2. Are any of the highways a toll road or an interstate highway?

3. What is the distance in miles to your destination city?

4. Assume that you travel to your destination at an average speed of 55 miles per hour. How long will the trip take if you do not make any stops?

5. If the trip requires more than six hours, where would you most likely spend the night after about six hours of driving time?

6. If your car averages 20 miles per gallon of gasoline, how many gallons will the trip require? What will be the cost of the gasoline if the average price is $1.25 per gallon?

Sooner Trivia

. . . The locally made Tulsa 4 automobile was designed to withstand "the almost unbelievable shock and strain of rapid driving over oil field roads."

. . . The winner of the 1923 Kentucky Derby was Zev, owned by Tulsan Harry Sinclair. The runner-up was Martingale, owned by Tulsa oil man Josh Cosden. The 1924 winner was Black Gold, owned by Rosa M. Hoots of Tulsa.

. . . The most organized publishing venture in the state began in 1929 when the University of Oklahoma Press began. The Press would become known for its books on Southwestern, Indian, and cowboy history.

. . . The legislature passed the state's first gasoline tax in 1924. The 2.5¢-a-gallon tax was to be used for highway construction.

. . . The call letters for radio station KFRU stood for "Kind Friends Remember Us."

CHAPTER FIFTEEN

THE GREAT DEPRESSION AND WORLD WAR II

Back in nineteen thirty-three,
Old dust storms was a-killin' me.
Nineteen hundred thirty-four
Dust had rose and blow'd some more.
Nineteen hundred thirty-five
Figger'd I was lucky just to be alive.

—Woody Guthrie, "Bonneville Dam"
Sanga Music, Inc., © 1959

I N THE 1930S, THE UNITED STATES SUFFERED the worst economic depression in its history. The farmers had been suffering for several years; the stock market crash of 1929 moved the depression to the city. Industry declined and unemployment spread. When hot, dry weather continued season after season, Oklahoma farmers were devastated.

The Great Depression was too big a problem for a city, a state, or even a country to handle. It was hard to imagine such a prosperous country in such terrible trouble. But all anyone had to do was look at the people on the street, the going-out-of-business signs, the business-men selling apples on street corners. The government—federal, state, and local—tried various measures to ease conditions, but did not end the depression. What did end it was the United States's entry into World War II.

Two men struggle to free their car from the sand near an abandoned Dust Bowl farm in Cimarron County.

During an economic depression, sales of goods and services slow down, prices fall, manufacturing decreases, businesses close, banks fail, and people lose their jobs. Although there had been constant ups and downs in the economy, there had usually been pockets of prosperity, areas or types of businesses that seemed less affected. With "The Great Depression" of the 1930s, every area and type of business was affected. A number of factors contributed to the depression.

SETTING THE STAGE FOR TROUBLE

Before 1910, most manufacturers produced goods for large industries: railroads, shipbuilders, textiles, construction. In the 1920s, manufacturers started producing **consumer goods** (goods for family or personal use): radios, refrigerators, toasters, and so on. But these goods often cost more than most workers could afford to pay. This had two important results: overproduction and changes in credit.

Some **economists** (specialists who study the economy) believe that this consumer economy grew too quickly. With more consumer goods than people could buy, factories had to cut back production (and jobs), make products that people could afford, or find new markets. Some excess goods could be sold to people in other countries. But after World War I, many of these countries had little money available to spend on American goods. Then, in the 1920s, Congress passed high tariffs, which made it difficult for foreign businesses to sell their products in America and buy American products. As a result, **international trade** (trade between countries) declined.

In the past, the United States had been a cash society. There were exceptions, such as miners who bought goods at the company stores against their month's wages. But buying consumer goods on credit was a new idea. **Credit** enabled people to buy goods and pay for the items over a period of time. This meant more goods would be purchased, and more goods could be produced. Thus, the American system of credit was born. It had its downside, though. The business person who sold consumer goods on credit had to find a way to pay the manufacturers. If the manufacturer would not extend credit, the business owner had to turn to the banks. This drove up the cost of goods.

Until this time, bankers had usually dealt with people who had money or goods to back up loans. Now they had to deal with business people who depended on someone else's promise to pay. Loans to these businesses were more risky. The American banking system was not well regulated, and inspectors sometimes overlooked violations. Accounts were not insured. Depositors could cause a run if they felt a bank was in trouble. When a run occurred, a bank might shut its doors until enough cash came in to do business. If a bank could not reopen, the money in people's accounts was "frozen," perhaps for years.

The stock market was another weak area. A **stock market** is a place where the stock (shares of ownership) of corporations is bought and sold. Most of the trading in the country was done on the New York Stock Exchange. Stock price is supposed to be related to its profitability or value; it may also be based on its *perceived* value. Throughout the 1920s, millions of investors bought and sold stock. They usually tried to buy stock at low prices and sell at high prices. Many people also began to buy stock on credit. They were betting that the economy and stock prices would continue to go up; it seemed a good bet. Westinghouse stock, for example, sold at $92 a share in March 1928. By September 1929, it sold at $313 a share.

On September 3, 1929, stock prices on the New York Stock Exchange reached an all-time high. Then prices began to decline, slowly at first, then more quickly. On October 24 (called "Black Thursday"), the stock market "crashed" and stock prices plunged. Five days later on October 29 ("Black Tuesday"), prices dropped again. By November 13, Westinghouse stock, for example, had fallen to $102 a share. Thousands of businesses and investors lost fortunes. Many were in debt without any hope of being able to climb out. When President Herbert Hoover announced, "The fundamental business of the country...is on a sound and prosperous basis," few believed him, certainly not the 3 million Americans out of work in the spring of 1930.

This caricature of President Herbert Hoover was published the year he left office. Many people blamed Hoover for their financial troubles.

OKLAHOMA'S PLIGHT

Oklahoma was hit hard by the Great Depression. The state's economy centered around agriculture and oil; when those areas suffered, the entire state suffered.

Oklahoma had never been an easy land in which to raise crops, gardens, or livestock. Even farming experts found that techniques acceptable elsewhere did not apply on the Plains. In the 1920s and 1930s, farming became even more difficult due to climate changes. Floods in 1923 and 1925 were followed by drought. In 1929, the year the Better Farm Bureau introduced Oklahoma farmers to peanuts, it rained so much that the crops rotted in the ground. When spring came, temperatures soared, hitting 100° for days on end, even as late as October. The next summer the cycle started all over again. Conditions were so bad that an informal relief tour, headlining Will Rogers, raised money

Oklahomans were taking to the air. In June 1931, Wiley Post (left), seen here with his plane "Winnie Mae," and Harold Gatty set a record for an around-the-world flight. Post set records again in 1933.

for the drought-stricken farmers. Even when something could be grown, the yield was poor. By 1931, the price for cotton, the state's principal agricultural crop, was down to 5¢ a pound, less than it cost to produce it. Related businesses, such as textiles, shut down or were bought out by other companies.

In 1925, there were over 180 mines in the Tri-State District producing zinc and lead. Five years later, production had decreased and by 1932 there were only 5 mines still operating in Ottawa County.

After the stock market crash of 1929, the price of a barrel of oil sank to 29¢. Oklahoma technology had brought innovations in drilling, such as injecting water under high pressure to force oil into the sands of nearby wells. This revolutionized the oil industry and its ability to recover oil more easily. But as it helped produce more oil, the increased production drove prices down.

Oklahoma's only other industry was aviation. When the depression set in, people stopped buying planes. In Tulsa, Spartan Aircraft began producing planes for flight training schools. Trans-Continental and Western airlines provided important airmail contracts.

Retail businesses—such as clothing, furniture, and drug stores—suffered as there was less money to go around. Going-out-of-business signs went up throughout the towns. When stores closed, landlords and landowners found themselves with empty buildings. Construction crews were idle as more people were selling homes than buying.

There was not enough work for all the homeless and jobless and those without skills. Even those who had skills were being laid off as overproduction in the oil fields drove down prices in all kinds of businesses. State officials knew they had to do something. Oklahoma was the first state to set up a direct-aid program for its citizens. The legislature created the Oklahoma Emergency Relief Board in 1931 and set aside $300,000 to buy food and clothing for needy citizens. Another $300,000 was set aside to purchase seed for farmers. The first federal relief funds arrived in Oklahoma shortly after the presidential election in November 1932. By 1932, there were 700,000 Oklahomans on relief and 150,000 unemployed.

The state was also struggling. When oil prices plunged to 15¢ a barrel, the entire state government faced financial ruin because most of the state's revenue came from a production tax on oil. On August 4, 1931, Governor William H. Murray (who was elected in 1930) placed more than 3,000 wells under martial law for almost two years. Production stopped until a quota system assigning so many barrels per well was instituted. The Interstate Oil Compact was signed with several other states to enforce quotas throughout the region.

The state had over $13 million in outstanding warrants (authorizations for payments) but no money with which to pay them. The legislature quickly passed a law permitting the state to issue bonds (long-term promises to repay a debt with interest) in exchange for the warrants. A second law provided funds from gasoline taxes to pay the bonds. The legislature passed a series of bills restructuring the state tax system under a State Tax Commission.

On May 5, 1933, the governor signed the Oklahoma Credit Union Act. **Credit unions** are cooperatives that promote savings among members and make loans to members at low rates of interest. This was an important step for average working people who had never had access to credit. Following Oklahoma's lead, a federal credit union act was passed in June 1934.

Education suffered during the depression. In some rural areas, just attending school was a challenge. There were no federal or state lunch programs. Some children had no food to bring for lunch. It became almost a tradition during these hard times for each woman in the community to donate one extra vegetable or a little scrap of meat to the schools. They were placed in a pot on the wood stove in the middle of the classroom, where the ingredients simmered until all could share a school lunch. Often, there was only one high school in a school district, and that was in the city. Families who could spare an older child from work often sent the child to live with relatives or friends in town so the young person could attend school. By 1938, Tulsa's Central High School was one of the largest schools in the nation with more than 5,700 students.

Between 1929 and 1933, more than 9,700 U.S. banks closed their doors temporarily or permanently. The Exchange National Bank, the oil man's bank and the biggest in the state, teetered on the brink of disaster. Investors tried to save it, but it failed in 1933. It was reorganized and reopened as National Bank of Tulsa (and later became the Bank of Oklahoma). There were so many rumors about bank failures, that a state banking **moratorium** (temporary delay of any action or business) was called on March 2, 1933. On March 6, 1933, President Roosevelt ordered a national banking moratorium, which lasted more than a week. Business nearly ground to a halt.

William H. Murray was elected governor in 1930, twenty-four years after serving as president of the state's Constitutional Convention.

Do You Remember?

1. Why did international trade decline in the 1920s?
2. What happened to the U.S. economy on "Black Thursday" in October 1929?
3. How did new technology affect oil production?

As Franklin D. Roosevelt campaigned for president in 1932, he spread a feeling of optimism that times would get better.

THE NEW DEAL

In November 1932, American voters elected Franklin D. Roosevelt president. When he accepted the Democratic nomination in July 1932, he called for a "new deal for the American people." He and his wife Eleanor were committed to easing the burden of the depression. President Roosevelt urged Congress to pass a number of programs designed to create jobs, strengthen the economy, and build the **infrastructure** (basic facilities, equipment, and services) of the nation. These programs came to be called the **New Deal**. There were so many programs—most of them known by their initials—that the New Deal was sometimes referred to as "Alphabet Soup."

WORK RELIEF

The Federal Emergency Relief Administration (FERA) gave money to the states to provide jobs, food, and clothes. Farmers were among the first to receive aid, and Oklahoma was one of the first states to receive aid. The Farm Credit Administration (FCA) stopped farm mortgage foreclosures by refinancing the loans through federal land banks. The Agriculture Adjustment Act of 1933 (AAA) was an emergency plow-up campaign. Farmers had bumper crops in many states, causing prices to drop. The AAA provided **price supports** (guaranteed higher prices) to farmers who cut back or who destroyed part of their crop. In 1936, the U.S. Supreme Court ruled that the AAA was unconstitutional, but it was soon replaced with the Soil Conservation and Domestic Allotment Act.

The Public Works Administration (PWA) built useful public projects to help the economy recover. The Civil Works Administration (CWA) put thousands to work repairing schools, fairgrounds, athletic fields, post offices, libraries, city and county offices, airports, parks, sewer systems, and waterworks. The Civilian Conservation Corps (CCC) employed young men to work on conservation projects. These projects included clearing forests, building roads and recreation spots, working to protect trees from fire and plant disease, and filling in badly eroded lands. In 1935, Congress created the Works Progress Administration (WPA) to provide jobs for workers as quickly as possible. WPA projects included constructing school buildings, parks, roads, and airports. They also repaired library books and operated sewing rooms. Nearly 90,000 Oklahomans worked on 1,300 WPA projects.

The government also wanted to do something to help those who could not work and to protect workers in case of unemployment. In 1935, Congress passed the **Social Security Act**, one of the most significant long-term programs of the New Deal. Through it, the federal government provided retirement benefits, financed by taxes on both workers and employers. The legislation also provided financial aid to children, the blind, widows with small children, and the elderly. It established a system of state-administered unemployment assistance.

The flurry of New Deal programs early in Franklin D. Roosevelt's presidency gave political cartoonists many opportunities to ply their trade.

FINANCIAL REFORM

The New Deal tried to correct weaknesses in the economy that may have added to the depression. One important reform was the creation of the **Federal Deposit Insurance Corporation** (FDIC) in June 1933 to insure depositors' accounts in banks. Oklahoma had had a bank guaranty program for many years, but it had not been big enough to handle the volume of failures.

Congress passed the Securities Exchange Act of 1934 to eliminate abuses on the stock exchanges. One abuse was *insider trading*, by which people "inside" corporations or stock exchanges used information they knew about the companies to make fortunes or avoid losses. Another problem was giving out false information about corporations in order to sell stocks. Congress also discovered that investors bought too much stock with borrowed money.

A PEOPLE'S ART

Artists and writers were particularly hard hit during the Great Depression because no one had money to buy art. The federal arts project was suggested by a friend of President Roosevelt who felt that buying public art with taxpayer dollars would create "living monuments to [Roosevelt's] social ideas." The federal government set up the Treasury Relief Art Project (TRAP), Works Progress Administration (WPA) federal arts project, and the Section of Fine Arts. Musicians and actors were hired to tour the country, and writers wrote a series of guidebooks about each state.

The program that had the most impact, however, was the Public Works of Art (PWA), which sponsored art in public buildings. Over a ten-year period, the federal government spent almost $40 million on the program. It paid 14,000 artists to produce about 4,400 murals, 117,000 paintings, 19,000 sculptures, and over 300,000 graphic art designs. Since the artists consulted with the local people on the subjects, the murals were truly a "people's art."

Forty artists painted fifty Oklahoma murals. They showed pioneer and Indian history—buffalo hunts, war dances, medicine men, cowboys, and the land rush. Many of these artists were Indian,

These WPA murals depicting various Oklahoma tribes, on display in the Oklahoma State Museum of History (above), were painted by Monro Tsotoke and Spencer Asah in 1934. The details show Monro Tsotoke's paintings of the Osage (top) and Kiowa (opposite page) tribes.

and many later became famous: Monro Tsotoke, Stephen Mopope, Woody Crumbo, Dick West, Solomon McCombs, Acee Blue Eagle, Randall Davey, Joseph Flick, and Manuel Bromberg. For the Pawhuska post office, Olive Rush painted an Osage Indian chief, a white Indian agent, and a cowman. For the Poteau post office, Joan Cunningham depicted the importance of cotton. The Claremore post office mural showed the life of Will Rogers. A series of six murals done for Vinita traced early Cherokee history. In Stilwell, Olga Mohr painted Indian farmers at work. These and other works of public art can still be seen in many post offices and federal buildings in the state.

IOWA

192C

Tsotoke
34

This farmer and his two sons (top) were caught in a dust storm in Cimarron County in the mid-1930s. These dust storms turned the Great Plains into the "Dust Bowl" in the late 1930s. The photograph (above), taken near Sallisaw, reflects the plight of Native Americans during the 1930s.

More than a dozen holding companies controlled three fourths of the power companies in the nation. Investors in these holding companies took the profits out of the businesses, leaving little money for growth. This led to higher rates for customers. Congress passed a law abolishing the holding companies and authorizing the government to organize power companies into regional systems to provide power more cheaply and efficiently.

In 1935, the Rural Electrification Administration (REA) was formed. In the 1920s, power companies ran electrical lines to towns and cities. Because the rural population was spread out, power lines were expensive to build and maintain. In 1935, about 11 percent of American farmers had electricity, but less than 3 percent of Oklahoma's farmers did. The REA allowed people to form cooperatives to bring electrical lines into remote areas. The Grand River Dam Authority was organized in 1935 to develop water power and generate electric energy for irrigation, reclamation, and conservation. When electricity finally arrived late in the decade, it completely changed living conditions in the rural areas. It opened the way for lights, milking machines, appliances, irrigation equipment, and deep water wells that made farm life easier.

HELP FOR AGRICULTURE

During the mid-1930s, disaster struck farmers on the Great Plains. Oklahoma winters were mild, and summers were hot with little rain. Crops burned up, leaving bare dirt. Rain finally arrived in August 1934, but it was too late. Much of the topsoil had turned to powder. When the winds came in February 1935, the soil swirled into the skies in great dark clouds that blotted the sun. On April 10, 1935, the worst dust storm in the history of Oklahoma hit. Temperatures climbed to 100°, 110°, then higher. For the next three days, dust covered the state. Millions of tons of airborne powdery topsoil turned the Great Plains into the "Dust Bowl" for most of the late 1930s.

The Czechs, many of whom had settled in the western part of the state, were model farmers who fertilized their land, rotated crops, and grew feed and cover crops to replenish the soil. Their techniques helped them survive. Ellard Anderton near Carter plowed up ridges 20-30 feet apart across his fields to keep the soil from blowing away. Neil Horn's mother had received a dozen canna (flower) bulbs in 1930. They multiplied, covering a whole field. The family traded bulbs for food and then developed a bulb business that lasted for more than fifty years.

Deep in the woods, where many of the full-blood Indians lived, hundreds of Indians were on the verge of starvation, living on what little they could find to hunt or fish. Conditions were worse than in the first years in Indian Territory.

A sharecropper and his family (bottom) make their way from Idabel to Krebs after losing their farm. Many others packed up and headed west (below) to California in search of a better life.

Top: The panoramic view of the state capitol festooned with oil derricks dramatizes the state's dependence on the oil industry. Above: Woody Guthrie, a young songwriter and storyteller from Okemah, captured the plight of the migrant families of the era in his songs.

The long, hard drought and dust storms robbed the land of its richness and the farmers of their livelihood. When farmers could no longer pay their bank debts, the farms were repossessed and sold at auction. Once-proud landowners were now reduced to renting or sharecropping. By 1936, farmers in Oklahoma were literally starving. And then the handbills arrived. Work in California, they said; farmhands wanted to pick fruit and vegetables. Thousands took to the roads without money or transportation, thumbing their way west; some rode the rails. Many young families packed their children and what few possessions they had left on whatever vehicle was still running and rumbled down Route 66 toward California. They arrived broke, without work, with no place to go, and no place to go back to. A few were lucky enough to find a spot in the government camps where there were schools, organized activities, showers, and latrines. Most did not. Between 1936 and 1940, 309,000 people left Oklahoma.

Two men recorded the conditions of these displaced people. Author John Steinbeck's *Grapes of Wrath* was a tragic drama of one Oklahoma family; its success brought the term *Okie* into the language. Although the work was fiction, it did not exaggerate the conditions. Woody Guthrie, a young storyteller and songwriter from Okemah, followed the hobos and migrant families, writing songs about their plight. He popularized the "talking blues" and wrote more than a thousand songs. "This Land Is Your Land" is probably his best known.

Do You Remember?

1. What was the purpose of the New Deal?
2. Identify four federal programs designed to put people back to work during the Great Depression.
3. Name two men who publicized the plight of Oklahomans.

Oklahoma Politics

In 1934, former oil man E. W. Marland was elected governor by the largest majority in the state's history. Marland had been one of Oklahoma's wealthiest businessmen, and he approached government with the same shrewd methods he had used to build a company. He tried to organize a program of state aid, but the legislature was bent on cutting back; few of his "Little New Deal" ideas became laws. He doubled the state income tax rate (to 2 percent) in order to receive matching federal funds for relief efforts. He also set up a State Planning Board to find ways to expand the state's economy.

Marland was responsible for bringing in a new, much needed revenue source. He was certain there was oil on the capitol grounds, but the Oklahoma City Council balked at placing wells inside city limits. Finally, Marland called out the National Guard, put the state capitol grounds under martial law, and showed the drillers where to drill. The drillers struck oil in October 1935, and money started flowing into the state treasury.

In the midst of the depression woes, Oklahoma lost two of its famous sons. In August 1935, Will Rogers and Wiley Post took off on a much publicized trip to Alaska. Post was an experienced pilot but was flying a plane that had been pieced together with second-hand parts. On August 15, "death, reaching through an Arctic fog, overtook Will Rogers, peerless comedian, and Wiley Post, master aviator, as their rebuilt airplane faltered and fell into an icy little river Thursday night near this bleak outpost of civilization," the Associated Press wrote.

They had just taken off for a trifling 10-minute flight from their river position to Point Barrow. Sixty feet in the air the motor misfired. The

Determined to find additional money for the struggling state, Governor E. W. Marland placed the capitol grounds under martial law and put drillers to work. Oil was discovered and money started flowing into the state treasury.

plane heeled over on its right wing. The lives of both the gentle master of the wise-crack and the champion aerial globe trotter were crushed out instantly as the impact drove the heavy motor back through the fuselage.

Eskimo natives recovered the bodies, and they received a state funeral that rivaled any president's.

POPULAR CULTURE

People looked to popular culture to take their minds off their troubles. Almost every town had a radio station offering afternoon soap operas, world news and commentaries, religious programs, drama, comedy, westerns, adventure shows, and science fiction drama. The stations drew on local talent, helping to create a generation of talented musicians and entertainers. Jazz musicians from Oklahoma were popular in California, Canada, and Europe. Many were members of some of the best-known orchestras of the time—those of Benny Goodman, Count Basie, Cab Calloway, Lionel Hampton. The sound that jazz guitarist Charlie Christian mouthed while he played ("be-bop, be-bop, be-bop") became the name given to the music of the 1940s. Oklahoma's country musicians popularized a new type of music called "western swing," which combined big band, Mexican horn, black blues, black horn, and southern country music. The most popular of the western swing groups was Bob Wills and his Texas Playboys, who would influence music for the next forty years. The group toured the country and made numerous movies.

Radio was such a powerful medium that President Roosevelt used it for his "fireside chats," which were broadcast on Sunday evenings.

The first fireside chat was on March 12, 1933. Roosevelt's weekly broadcasts kept the nation informed and gave people confidence.

Movies were a good way to forget troubles and enter a world where all women were beautiful and all men wealthy—except, of course, for those criminals who usually got their "comeuppance" in the end. Cash was dear, but Saturday matinees were a dime for a double feature, at least one serial, and three or four cartoons. To make sure that people came even in hard times, small-town theaters held local talent shows and dish giveaways. The theater was also the only air-conditioned building in most towns.

Poverty, uncertainty, lack of jobs—all contributed to a crime wave that spread across the country. Oklahoma was right in the middle of it. Gangsters and criminals who operated out of Oklahoma included George "Machine-Gun" Kelly, Bonnie Parker and Clyde Barrow, Charles "Pretty Boy" Floyd, and Kate "Ma" Barker and her boys—Freddie, Herman, Lloyd, and Arthur ("Doc").

Jazz musicians from Oklahoma were members of some of the best-known orchestras of the time. Jimmy Rushing (left) was a vocalist with Count Basie (center).

Do You Remember?

1. Name two ways in which Governor Marland was able to finance state government and its programs during this period.
2. What two Oklahoma heroes died in a plane crash in 1935?

WORLD WAR II

While the United States struggled with the problems of the Great Depression, four other nations were expanding their power and territory—Japan, Italy, Germany, and the Soviet Union.

INCREASING TENSIONS IN ASIA AND EUROPE

Japan was an expanding nation that lacked the basic raw materials to become an industrial power. In 1931, the Japanese army took over Manchuria, a province of China, and six years later seized most of the coastal area of China. In 1938, the Japanese announced a "New Order in East Asia." Japan would no longer permit free trade with China but would instead use its coal and iron to fuel the Japanese economy.

In the Soviet Union, Joseph Stalin was proving to be a brutal **dictator** (a ruler with complete control), purging the government and country of his opponents. Under a new economic plan, Soviet factories turned to producing weapons rather than consumer goods.

World War I had left Germany with heavy war debts and inflation that was out of control. People looked for leaders with answers; and dictators such as Benito Mussolini in Italy and Adolf Hitler in Germany stepped up. Hitler and the leaders of the National Socialist party (Nazis) promised to make Germany a great nation again and to regain the territory it had lost after World War I. More important, Hitler talked of food and jobs and preached of German superiority and a return to strong family values and morality.

Adolf Hitler (above) came to power talking of German superiority and a return to strong family values and morality. In a quest for power, he tried to unite all Germanic people. His invasion of neighboring countries led to World War II. Hitler (right) salutes his followers at a rally at Nuremberg.

In his quest for power, Hitler tried to unite all the Germanic people in Europe. In 1936, he seized the Rhineland (the area between Germany and France). He forced the government of Austria to turn over power to the Austrian Nazi party. Next he targeted the Sudetenland, a part of Czechoslovakia where 3 million Germans lived. Great Britain and France were alarmed, but they agreed to let Hitler have the Sudetenland on condition that he seize no more territory. However, Hitler took over the rest of Czechoslovakia less than a year later. Meanwhile, Mussolini invaded the African nation of Ethiopia, and in 1939 Italian troops sailed across the Adriatic Sea to conquer Albania.

THE WAR BEGINS

Hitler next turned against Poland. He charged that Poland was abusing Polish Germans and made plans to invade. Before doing that, however, he made a secret pact with the Soviet Union in which they agreed not to attack each other. In exchange, Hitler promised to divide Poland with the Soviet Union. On September 1, 1939, German troops invaded Poland. Shortly thereafter, Great Britain (which had an alliance with Poland), France, Australia, New Zealand, Canada, and South Africa declared war on Germany. Before these countries could react, the Soviet army took over Estonia, Latvia, and Lithuania and then invaded Finland. World War II had begun.

By May 1940, the German army had taken over Denmark, Norway, Holland, Belgium, Luxembourg, and a large part of France. The British army, which had been fighting on the European mainland, barely escaped across the English Channel, leaving their weapons behind. Hitler began bombing Great Britain in August 1940 in preparation for an invasion. The efforts of the Royal Air Force (RAF), however, held off the German invasion.

THE UNITED STATES ENTERS THE WAR

President Roosevelt watched with alarm as Japan, Italy, the Soviet Union, and Germany carved up the world. In the early 1930s, Congress had passed laws to keep the United States out of another war and to prevent the president from selling arms to a nation at war. Roosevelt felt strongly that if Great Britain fell, the United States would be next. In 1939, Roosevelt managed to push through a law that allowed Great Britain and France to buy arms from the United States if they paid cash and carried them in their own ships.

In June 1941, Hitler turned on and invaded the Soviet Union, despite their agreement. When the British ran out of cash, Congress authorized Roosevelt to lend or lease arms and other supplies to them

Hitler forced the government of Austria to turn over power to the Austrian Nazi party. Austrians welcomed German troops to Vienna once the Nazis were in power.

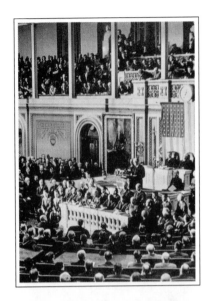

Top: Following the Japanese attack on Pearl Harbor, President Franklin D. Roosevelt asked Congress to declare war. *Above:* The sign on the door of an Oklahoma City business indicates the willingness of all Americans to go to war to protect freedom.

and to the Soviets. Roosevelt also ordered the U.S. Navy to escort British ships across the Atlantic. In October 1941, German submarines sank the *Reuben James*, an American destroyer.

Americans began to gear up for war. In 1940, Oklahoma City manufacturers had $3 million in defense contracts; by the next year they had $30 million. Plans were underway for Tinker Field in Oklahoma City. Douglas began building a plant in Tulsa to assemble bombers. A sister plant in Oklahoma City produced cargo planes.

Meanwhile, American-Japanese relations were strained. To protest Japanese aggression, the United States froze Japanese assets in the United States, which stopped Japanese-U.S. trade. Japan badly needed the oil that Roosevelt had cut off. Negotiations between the two countries deteriorated and war seemed imminent (about to happen).

On December 7, 1941, the Japanese bombed Pearl Harbor, a U.S. naval base on the Hawaiian islands. The first battleship hit was the *USS Oklahoma*. "When they fired the three torpedoes, we watched the side of the ship cave in on the third deck," said Oklahoman Charles Burns. The ship was already rolling over by the time the men got word to abandon ship; 448 sailors on the ship lost their lives. More than 2,400 American soldiers, sailors, marines, and civilians were killed in the attack, nearly 1,200 wounded, and the fleet almost destroyed. President Roosevelt called it a "day that shall live in infamy." On December 8, 1941, the United States declared war on Japan. Three days later, Germany and Italy declared war on the United States.

Do You Remember?

1. What four nations were expanding their power in the 1930s?
2. Why did Japan feel the need to expand her territory?
3. Why did President Roosevelt want to help the British?
4. What event finally led the United States to enter the war?

OKLAHOMANS AND THE WAR

More than 193,000 Oklahomans enlisted in the armed forces. Another 300,000 were drafted. Nearly 125,000 women served in the military and navy during the war. There were Army WACs, Navy WAVES, U.S. Coast Guard SPARs, and Army Air Force WASPs. The WASPs were active-duty pilots from 1942 to 1944. They ferried planes, towed targets for artillery practice, and served as test pilots.

Oklahoma had three top-ranking officers in the Navy: Mark Mitscher of Oklahoma City, A. S. Soucek of Medford, and Joseph James Clark of Pryor, the highest-ranking Indian in the armed forces. Ira Eaker served as deputy commander of the Army Air Forces.

The Oklahoma National Guard 45th Division, under the command of Major General William S. Key, was active in some of the fiercest battles of the European crusade—Sicily, Messina, and Palermo. General George S. Patton called the 45th "one of the best, if not the best, division in the history of American arms."

Lieutenant General Raymond S. McLain of Oklahoma City was a field artillery commander who had been with the 45th Infantry Division since 1924. He also commanded the 19th Corps of the Ninth Army and the 30th Division Field Artillery. General Lucian K. Truscott succeeded General Patton as head of the Third Army.

One platoon sergeant with the 45th became the hero of the common soldier during the war. Rayson Billey, a Choctaw, became the model for Willie of the "Willie and Joe" cartoon characters popular during the war. Billey was awarded two Bronze Stars and was nominated for the Congressional Medal of Honor.

Because of its location and mild climate, Oklahoma was ideal for military installations. Fort Sill served as an artillery center. There were twenty-eight army camps; several army air corps bases, one at Will Rogers Field near Oklahoma City and another at Cimarron Field near Yukon. Vance Air Force Base at Enid trained aviation cadets, with other aviation programs at Ardmore, Ponca City, and Okmulgee. There were thirteen naval bases, including the Technical Training Center adjoining the University of Oklahoma at Norman; Clinton was a naval flight training school. Camp Gruber near Muskogee was used to activate army divisions. Tinker Air Force Base (named for Major General Clarence L. Tinker, an Osage from Pawhuska) opened near Oklahoma City as the largest air materiel depot in the world.

Top: Tinker Air Force Base opened near Oklahoma City and served as the largest air materiel depot in the world. Bombers were also repaired at Tinker. **Above:** Admiral Joseph James Clark of Pryor was the highest-ranking Native American officer in World War II.

These World War II posters were typical of the effort to encourage Americans to support their country and to endure whatever hardships were necessary to win the war.

Oklahoma's manufacturing operations turned to the war effort. At Pryor, the federal government produced smokeless powder. A naval ammunition depot operated near McAlester. Tulsa's aircraft plants produced B-24 and B-26 bombers, the A-24 dive bomber, the twin-engine A-26 "Invaders," and a special type of the B-17 Flying Fortress.

The War Emergency Pipeline projects were a government-industry venture to build oil pipelines to the East Coast from the Southwest, including tie-ins to major Oklahoma fields. The industry developed high-octane aviation gasoline and synthetic rubber, and Clarence Glasgow of Tulsa designed an oil and gas separator that doubled the amount of oil that could be moved through a pipeline at any time. During this time, the giant West Edmond oil field opened not far from Oklahoma City.

Several dams were built to produce hydroelectric power for the wartime industries. The U.S. Army Corps of Engineers completed the Grand River Dam Authority (GRDA) and Pensacola Dam, as well as the Denison Dam on the Red River. These dams created reservoirs, which provided a steady water supply and controlled flooding.

Because of the war effort, civilian goods were in short supply. Oil and gas were rationed. New car production was stopped, and new car sales banned. Food stamps were issued, allowing families to purchase only certain amounts of items, such as coffee and sugar. Butter, steak, and milk became luxuries. Families returned to growing their own vegetables in "victory gardens."

Farmers and ranchers were called on to produce more livestock and more crops. Rural electrification was halted since the copper needed for wiring went to the war effort. Farmers were desperately shorthanded until later in the war when many of the prisoners of war (POWs) were allowed to work on Oklahoma farms and ranches. The state had nine POW compounds. Fort Sill and Fort Reno were the largest, with smaller ones at Tonkawa, Chickasaw, Alva, Tipton, Okmulgee, and Camp Gruber near Muskogee. About 3,000 German officers were held at a camp near McAlester.

The watchword of the day was "Use it up, wear it out, make it do, or do without." Schoolchildren collected metal to recycle. Women knitted socks and made clothes for children in the war countries. War bonds were sold across the state to help finance the war effort. Children saved money through the post office by buying savings stamps. The war even changed fashions. Women gave up their nylon stockings for cotton and rayon or went without. Skirts were shorter because they used less fabric. Pants were popular because they were easier to wear in the factories where so many women now worked.

ENDING THE WAR

On June 6, 1944 (D-Day), the Allies began a massive counterattack, landing their forces on the beaches of Normandy, France. The Allied march across Europe was more than the German army could repel. In April 1945, the city of Berlin fell. Germany officially surrendered May 8, 1945.

The war with Japan on the eastern front was brutal, with Allied forces pushing the Japanese back one island at a time. To avoid an invasion of Japan's home islands, the United States decided to drop the newly developed atom bomb on Japan. On August 6, 1945, the *Enola Gay*, an airplane outfitted at Tinker Field, dropped the bomb on Hiroshima, a major assembly point for convoys of the Japanese navy and the site of numerous war plants. On August 9, a second bomb was dropped on Nagasaki, a ship-building and torpedo-factory center. Japan officially surrendered on September 2, 1945, on the battleship *Missouri*. During the war, Oklahoma lost 6,500 military personnel, and 11,000 more were wounded. Thirteen Oklahomans were awarded the Medal of Honor, the highest U.S. military decoration.

Do You Remember?
1. How did women serve in the military during World War II?
2. What was Oklahoma's famous fighting division?
3. What event caused the surrender of Japan?

Only those involved in war, such as the troops coming off the landing craft on D-Day (top) know the fears and devastation, such as that caused by the atomic bomb at Hiroshima (above).

CHAPTER REVIEW

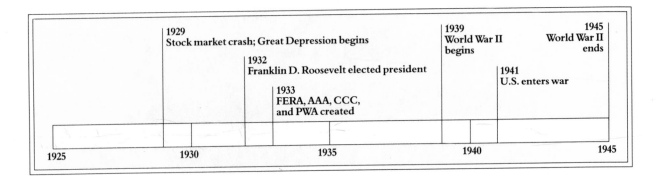

1929
Stock market crash; Great Depression begins

1932
Franklin D. Roosevelt elected president

1933
FERA, AAA, CCC, and PWA created

1939
World War II begins

1941
U.S. enters war

1945
World War II ends

1925　1930　1935　1940　1945

At the Same Time

1931　"Star Spangled Banner" became the national anthem

1936　*Gone With the Wind* released

1942　First daylight savings time

1943　*Oklahoma!* opened on Broadway

1945　President Roosevelt died; Vice President Harry S Truman became president

Summary

The stock market crash of 1929 brought the worst economic depression that America had ever seen. Every area and type of business was affected; unemployment spread. It was not until President Franklin D. Roosevelt's New Deal programs began that any headway was made. But the state—and the rest of the country—would not come out of the depression until World War II.

The actions by Japan, Italy, Germany, and the Soviet Union led to the war. The United States was at first neutral, although President Roosevelt initiated several programs to aid the Allies. The United States finally entered the war in 1941 when Japan attacked the fleet at Pearl Harbor.

Oklahoma made significant contributions to the war effort. It was an important training area for military personnel. Thousands served on the front lines; thousands more worked in the war plants. And it was oil industry know-how—much of it developed from Oklahoma—that kept the war fueled.

Reviewing People, Places, and Things

Define, identify, or explain the importance of the following.

1. consumer goods
2. credit
3. credit union
4. dictator
5. economist
6. Federal Deposit Insurance Corporation
7. infrastructure
8. international trade
9. moratorium
10. New Deal
11. Pearl Harbor
12. price supports
13. Franklin D. Roosevelt
14. Social Security Act
15. stock market

Understanding the Facts

1. What conditions in the American economy led to the Great Depression?
2. What was the CCC and what did it do?
3. What conditions eventually resulted in the Dust Bowl in the Great Plains?
4. Why did so many Oklahomans decide to go to California?
5. What event dramatically increased production and employment and brought the United States out of the Great Depression?

Developing Critical Thinking

1. When Franklin D. Roosevelt was inaugurated president in 1933, he said, "The only thing we have to fear is fear itself." What do you think he meant by that?
2. Few Oklahoma farms had electricity in the 1930s. Name at least five important things they would not have had then.

Using Your Skills

1. Westinghouse stock sold at $92 a share in March 1928. By September 1929, it sold at $313 a share. By November 13, Westinghouse stock had fallen to $102 a share.
   a. If an investor had bought 100 shares of the stock in March 1928, how much was it worth by November 13, 1929? How much had the investor gained or lost?
   b. How much had the investor gained or lost if the stock had been purchased in September 1929?
2. On a map of Oklahoma, identify where the military installations mentioned in the chapter were located. Which military operation was closest to where you live? What did that operation do? Check your library and find out more details about it.

Special Projects

1. Wiley Post is considered one of the first "astronauts." Find more details about Post and his contributions to aviation. Share your findings with the class.
2. Write a poem or short story about life during the Great Depression.
3. Tinker Air Base was named for Clarence Tinker. Prepare a report about him.
4. Find pictures of the airplanes that were manufactured in Oklahoma during World War II. How do they differ from the planes produced today? How do they compare in speed? size? capabilities?

Building Skills: Reading Circle Graphs

There are many ways to visually present numerical data. Charts, graphs, and tables may all make it easier to see and understand the data, trends, or relationships.

Choosing the best type of graph to illustrate the relationships between sets of numbers is important. Bar graphs are a good choice when comparing two sets of numbers over time. Line graphs are useful for showing trends. Circle graphs are best when comparing the parts to the whole.

The following circle graph shows the art projects sponsored by the Public Works of Art (PWA) in Oklahoma over a ten-year period.

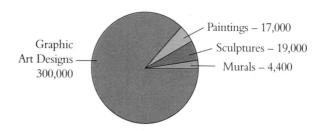

Graphic Art Designs — 300,000

Paintings – 17,000
Sculptures – 19,000
Murals – 4,400

1. What was the total number of pieces of art sponsored by the Public Works of Art program?
2. What percentage of the total pieces were murals? graphic art designs? paintings? sculptures?

Sooner Trivia

. . . On June 23, 1931, Wiley Post, with Harold Gatty as navigator, took off from New York in his monoplane. They flew 16,000 miles around the world in 8 days, 15 hours, and 51 minutes, a new record.

. . . Robert S. Kerr, Democrat, was elected Oklahoma's twelfth governor in 1942. He was the state's first native-born governor. He was born in a log cabin in the Chickasaw Nation and trained as an attorney.

. . . The parking meter was invented by Carl Magee, former editor of the *Oklahoma News,* in 1938. The engineering staff and faculty at Oklahoma A&M College at Stillwater put the finishing touches on it. A plant in Sand Springs produced them.

WINDS
OF
CHANGE

AFTER WORLD WAR II, Oklahoma found itself trying to adjust to major social and technological changes. The need for—and use of—both natural and people resources had changed. It was now the job of responsible politicians and government officials to find ways to lift Oklahoma beyond its past images of wild oil boomtowns, Okies, and the Dust Bowl. This would not be an easy task because so much needed to be done to repair the damage of decades. The world had become more complex, and it would take a great deal of effort—and enthusiasm—to forge ahead.

You have followed the growth and changes in Oklahoma City over the years through the photographs in this book. The photograph below is a 1994 view of Oklahoma City with Myriad Gardens in the foreground. How can you find the other photographs of Oklahoma City in this book? On what pages are they?

CHAPTER 16

OKLAHOMA FACES THE MODERN WORLD

Oklahoma is a rare event.
——Tom Hall, University of Oklahoma sociologist

O KLAHOMA CELEBRATED THE END OF WORLD War II. Its returning men and women were eager to begin new lives and new families. The state had been through almost two decades of hard times; it too was ready for a new start.

But after the war hostilities arose between the United States and its allies and the Soviet Union and its allies. Those hostilities lasted until the 1980s.

Oklahoma's economy became more diversified, but its boom-and-bust history contributed to a financial disaster that almost brought down the entire banking system.

COMING HOME

The young men and women returning from the war were ready to move ahead with their lives. After the lean years of depression and war, they wanted everything: families, cars, jobs, homes, and an education. Many were able to accomplish their goals with the help of what is commonly called "the GI Bill." Passed in 1944, the legislation offered low-cost loans for veterans who wanted to go to college, buy homes, and start businesses.

Millions of young people, many of them married veterans, enrolled in college. Universities could not put up buildings fast enough. Across the country, second-hand military quonset huts dotted every campus. At Oklahoma State University, the Veterans Village had more than 5,000 residents, complete with a community government, a mayor, grocery store, fire station, and sidewalks.

Other veterans joined the work force immediately. With their wages and the GI Bill, they could afford to buy a house. Developers began

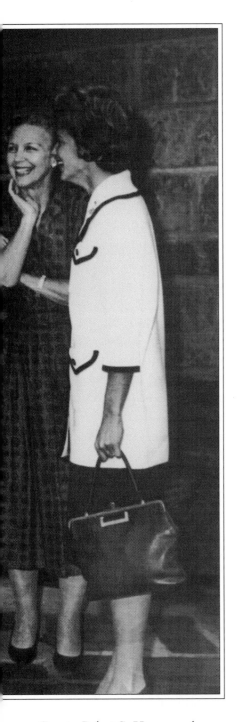

Senator Robert S. Kerr, seen above with President John F. Kennedy, was one of the most influential legislators in Washington. He was responsible for much of the federal money spent in the state.

In 1951, President Truman faced a firestorm of controversy for firing General Douglas MacArthur as commander of allied forces in Korea. MacArthur had criticized Truman's containment policy.

buying land just outside cities, where land prices were low. They built entire blocks of houses at one time, often using the same floor plan. These new subdivisions were nicknamed **suburbs** (residential areas outside city limits). Houses could not go up fast enough to meet the demand. J. Paul Getty, who owned Spartan Air Craft of Tulsa, decided to create movable housing—house trailers. They were an instant hit all around the country, and trailer parks sprang up in open fields.

By 1950, 51 percent of Oklahoma's population was urban. The three largest cities were Oklahoma City, Tulsa, and Lawton. Oklahoma City had its roots in agriculture and served as the political center of the state. Tulsa's roots were in the petroleum industry and served as the cultural center. Lawton supported its military neighbor Fort Sill.

THE COLD WAR

Almost immediately after World War II, the alliance with the Soviet Union broke down. The Soviet Union's expansion into eastern Europe increased U.S. fears of **communism**, a system in which the community (as represented by the Communist party) owns and controls all property and means of production. The term *iron curtain* was used to describe the boundary between the free world and the area taken over by the Soviets. The United States and its allies were determined to oppose further communist expansion.

People became worried that communist influence might make its way into American life. The "red scare" led the Oklahoma legislature to pass a law requiring all elected officials and public employees to take an oath of allegiance to the United States and to the state of Oklahoma. The so-called cold war turned hot in the 1950s and again in the 1960s.

THE KOREAN CONFLICT

After World War II, Korea had been divided. The United States supervised the government of South Korea; the Soviet Union supervised the government of North Korea. In 1950, communists from North Korea invaded South Korea. Although the U.S. government never officially declared war on North Korea, various units of Oklahoma-based military forces were ordered to active duty with the United Nations forces. Oklahoma's National Guard—the 45th Division—was called up and fought in Korea. Activity at several of Oklahoma's military installations briefly increased. Tinker Air Force Base, for example, had more than 23,500 employees, making it the largest employer in the state. A cease-fire was signed July 27, 1953, ending the fighting. About 450 Oklahomans died while serving in Korea.

The Korean conflict had several important results. First, blacks and whites served together in the same military units for the first time. Second, the war stimulated industry, keeping prices and wages high. It also helped to elect Dwight D. Eisenhower as the U.S. president in 1952.

The stark contrast of a country faced with a liberating army on one side and fleeing refugees on the other is a literal picture shown here during the Korean conflict.

THE VIETNAM WAR

The Vietnam war was also an undeclared war. Like Korea, Vietnam was a divided nation, with North Vietnam controlled by the communists. American "advisors" were sent to Vietnam as early as the 1950s. In 1960, North Vietnam began supporting communist rebels in South Vietnam. The United States increased economic aid to South Vietnam and in 1965 began sending combat troops. By 1968, there were almost 600,000 Americans serving in Vietnam. It was not a popular war, and Americans were bitterly divided over it. Some young men felt so strongly that they moved to Canada rather than be drafted.

For the first time, television provided graphic images of the fighting and of the antiwar protests at home. Oklahoma campuses were relatively quiet, until May 1970 when four students were killed by soldiers at Kent State University in Ohio during a demonstration. Oklahoma students also demonstrated against the Office of Inter-Agency Coordination (OIAC), which state officials had organized to monitor those suspected of "radical tendencies."

The effort of carrying on the war in Vietnam while enacting social programs at home was a heavy financial burden for the country. That

The U.S. 7th Cavalry was involved in many search-and-destroy missions in Vietnam. The rugged terrain nullified the superior technology and numbers of U.S. forces.

fact, plus the growing antiwar sentiment, brought an end to U.S. involvement. Peace talks began in 1968, but an agreement to withdraw U.S. troops was not reached until 1973. About 950 Oklahomans died in Vietnam, with many more wounded.

THE END OF THE COLD WAR

In the late 1980s and early 1990s, the Soviet Union suddenly, quickly, and dramatically fell apart. The Soviet empire broke up into a number of independent countries. Countries under Soviet influence, such as Hungary, Poland, and Romania, became independent and democratic. Others, such as Czechoslovakia and Yugoslavia, chose to break up and form "new" nations based on different ethnic groups and old boundaries. The wall between East and West Germany fell, and the two Germanies were reunited. The cold war was over, but regional tensions around the world have led to outbreaks of fighting in which the United States has sometimes become involved.

Do You Remember?
1. What was the GI Bill?
2. What was the "iron curtain"?
3. Name at least two ways in which the Korean conflict affected Oklahoma.

A CHANGING ECONOMY

Oklahoma's economy had been driven by war needs for more than five years. After World War II, the state had to find other ways of stimulating its economy. The Civil Aeronautics Administration moved its field training and servicing center to Tinker Air Force Base in Oklahoma City.

In 1946, native Oklahoman Roy Turner was elected governor. A rancher and oil man, he called for economy in state government and development of state resources and recreation. He pushed the legislature to reduce corporate taxes to attract more business. He organized a tour that featured Oklahoma products and promoted Oklahoma communities as places for businesses to relocate. The tour advertised Oklahoma's low-cost fuel, central location, access to transportation, pro-business attitude, and experienced, well-trained workers. By 1948, the state's total industrial development had jumped more than 36 percent, compared to a national increase of only 10 percent.

Senator Robert S. Kerr also helped bring federal monies to the state. By the 1960s, 30¢ of every dollar spent in Oklahoma came from federal grants. Most of that money went to welfare (33 percent), highways (25 percent), and education (30 percent).

While agriculture and oil remain important, Oklahoma's economy has become much more diversified.

Oklahoma Governor Roy Turner, seen above with President Harry S Truman, pressed for economy in state government and development of state resources and recreation during his term. He also asked for reduced corporate taxes in order to lure new businesses to the state.

AGRICULTURE

During and after World War II, many young people left the farms, never to return. Luckily, gasoline-powered equipment (such as the tractor, cotton picker, and combine) made it possible for fewer farmers to do the work of many. As new synthetic fibers replaced cotton for clothing, the market for cotton shrank. Many farmers switched to livestock, which became the principal agricultural focus across the state.

As the farm population decreased, the farms were often sold to other farmers who consolidated and made larger farms. By 1960, only ten states had more land in farm acreage than Oklahoma did. Cattle were the number one money producer for farmers. Wheat and cotton were still important agricultural crops; but agricultural crops were always subject to weather conditions and the laws of supply and demand: When crop yields were up, overproduction brought prices down. When crop yields were down, prices might go up, but there was less for the farmer to sell.

The Agricultural Act of 1964 provided some help for Oklahoma farmers. It set price supports for wheat and cotton and controlled surplus production. It also paid farmers to leave some of their acreage unplanted for soil conservation.

Beginning in the 1940s, farms changed from self-sufficient operations to operations that specialized in one or two crops. This tended to increase production, which created surpluses that lowered farm prices. The 1960s saw the beginning of a period of inflation. **Inflation** occurs when the money supply increases rapidly and there are not enough goods and services on which to spend it. Prices therefore rise. Oklahoma farmers were caught in a squeeze. They were able to stay in business by borrowing money against their land, which increased in value as inflation raised prices. In 1985, President Ronald Reagan signed the cost-

In 1988, cattle and calves represented more than half of Oklahoma's total agricultural receipts.

liest farm bill in history; but the bill also reduced income and price supports to farmers for the first time since 1933.

In 1988, cattle and calves were still the leading agricultural product. There were over 5 million cattle on the state's farms and ranches. Animal hides and skins were the state's third largest export. Winter wheat was the state's second most important agricultural product. Drought and heavy rains affected the yield, but Oklahoma still ranked second in the nation for that crop. Wheat was the state's chief export, and Oklahoma exported more wheat to the Soviet Union than any other state. Hay and alfalfa hay were the state's third most important agricultural crop. Hay is grown in all areas of the state except the Panhandle. Other leading agricultural products included milk, eggs, peanuts, hogs, and cotton. Oklahoma farmers also harvested grain sorghum, rye, oats, soybeans, mung beans, and mushrooms.

MINING

After the war, oil and gas were still the state's leading businesses. Oklahoma was fourth in both total petroleum production and total gas production. The oil fields had spread further across the state; the four largest oil fields were Velma and Sholem-Alecham in south-central Oklahoma, Elk City, and Oklahoma City. There were 3,600 producing gas wells in the state. The biggest were in the Guymon-Hugoton field in Texas County.

Synthetic fibers (such as polyester) made from petroleum products were in demand, and oil consumption rose faster than domestic crude production. In 1948, for the first time, the United States began to import more oil than it exported. It was the beginning of a major change in the petroleum industry. The cost of foreign oil was so much less than domestic oil that foreign oil from Venezuela and the Middle East soon flooded the market.

For years, the prices of oil around the world had been kept stable by a group of companies known as the "Seven Sisters" (Standard of New Jersey, Standard of California, Texaco, Gulf, Mobil, Royal Dutch/Shell, and British Petroleum). They set prices, negotiated contracts with American and world markets, and generally controlled the amount of oil in the market. They paid the countries in which they drilled a royalty or percentage of the profits. Their hold on the oil industry broke down in 1951 with revolution in Iran. Oil companies that had been operating in Iran were **nationalized**; that is, they were taken over by the government. The Shah of Iran contracted with companies to drill and operate the wells. Other oil-rich nations soon followed Iran's example.

By 1960, there were 190 American petroleum or oil-related companies operating in 91 countries. So many nations were selling petroleum on the international market that prices fell. To maintain bargaining power, the five major oil-exporting nations (Venezuela, Saudi Arabia, Iran, Iraq, and Kuwait) formed the **Organization of Petroleum Exporting Countries** (OPEC). OPEC would have long-term effects upon oil prices around the world and in Oklahoma.

On the domestic market, drilling for oil in the United States reached its peak. New techniques allowed deeper and more difficult drilling. Companies such as Tulsa's Reading and Bates Corporation used the new technology to look for new fields in the Gulf of Mexico and off the shore of Louisiana. The deep Anadarko Basin in western Oklahoma had been discovered, and Mustang Fuel Corporation built the first gas transmission line into the basin in 1961. Three years later, it extended the gas line to the Arkoma Basin in the eastern part of the state. The company also built one of the largest gas-processing facilities in the state at Calumet.

The State Capitol in Oklahoma City is one of the few in the nation without a dome—and probably the only one in the world with a working oil well on its grounds.

The Energy Crisis and Penn Square

The story of how an Oklahoma bank almost destroyed the nation's banking industry is tied to Oklahoma oil and gas, to environmentalists, to OPEC, and to bankers all across the country.

In February 1969, environmentalists raised a tremendous outcry against all oil operations, as a result of an oil well blowout that caused a huge oil slick along the California coastline. The government's reaction was to impose stricter controls and regulations on drilling. The added controls and regulations, coupled with price regulations, kept producers from looking for oil in the United States. American oil companies began buying foreign oil because it was cheaper.

When war erupted between Egypt and Israel in the Middle East on October 7, 1973, OPEC embargoed oil shipments to the United States. The embargo lasted for six months, and the U.S. supply of oil and gas dwindled quickly, causing long lines at gas stations.

In October 1973, war broke out in the Middle East between Egypt and Israel. U.S. support for Israel caused OPEC to cut oil production and to place an embargo on oil to the United States. An **embargo** is an order forbidding trade with a particular country. By the time the embargo was lifted in March 1974, America's supply of oil and gas had dwindled significantly. There were long lines at gas stations, and prices soared. Congress passed a law reducing the speed limit on interstate highways to 55 mph. Yet, because of environmental restrictions, little could be done to search for and erect new oil wells, open up old ones, or increase refinery capacity.

The embargo did have one positive result. The United States began a program to become energy self-sufficient. One aspect of that program was the approval of the trans-Alaskan oil pipeline. Much of the technology to build the Alaska pipeline came from Oklahoma companies and Oklahoma workers.

Oklahoma oil men had always financed their operations through loans from banks in Chicago, Dallas, or Houston because no Oklahoma bank was large enough. In 1976, Billy Paul Jennings purchased Penn Square Bank in Oklahoma City and set about creating a bank to serve the oil and gas industry. From that point, oil men flocked to Penn Square Bank.

In 1977, President Jimmy Carter and Congress established a Department of Energy. Natural gas was **deregulated** as an incentive for new exploration; that is, government rules and restrictions were removed. Increased demand meant higher prices, which made even small wells profitable. Thousands of new wells, oil and gas, were drilled in Oklahoma in 1977-1978, and thousands of people rushed to the Sooner State to work in the oil fields. However, there were not enough refineries to process the oil and gas.

While the oil industry in Oklahoma seemed to be making a comeback, Penn Square Bank was heading into trouble. The bank had made too many loans, putting it beyond its limit. A common occurrence, a bank usually called a larger bank and asked it to buy some of the loans. Penn Square managed to sell its loans to banks in such cities as Seattle, Chicago, and New York. All the while, Penn Square continued to make riskier and riskier loans. People in the oil business believed that the price of oil and gas would continue to go up. But around 1980 Oklahoma's boom turned into a bust; independent producers had pumped so much oil that the prices plunged. The value of Penn Square Bank's loans dropped, making it harder and harder for the bank to even raise the money to pay the interest on its certificates of deposit (CDs).

Billy Paul Jennings purchased Penn Square Bank in order to create a bank to serve the oil and gas industry. The bank approved a number of high-risk, questionable loans. When oil prices dropped, the bank was on the verge of collapse. Depositors who had more money on deposit than that insured by the FDIC are shown above standing in line to try to withdraw their excess funds.

By the time everything began to unravel and the Federal Deposit Insurance Corporation (FDIC) stepped in, Penn Square had sold loan paper to most of the banking community in the United States. The FDIC closed down the bank in the summer of 1982, forcing hundreds of oil and gas companies into bankruptcy.

The Penn Square case changed the way banks are regulated and affected decisions by the savings and loan industry. When many small banks closed, oil and gas companies could not borrow the money they needed to operate. By 1992, drilling in Oklahoma reached an all-time low.

Mining at the End of the Century

In 1989, the U.S. Commerce Department found that the national security of the United States is threatened when 39 percent of the country's oil is imported. By 1993, the United States was importing

The Anadarko Basin is one of the bright spots in the oil and gas industry. With the demand for natural gas increasing and a federal tax credit available to natural gas producers, new wells, such as the one above, are a familiar sight.

nearly 50 percent of the oil needed to run the economy every day. Import levels were at their highest level since the mid-1970s, when Arab oil embargoes created an energy crisis. In February 1994, the United States was importing 8.17 million barrels a day, compared to U.S. production of 6.78 million barrels a day.

Between 1983 and 1993, the U.S. oil industry lost more than 400,000 jobs. Oil prices were at historically low levels. Many domestic producers could no longer afford to operate, and domestic oil production declined to a 35-year low.

What little drilling for oil and gas there was was concentrated in low-risk areas. One area that became important is in Major County near Ames. This is considered a giant oil field, one of fewer than twenty such fields in the state. By early 1994, more than one hundred wells had been drilled in the area, some as deep as 8,000 feet.

Horizontal drilling was instituted to exploit existing reservoirs. With this technique, a well is first drilled vertically from the surface. When the oil-producing rock formation is reached, the well bore is turned horizontal. Horizontal drilling allows the company to recover a greater percentage of the total oil available. Several hundred horizontal wells have been drilled in the state. Many of Oklahoma's oil firms now spend more time in other countries than they do in the United States. Several firms are heavily involved in drilling in the North Sea and Alaska.

Many of the state's refineries shut down in the 1970s and 1980s, particularly those that were older or smaller and could not justify the cost of being brought up to the new environmental standards. The largest refinery in the state is owned by Conoco Inc., in Ponca City. Tulsa's Sun Refinery, the second largest, no longer refines gasoline but only related products such as motor oil, naptha, and paving materials. Other refineries are located at Cyril, Wynnewood, and Ardmore.

One bright spot is natural gas production. While demand for oil has been declining, demand for gas is growing. Drilling goes on in the Anadarko Basin, a result to a great degree of a federal tax credit given to natural gas producers.

About 5 percent of Oklahomans are employed in mining. In 1986, the annual mineral production from Oklahoma was valued at $5.5 billion. In addition to coal, companies in the state mined copper, granite, gypsum, helium, limestone, sand, gravel, and stone. Of lesser value were bentonite, clays, glass sand, lime dolomite, salt, silver, tripoli, and volcanic ash. The soft coal found in Oklahoma cannot be used in the state because of environmental regulations. Any coal burned in Oklahoma must, therefore, be imported from other areas of the country, thus driving up the cost. This has kept coal from being a viable alternative fuel source.

Do You Remember?

1. What did Governor Turner do to increase Oklahoma's economic development?
2. How did agriculture change after 1945?
3. How did imported oil affect the Oklahoma oil industry? How did it affect the Oklahoma economy?

BUSINESS AND INDUSTRY

In the 1950s, the principal industries in the state were refining, aircraft manufacturing, flour milling, meat packing, zinc smelting, and lumber processing. Because of the Douglas plant, Tulsa was able to attract American Airlines' Maintenance & Engineering Center. Governair Corp., which made water-cooled air conditioners before the war, developed giant industrial cooling systems after the war. In 1956, it built the world's first 100-ton-cooling-capacity air-conditioning unit for The Market Place mall in Philadelphia. Other notable Oklahoma businesses of the period included OTASCO, the T.G.&Y. variety store chain, the Humpty Dumpty grocery chain, Fleming Companies (a wholesale grocery firm), Bama Pie Ltd. of Tulsa, Brown Manufacturing Company in Oklahoma City, and O. W. Coburn.

Nevertheless, the state wanted to expand manufacturing and industry to provide a more stable base. The Oklahoma Industrial Finance Authority was formed to issue bonds to local agencies for industrial development.

Since the 1980s, about 14 percent of the total jobs in the state have been in manufacturing. The largest industry is still aviation.

Since the 1980s, about 14 percent of the total number of jobs in the state have been in manufacturing. The Xerox plant (below) outside Oklahoma City is just one of the many facilities operated by international companies in Oklahoma.

*Above: W. H. Braum is a familiar sight to Oklahoma's fast food diners. Fast food businesses are one of the fastest-growing areas of the service sector of our economy. **Opposite page:** One of the highlights of the Anadarko Indian Exposition is the dance competition. These two photographs were taken during one of the competitions. The exposition is held annually at Anadarko.*

Tulsa has a number of sophisticated online information processing facilities. The expertise came from the oil companies and their refinery automation and pipeline metering capabilities. Tulsa is also an important center for seismic data processing.

Oklahoma boasts several international manufacturing operations. Businesses in Oklahoma manufacture automobiles, fishing rods and reels, construction equipment, and freshwater sonar gear. Many smaller companies provide strategic parts to various industries. The first foreign-owned manufacturer to locate in Oklahoma was Hilti, Inc., whose headquarters are in Liechtenstein. The company manufactures products for the construction industry: drills, power tools, fasteners, anchors, electric screwdrivers, and pneumatic fastening tools.

In the 1980s, service industries began to provide most of the new jobs in the state. Several large employers, such as Southwestern Bell Telephone, are in the communications field. However, most of the new service jobs, such as those in fast food businesses, offer low pay and little potential for growth.

Retail businesses (businesses that sell products directly to the consumer) account for about 19 percent of the jobs in the state. Wal-Mart Stores, Inc., is the largest retail operation in Oklahoma.

GOVERNMENT AND THE MILITARY

Government and the military have been major employers in the state since World War I. The largest employer is the Oklahoma City Air Materiel at Tinker Air Force Base, with more than 5,000 employees. The U.S. Air Force maintains Altus Air Force Base, Tinker Air Force Base/Oklahoma City Air Logistics Center, and Vance Air Force Base in Enid. The U.S. Army maintains the U.S. Corps of Engineers at Tulsa, Fort Sill (the U.S. Army Field Artillery Center), and the Ammunition Depot at McAlester. The U.S. Navy maintains two Naval and Marine Corps Reserve Centers in Midwest City and Broken Arrow.

Other large government employers in the state include the University of Oklahoma, Oklahoma State University, the Tulsa Public Schools, and the Oklahoma Department of Human Services.

TOURISM

Until the end of the nineteenth century, Oklahoma was known as Indian Territory. Still the home of more Native Americans than any other state, Oklahoma is rich in the cultural traditions and artistic expressions of sixty-seven tribes. The Five Civilized Tribes Museum in Tahlequah and the Great Plains Museum in Anadarko document Native American life in Oklahoma. The Red Earth Celebration in

Oklahoma City each June has become the largest gathering of Native Americans in the United States.

The Oklahoma government has established a Department of Tourism whose mission is to "sell" Oklahoma as a vacation destination. As a consequence, tourism has become the state's third largest industry. The state's unique history is celebrated in more than three hundred museums and historic sites ranging from art-filled treasures like the Gilcrease and Philbrook museums in Tulsa to the National Cowboy Hall of Fame in Oklahoma City to smaller museums such as the Mabee Gerrer Museum of Art in Shawnee and Price Tower Arts Center in Bartlesville. The Firefighters Museum, Zoo, Softball Hall of Fame, and Omniplex are popular attractions for visitors to Oklahoma City.

The University of Oklahoma in Norman boasts the world's largest university-affiliated natural history museum and the largest history of science collection in the world. The library on the OU campus is the only place in the United States where you can hold Galileo's written words in your own hand.

Oklahoma's rich African-American heritage includes a sound the rest of the nation envied—jazz. Visitors can share in that proud legacy at the Jazz Hall of Fame in Greenwood, near Tulsa, and at Deep Deuce in Oklahoma City.

Tourism has become the state's third largest industry. If you like fire engines, one attraction you will want to visit is the Firefighters' Hall of Fame in Oklahoma City.

Oklahoma's cowboy image is still strong. In fact, Oklahoma has more horses than any other state. Visitors can experience cowboy life in many ways—rodeos, guest ranches, and trail riding. For a slightly different experience, visitors can enjoy the horse racing at Remington Park in Oklahoma City.

Route 66 enthusiasts routinely travel the "mother road" as it makes its way across Oklahoma for over four hundred miles. Neon-lit diners, drive-in theaters, mom-and-pop gas stations, and rustic trading posts lure travelers seeking a taste of nostalgia.

Those who love the outdoors and the beauty of nature will delight in Oklahoma's fifty-one state parks, numerous wildlife refuges, and many recreation areas. Featuring twelve distinct ecosystems, the state's landscapes range from mesas and sand dunes to wetlands and waterfalls, with mountains and prairie in between.

Oklahoma's state parks draw thousands of visitors each year. At Heavener Runestone State Park, you will see this view of Poteau Mountain. You can also see a 12-foot stone with rune carvings.

Do You Remember?
1. For what purpose did the state create the Oklahoma Industrial Finance Authority?
2. What percentage of Oklahomans work for retail businesses?
3. Who is the state's largest employer?

THE OKLAHOMA CITY BOMBING

On April 19, 1995, world attention was suddenly focused on Oklahoma. At 9:02 a.m., an explosion heard and felt for miles shook downtown Oklahoma City. A rented truck, rigged with a powerful fertilizer bomb, exploded outside the Alfred P. Murrah Federal Building in Oklahoma City. One hundred sixty-eight people were killed, nineteen of them children. Two men were later arrested, tried, and convicted in federal court for the worst-ever terrorist attack on U.S. soil. Timothy McVeigh received the death penalty, and Terry Nichols received a life sentence.

The bomb that destroyed the Murrah Building on April 19, 1995, took the lives of over 160 persons. The building was later demolished.

The shock and horror of the bombing has been forever etched in the hearts and minds of many by the photograph of a severely injured small child cradled in the arms of an Oklahoma City firefighter. The Oklahoma City firefighters and the others from around the country who came to help became instant heroes and the symbol of community and team effort.

Amid the devastation and loss, a new image of Oklahomans emerged— that of a caring, heroic people who responded to a crisis with unyielding determination. This show of strength echoed across the land.

In the aftermath of the bombing, Oklahoma City mayor Ron Norick appointed a task force to develop an appropriate memorial to honor those touched by the event. Both survivors and the public expressed a wish that the memorial complex be a place of: remembrance, peace, spirituality and hope, cherished children, comfort, recognition, and learning. The task force chose as their mission statement the following:

> *We come here to remember those who were killed,*
> *Those who survived and those changed forever.*
> *May all who leave here know the impact of violence.*
> *May this memorial offer comfort,*
> *Strength, peace, hope and serenity.*

A crude chain-link fence was erected around the bomb site to protect the crime scene and to prevent accidents and souvenir hunting.

Soon, people gathered at the fence, attaching flowers, teddy bears, toys and other items to honor those who had lost their lives in the bombing. This fence became a shrine where family members, friends, and people from all over the world came to pay tribute to those who had died. A section of that fence has been saved and is part of the Oklahoma City National Memorial, which was dedicated on April 19, 2000, the fifth anniversary of the bombing.

Two gates stand at either end of the memorial. On the eastern gate is carved "9:01," and on the western gate is "9:03." They frame the moment in time when lives changed forever. The site of the Murrah Building is covered with soft green grass. Evergreens stand watch over 168 empty glass chairs, which convey the deep sense of loss of those who died. The chairs are in nine rows, representing the nine floors of the building. The chairs are illuminated at night to represent beacons of hope. The memorial also has a place for the survivors of the attack. The so-called Survivor Tree, which somehow lived through the violence of the moment, stands to the north and commemorates strength and endurance. Cascading terraces under its canopy offer a peaceful setting for thought and contemplation. The empty chairs, the Survivor Tree, and the terraces meet at the reflecting pool, which represents healing.

The members of the honor guard salute the 168 chairs that represent those who died in the 1995 bombing of the Murrah Federal Building in Oklahoma City. Survivors, families of victims, friends, and rescue personnel gathered to officially dedicate the Oklahoma City National Memorial on April 19, 2000.

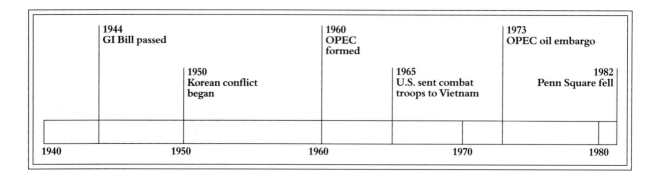

1944 GI Bill passed	**1960** OPEC formed		**1973** OPEC oil embargo
	1950 Korean conflict began	**1965** U.S. sent combat troops to Vietnam	**1982** Penn Square fell

1940 — 1950 — 1960 — 1970 — 1980

At the Same Time

1948   State of Israel founded

1959   Fidel Castro took over Cuba

1961   Berlin Wall built

1963   President Kennedy assassinated; Lyndon Johnson became president

1978   Egypt and Israel signed Camp David Peace Accords

1991   Persian Gulf War; breakup of USSR

Summary

World War II had brought manufacturing, aviation, and the aerospace industry to Oklahoma. When it ended, there was an economic adjustment, and the state looked for new ways to improve the economy. Thousands of military personnel returned and, with the help of the GI Bill, began to buy houses, get an education, and start businesses. This stimulated the economy as houses went up everywhere and the baby boom began.

The cold war with the communists grew warmer with the Korean conflict in the 1950s and the Vietnam war in the 1960s.

Agriculture became more mechanized, and the state's farmers turned to livestock. Oil and gas continued to be important, but foreign oil led to a decrease in domestic production. The state's boom-and-bust cycle unleashed the Penn Square Bank crisis. That failure could have taken down the American banking industry had not the FDIC stepped in to save the correspondent banks. It was a disaster that wiped out thousands of honest investors and bankrupted hundreds of companies across the United States.

Reviewing People, Places, and Things

Define, identify, or explain the importance of the following.

1. communism
2. deregulate
3. embargo
4. inflation
5. nationalize
6. Organization of Petroleum Exporting Countries
7. retail business
8. suburb

Understanding the Facts

1. Why were suburbs created?
2. What new type of housing was developed in Oklahoma?
3. What was the "red scare" of the late 1940s?
4. What event ended the cost war?
5. Name four of Oklahoma's most important agricultural products.
6. What was the significance of the "Seven Sisters"?
7. How did California environmentalists affect Oklahoma's oil industry?

8. America currently uses both imported and domestic oil. Define the two terms.
9. How did the embargo by OPEC nations in 1973 affect the United States?
10. Why was the Penn Square Bank important to the oil industry?
11. What is Oklahoma's largest industry?
12. How does tourism rank among the state's industries?

Developing Critical Thinking

1. Broken Arrow is an example of one of the new suburban areas that developed in Oklahoma during the 1950s. What advantages did suburban living offer? Disadvantages?
2. What does the term *cold war* mean, and how does it apply to the post-World War II years? Why do you think people were so concerned about communism at this time?
3. Compare the energy problems President Carter faced in 1977 with the problems faced by the United States today.

Using Your Skills

1. Oklahoma's population declined from 2,346,000 in 1940 to 2,223,351 in 1950. What was the amount and percentage of decrease?
2. On a world map, identify those countries that are members of OPEC.
3. On a map showing Oklahoma counties, indicate those counties where oil or natural gas are produced.

Special Projects

1. Prepare an economic survey of your community or county. Where are businesses locating: downtown, at shopping centers, along major streets and highways? Where do businesses like motels, grocery stores, restaurants, and discount stores tend to locate?
2. Sonic Industries and McDonald's are both franchises. A *franchise* is a business that has the right to market a company's products or services in a certain area. What are some of the franchises in your area? Find out how franchises work. What do people pay for them? What do they get in return for their investment?

Building Skills: Reading for Details

Reading for details often requires different techniques than reading for an overview or the big picture. To read for details, do the following:

1. Slow down in your reading. Use a ruler or a guide of colored paper or cardboard to help you read line by line, concentrating on a few words at a time.
2. Look for verbal clues. The first sentence usually gives an idea of what the paragraph is about. Details and examples follow this topic sentence. Look for words like *for example, such as,* and *that is.*
3. Look for visual "tricks." Numbers, dashes, and other graphic devices are sometimes used to mark major points or details.

Re-read the section on "The Energy Crisis and Penn Square." Answer the following questions based on the details in this section.

1. When was the OPEC oil embargo lifted?
2. Congress enacted a speed limit on interstate highways in order to conserve gasoline. What was that speed limit?
3. Banks in which three cities purchased loan papers from Penn Square Bank?
4. When did the FDIC close down the Penn Square Bank?

Sooner Trivia

. . . Oklahoma's worst tornado occurred on April 9, 1947. It entered Oklahoma in Ellis County near Shattuck and struck Woodward just before 9 p.m. At Woodward, its path was nearly two miles wide. The tornado stayed on the ground for 221 miles, killing 101 people and injuring 782 in Oklahoma alone. Property damage totaled nearly $10 million.

CHAPTER SEVENTEEN

A CHANGING OKLAHOMA

The clock is ticking fast on America as the last important stronghold of the democratic system. We cannot allow segregation, injustice, and discrimination to weaken it.

—Jake Simmons, president, Oklahoma NAACP

THE CHANGES THAT HAD OCCURRED during the war were permanent changes in the structure of the state and its societies. Since the 1960s, the changes—social, economic, technological, cultural, political—that have affected our lives have seemed to increase at breakneck speed. More people now lived in cities, fewer on farms. Schools and higher education were more important than ever. Technology was changing daily life and entertainment as well the nature of work and the workplace. Sports have become an important part of Oklahomans' lifestyles, both as observers and as participants. The issues the state faced were both old and new. Roads were poor. Housing was inadequate. New jobs were needed, and new training for those jobs. Citizens needed better schools.

Blacks, Indians, and people from other ethnic cultures have worked hard to be able to participate more fully in the American culture. The roles of women in our society have changed greatly since World War II. They too have sought to achieve equal rights.

EDUCATION

Since World War II, progress has been made in improving all levels of education in the state.

PUBLIC SCHOOLS

In the late 1940s, Oklahoma's common (public) school system was barely mediocre. Public school teachers were so poorly paid and conditions were so bad in Oklahoma's rural districts that many teachers left the state immediately after the war. In 1947, there were 4,450 school

The civil rights marches of the 1960s, such as this one in Oklahoma City, were used to get their message of equality across to all Americans.

districts in the state, some so poor that they could stay open only a few months each year.

Because of the growing number of families with young children, however, the amount of money Oklahoma set aside for education steadily began to increase. By 1950, only six other states had more thoroughly trained elementary teachers. And only six states had a greater percentage of the population with high school diplomas.

The state also sought to improve its schools by combining smaller, poorer schools into fewer, larger schools. The issue of **consolidated schools** was hotly debated in the legislature and the towns. No community wanted to lose its school. However, despite the opposition, consolidation passed. The number of districts was cut in half. More funds were available to each school, and more teachers were hired who specialized in one subject, such as art, music, and business. By 1955, there were 1,800 school districts in the state, including 800 high schools, with an enrollment of about half a million students. One other effect of con-

solidation was increased busing: about one third of the entire school population rode buses to school compared to less than one tenth in 1930.

When Raymond Gary of Madill was elected governor in 1954, one of the first challenges he faced was the requirement to integrate the public schools. **Integration** is the process of bringing different groups (races) into society as equals. A U.S. Supreme Court ruling in 1896 had legally established the separate-but-equal concept allowing states to pass laws to segregate public facilities for blacks and whites. In 1954, the Supreme Court ruled (in *Brown v. Board of Education*) that the separate-but-equal concept was unconstitutional. The court reasoned that the fact of segregation created a feeling of inferiority in the minds of black children. Thus, even the best black schools could not be equal to white schools. The ruling meant that schools must integrate.

Integration orders brought violence in other states. But in Oklahoma, Governor Gary gave the school district officials an **ultimatum** (a final statement of terms offered by one party to another): Obey the law or lose state funding. Poteau integrated its classes in 1954, the first Oklahoma school district to do so. By the fall of 1955, 273 school districts followed. But integration did have one adverse effect: When the black schools closed, black teachers lost their jobs. It was several years before the teaching staffs were also integrated.

*Opposite page: The first challenge Raymond Gary faced in 1954 as governor was the requirement to integrate public schools. Although that requirement brought violence in other states, Governor Gary's ultimatum to obey the law or lose state funding resulted in a peaceful integration of Oklahoma's public schools. **Above:** Because of the growing number of families with young children, the state began to set aside increased amounts for education. A kindergarten class, like this one in 1957, might not have been available to Oklahomans a decade earlier.*

In the late 1950s, *Life* magazine wrote a series on the "Crisis in Education." The editors criticized American schools for poor curricula, overcrowded classrooms, poorly paid teachers, and a lack of proper professional attention to important matters. This was a call to arms. Congress passed laws providing funding for vocational-technical schools. Foreign languages were introduced in grade schools. President Lyndon Johnson's "war on poverty" in the early 1960s included such education and training programs as the Job Corps, Neighborhood Youth Corps, VISTA, and preschool Head Start. The state set standards for public libraries and created the Oklahoma Educational Television Association (OETA) to improve educational instruction. An Arts & Humanities Council was established to send artists into rural communities. In 1968, a school improvement program was adopted to bring Oklahoma up to standards.

HIGHER EDUCATION

Integration in Oklahoma schools of higher education actually took place much earlier—in 1946. Ada Lois Sipuel Fisher, a Langston University graduate, applied for admission to the University of Oklahoma Law School. She was turned down because Oklahoma had strict segregation laws and OU staff members and President George L. Cross could have been imprisoned and fined if they admitted her. She appealed the decision, and the U.S. Supreme Court ruled that black university students must be provided the same education privileges as whites. The legislature set up the "Langston University of Law for Negroes" in the state Capitol. Fisher fought that and she was finally admitted to the OU School of Law.

Top: *In 1946, Ada Lois Sipuel Fisher was the first black admitted, under court order, to the OU Law School.* ***Above:*** *George McLaurin was ordered admitted to the OU graduate school in 1948.*

Meanwhile, six blacks were denied enrollment in the University of Oklahoma graduate college. George McLaurin, one of the six, sued in federal court in June 1948. The court ordered McLaurin admitted. McLaurin was seated in a special roped-off area of the classroom and had to eat in a segregated area of the student union. White students ignored the signs and cut the rope barriers in protest.

These two cases were important because they not only brought about the complete desegregation of higher education in Oklahoma, but also institutions across the nation. Thurgood Marshall was the NAACP attorney who represented Fisher and McLaurin before the Supreme Court. He went on to represent Brown in *Brown v. Board of Education of Topeka*, which forced elementary and secondary schools to integrate. Marshall was appointed to U.S. Supreme Court later.

The Oklahoma State System of Higher Education oversees twenty-five colleges and universities and nine related educational agencies.

The two major universities in the state are the University of Oklahoma (OU) at Norman and Oklahoma State University (OSU) at Stillwater. Each school enrolls over 25,000 students. The University of Oklahoma includes a School of Medicine and a School of Law. OSU has a School of Veterinary Medicine, a School of Business Administration, and seventeen regional agricultural stations, making it one of the leading schools in the field of agricultural research.

There are eighteen junior colleges in the state. The largest are Tulsa Community College, Rose State College, and Oklahoma City Community College. The state also has over two dozen vocational-technical districts, which serve one or more counties. There are approximately fifty technical centers offering a wide variety of programs for trade and industrial occupations, technology occupations agricultural occupations, health occupations, legal support occupations, and other occupations that require skills but not college classwork.

A civil rights march in front of the state capitol in the 1960s.

Do You Remember?

1. Why was school consolidation difficult?
2. Why did Ada Lois Sipuel Fisher take Oklahoma to court in 1946?

CIVIL RIGHTS MOVEMENTS

The term **civil rights** refers to the personal liberties guaranteed to the citizens of the United States by the U.S. Constitution. There is no complete list of these rights, but most people include the following: free speech, freedom of religion, the right to own property, the right to a trial by a jury of one's peers (equals), the right to vote, access to jobs, the right to privacy, and the right to travel wherever one wishes inside the country.

The phrase *civil rights movement* is generally used to refer to the struggle for equal rights by blacks. It can also be applied to the struggles by Indians, other ethnic groups, and women.

BLACK AMERICANS

In 1955, in Montgomery, Alabama, a tired Rosa Parks refused to give up her seat on a bus to a white man who was standing. When she was arrested, leading blacks in the city called for a boycott of the city buses. Reverend Martin Luther King, Jr., was a leader of that boycott, which lasted for almost a year. The standoff ended in 1956 when the U.S. Supreme Court ruled that segregation on buses was unconstitutional. That same year, the Oklahoma State Regents for Higher Education directed that the state's schools of higher education be desegregated. At least one school—Oklahoma A&M—had opened its dormitories and cafeterias to blacks the year before.

In the late 1950s, few restaurants in Oklahoma served blacks. If the restaurants did serve them, blacks had to take the food outside. In May 1957, the local chapter of the National Association for the Advancement of Colored People (NAACP) began a campaign to end that injustice. In August 1958, a group of black youths in Oklahoma City staged a sit-in at the lunch counter of Katz Drug Store. A **sit-in** occurs when a group of people enter a public facility and refuse to leave until they are recognized or their demands are met. The demonstration was led by Clara Luper, a schoolteacher. The young people sat at the counter quietly for two days. Finally, the manager ordered waitresses to serve them. The first barrier was broken.

In Oklahoma, blacks split into two groups, almost along age lines. The young people Clara Luper had organized in 1958 marched and held sit-ins all across the

Top: *Clara Luper, a schoolteacher, led a group of black youth who staged a sit-in at the lunch counter of Katz Drug Store in Oklahoma City.* ***Above:*** *Jake Simmons, president of the Oklahoma NAACP, introduces his granddaughter to Hubert H. Humphrey, vice president of the United States.*

state. The second group consisted of older blacks who held positions of power in the state. Jake Simmons, a well-to-do black oil man, convinced most of Muskogee's hotels and restaurants to integrate in 1960 simply by hinting that if they did not, Luper and her "kids" would show up on their doorsteps. That year Simmons was chosen Muskogee's only delegate to the Democratic National Convention in Los Angeles. In 1962, he was named state president of the NAACP.

Simmons believed that integration was an economic issue. "Men must have a chance to work to make a living," he told a *Daily Oklahoman* reporter in 1963, "or they will turn to socialism to answer their needs." He called on blacks to use peaceful demonstrations and all possible legal means to gain their rights. He also lambasted Southern politicians who had "played on prejudice, have played Negro against white. We should get rid of such men now."

In August 1963, more than 200,000 blacks marched on Washington in support of desegregation and equal rights. Among the speakers was Reverend King, who told the audience, "I have a dream that one day this nation will rise up and live out the true meaning of its creed . . . that all men are created equal." Unfortunately, the optimism generated by the march on Washington did not last. Just a few weeks later, in Birmingham, Alabama, four young black girls were killed in a bombing.

President Lyndon Johnson signed the comprehensive **Civil Rights Act of 1964**. The law required any business involved in interstate commerce to open its doors to people of all races. In 1964, the federal government demanded that Oklahoma's election districts be reapportioned (to have the borders redrawn) to ensure black districts. For the first time, blacks in Oklahoma City would be able to elect a black representative. Edward M. Porter, head of Oklahoma City's NAACP, decided to run against F. D. Moon, a black leader of the old guard. Porter had to raise money at cookie sales and other small fund-raisers, but he won.

In the southern United States, there were riots and violence as blacks marched for their rights. There was so much animosity in the South that Reverend King was assassinated in Memphis, Tennessee, on April 4, 1968. Some black leaders began to talk of "black power" to counter Reverend King's nonviolent, civil disobedience approach. The Black Panthers movement used violence to call attention to the problems of urban blacks, particularly in New York and California. Black Muslims adopted Arabic names and called for removing themselves from white society. But men such as Jake Simmons, who constantly trained blacks and helped them find jobs, made the big difference in Oklahoma. Luper, Simmons, Porter, and others like them gave direction to the young people and the civil rights movement in Oklahoma.

In Chapter 14, you read about the 1921 Tulsa race riot. After nearly eighty years, the 2000 Oklahoma State Legislature took steps to make restitution by establishing the Tulsa Race Riot Commission. The commission will put together a historical record of persons who were actual residents of the Greenwood community during the time of the riot and who lost lives or property. The commission will make recommendations about whether reparations should be made. The Tulsa Race Riot Reconciliation Memorial Design Committee will develop and construct a memorial to commemorate the lives of the victims and honor the survivors of the race riot.

Rivals in the 1964 election for the congressional seat for Oklahoma City were Edward Porter (top), head of the city's NAACP, and F. D. Moon (above), a black leader of the old guard

NATIVE AMERICANS

Unrest was growing among young Native Americans in the 1960s. The tribes had been working to restore tribal government since the 1930s. But their efforts were complicated by the Bureau of Indian Affairs (BIA). In 1953, Congress decided that the Indians should be integrated into mainstream society and adopted a resolution to "end [Native Americans'] status as wards of the United States." Over the next thirteen years, Congress ended its relation with more than one hundred tribes. More than 11,000 lost their status as recognized Native Americans. Many were relocated, especially to cities, weakening their ties with their Indian culture and community.

The Indians and their tribal governments were called upon to become self-supporting almost overnight. They were eligible for job training under the 1962 Manpower Development and Training Act, and they could get help starting new businesses under the Economic Opportunity Act, which was expanded to cover Native Americans in 1964. But these programs mainly helped those in urban areas, not in the remote rural areas where so many Oklahoma Indians lived. Young, well-educated Native Americans, such as the members of the National Youth Indian Council, protested the government's termination policy. They claimed that even well-meaning organizations, such as the newly formed Western Plains Indians Arts and Crafts Commission in Anadarko, exploited their arts and crafts at the expense of the people. The U.S. Congress enacted the Indian Civil Rights Act in 1968, giving Native Americans the same rights as other U.S. citizens. Freedom to practice traditional religion was not included, however.

In 1968, the **American Indian Movement** (AIM) was founded in Minneapolis and included Native Americans from tribes throughout the country. AIM was a militant organization that demanded "Red Power," freedom from BIA domination, and a return to traditional Native American culture. In November 1969, a small number of Native Americans seized Alcatraz Island in San Francisco Bay, the site of an abandoned federal prison, in an effort to make Americans aware of the problems faced by Native Americans throughout the country. Among the group was Wilma Mankiller, a Cherokee whose family had been removed from their Oklahoma lands under the government's termination policy. In 1973, AIM members occupied the historic village of Wounded Knee, South Dakota, where U.S. Army troops had massacred three hundred Sioux men, women, and children in 1890.

In 1970, a new era began for the Indian tribes. Since the 1930s, tribal chiefs had been appointed by federal officials. Now, the U.S. government returned to the tribes the right to hold elections and choose their

A small group of Native Americans seized Alcatraz Island in 1969 in an effort to make America aware of the problems faced by Native Americans.

own leaders. Oklahoma had actually set up an Indian Affairs Commission in 1967 to help tribes work together. The federal government also agreed to give tribal governments more authority over funds and schools, to hire Native American teachers in reservation schools, and to restore the teaching of tribal language and culture. The government also agreed to provide loans to attract businesses and jobs. These early years were important to all the tribes. They not only had to forge new constitutions and laws and find new leaders, but they also had to set new goals: to find ways to survive as a nation, to create jobs, and to meet the social needs of the tribal members.

The Cherokee were one of the first tribes to work out political problems and move toward self-support. The Cherokee are the second largest tribe in the United States, outnumbered only by the Navajo in the Southwest. In 1949, William W. Keeler had been appointed to head the Cherokee. When the first election was held in 1971, Keeler was chosen chief, the first chief elected by all the Cherokee people since 1903. In 1975, he was succeeded by Ross O. Swimmer, an attorney and president of First National Bank of Tahlequah.

In 1970, Keeler appointed a committee to draft a new constitution, which was finally approved by the U.S. Department of the Interior and

In a continuing effort to expose the plight of Native Americans, AIM members occupied the historic village of Wounded Knee, South Dakota, in February 1973.

The Creek Council House Museum, located in Okmulgee, houses displays of Creek tribal history. This building was the capitol of the Creek Nation.

ratified by the Cherokee in June 1976. The new constitution established a checks-and-balances government consisting of three branches. A principal chief and a deputy principal chief, elected every four years, are the executive branch. A fifteen-member tribal council acts as the legislative branch. A three-member judicial appeals tribunal serves as the judiciary branch. The constitution promises "speedy and certain remedy" to all Cherokee who suffer wrong or injury and allows all registered Cherokee to vote in tribal elections.

In 1981, Wilma Mankiller was the first woman to be elected deputy chief of the Cherokee. In 1985, Chief Ross Swimmer agreed to head the BIA and serve as Assistant Secretary of the Interior for Indian Affairs. By virtue of the Cherokee constitution, Mankiller became principal chief of the Cherokee and was sworn in December 5, 1985. Wilma Mankiller's work has extended beyond her tribe. She is credited with improvements in employment, education, and health services for Native Americans. In 1993, she was inducted into the National Women's Hall of Fame. In 1998, President Clinton honored her with the Medal of Freedom, the highest honor awarded to a non-military citizen.

As their **autonomy** (self-government) has grown, the tribes have hunted for ways to raise money to support their governments and find ways to create jobs for their citizens. In the urban areas, where jobs already exist, the tribes are involved in job-training programs and education. In the more remote rural areas, they have tried to attract industry. Elk City has attracted a furniture manufacturing facility. Some tribes have built recreation or tourist attractions, ranging from tribal museums to hotels. One revenue-producing business—casinos—has been both controversial and successful. Since the passage of a 1988 federal law allowing Indians to establish casinos on their tribal lands, more than three hundred gaming operations have been set up across the United States under tribal economic development programs. Gambling has become a multibillion-dollar industry. One of the most successful casinos in Oklahoma is Creek Bingo, located on the outskirts of Tulsa.

The tribes have not ignored education. All of the Oklahoma tribes are working with local school systems and the Oklahoma Department of Education to develop **curricula** (specific educational programs) to teach tribal language and culture in schools across the state. The Education Reform and Tax Act of 1990 allows public schools to offer native languages as part of their language provision. Schools offer courses in the Otoe-Jiweda, Creek, Kiowa, and Cherokee languages. Classes in tribal music, songs, dances, rituals, and history are also offered. Tulsa has the largest Indian student population in Oklahoma and the third largest in the nation.

The University of Oklahoma has the nation's most extensive native language program in higher education. It has offered Cherokee, Creek, Choctaw, Kiowa, Lakota, and Comanche. OU is one of the few major institutions of higher learning to accept native language coursework for foreign language requirements. A Native American Studies degree has nine native language options — Modoc, Miami, Ottawa, Quapaw, Seneca-Cayuga, Eastern Shawnee, Wyandotte, and Peoria.

Today there are thirty-seven federally recognized Native American tribes in the state. There are also another thirty tribes that have only a few members. The Indian population in 1990 was over 252,000.

OTHER ETHNIC CULTURES

The rich cultural diversity within the state helps define the social uniqueness of Oklahoma. As the twenty-first century began, the Hispanic population of the state was the fastest-growing ethnic group. The Spanish presence in Oklahoma dates back to Coronado. During the cattle drives of the nineteenth century, many of the cowboys were Mexican. But it was not until the mid-1920s that the Hispanic population in Oklahoma really begin to grow.

Wilma Mankiller became principal chief of the Cherokee in December 1985. She is seen above speaking during the rededication of the Cherokee Capitol Building.

Impoverished conditions in Mexico at the beginning of the twentieth century caused men to cross the border seeking work to support their families. They drifted northward into Oklahoma. Soon, however, they became firmly established as railroaders, miners, packing house workers, and farm laborers. With some semblance of permanency in their work, whole families began to move to the state.

Hispanics too have experienced discrimination in Oklahoma. Opportunities for Hispanics to establish their own institutions and social groups have been hindered in two ways. First, most spoke only Spanish; second, the mobility of their work as laborers prevented home ownership. However, through the efforts of the Catholic Church in Hispanic communities, ethnic solidarity has been strengthened and is commemorated in fiesta celebrations. Today, Hispanics have settled mostly in the urban areas of Oklahoma City and Tulsa. Hispanics are leaders in the business world and in the political arena of Oklahoma. The Hispanic population in Oklahoma in the 1990 census was 86,160.

Before the Vietnam war, there were few Asians who called Oklahoma home. The 1990 census reported 32,000 Asians living in Oklahoma, the larger portion being Vietnamese. The Vietnamese were **refugees**, those who fled from war or political oppression in search of a place of refuge. Coming to the United States was not really the choice of the refugees; its only purpose was survival. The U.S. government set up a sponsorship program that spread the Vietnamese out across the country. The sponsorship program worked well in Oklahoma and especially in Oklahoma City, which has the largest Vietnamese population in the state.

Among the Vietnamese refugees, and the family members who later joined them, were professional people, physicians, and businessman. Faced with a new language, strange food, a very different culture, and the task of finding employment, the Vietnamese accepted the challenge of adjustment. Today, the Vietnamese operate businesses such as restaurants, grocery stores, and cleaning and clothing establishments. Yet, they have not abandoned their cultural ceremonies that honor ancestors and reinforce traditional values.

Many rallies were held for and against the Equal Rights Amendment. It ultimately failed to be ratified by enough states for it to become law.

THE WOMEN'S MOVEMENT

Women took a lesson from the methods used by blacks and Native Americans to gain equal rights. The Civil Rights Act of 1964 also made it illegal to discriminate against women in hiring practices. **Affirmative action** programs increased the number of women and other minorities hired and promoted. But women have rarely been paid the same salaries as men in the same positions. And women have often encountered unfair treatment, discrimination, and harassment on the job.

A national movement began to grow seeking equality for women in the workplace. On a national basis, the best-known women's organization was the National Organization of Women (NOW), which worked for legal and institutional changes to benefit women. The National Women's Political Caucus worked to get more women into political office. These women's organizations supported a drive to add the Equal Rights Amendment (ERA) to the U.S. Constitution in the 1970s. The proposed amendment read "Equality of rights under the law shall not be denied or abridged by the United States or by any state on account of sex."

Rallies were held on local campuses, and the nation's women marched on Washington in 1978 to show their support. Congress passed the amendment and presented it to the states for ratification. Three fourths of the state legislatures (38) had to approve it for the amendment to become law. Almost as many Oklahoma women opposed the ERA as supported it. Opponents argued that equal rights would undermine the family, send women into combat, and require a common restroom for both sexes. Many did not like the tactics of NOW. In the end, Oklahoma did not ratify the ERA, and the amendment failed by three votes.

This did not stop Oklahoma women from going ahead with their lives—whether raising families; working in such traditional roles as teaching, nursing, secretarial, and legal secretarial positions; or working in the professions as lawyers, doctors, scientists, and researchers.

The nation's women marched on Washington in 1978 to show their support for the Equal Rights Amendment

Do You Remember?

1. What did Rosa Parks's actions in Montgomery, Alabama, lead to?
2. What resulted from the 1953 government decision to terminate financial support for the Indian tribes?
3. Why didn't the Equal Rights Amendment become part of the U.S. Constitution?

The last half of the twentieth century brought changes that have affected the daily lives of Oklahomans.

SPORTS

Oklahoma's culture is built on the work ethic, which allows little time for leisure. Sports, however, were readily accepted as leisure activities because they are related to work and exhibit the hard-working spirit that helped Oklahomans settle the frontier.

Rodeo is one of the most popular sports across the state. The rodeo developed during the cattle drive era when the cowboys would gather at end of a trail drive to challenge each other on a variety of skills. The contests provided both relaxation and entertainment. Oklahoma has produced many rodeo champions, including Jim Shoulders of Henryetta, who holds the greatest number of world championships.

Oklahoma's image has been affected by cowboys and Indians, the Dust Bowl, the Great Depression and Okies, and the boom-and-bust economic conditions. State leaders wanted to change that image by using our love of sports. They believed Oklahomans' morale could be raised by college football, specifically the University of Oklahoma Sooners team. This emphasis on football opened doors for high school players by making available to them college scholarships.

Troy Aikman played high school football at Henryetta. He went on to play professional football as a quarterback for the Dallas Cowboys. Troy has not forgotten his hometown, and in 1991 pledged to match any funds raised to build a health and fitness center for the Henryetta schools. Aikman also sponsors a scholarship at his old high school for students who want to attend college but cannot afford it. The Troy Aikman Foundation was established to benefit children's charities. In hospitals in Dallas and Oklahoma City, the Foundation has funded "Aikman's End Zone," an interactive playroom and education center for children who must endure long hospital stays.

Barry Sanders, from a family of eleven children in Wichita, Kansas, attended Oklahoma State University on a football scholarship. Pat Jones, his OSU coach, was greatly impressed by Sanders' rare combination of talent and humility. Sanders has gone on to play professional football for the Detroit Lions and is considered the greatest running back the game has ever had.

Although there are some disputes about the origin of baseball, it has always been considered "America's pastime" and a part of America's culture. In Oklahoma, the game is a common schoolyard game, and

municipalities sponsor youth baseball leagues. Two minor league teams of the Texas Rangers—the RedHawks in Oklahoma City and the Drillers in Tulsa—keep Oklahoma baseball fans singing "Take me out to the ballgame." Many professional baseball players had their start on sandlot, high school, and college teams. One of those players stands out—Mickey Mantle. One of the greatest major league players, Mickey Mantle was born in Spavinaw. His achievements on the baseball diamond were exceeded only by his generosity in establishing the Mickey Mantle Foundation. In cooperation with the New York Health Science Center, the Foundation promotes organ and tissue transplants and donor awareness.

A pitcher and a catcher are among other baseball greats who have made Oklahoma proud. Allie Reynolds, a Creek Indian from Bethany, was known as "Super Chief." He pitched in fifteen World Series games for the New York Yankees. In the seventies, Johnny Bench, a catcher from Binger, hit more home runs than any catcher in major league history.

In 1912, the eyes of the world were turned toward the Olympic Games in Stockholm, Sweden, and especially upon a Native American from Oklahoma. Jim Thorpe, a Sac-and-Fox athlete from Prague, won both the pentathlon and decathlon—a feat that has never been repeated. Many consider him to be the greatest athlete of all time.

Opposite page above: Bud Wilkinson made Oklahoma and football synonymous. In the seventeen years he coached at the University of Oklahoma, his teams won three national championships. **Opposite page below:** *Oklahoman Jim Thorpe, a Sac-and-Fox Indian, was named the world's greatest athlete at the 1912 Summer Olympics.* **Above:** *The National Softball Hall of Fame is located in Oklahoma City.*

It is most appropriate that Oklahomans would enjoy horse racing. The state has two major horse racing facilities: Blue Ribbon Downs in Sallisaw and Remington Park (above) in Oklahoma City.

Oklahomans have continued to be successful in the Olympic games. John Smith of Del City won his second Olympic gold medal in 1992. Having won six world championships, Smith is the most decorated wrestler in American history and may be the greatest American wrestler ever. Oklahoma athletes have also scored big in the field of gymnastics. Bart Conner of Norman is the only American gymnast, male or female, to win gold medals at every level of national and international competition. In 1976, Nadia Comaneci became the first woman to score a perfect 10 on her way to winning three gold medals, one silver medal, and one bronze medal. In 1998, she was selected one of the one hundred most important women of the twentieth century. Although Nadia Comaneci was not an American when she achieved her Olympic feats, she now calls Oklahoma home and proudly represents the state in the gymnastic arena. Edmond's Shannon Miller is the most decorated gymnast in American history. She has seven Olympic medals and nine world championship medals to her credit. In 1996, she led the U. S. Olympic team to a first-ever team gold and was also the first American to take the gold on the balance beam.

Golf as a spectator sport began to command attention in the twentieth century, leading Oklahoma colleges to field teams. Bob Tway of Oklahoma State University was a three-time All-American and member of two national championship teams. He joined the Professional Golf Association in 1981 and has consistently finished on the money list. Dr. Gil Morgan, another of golf's greats, was born in Wewoka and attended college at East Central University in Ada. He has a long list of victories to his credit and recently was among the top three in half of his twenty-five starts on the Senior Tour. Both Tway and Morgan play out of Oak Tree Country Club of Edmond. Oak Tree and Southern Hills Country Club of Tulsa have both hosted the PGA tournament.

Team sports for women are mostly confined to the high school and college levels, but the competition in these areas is strong. Women have excelled in college golf from the beginning; Susan Maxwell Berning playing for Oklahoma University was named national women's open champion three times.

ENTERTAINMENT

After World War II, radio was still the most popular and affordable entertainment. Television, however, was about to make a profound impact on American life. Television had been around before the war, but Oklahoma had no television stations until 1949. That year, both Oklahoma City's WKY and Tulsa's KOTV made their first broadcasts. General manager for KOTV was M. H. (Helen) Alvarez, who built the transmission tower atop the downtown National Bank of Tulsa building before competitors caught on to what was happening. She was the only woman in television management in the country at the time and was very successful. For the first two years, all programming on

In 1949, Oklahoma City's WKY made its first television broadcast. That same year Tulsa's KOTV went on the air and Oklahoma entered the age of television. All programs on the two stations were local and live for the first two years until they joined national networks.

Right: The age of television brought the day's news into living rooms around the nation. Today, satellites make it possible to see the news as it is actually being made. **Below:** One of the most popular TV shows was "I Love Lucy."

Oklahoma stations was local and live; it was not until 1952 that they were able to tie into the national networks.

Television has been a powerful instrument of popular culture. The medium caught on quickly, drawing people away from radio and movies. The earliest programs were old movies, including early cowboy films of Oklahomans Tom Mix, Jimmy Wakely, and Gene Autry. The most popular television shows of the mid-1950s included "I Love Lucy," "Dragnet," and "The Milton Berle Show." The first "Tonight Show" aired in 1953 and changed sleeping habits across the country. By the mid-1950s, 86 percent of families owned a television set and watched 42 hours a week. Children were watching television more hours than they spent in the classroom. Since that time, television has continued to have a major impact on our culture. Cable stations and satellite dishes have dramatically increased the kinds of television programming available.

TECHNOLOGY

The "baby boom" and the housing boom of the 1950s increased the demand for consumer goods. Electric cookers, irons, refrigerators, and freezers were all in demand. The electric washing machine was a real luxury.

The postwar period also brought remarkable technological change. **Technology** is the practical use of scientific knowledge, especially in business and industry. American technology has brought us labor- and time-saving appliances and equipment and helped us explore the outer reaches of space. Some of these accomplishments would not have been possible without the aid of computers.

In 1957, the Soviet Union launched Sputnik, the world's first **satellite** (an artificial object that orbits Earth). The exploit created a tremendous increase in scientific education and led to the so-called space race. Oklahoma businesses, institutions, and people were very involved in the new technology.

The OSU Research Foundation in Stillwater played a leading role in rocketry and upper-air research and was a major contributor to Explorer, the United States's first satellite. University scientists developed instruments to receive information about cosmic rays and micrometeorites. A self-contained, water-moderated nuclear reactor was installed on campus to study the biological effects of radiation. In 1969, the National Science Foundation presented OSU with the Center of Excellence Award, the first time the award had been given to an institution of higher education in mid-America. It was also chosen as the headquarters for the National Aeronautics and Space Administration (NASA) Space Science Education Project.

One of the original seven American astronauts was L. Gordon Cooper, Jr., from Shawnee. In 1963, he was the fourth American in orbit, completing twenty-two orbits around Earth aboard the capsule *Faith 7*. Cooper was also the first astronaut who made a second trip into space. Rockwell International opened in Tulsa with 250 employees, bringing even more space-age technology. At the time, it was the most modern aerospace manufacturing capability in the world. One of every six employees was either a scientist or an engineer. In 1963, North American Aviation, a division of Rockwell, signed a contract with NASA for work with the Apollo space program.

Water

The construction of dams that was begun during World War II continued after the war. The Tenkiller and Fort Gibson dams near Muskogee and the Upper Spavinaw Dam near Grove were among those completed in the early 1950s. In addition to the major lakes created by the new dams, the state built 1,800 small reservoirs and almost 200,000 farm ponds. Oklahoma's ratio of water to land exceeded that of Minnesota.

The dams transformed Oklahoma in three ways. First, they spread electricity to rural Oklahoma. The dams allowed the Southwestern Power Administration to sell power to a dozen rural electric cooperatives. By 1950, nearly 66 percent of Oklahoma farms had electricity, compared to only 4 percent twenty years before. Second, electricity made irrigation practical. In 1950, there were only 35,071 acres of land being irrigated. By the end of the decade, that number had jumped to 197,237 acres. Third, dams led to an entirely new form of recreation

The state of Oklahoma has played a role in America's space exploration. In 1963 Astronaut L. Gordon Cooper (top) from Shamrock was the fourth American to orbit Earth and was the first astronaut to make a second trip into space in 1965. North American Aviation, a division of Rockwell, worked on one Apollo space program (above).

THE NATION'S INLAND WATERWAY

Early settlers who had to struggle up the area's rivers and streams dreamed of an inland waterway that would rrn from the Gulf of Mexico up the Arkansas River. As early as 1909, engineers surveyed the Arkansas River to see whether it could be navigated. There was, they said, some proof that it could be done. Will Rogers quipped that "paving the Arkansas would be cheaper than making it navigable."

Leaders in Fort Smith and Tulsa, however, were determined. When the idea was finally presented to Congress in the 1940s, people called it a pork-barrel project (a project that an elected politician uses to keep people in her or his district happy even though it may have very little real value). Politicians were able to get enough support in 1946 to pass the River and Harbor Act, which authorized the McClellan-Kerr Arkansas River Navigation System project. Actual construction did not begin until 1957, and it took nearly twenty years to finish the project. By the time it was completed, it had cost over $1.32 billion.

It was the largest civil works program ever undertaken by the U.S. Corps of Engineers and one of most challenging engineering feats in history. The project called for a navigation route from the Mississippi River through Arkansas and Oklahoma to Catoosa, just north of Tulsa. On paper, it was almost 450 miles long. The project, which affected twenty-eight counties in Arkansas and Oklahoma, would control flooding, produce electricity, and create lakes for recreation. It included two rivers, eleven lakes, and seventeen locks and dams.

The McClellan-Kerr Arkansas River Navigation System connects 25,000 miles of inland waterways to the ocean. There are five major public ports and more than twenty-five private ports along its banks. Port authorities were established for Muskogee, Sallisaw, and Tulsa-Rogers County. There are river terminals at Fort Smith, Port Carl Albert (Keota), Webbers Falls, Muskogee, Wagoner, and Catoosa.

Will Rogers was correct when he quipped that "paving the Arkansas would be cheaper than making it navigable." The McClellan-Kerr Arkansas River Navigation System cost $1.32 billion to complete. Lock and Dam #15 (above) is located at Cowlington.

In January 1971, the first commercial goods—a bargeload of news-print paper—arrived at the Port of Muskogee. By 1987, over 142 million tons of goods had been shipped on the waterway. Today, barges carry bauxite, lumber, petroleum, coal, chemicals, stone, sand, steel, fertilizer, paper, grain, and other commodities. In terms of flood control, the U.S. Army Corps of Engineers calculated that, by 1987, the system had prevented $1.3 billion in flood damage.

Tornadoes are a part of Oklahoma weather. Technology and better storm-chasing skills are helping to save lives by putting out earlier warnings.

and tourism. Oklahoma began to build parks and recreational areas centered around water.

Weather Watching

In referring to Oklahoma, Will Rogers supposedly said, "If you don't like the weather, wait a minute." All who have spent any time in Oklahoma will attest to the truth of that statement. Weather in Oklahoma is changeable. Weather has always been important to the people of Oklahoma, monopolizing much of our conversation. Whether it is a gully-washer spring rainstorm, a hot sultry summer day, a spectacular winter snowstorm, or an Indian summer fall day, we talk about it. Sometimes the weather can be dangerous.

New technology and storm-chasing skills are helping meteorologists (those who study the weather) save lives. On May 3, 1999, a devastating tornado cut a huge path through south Oklahoma City, while many smaller tornadoes ripped across the state. Hundreds of homes and buildings were destroyed, and forty-four people died. More people would have died had it not been for the best warning system in the world. Norman is home to the National Severe Storms Prediction Center, the National Severe Storms Laboratory, and the National Weather Service's regional forecast center. The services of these agencies are augmented by the major television stations, which have developed multimillion-dollar weather facilities.

Meteorologist Gary England of KWTV in Oklahoma City was responsible for the development of Doppler radar, a sophisticated system that shows storm movements and windshifts that produce tornadoes. Digital storm-tracking photos and computer software help project the path and arrival of severe storms. Destructive tornadoes are a part of Oklahoma's history and future. New technology and dedicated meteorologists will continue to sound the warning signals to save lives.

TRANSPORTATION

After the war, the country faced a transportation revolution, and it was the automobile that most changed society. America's credit system enabled more and more people to buy automobiles. Reliable cars, inexpensive gasoline, and good roads allowed people to **commute** (go to and come from workplaces) from the suburbs. Automobile manufacturers could not keep up with the demand.

There were 7,000 miles of paved roads in the state in 1947, four times as many as twenty years earlier—but still not enough. Because the state could not finance all the roads needed, it created the Oklahoma Turnpike Authority in 1948. A **turnpike** is a pay-as-you-drive system. By 1950, the Turner Turnpike had been financed, but it took three more years to build. Today, there are more than 100,000 miles of paved roads in the state. Oklahoma has several **interstate highways** (limited access highways that extend through more than one state and are therefore part of the federal highway system) that connect various parts of the state.

Oklahoma cities were so spread out that neither bus companies nor interurbans could afford to service suburbs. Residents became more dependent on automobiles, which led to decreased use of buses, which led to increased numbers of cars. Streets grew more crowded, and parking became a problem. Businesses realized that stores needed to be closer to the suburbs, and they began building the first suburban shopping centers. The first shopping center in the state was the elegant Utica Square in Tulsa. This concept changed the way people shopped and the way cities developed. It also contributed to the deterioration of the downtown areas as more stores moved out.

After World War II, larger airplanes were adapted for passenger flight. Douglas Aircraft manufactured the DC-6, which could handle 70 passengers and travel 300 miles an hour carrying cargo. Airports across the state expanded. Tulsa's airport was one of the country's best and largest.

Rail travel all across the country declined as automobiles increased. Fewer passenger trains came through the state; by 1978, railway passenger service had disappeared in Oklahoma. In 1999, passenger service was restored between Oklahoma City and Fort Worth, Texas. The railway industry remained as a freight carrier, with Union Pacific the largest carrier. Trucks, however, have taken over that market.

After World War II, the country faced a transportation crisis. The need for roads outstripped the tax revenues available to build them. The Oklahoma Turnpike Authority was created in 1948 and Turner Turnpike was the first turnpike completed.

Do You Remember?

1. With interest in which sport did Oklahoma leaders hope to raise citizens' morale and self-image?
2. What were the first televisions stations in Oklahoma?
3. What was the world's first satellite, and which country launched it?

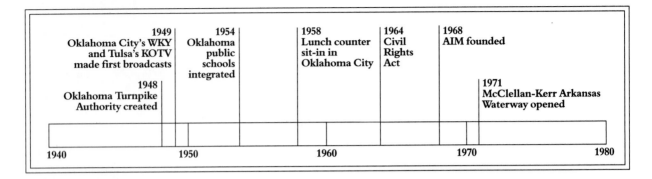

At the Same Time

1947   Jackie Robinson became first black to play major league baseball

1950   FCC authorized color television broadcasting

1959   NASA selected first seven American astronauts

1968   Dr. Martin Luther King, Jr., assassinated

1981   Sandra Day O'Connor first woman appointed to the U.S. Supreme Court

Summary

During the 1960s and 1970s, blacks, Native Americans, and women all demanded equal opportunities and took their cases to the courts and campuses. While great strides have been made by each group, their struggles continue.

At the end of the twentieth century, sports played an increasingly important role in the lives of Oklahoma citizens, and Oklahoma can count numerous Olympic and professional stars among its sons and daughters. Automobiles and television drastically changed the culture, and technology has brought both labor-saving and life-saving devices.

Reviewing People, Places, and Things

Define, identify, or explain the importance of the following.

1. affirmative action
2. American Indian Movement
3. autonomy
4. civil rights
5. Civil Rights Act of 1964
6. commute
7. consolidated school
8. curricula
9. integration
10. interstate highway
11. refugee
12. satellite
13. sit-in
14. technology
15. turnpike
16. ultimatum

Understanding the Facts

1. Why was the Court's decision in *Brown v. Board of Education* important?
2. Why did young people stage a sit-in in Oklahoma City in 1958?
3. What government agency is responsible for working with Native Americans?
4. How many Native American tribes in Oklahoma are recognized by the federal government?
5. What Oklahoma athlete is considered by many to be the greatest athlete of all time?
6. In what three ways did building dams transform Oklahoma?
7. What weather-related agencies are located in Oklahoma?

Developing Critical Thinking

1. How have the attitudes about Indian language and culture changed from the days of Indian boarding schools?
2. Why do you think sports have become so popular in our society in recent years?
3. How did the automobile and television change American life?

Using Your Skills

1. On a map showing Oklahoma's major rivers, identify and highlight the state's major ports.
2. On a map of Oklahoma, locate the dams and manmade lakes in your county or in surrounding counties.

Special Projects

1. Compile a list of the civil rights guaranteed to U.S. citizens by the U.S. Constitution and its Bill of Rights. Article 2 of the Oklahoma constitution is also a bill of rights. How do the two overlap? What are the differences?
2. Get a copy of the Reverend Martin Luther King, Jr.'s "I Have a Dream" speech. With at least one classmate, read Dr. King's speech to your class.
3. Contact a local radio or television station. Find out when the station began operation and what type of programming it broadcasts. How has its programming changed over the years? Why? Share your information with the class.

Building Skills: Detecting Bias

Everyone has certain opinions or ideas about certain topics or subjects. For this reason, written material is not always objective (free from the writer's personal opinions). Even though a writer may try hard to be objective, what he or she writes or says may show *bias,* a highly personal, and sometimes unreasonable, opinion about something or someone. Bias can be either for or against an idea or individual.

To be a good and thoughtful citizen, you need to learn how to detect bias in both written and oral materials and in materials from both the past and the present. Asking the following questions may help you.

- When and why was the material written or the statement made?
- Did the writer or speaker use certain phrases for emotional impact or try to play on your emotions rather than present facts?
- Does the writer or speaker tend to show one group as good and the other group as evil?

Both of the following statements describe the impact of the U.S. Supreme Court's *Brown* decision. Identify any bias you believe exists.

The court had restored to the American people a measure of the humanity that had been drained away in their climb to worldwide supremacy. The Court said, without using the words, that when you stepped on a black man, he hurt. The time had come to stop.

— Richard Kluger, *Simple Justice*

This unwarranted exercise of power by the court, contrary to the Constitution, is creating chaos and confusion in the state principally affected. It is destroying the amicable relations between the white and Negro races that have been created through ninety years of patient effort by the good people of both races. It has planted hatred and suspicion where there had been heretofore friendship and understanding.

— From the "Southern Manifesto"

Sooner Trivia

. . . In 1968, N. Scott Momaday, an Oklahoma Kiowa, received the Pulitzer Prize for his fiction work *House Made of Dawn* and published *The Way to Rainy Mountain*. Both books dealt with Indian traditions and values.

. . . When it was built in 1952, KWTV's broadcasting tower was the tallest manmade structure in the world.

. . . Roger Miller from Erick won five Grammy awards in 1965 for his hit "King of the Road."

CHAPTER EIGHTEEN

CHALLENGES FOR THE TWENTY-FIRST CENTURY

We've always been able to depend on land, oil, and agriculture, but I would like to see us put our security in our real livelihood—our children.

— Alfre Woodard

Today, Tulsa has an abundance of parks and gardens that soften the urban landscape. The area has truly earned the nickname of "Green Country."

A T THE DAWN OF THE TWENTIETH CENTURY, Oklahoma was separated into twin territories—Indian Territory and Oklahoma Territory. Those two territories were united, and Oklahoma became the forty-sixth state of the Union in 1907. The pioneers who defied the emptiness of the prairie to seek a better life brought with them a spirit of determination to succeed that has become a cultural trait. Tested by drought, depression, and destructive tornadoes and challenged by the diversity of cultures, that spirit of determination has remained strong. As the twenty-first century dawns, Oklahoma pioneers are leading the nation in space exploration, medical research, technology, and aviation.

REVITALIZATION OF OUR URBAN LANDSCAPE

Angie Debo, the great Oklahoma author and historian, wrote about Tulsa, "Thus steady, alert and undismayed the city goes out to meet the future, confident that the light that strikes its shining towers still comes from a rising sun." Over the past thirty-five years, the Tulsa Development Authority (TDA) has been busy keeping Tulsa aligned with the future. With its slogan "Helping Tulsa to be a better place to live," the TDA has taken on the task of revitalizing declining areas, encouraging private reinvestment and economic growth through redevelopment and removing blight. **Revitalization** is the process of restoring the livability and economic viability of an area, particularly an inner city area.

A variety of new housing styles and price ranges has brought about dramatic changes in inner city housing. Throughout the year, festivals are held on the Main Mall of Bartlett Square, a TDA contribution to downtown open space and pedestrian-oriented areas. The city's "Paint the Town" program encourages young people to volunteer to paint over graffiti. The citizens of Tulsa have made a determined effort to keep Tulsa among the nation's most beautiful cities.

One of the fastest growing cities in Oklahoma, Edmond has learned to use its greatest asset—people—to plan for its present and its future. Education is the major industry in Edmond. Edmond's good public schools help sell the real estate that keeps Edmond booming. When the time came to plan for the twenty-first century, a committee of community volunteers set in motion a plan to strengthen the character and image of downtown. The Central Edmond Urban Development Board (CEUDB) was charged with creating a pedestrian-friendly downtown. Among other plans are an outdoor festival activity space and connecting open space areas with the city's historic places. The University of Central Oklahoma (UCO), an important part of Edmond's economy, is working to strengthen the connection between the university and downtown. Similar projects are taking place in other Oklahoma cities.

MAIN STREET AMERICA

The small town image is typical Oklahoma. The lifeblood of these communities has always been the agriculture and oil industries. But as these industries fell on hard times, the small towns suffered. In small towns all across the state, retail businesses closed their doors and cafes were boarded up. The Main Street Program of the National Trust for Historic Preservation (NTHP) was designed to help such cities and towns revitalize their downtown or historic areas. Cities and towns taking part in the program receive technical assistance from the NTHP, but the strategy, funding, and organization are all locally provided. Cordell, Cushing, Durant, and Perkins are among those Oklahoma cities and towns participating in the Main Street Program. Those towns are experiencing growth, as well as a renewed confidence in the community and its future.

In 1985, the mayor, city council, Chamber of Commerce president, and other business leaders in Duncan appointed a task force to look into the deterioration of its downtown business area. The area had few business, little traffic, and numerous empty buildings with broken and boarded-up windows. The county's major employer had eliminated 2,500 jobs and transferred hundreds of others, resulting in an exodus of working families. When Oklahoma joined the National Main Street

CHAPTER PREVIEW

Terms: revitalization, distance learning, specialty school, charter school, exports, North American Free Trade Agreement (NAFTA), genome, downsizing

People: Dr. Jordan Tang, Dr. Kenneth Cooper, Dr. Kenneth Copeland

Places: Edmond, Cordell, Durant, Perkins, Duncan, I-35 Corridor

Program, Duncan was the first town to request designation as a Main Street community.

Over eighty buildings in the downtown area have been renovated. The Patterson Hospital building, scheduled for demolition, was renovated and is now on the National Register of Historic Places. The renovation projects have provided jobs for local contractors and craftsmen and boosted Duncan's economy. The Main Street Program has also made it possible for local people to become business owners. Downtown is a major employer, replacing the town's former dependency on oil industry companies. Duncan entered the twenty-first century as a thriving community that is proud of its downtown.

Thanks to the National Main Street Program, Duncan's downtown is once more a thriving area. Its picture-book Main Street is home to antiques, shops, a drugstore with a soda fountain, and the White Horse Inn.

MAPS

After World War II, downtown Oklahoma City begin to deteriorate as retail shops moved out to the new shopping centers. Businesses abandoned the downtown office buildings for the suburbs. Downtown Oklahoma City soon became a mere shell of its former self. In 1993,

Oklahoma City is both cosmopolitan and comfortable. The recent MAPS project has made the city even more tourist-friendly.

the citizens of Oklahoma City approved a temporary one-cent sales tax to fund a program called MAPS, the Metropolitan Area Projects. The MAPS program planned to revitalize the downtown area through a series of projects that would add new buildings and renovate the downtown area. The projects were expected to improve Oklahoma City's economy and quality of life and enable Oklahoma City to compete with other cities for convention and tourism dollars.

As the twenty-first century opened, Oklahoma City was teeming with activity. The Bricktown Canal provides the setting for a leisurely stroll along the Riverwalk or a water taxi cruise. Restaurants and retail businesses are found along its banks. A RedHawks' baseball game can be enjoyed at the Bricktown Ballpark. The Myriad Convention Center has been renovated and expanded to accommodate more conventions. The Civic Center Music Hall has been renovated to attract Broadway-quality programs, and a new multiple-use arena is being constructed. Other MAPS projects include the Metropolitan Library/Learning Center and renovation of the Fairgrounds Complex. The Crystal Bridge and the Oklahoma City National Memorial, although not MAPS projects, also draw residents and tourists into the downtown area. To borrow from the lyrics of an old song about Route 66, "Oklahoma City is mighty pretty."

EDUCATION

As Oklahoma's education system moves into the new century, it continues to be plagued by age-old problems—lack of money, the unequal distribution of students across the districts, and teacher shortages. Math and science teachers are being wooed away from the classrooms by private business, creating critical shortages in these important areas.

Educational leaders across the state are expecting technology to help with these serious problems. In 1995, the state legislature created OneNet, a telecommunications and information network for education and government. The system has the potential to link every school district to the Internet and to video courses. Students and schools can use OneNet for **distance learning**, allowing them to take classes taught by instructors miles away.

Several Oklahoma school districts are establishing **specialty schools**, schools that cater to students interested in a particular subject area. Math, science and technology, and health and research are common specialty schools, while performing arts or foreign language immersion schools are also emerging. The specialty schools have limited enrollment with a strict admission criteria and are more expen-

sive to operate than a regular curriculum school. The Oklahoma Department of Education and the state legislature will have to address this issue for the future of education.

Charter schools are also catching the attention of educators, parents, and business. Charter schools are independent public schools that give parents, businesses, community groups, and others the freedom—and the tax money—to run their own school. The school operates under a charter (or contract) with a sponsoring school district and generally does not have to deal with the bureaucratic and regulatory red tape other public schools do. Oklahoma's first charter school was approved by the Oklahoma City School Board in March 2000.

Kindergarten at age four, year-round school, and standardized testing will all be on the agenda for future discussion. If changes come in the basic formula for public education, however, they will be gradual.

Oklahoma has always been a leader in vocational-technical education. To meet the challenges of the twenty-first century, the fifty-four vocational-technical campuses throughout Oklahoma have become "technology centers." These technology centers, funded mainly by local property taxes, are the economic development arm of the state's public education system.

The Red River Technology Center is one of about fifty vo-tech campuses in the state.

Future needs for technology and research workers are leading the corporate world to become more and more involved in higher education. The private sector ties help pay the bills and provide avenues to the necessary skills for the future. President David Boren of the University of Oklahoma believes education's greatest challenge for this century is to be the connecting link between the cultural values of our society and technology.

Do You Remember?

1. What has been the objective of the TDA?
2. What town in Oklahoma was the first to apply for participation in the Main Street Program?
3. Name two types of specialty schools.

ECONOMY

For much of its history, Oklahoma's economy has been based on two or three industries. In the future, however, the state's economy will become more diverse.

Wheat fields such as this one in Logan County are a familiar sight in the state. Oklahoma is second in the nation in winter wheat production.

AGRICULTURE

Oklahoma is most often thought of as being an agricultural state. Although agriculture is still important to the state, it no longer claims the number one or number two ranking.

Technology and irrigation have helped Oklahoma farmers in their struggle against the unpredictable weather, resulting in a longer growing season with less crop loss. Winter wheat is grown on more acres than any other crop, making Oklahoma second in wheat production in the nation. Approximately 40 percent of all wheat exported comes from Oklahoma. **Exports** are products sent outside the country to sell. The largest shipments of Oklahoma wheat are exported to Russia.

In the Panhandle area of Oklahoma, once wheat and cattle country, a variety of crops are grown to support a large cattle-feeding industry and the expansion in hog production. Oklahoma ranks fourth in the nation in beef cattle production for domestic use.

The number of small farms increased in the late 1990s, as more and more people grew weary of city noises and sought the benefits of a rural lifestyle. The trend of continuing to work in the cities to supplement a rural lifestyle is becoming attractive to more and more Oklahomans.

Technology has also taken the backache out of cotton farming, and Oklahoma's southwest corner offers a warm climate and a long growing season that is favorable for cotton production. The climate of the eastern counties provides a year-round growing season for a wide variety of crops—vegetables, fruits, soybeans, corn, and peanuts. Dairy and poultry production are also important to this region. Poultry is fast becoming a major commodity in Oklahoma's agricultural industry.

Hay and alfalfa were once the state's third most important agricultural product. Hay fields can still be seen in all parts of the state except the Panhandle.

BUSINESS AND INDUSTRY

The **North American Free Trade Agreement** (NAFTA) was passed by the U.S. Congress in November 1993. In June 1995, the Oklahoma legislature signed a resolution allowing Oklahoma to work with other states and the federal government to create an international NAFTA superhighway. The superhighway, now known as the I-35 Corridor, gives Mexican trucks access to the four states that border Mexico and American trucks access to bordering Mexican states. This "high priority corridor" is expected to greatly benefit Oklahoma's economy. However, commuters and those who regularly use I-35 will have to endure heavier traffic as detours and construction get underway for additional lanes and relief routes for the heavy trucks.

In anticipation of the increased traffic and business, cities along the corridor, such as Edmond, are studying how best to take advantage of the international trade route while avoiding environmental blight.

Ordinances to control signage, structure and style of buildings, and the removal of native trees have all been put in place.

Spurred by growth rates in Oklahoma's two largest metropolitan areas—Oklahoma City and Tulsa—the state's economy is on the upswing. In 1998, the Oklahoma Department of Commerce reported the three largest industries in the state to be (1) services, (2) wholesale and retail trade, and (3) finance, insurance, and real estate. This same report stated that Oklahoma had outpaced the nation in manufacturing and business services in the last five years.

Manufacturers and businessmen who are thinking of relocating are attracted by Oklahoma's geographic advantage. The state is equidistant from the two coasts, as well as being at the midpoint of the I-35 Corridor. In 1997, *Financial World* listed Oklahoma as the second lowest cost-of-doing-business state, while a Young & Leventhal study showed Oklahoma City and Tulsa to be the two least expensive housing markets among the seventy-five major areas in the nation. These comparisons are major factors in the ability of the state's Department of Commerce to attract new industries.

Above: In 1993, President Clinton signed the North American Free Trade Agreement, which links Canada, the United States, and Mexico in a "free-trade zone."
Opposite page above: Dr. Jordan Tang has been instrumental in the research on Alzheimer's disease.
Opposite page below: Dr. Kenneth Cooper is a strong proponent of exercise programs. He was the developer of aerobics.

OKLAHOMA AND MEDICAL RESEARCH

Medical research has been referred to as Oklahoma's "hidden treasure." The Oklahoma Medical Research Foundation (OMRF) was chartered in 1946 as a private, nonprofit corporation. That is, it was built and is maintained with no direct funding from local, state, or federal governments. Its mission is biomedical research and training, and its focus on critical areas of research has advanced medical technology in the treatment of cancer, heart disease, diabetes, and lupus among others.

Overweight mice with dirty blonde coats are playing a role in an all-Oklahoma success story. A recent study on human obesity and possible treatments to arrest it was conducted by the OMRF and funded by two Oklahoma corporations.

In 1959, while still a graduate student, Dr. Jordan Tang discovered an important enzyme that set the stage for accomplishments in biomedical research. An announcement was made in February 2000 that Dr. Tang and his team of scientists had positively identified the enzyme that is directly related to Alzheimer's disease. "It is possible that we will soon develop the medical technology to detect Alzheimer's before its onset," Dr. Tang said.

The Oklahoma State University is also busy with research to help people live longer, healthier lives. Researchers studying the human immune system are looking for ways to control AIDS and AIDS virus tuberculosis. As a spin-off of this research, scientists are exploring ways to control the immune system's reaction to organ transplants.

Oklahoma University ranks fourth in the world in total basic sequence human genome projects, and the Oklahoma University Health Science Center is second in micro-genome projects. A **genome** is a complete collection of an organism's genetic material. The human genome is composed of about 50,000-100,000 genes located on the 23 pairs of *chromosomes* in a human cell.

Perhaps the overweight, dirty blonde mice you read about earlier should meet Dr. Kenneth H. Cooper. This Oklahoman can properly be credited for the international fitness craze, because he is the man who invented aerobics. He has made advancements in medical research, including the treadmill stress test to determine heart health and routine early screening for osteoporosis. Dr. Cooper was born and educated in Oklahoma City. He attended public school at Putnam City, and has a degree from the University of Oklahoma. In 2000, Dr. Cooper was named by *Oklahoma Today* magazine as one of "50 Oklahomans of the Century."

Children suffering from juvenile diabetes have new hope from the research conducted at Children's Hospital of Oklahoma. Dr. Kenneth Copeland, director of the hospital's diabetes and endocrinology program, oversees clinical trials to determine the safety and effectiveness of insulin delivered into the lungs of children by an inhaler. If all trials are successful, it would be good news for the 127,000 children with juvenile diabetes who must be injected with insulin up to six times a day.

The I-35 Corridor is expected to put Oklahoma's leadership in research in the national spotlight. The Sooner State's world-class biomedical research centers are located along the I-35 Corridor between Ardmore and Stillwater. One day the area may be as well known for biomedical research as California's Silicon Valley is in the computer world. Medical research is a journey toward a better quality of life for all mankind, and Oklahoma scientists are a dedicated part of that journey.

The military has been a major employer in Oklahoma since World War II. Among the military bases in Oklahoma is Fort Sill near Lawton. The artillery rockets shown above are on display at the fort.

THE ECONOMIC ROLE OF THE MILITARY

Oklahoma will be home to an increasing number of soldiers, pilots, and other military personnel in the twenty-first century. The Pentagon's **downsizing** (reducing the number of personnel or employees) has had the opposite effect on Oklahoma, as each of its four military bases is projected to grow. Tinker Air Force Base will soon be the largest of three air logistics centers in the country. Three major projects in the Fort Sill area will bring much-needed jobs to the region and add millions of dollars to Oklahoma's economy. The construction of a national cemetery at Fort Sill is expected to add a tourist attraction to the area. Vance Air Force Base is one of three Air Force student pilot training bases in the country. It the largest employer in Enid, a city in the northern part of the state. The availability of jobs with commercial airlines is attracting young adults to the Air Force. This trend is expected to continue through the early part of the twenty-first century.

The economic base of southwest Oklahoma is Altus Air Force Base. Half of the population of Altus are military personnel. The military families are involved in the community, thus providing a stable market for retail businesses.

MINING/PETROLEUM/NATURAL GAS

Petroleum and natural gas continue to be important to the economy of the state. Oklahoma, which exports about half of its natural gas, ranks third in the nation in the production of natural gas. But it faces pro-

duction challenges from Louisiana and New Mexico. Oklahoma operators also face greater price fluctuations because many are small independent operators. These independent operators cannot compete with the larger producers from neighboring states.

Oklahoma has endured the boom-and-bust cycle in the petroleum industry for over a hundred years. The decline in the 1990s is probably one that will not turn around anytime soon. However, Oklahoma crude oil production is still important to the nation's energy needs.

Thousands of businesses remain actively involved with the oil business and are proud of their heritage. Through the Oklahoma Energy Resources Board (OERB), the petroleum industry has undertaken the only voluntary environmental cleanup program in the nation. This program not only restores abandoned well sites, but also emphasizes education for future generations about the importance of energy in our lives.

Oil—"black gold"—brought great wealth to Oklahoma. Even today, thousands of businesses across the state are involved in some way with the petroleum industry.

Do You Remember?
1. What is the most important agricultural crop in Oklahoma?
2. What were the three largest industries in the state in 1998?
3. What is the outlook for Oklahoma's four military bases in the twenty-first century?

PRESERVING NATURAL HABITATS

As a result of the combined efforts of many groups, the Illinois River (opposite page) in the northeastern part of the state remains pristine and undammed. The Nongame Wildlife Improvement Program is aimed at preserving nongame species such as the eagle (above).

Oklahoma was one of the first states to become concerned about ecology. As early as 1895, the territorial legislature passed laws to prevent the killing out of wild game and insect-eating birds. In 1909, the second Oklahoma legislature adopted a general game and fish code.

In 1956, a constitutional amendment created the Department of Wildlife Conservation and the Wildlife Conservation Commission. The Wildlife Game Division of Oklahoma's Department of Wildlife Conservation is responsible for watching over the wildlife populations in the state, introducing new species, and restoring depleted populations. The state adopted a comprehensive code on wildlife in 1974. In 1988, the state passed a law providing for fines of up to $20,000 and five years in prison for anyone convicted of disturbing an endangered species.

In 1981, Oklahoma began a Nongame Wildlife Improvement Program, only the eighth state in the country to do so. The legislation is aimed at preserving nongame species—songbirds, eagles, and reptiles. Through this act, urban wildlife programs such as nature trails and nature centers were started. The program is funded by donations.

The Oklahoma Department of Wildlife Conservation's Fisheries Division manages seventeen public fishing lakes, fisheries, and fish hatcheries. About 95 percent of hatchery fish go into public waters; 5 percent goes to stock private ponds. There is also a research laboratory at Norman.

The U.S. Forest Service works to control forest insects and diseases and to make sure the range is not overgrazed. It also works with the state Division of Forestry to control fires. The Oklahoma State Forestry Department educates the public about forest conservation and polices forest areas to keep timberland from being destroyed.

Citizens have also taken on the responsibility of preserving the land. As a result of the combined efforts of many groups, the Illinois River in the northeastern part of the state, the last free-flowing stream in America, remains pristine and undammed. North, in the Osage prairie land, the Nature Conservancy's new Tallgrass Prairie Preserve hopes to recreate the ecosystem that has all but disappeared from the Great Plains.

CHAPTER REVIEW

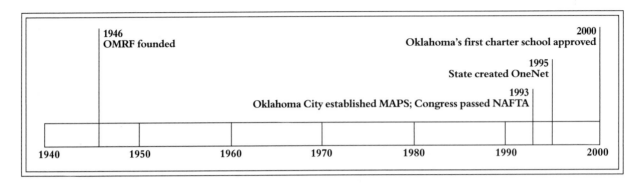

1946
OMRF founded

2000
Oklahoma's first charter school approved

1995
State created OneNet

1993
Oklahoma City established MAPS; Congress passed NAFTA

1940   1950   1960   1970   1980   1990   2000

At the Same Time

1993   World Trade Center bombed

1994   Announcement that President Ronald Reagan has Alzheimer's disease

1995   Trial of O. J. Simpson

1997   Timothy McVeigh and Terry Nichols convicted in Oklahoma City bombing

1998   John Glenn returned to space at age 77

Summary

As the twenty-first century dawned, Oklahoma's economy is experiencing a boom cycle. Cities across the state are rebuilding their downtown and historic areas. The state's educational system is responding to technological changes and exploring new options, such as specialty and charter schools.

Agriculture and oil are still important, but the state's economy is becoming more diverse. The I-35 Corridor, which connects Mexico, the United States, and Canada, promises to play an important role in Oklahoma's economy. Services and whole-sale and retail sales are now the top-ranking industries in the state, while finance, insurance, and real estate are also on the rise. Medical research is becoming an important, new field. The military continues to appreciate Oklahoma's favorable geographical location, as well as the quality of life communities offer military personnel. Downsizing of the military has only helped to increase military presence in the state.

Reviewing People, Places, and Things

Define, identify, or explain the importance of the following.

1. charter school
2. distance learning
3. downsizing
4. exports
5. genome
6. NAFTA
7. revitalization
8. specialty school

Understanding the Facts

1. What happened to small cities and towns in Oklahoma when the oil and agriculture industries fell on hard times?
2. How is the Main Street Program helping Oklahoma's small towns and cities?
3. What is the ultimate objective of the MAPS project?
4. What are three problems that plague Oklahoma's educational system?
5. What is the role of the technology centers in the Oklahoma educational system?
6. How has Oklahoma agriculture diversified?
7. What project has the OERB undertaken?

Developing Critical Thinking

1. Do you think the revitalization of downtown areas should be a tax-supported activity or

should those who own the downtown businesses pay the cost?

2. Do you think specialty and charter schools will be good for education? Are there disadvantages or dangers?

3. Why are some people unhappy about the NAFTA Corridor? Suppose you owned property along the I-35 Corridor. How would you react to a city government's plan that restricted how you could develop that property?

4. Suppose that you are working for Oklahoma's Department of Commerce. How would you "sell" your hometown to a men's clothing factory that was looking to relocate?

Using Your Skills

1. On an Oklahoma map showing county boundaries, locate the cities under "Revitalization of our Urban Landscape."

2. On an Oklahoma map, trace the I-35 Corridor and other highways that intersect the Corridor. Identify your hometown. How many miles is your hometown from the Corridor?

Special Projects

1. You have read of the many achievements the state has made over the last decade. Write a poem, song, essay, or commercial to express pride in Oklahoma's leadership.

2. Interview six friends or classmates. Ask them whether they would like to attend a specialty school or a charter school. Why or why not? Interview six parents and ask them whether they would enroll their children in a specialty school or a charter school. Why or why not? Report your findings to the class.

3. You have read that services are Oklahoma's economic base today. Survey your hometown for help wanted signs and check the local newspaper for jobs in the service area. Based on your findings, write a statement to support the services role in Oklahoma's economy.

Building Skills: Comparing Costs and Benefits

One of the responsibilities state and local governments have assumed is to provide essential services for the people. Examples of these services include education, environmental protection, road construction and repair, and health services. None of these services is, of course, free, and one of the ways to raise revenue to pay for the services is by levying taxes. The property tax and sales tax are two taxes used by state and local governments.

While citizens are usually willing to accept increased services, the decision to raise taxes is often met with a fair amount of resistance. Lawmakers are increasingly being forced to choose between services they can provide with limited revenues. One way to decide is to compare the costs and benefits of each service. Generally, the benefits that a community expects to receive from a particular service should outweigh the costs to provide that service. This is not as easy as it sounds; not all benefits or costs can be measured in monetary terms.

Suppose you are a member of the governing body of your local community. Suppose too that your community provides the following services: police and fire protection; trash removal; schools; public libraries; parks and recreational facilities; road building, maintenance, and repairs; emergency management; licensing and inspection services. For this exercise, assume that the cost of each service is $1,000. Your community expects annual revenues to be $7,000 from the property tax this year. How would you deal with the shortage? you may wish to form a "committee" of several classmates to discuss your options.

Can you think of any services for which you would be willing to pay higher taxes? If so, list them and give your reasons.

Sooner Trivia

. . . Among comprehensive public universities, the University of Oklahoma ranks first in the number of National Merit Scholars.

CHAPTER NINETEEN

INFLUENTIAL OKLAHOMANS

Oklahoma has given me everything. You have seasons in your life.
I'm at the point in my life when I can start giving back to Oklahoma.
— David Boren, President, University of Oklahoma

I N THIS CHAPTER, YOU WILL READ ABOUT
Oklahoma men and women who have made contributions to our state, the nation, and the world. Wherever their field of endeavor has taken them, they are
proud of their Oklahoma heritage. All would agree with
the above quotation that it is important to give back to the
state that has given them so much. As you read about these
people, may their lives serve as the inspiration you need to
achieve your goals.

POLITICS

Like wind, rain, storms, and red dirt, politics is a part of
Oklahoma. It played a role in the government's treaties
with the Indians, in the land runs, and in the quest for statehood. Oklahoma's leadership in the political arena has always
been strong.

Mike Monroney, a native Oklahoman, served in the U.S.
House of Representatives and later in the U.S. Senate. Mike
is known as "Mr. Aviation" because he is largely responsible
for the legislation that created the Federal Aviation Administration. He championed aviation for his home state, playing a major role in bringing Tinker Air Depot to Oklahoma.
As a result of Mike Monroney's influence, aviation is among
the most important industries in the state.

Robert S. (Bob) Kerr was born in a log cabin near Ada and educated
in the public schools and colleges of the state. Kerr became a multi-
millionaire in the oil industry. In 1942, he became the first native Oklahoman to be elected governor. During World War II, he successfully

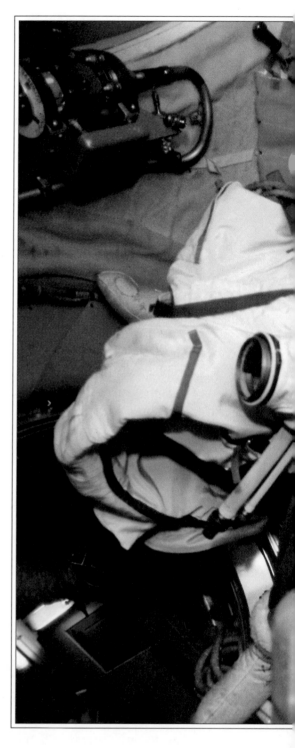

*At one point during the three months
she spent aboard the Russian space
station* Mir, *Shannon Lucid showed
her space suit to viewers.*

Above: A. S. "Mike" Monroney served Oklahoma in Congress from 1939 to 1969. In this photograph, he is seen giving a speech at the National Press Club. *Opposite page:* Bob Kerr was elected to the U.S. Senate after serving as Oklahoma's governor. He was a strong supporter of President Truman and is here seen leaving the White House after a meeting with Truman.

channeled military money into the state and raised his voice in favor of bills to aid Oklahoma farmers. In 1948, he was elected to the U.S. Senate. Kerr had dreams of progress for his state and worked diligently to fulfill those dreams. Often referred to as the "uncrowned king of the Senate," he guided bills through Congress that were important to the nation but that also benefited Oklahoma.

It has been said that Bob Kerr was the finest orator Oklahoma ever produced or the Senate ever heard, and he never failed to take advantage of his ability to charm an audience. In speeches around the state and on the Senate floor, Kerr spoke often about harnessing Oklahoma's natural resources—"land, wood, and water." His plan for making the Arkansas River navigable became a joke to many, but Kerr was not discouraged. The McClellan-Kerr Arkansas River Navigation System, an asset to Oklahoma's economy, is the result of his determined efforts.

"Society has never barred women from bread-winning roles, but only from economic roles that are profitable and respectable." These are the words of the first woman to serve as the U.S. Ambassador to the United

Nations. Born in Duncan, Jeane Kirkpatrick has helped shape U.S. foreign and defense policy for more than twenty years. This Medal of Freedom winner has distinguished herself as a university professor, syndicated columnist, and White House cabinet member. During the cold war years, she stood firmly opposed to communism.

Hannah Atkins would probably agree with Jeane Kirkpatrick about society's assignments for women. She would also probably note that she has encountered not one but two obstacles—one because she is a woman and the other because she is black. Her strength and determination to be who she was at all costs and a desire to be of service to her state and nation have helped Hannah Atkins achieve a number of firsts. She was the first black woman elected to the state legislature. While serving in the Oklahoma legislature, she authored a bill requiring that children have up-to-date immunization records to enroll in school. She also served

Jeane J. Kirkpatrick is a scholar, diplomat, syndicated columnist, author, political scientist, and an expert on international affairs. She has been honored with numerous awards, including the Medal of Freedom and the Distinguished Public Service Award.

as Oklahoma's secretary of state, the highest government office ever held by an African American in the state. She was a U.S. delegate to the thirty-fifth General Assembly of the United Nations.

Perle Mesta, who called Oklahoma City home, held an unusual position of influence in the nation's capital. Dubbed the "hostess with the mostess," this Washington socialite entertained with lavish parties the business and political elite of the world, bringing together prime ministers, presidents, kings, and potentates. From the 1930s to the 1950s, men and women of different cultures, religions, and languages laughed and talked together at a Mesta party. She used her influence to raise funds for Harry Truman's presidential campaign. After his election, he appointed her to the position of first minister to Luxembourg. In this role, she continued to live up to her reputation for entertaining, thus introducing a new diplomatic style. In 1950, Irving Berlin wrote the score for the musical comedy *Call Me Madam* based on her life.

Oklahoma's most distinguished statesman, Carl Albert was born in Bugtussle and went on to Oxford University and the most coveted position in the U.S. House of Representatives. Albert, known affectionately as "the little giant from Little Dixie," served longer in Congress and held more power than any other Oklahoman. As the speaker of the house, Albert presided over the House of Representatives during the Watergate crisis, and for a short time he was directly in line for the presidency.

Albert often spoke of his education in Bugtussle and of the elementary class where he learned that a person with a simple upbringing, such as he, could aspire to Congress. He often paid tribute to his teachers and to public education for providing him the opportunity to succeed. Once a reporter referred to Albert's political power as having roots in an Oxford University education. Albert remarked, "No, Bugtussle." Albert used his power the way he lived—with determination to do good and with the dignity that was his Oklahoma heritage.

African-American J. C. Watts, Jr., often reminds people of his heritage. "I grew up in a poor, black neighborhood on the east side of the railroad tracks." But the Watts family instilled in their children a belief in education and a strong value system. J. C. Watts learned to apply himself in order to succeed in life. While at the University of Oklahoma, he became the quarterback on the Sooners' national championship football team. His leadership on the football field also established him as a role model for young people across the nation. Because of his reputation as an honest, hard-working community leader, he was urged to run for Congress. Watts was first elected in 1994. In 1998, he was elected by his fellow congressmen and women as the chairman of the conference committee. His message to people of all ages is to be responsible, caring members of their communities.

Carl Albert (left) was known as "the little giant from Little Dixie" because his work in Congress outweighed his small stature. He represented the Third District in the U.S. House of Representatives from 1947 to 1976.

Ralph W. Ellison was born in Oklahoma City. He became one of the most influential African-American writers of the twentieth century. In 1953, his novel The Invisible Man *won the National Book Award for fiction.*

Whether they were born and educated in Oklahoma or chose the state later in life, Oklahomans are among those who have accepted the challenge of using the written word to inform and entertain. These writers agree that reading is a skill that opens up the world.

"To discover truth and publish it," was the stated goal of the "first lady of Oklahoma history." Angie Debo came to Oklahoma as a child with her parents in 1899 and endured the sparse lifestyle of the prairie. In Marshall, where she lived, there was no library and few books and magazines. Eager to read and learn, Debo waited for the opening of Marshall's first school. After completing the elementary level, she waited again for a high school to be built. It opened one grade at a time. When Debo finally graduated from high school, she was twenty-three years old. She continued to pursue an education, working as a teacher to earn money for tuition to the University of Oklahoma and later Chicago University.

A doctoral degree did not help Debo find employment during the Great Depression, when jobs were scarce for men and almost nonexistent for women. To occupy her time, she continued her research and writing on a subject with which she had become intrigued—Oklahoma's Five Civilized Tribes. When her research uncovered serious abuse of the Indians by the government, particularly in land dealings, Debo wrote the story in *And Still the Waters Run*. She had difficulty finding a publisher. When the book was finally printed, many newspapers refused to review it, and Oklahoma libraries banned it. Debo continued her research and writing, but it was many years before historians and scholars recognized Angie Debo as the great historian she was. The state of Oklahoma has honored Angie Debo by hanging her portrait in the Capitol rotunda alongside that of Jim Thorpe.

Another greatly respected historian is an Oklahoman whose expertise in black history has brought him many honors. John Hope Franklin was the first African American to serve as president of the American Historical Association. He has taught at some of the nation's most prestigious universities, and in 1997 was inducted into the Oklahoma Hall of Fame.

The parents of Ralph Waldo Ellison left the South to claim the promise of a better life for their children in Oklahoma. The frontier spirit shaped Ellison into one of the most important American writers in the twentieth century. About his Oklahoma background, he said, "In Oklahoma, the atmosphere of the place, there was a sense that you have to determine your own fate, and that you have a chance to do it." Ellison's classic novel *The Invisible Man* is a compelling exploration of the conflict between the freedom promised by the American dream and the reality of the African-American experience. At the dedication of the Ralph W. Ellison Branch Library in Oklahoma City in 1975, Ellison spoke of the sense of possibility that came from Oklahoma and the power of language to make men free.

N. Scott Momaday's Indian storytelling heritage is reflected in his colorful tales, which bring together the traditions of his culture and the modern world. In 1969, his *House Made of Dawn* won the Pulitzer prize for fiction. S. E. (Susan Eloise) Hinton draws upon her experiences growing up in Tulsa to tell her stories for teenage readers. The literary world has given her credit for singularly establishing young adult

As a child, N. Scott Momaday heard many stories of his Kiowa Indian culture from his father and others. As an adult, Momaday has tried to safeguard that oral tradition and other aspects of Indian culture.

literature. Hinton's first book, *The Outsiders*, was published when she was seventeen, and it became an instant hit with teens. She has since written seven novels, and her work continues to be popular with readers.

If asked how to become a successful writer, Billie Letts would answer, "Write what you know." Like Momaday and Hinton, Letts weaves her stories around the strong sense of community that is an Oklahoma trait. Her book *Where the Heart Is* became a best seller immediately after being selected by Oprah Winfrey's Book Club. Letts taught creative writing at Southeastern Oklahoma State in Durant, where she makes her home. She continues to write what she knows—life in small town Oklahoma.

Carolyn Hart, an accomplished master of mystery, is a best-selling novelist who lives in Oklahoma City. She is known for her *Death on Demand* series, and she is also the creator of the highly praised *Henrie O* series. Hart's mysteries have won multiple Agatha, Anthony, and Macavity awards.

JOURNALISM

As a teenager, Paul Harvey hung around radio station KVOO in Tulsa until the station manager finally hired him. Today, he is the most listened-to person on radio, with broadcasts that reach more than 20 million listeners each week.

"And now you know the rest of the story." "Paul Harvey, good day!" Those familiar words are carried over the air waves throughout the day as journalist Paul Harvey comments on current events and historical stories. Harvey, a native of Tulsa, may have the most recognized voice on radio, and he never fails to use its resonance to praise his home state. Another famous voice is that of Walter Cronkite. Early in his career, he lived in Norman and was the radio voice of the University of Oklahoma football team. He was hired by E. K. Gaylord for WKY radio in 1937.

Gaylord came to Oklahoma in 1903 with a determination to own his own newspaper. He not only fulfilled his dream, he shaped the state of Oklahoma while doing it. He was twenty-nine years old when he began publishing *The Daily Oklahoman*. Within a few years, he had developed it into a national media giant. His influence was also felt in the political scene; it was difficult to be elected without a Gaylord endorsement. Gaylord was a pioneer in broadcasting. He was the owner-operator of

WKY Radio and the first to offer television to Oklahoma. Gaylord believed that respect was earned by working up to one's fullest potential. He continued to guide his publishing empire until his death at age 101. The Gaylord Foundation has endowed a scholarship fund for the development of a College of Journalism at the University of Oklahoma.

Although not an Oklahoman, Bill Mauldin is closely associated with Oklahoma's 45th Division, having served with that unit during World War II. He enlisted in the U.S. Army and was sent to Fort Sill in Lawton for infantry training. After his cartooning ability was discovered, he joined the staff of the 45th Infantry Division News. He was shipped overseas and assigned to the Army newspaper *Stars and Stripes*, where he introduced his famous cartoon characters Willie and Joe. Mauldin humorously depicted the horrors of war through the antics of two riflemen of the 45th Division. He won a Pulitzer Prize for his cartoons of battle-weary troops. Mauldin's entire *Willie and Joe* collection is on display at the 45th Division Museum in Oklahoma City.

Left: Bill Mauldin developed his Willie and Joe cartoon characters while serving with Oklahoma's 45th Infantry Division in World War II. *Top:* E. K. Gaylord was a pioneer in communication in Oklahoma. In 1973, he received the Henry G. Bennett Distinguished Service Award. *Above:* Early in his career, legendary broadcaster Walter Cronkite was the radio voice of the OU football team.

LAW

Judge Vicki Miles-LaGrange and Judge Luther Bohanon are probably the state's most influential jurists. Both have contributed solutions to controversial problems in a positive way.

Judge Luther Bohanon was charged with overseeing the integration of the Oklahoma City schools.

The Honorable Vicki Miles-LaGrange, a U.S. district court judge for the Western District of Oklahoma, has a number of "firsts" to her credit. In August 1986, Miles-LaGrange was the first African-American female elected to the Oklahoma State Senate. While in the senate, she was an advocate of issues affecting children, families, law, and justice. She is the first African-American federal judge in the six states (including Oklahoma) that make up the Tenth Circuit. Judge Miles-LaGrange was the first woman to serve as U.S. attorney in Oklahoma and one of the first in the nation. She has also taught and lectured at universities in China.

Judge Bohanon's greatest challenge was in dealing with the integration of the state's public schools, particularly those in Oklahoma City. Faced with a court order and an executive directive, Judge Bohanon ordered implementation of the busing plan that sent thousands of students to schools miles outside their neighborhoods. Unwilling to accept the adjustment necessary to integrate the schools, angry parents and students blamed Bohanon. The judge received death threats, harassing telephone calls, and garbage dumped on his lawn. Many families moved to the suburbs where integration was not a problem. This "white flight" caused overcrowded conditions in the suburban schools and a deterioration of the inner city schools. Judge Bohanon is also credited with revolutionary changes in the state prison system. This too was controversial, but Bohanon held to his convictions and continued to do what the law required. Those who knew him best speak admirably of his convictions whether they agreed with him or not.

SCIENCE AND MEDICINE

The walls of the office reception area of the Renewal Centre in Oklahoma City are covered with large oil paintings. The rugs are of beautifully textured fabric, and the cold drink served while you wait is in a crystal tumbler. Surrounded by softness and beauty, the special clients of Dr. Lori Hansen sometimes feel out of place because their lives have been void of beauty. A former Miss Oklahoma, Lori Hansen is the founder of Face to Face National Domestic Violence Project, a nationwide effort to reconstruct battered women's faces through plastic surgery. Women scarred by cigarette burns or whose noses were broken by fists are recipients of free plastic surgery. Hansen provides her professional skills on a *pro bono* (no charge) basis. She has found that a second healing technique is necessary. Plastic surgery can remove the physical scars, but a sense of self-worth is necessary to restore the motivation for a new life. Hansen has made some of the most famous women in the creative arts beautiful and youthful, but her greatest reward has been those faces that can smile again after years of abuse. Hansen has been named one of the two hundred most influential women in the United States by *Vanity Fair* magazine.

SPACE

Growing up on a poor farm in Maysville, Wiley Post followed his dream to reach the stars. Making his first solo flight in 1926, he continued to test the uncharted heavens, setting a new around-the-world record in 1931. The flight brought Post fame, but not fortune, and encouraged him to plan for greater feats. Setting his sights on altitude flying, he developed a pressurized suit that would allow a pilot to maintain normal atmospheric pressure and oxygen content in the stratosphere. He used the equipment to establish a new altitude record. Post's pressurized suit and helmet and the altitude record were forerunners of space travel.

Astronaut Thomas P. Stafford made his first flight on Gemini VI *in 1965. Ten years later, he was the Apollo commander for a joint space flight during which American astronauts and Soviet cosmonauts met for the first time in space.*

Oklahoma is the only state to have as many as six who have flown in space. L. Gordon Cooper, a Shawnee native, was the first of the distinguished six. In 1963, his *Mercury 9* flight set a world record for time in space. Thomas Stafford, born in Weatherford, was named to the second class of NASA astronauts in 1962. He made four space flights between 1965 and 1975, logging more than twenty-one days in space. As chief of research and development for the U.S. Air Force, Stafford played a key role in the design and implementation of the space shuttle, the world's first reusable spacecraft.

Owen Garriott of Enid was selected as a scientist-astronaut by NASA in 1965. He was the science-pilot for *Skylab 3*, which was the second manned *Skylab* mission. Traveling some 24 million miles, *Skylab 3* set a single mission world record. Garriott was also part of the first international space shuttle crew. William Pogue, who called Okemah home, was one of nineteen astronauts selected by NASA in 1966. He was the pilot of *Skylab 4*, which was the longest manned space flight by U. S. astronauts—1,214 revolutions of Earth. Stuart Roosa attended high school in Claremore and became an astronaut in 1966. He was the command module pilot on the *Apollo 14* mission to the moon January 31-February 9, 1971. Roosa was assigned to the space shuttle program until his retirement in 1976.

Shannon Lucid was born in Shanghai, China, but calls Bethany her home. Selected by NASA in 1978, she was the first female astronaut from Oklahoma. A veteran of five space flights, she spent 223 days in space. She holds the single mission space flight endurance record for service aboard the Russian space station *Mir*, where she performed numerous life science and physical science experiments. Lucid continues to hold the U.S. record for most flight hours in orbit by a woman.

ENTERTAINMENT

Country music is a natural for Oklahoma. The state has produced more influential country music singers, musicians, and songwriters than any other state in the union, including Bob Wills, Gene Autry, Roy Clark, Garth Brooks, Vince Gill, Reba McEntire, Toby Keith, and Brooks and Dunn. The unusual sounds of Kevin Welch and the honky-tonk tunes of Roger Miller have Oklahoma roots. The fiddle, guitar, and banjo all have southern Cajun origin, but the twang in the voice and the story-telling lyrics are pure Oklahoman. Once called hillbilly or honky-tonk music, country music is now big business, and the world has become its stage. Those who pick and sing are now called "artists."

Jazz is also an Oklahoma natural. Both the Greenwood district of Tulsa and the Deep Deuce district in Oklahoma City claim to have perfected this special sound and to have launched jazz artists. Charlie Christian played a special sound on the electric guitar that every jazz

Top: Owen Garriott's first flight into space was the 59-day Skylab 3 *mission. Above: Roger Miller grew up in Erick. He was elected to the Country Music Hall of Fame in 1995.*

guitarist tried to capture. Jazz greats Jimmy Rushing and Cecil McBee found their sound in the Greenwood district.

Grammy award winner Patti Page began her singing career in Tulsa with the country music style; she became the first artist to cross over to popular music. Leona Mitchell, from an Enid family of fifteen children, is one of the world's most requested opera sopranos. Since her Metropolitan Opera debut, she has given voice to a number of Verdi and Puccini heroines. Hanson, a Tulsa-based band, became an instant hit with the teen-age crowd. This group of three brothers began singing their own special brand of rock and roll while in their teen years.

Oklahomans fill the stage and movie and television screens with lead actors and actresses such as Tony Randall, James Garner, Rue McClanahan, Chuck Norris, Dennis Weaver, Alfre Woodard, and Kristen Chenoweth.

Left: Hanson—Tulsa brothers Isaac, Taylor, and Zachary—have received several Grammy nominations. Top: Enid's Leona Mitchell is a frequent performer at New York's Metropolitan Opera. Above: Norman's James Garner first gained attention when he starred in the television series "Maverick."

THE ARTS

Allan Houser's sculpture entitled As Long as the Waters Flow *stands in front of the State Capitol in Oklahoma City. Other sculptures by Houser stand in front of the U.S. Mission to the United Nations and the Russell Senate Office Building in Washington, D.C.*

Native Americans have a great appreciation for the arts. A people whose heritage is an understanding of nature, they translate that feeling into beautiful and unique works of art. The talents of five Anadarko students, known as the Kiowa Five, have given their name to a distinct style in painting. The artists' culture and history are dramatically incorporated in bright color and symbolism. The Kiowa Five were the first Native American artists to receive international recognition.

One of the most recognized Native American artists is Jerome Tiger. His rendition of the Trail of Tears is a familiar painting to Oklahomans. Unfortunately, this great talent was cut short by his death at the age of twenty-six.

A twenty-foot mural in the rotunda of the Capitol in Oklahoma City honors five Native American dancers for their graceful style as ballerinas. Yvonne Chouteau, Rosella Hightower, Moscelyne Larkin, Maria Tallchief, and Marjorie Tallchief have been honored as a group, as well as individually, for their talents. In 1997, Governor Frank Keating named the five women "Oklahoma Treasures."

On the front steps of the Oklahoma State Capitol stands a sculpture titled *As Long as the Waters Flow,* a remembrance of the government's promise to the Indians when they came to live in Oklahoma. This sculpture is the work of Allan Houser, a Chiricahua Apache. Houser was acclaimed one of the twentieth century's most important sculptors. His murals decorate the hallways and board rooms of both private and government buildings. In 1992, President Bush awarded Houser the National Medal of Arts.

MILITARY

Oklahomans have distinguished themselves in military service, ranging from the actions of an entire unit, such as the 45th Division in World War II, to the individual heroism of Robert Risner, a Vietnam prisoner of war. Born in Indian Territory, Patrick Jay Hurley began his military service in World War I. He was appointed secretary of war by President Hoover and served in that post for four years. At the onset of World War II, Hurley was promoted to brigadier general and assigned to the Far East. In that capacity, he relieved the beleaguered U.S. forces pinned down on the island of Bataan. Later, he served as a personal representative in various diplomatic roles. He was the first foreigner to visit Russia's Eastern Front. As U.S. Ambassador to China, he tried vigorously to reconcile nationalism and communism.

The nation's largest air depot bears the name of a soldier-airman who brought credit to his forebears, his state, and his nation. Clarence L. Tinker was born in Indian Territory of Osage Indian heritage. In 1908, Tinker began a long and distinguished military career finally reaching the rank of major general. In 1920, he joined the Air Force and was a pioneer of aviation in the military. In the early days of World War II, Tinker and his crew of ten were lost in action near Midway Island in the Pacific while leading a bombing mission against Japan.

William J. Crowe grew up in Oklahoma City and attended Classen High School, where he was president of his senior class. He attended the University of Oklahoma before receiving an appointment to the U.S. Naval Academy. He eventually achieved the rank of admiral, and in 1985 President Reagan named him to head the Joint Chiefs of Staff. Crowe became the first Oklahoman to reach the highest office in the armed services. Respected as an intellectual, he used his persuasive

Tinker Air Force Base was named in honor of Major General Clarence L. Tinker of Pawhuska. Tinker died early in World War II while leading an air strike against Japanese forces on Wake Island.

Admiral William J. Crowe is well known for his hat collection. You can see his collection at the Kirkpatrick Science and Air Space Museum at the Omniplex in Oklahoma City.

ability to mesh the armed forces into a unified force. Crowe retired in 1989, but in 1994 he became the U.S. Ambassador to the United Kingdom. He also headed the review board that investigated the Embassy bombings in Africa in 1998.

EDUCATION

Dr. Henry Bennett became president of Oklahoma Agricultural and Mechanical College (OAMC) in 1928 and immediately set into motion his vision of a university that would be an international force in agricultural research. He implemented a program to provide technical assistance to underdeveloped countries. Today, OAMC is Oklahoma State University (OSU) and a leader in agriculture and animal research, a credit to Dr. Bennett's vision.

A graduate of OSU, Wellston native Francis Tuttle is considered an international expert in the field of vocational-technical education. As director of the Oklahoma area vo-tech school system in Stillwater, Tuttle brought international attention to the state through his innovative ideas. Tuttle believed that industry and education are economically related and that the success of both required a positive and productive relationship. Oklahoma's decision to follow Tuttle's recommendation to build a system of vocational-technical schools has placed the state in a leadership role. Strategically located across the state, the vo-tech schools produce highly qualified technicians, a fact that encourages businesses and industries to locate here.

OIL MEN

There is something about gaining wealth from the depths of Oklahoma's soil that creates a philanthropic spirit. Four of Oklahoma's most successful and respected oil men are known for this "give back" attitude.

Dean A. McGee is referred to in the oil industry as the "geological genius of the Oklahoma oil fields." But McGee is also known for his generosity. McGee was the primary contributor to the Dean A. McGee Eye Institute, which is one of only seven such special eye research and examination clinics in the nation. McGee listed his personal involvement in the organization of the Oklahoma Health Science Center and Foundation as the achievement of which he was most proud. McGee's stature as a builder and leader is evident in downtown Oklahoma City; an office building, a park plaza, and a major street bear his name. Civic leaders credit McGee's generosity and talent for the beautiful Myriad Gardens, a showplace of Oklahoma City.

John Kirkpatrick's name also adorns Oklahoma City landmarks. Kirkpatrick was a decorated naval officer in World War II and founded Kirkpatrick Oil upon his return from duty. He credits Oklahoma oil and his own business acumen for his being able to help others. Kirkpatrick worked to bring science, medical research, arts, and education to Oklahoma City. Considered one of the nation's most generous philanthropists, Kirkpatrick channeled funds into a broad spectrum of projects through two family foundations and one community foundation.

Lloyd Noble founded the Noble Drilling Company, one of the state's premier oil companies. Lloyd Noble expressed his belief in people by creating one of the first employee profit-sharing plans in the oil industry. Across the state, the Noble family is remembered more for what they gave than for the fortune they made. Two buildings on the University of Oklahoma campus bear the Noble name: the Lloyd Noble

John E. Kirkpatrick's generosity and civic involvement have earned him a well-deserved spot in the Oklahoma Hall of Fame. In 1992, he received the Henry G. Bennett Distinguished Service Award.

Sports Complex and the Sam Noble Oklahoma Museum of Natural History. The Noble Foundation, established in the Depression Era to help destitute farmers, is now a multimillion-dollar institution and has grown to include medical research, education, and the arts.

"It's my aim always to leave something more beautiful than I found it," was the stated purpose of oil baron Thomas Gilcrease. Because his mother was of Creek ancestry, Gilcrease asked for and obtained his allotment of 160 acres when the federal government forced the Indians to give up their tribal lands. Gilcrease's land became part of one of Oklahoma's important oil fields. By age twenty-one, Gilcrease was a millionaire. It was then that he decided that man must leave "tracks" for others. To honor his Indian heritage, Gilcrease amassed a collection of art and objects depicting American Indian life and the development of the West. The Gilcrease Museum in Tulsa is the result of the "tracks" of this generous man.

TRANSPORTATION

Whether by airway or highway, Oklahomans have been influential in setting the standards. Cyrus Avery believed that safe roads and good water were the most important things in the world. He did not think he could do anything about the water, but as state highway commissioner in Tulsa he felt it was his responsibility to provide safe roads. He sketched out a plan for a major highway that would run across the heart of the United States from Chicago, Illinois, to Santa Monica, California. He took special care to make sure the highway went through Oklahoma in such a way as to be economically productive. Cyrus Avery's vision became Route 66, often called the "Mother Road or "the Main Street of America."

Paul and T. E. (Tom) Braniff turned a passion for airplanes into a business. In the late 1920s, the Braniff brothers organized an airline in Oklahoma City that shuttled oil men between Oklahoma City and Tulsa. It later became the thirteenth largest airline in the world. Along the way, these two entrepreneurs introduced the

use of flight attendants to the commercial airline industry. Paul and Tom Braniff were inducted into the Oklahoma Aviation and Space Hall of Fame in 1992

RETAIL BUSINESS

Reading through this chapter, you will notice a common thread—a firm belief in the work ethic. The belief that hard work is character-building defines C. R. Anthony, who was known to have worked sixteen hours a day, seven days a week until his death at age ninety-one. Undaunted by a childhood of poverty and orphaned at age twelve, Anthony set his sights on becoming a merchant. He opened his first store in Cushing in 1922. He continued to seek out small towns throughout Oklahoma to expand his business, which he called, "the friendliest store in town." To his creed of hard work, Anthony added civic duty, giving dollars as well as service.

Opposite page above: *Cyrus Avery of Tulsa has been called the "Father of Route 66."* **Opposite page below:** *Paul Braniff (right) treats his father T. A. Braniff to his first airplane ride in 1930.* **Above:** *Tom Braniff, see here in 1935 with an early Braniff plane, saw his airline grow from three employees to more than 4,000.*

APPENDIX A

OKLAHOMA COUNTIES

County	County Seat	1990 Population
Adair	Stilwell	18,421
Alfalfa	Cherokee	6,416
Atoka	Atoka	12,778
Beaver	Beaver	6,023
Beckham	Sayre	18,812
Blaine	Watonga	11,470
Bryan	Durant	32,089
Caddo	Anadarko	29,550
Canadian	El Reno	74,409
Carter	Ardmore	42,919
Cherokee	Tahlequah	34,049
Choctaw	Hugo	15,302
Cimarron	Boise City	3,301
Cleveland	Norman	174,253
Coal	Coalgate	5,780
Comanche	Lawton	111,486
Cotton	Walters	6,651
Craig	Vinita	14,104
Creek	Sapulpa	60,915
Custer	Arapaho	26,897
Delaware	Jay	28,070
Dewey	Taloga	5,551
Ellis	Arnett	4,497
Garfield	Enid	56,735
Garvin	Pauls Valley	26,605

OKLAHOMA COUNTIES

Marshall	Madill	33,433
Mayes	Pryor	16,779
McClain	Purcell	8,055
McCurtain	Idabel	10,829
McIntosh	Eufaula	33,366
Murray	Sulphur	12,042
Muskogee	Muskogee	68,078
Noble	Perry	11,045
Nowata	Nowata	9,992
Okfuskee	Okemah	11,551
Oklahoma	Oklahoma City	599,611
Okmulgee	Okmulgee	36,490
Osage	Pawhuska	41,645
Ottawa	Miami	30,561
Pawnee	Pawnee	15,575
Payne	Stillwater	61,507
Pittsburg	McAlester	40,581
Pontotoc	Ada	34,119
Pottawatomie	Shawnee	58,760
Pushmataha	Antlers	10,997
Roger Mills	Cheyenne	4,147
Rogers	Claremore	55,170
Seminole	Wewoka	25,412
Sequoyah	Sallisaw	33,828
Stephens	Duncan	42,299
Texas	Guymon	16,419
Tillman	Frederick	10,384
Tulsa	Tulsa	503,341
Wagoner	Wagoner	47,883
Washington	Bartlesville	48,066
Washita	Cordell	11,441
Woods	Alva	9,103
Woodward	Woodward	18,976

OKLAHOMA STATE SYMBOLS

Animal
BISON

Insect
HONEYBEE

State Fish
WHITE BASS

Bird
SCISSOR-TAILED
FLYCATCHER

Motto
LABOR OMNIA VINCIT
("Labor Conquers All Things")

Rock
BARITE ROSE
(ROSE ROCK)

Colors
GREEN AND WHITE

Musical instrument
FIDDLE

Soil
PORT SILT LOAM

Flower
MISTLETOE

Nickname
SOONER STATE

Song
"OKLAHOMA"

Grass
INDIANGRASS

Poem
"HOWDY FOLKS"

Tree
REDBUD

Monument
GOLDEN DRILLER, TULSA

Reptile
MOUNTAIN
BOOMER LIZARD

Waltz
"OKLAHOMA WIND"

OKLAHOMA INDIAN TRIBES

	Tribal Headquarters
Absentee Shawnee Tribe	Shawnee
Apache Tribe	Anadarko
Caddo Tribe	Binger
Cherokee Nation	Tahlequah
Cherokee-Shawnee Tribe	Tulsa
Cheyenne-Arapaho Tribe	Concho
Chickasaw Nation	Ada
Choctaw Nation	Durant
Citizen Band of Potawatomi	Shawnee
Comanche Tribe	Lawton
Creek Nation	Okmulgee
Delaware Tribe of Eastern Oklahoma	Bartlesville
Delaware Tribe of Western Oklahoma	Anadarko
Eastern Shawnee Tribe	Miami
Fort Sill Apache Tribe	Apache
Iowa Tribe of Oklahoma	Perkins

Kaw Tribe of Oklahoma .... Kaw City

Kickapoo Tribe .... McLoud

Kiowa Tribe .... Carnegie

Loyal Shawnee Tribe .... White Oak

Miami Tribe .... Miami

Modoc Tribe .... Miami

Osage Tribe .... Pawhuska

Otoe-Missouria Tribe .... Red Rock

Ottawa Tribe .... Miami

Pawnee Tribe .... Pawnee

Peoria Tribe .... Miami

Ponca Tribe .... Ponca City

Quapaw Tribe .... Quapaw

Sac & Fox Nation .... Stroud

Seminole Nation .... Wewoka

Seneca-Cayuga Tribe .... Miami

Tonkawa Tribe .... Tonkawa

United Keetoowah Band of Cherokee .... Tahlequah

Wichita Tribe .... Anadarko

Wyandott Tribe .... Wyandotte

Yuchi Tribe .... Okmulgee

Bureau of Indian Affairs .... Anadarko and Muskogee

APPENDIX D

GOVERNORS OF OKLAHOMA

Governors of Oklahoma Territory

Governor	Party	Term
George W. Steele	Republican	1890-1891
Abraham J. Seay	Republican	1891-1893
William C. Renfrow	Democrat	1893-1897
Cassius M. Barnes	Republican	1897-1901
William M. Jenkins	Republican	1901
Thompson B. Ferguson	Republican	1901-1906
Frank Frantz	Republican	1906-1907

Governors of the State of Oklahoma

Governor	Party	Term
Charles N. Haskell	Democrat	1907-1911
Lee Cruce	Democrat	1911-1915
Robert L. Williams	Democrat	1915-1919
James B. A. Robertson	Democrat	1919-1923

John C. Walton	Democrat	1923
Martin Edwin Trapp	Democrat	1923-1927
Henry S. Johnston	Democrat	1927-1929
William J. Holloway	Democrat	1929-1931
William H. Murray	Democrat	1931-1935
Ernest W. Marland	Democrat	1935-1939
Leon C. Phillips	Democrat	1939-1943
Robert S. Kerr	Democrat	1943-1947
Roy J. Turner	Democrat	1947-1951
Johnston Murray	Democrat	1951-1955
Raymond Gary	Democrat	1955-1959
H. Howard Edmondson	Democrat	1959-1963
George P. Nigh	Democrat	1963
Henry Louis Bellmon	Republican	1963-1967
Dewey Bartlett	Republican	1967-1971
David Hall	Democrat	1971-1975
David L. Boren	Democrat	1975-1979
George P. Nigh	Democrat	1979-1987
Henry Louis Bellmon	Republican	1987-1991
David Walters	Democrat	1991-1995
Frank Keating	Republican	1995-

APPENDIX E

OKLAHOMA STATE GOVERNMENT

Oklahoma's state government is composed of three branches: (1) the legislative branch, (2) the executive branch, and (3) the judicial branch.

THE LEGISLATIVE BRANCH

The Oklahoma Legislature is responsible for enacting, amending, and repealing laws for the state. The Legislature has two houses: (1) the state senate and (2) the house of representatives. The Legislature meets annually in a regular session that may be no longer than ninety legislative days. Extraordinary sessions may be called by the governor or by the Legislature itself.

State senators and representatives are elected by the voters in elections held in November of even-numbered years. State senators serve four-year terms and representatives serve two-year terms.

The state senate has 54 members. To be elected, a senator must be a registered voter and a resident of the district for at least six months. The lieutenant governor presides over and serves as president of the state senate. One senator is chosen by the senators to serve as president pro tempore. The president pro tempore (or "pro tem") presides over the state senate if the lieutenant governor is absent.

The house of representatives has 101 members. To be elected, a representative must also be a registered voter and a resident of the district for at least six months. The speaker of the house is elected by the representatives and presides over the house.

Each house of the Legislature has various committees that deal with special topics, such as agricul-

ture, appropriations, business and labor, criminal jurisprudence, county and municipal government, economic development, education, finance, general government, government operations and agency oversight, human resources, insurance, judiciary, natural resources, rules, standards and ethics, tourism, transportation, and wildlife.

HOW A BILL BECOMES LAW

A bill (a proposed law) may be introduced in either house of the Legislature. Once introduced, the bill follows the same procedure in either house.

After it is prepared by the bill drafting department, the bill is introduced by being read (first reading) in the house of origin. The following day, the bill is assigned to the appropriate committee in the house of origin (second reading) for study. Any changes made by the committee must be included when the bill is sent back to the house of origin. There it is read (third reading), discussed, and voted upon by the complete house of origin. The bill is then printed with any changes made by the house of origin and sent to the other house of the Legislature. There the bill follows the same procedure.

If the other house makes any changes in the bill, it must go back to and be voted upon by the house of origin. If agreed to by the house of origin, the bill is printed in its final form and considered for passage (fourth reading) and sent to the governor for his consideration.

If the two houses cannot agree with the changes made in the bill, the bill is sent to a *conference committee*. There the senators and representatives work out the differences between the two versions. The new version is sent back to both houses for another vote. The conference committee report goes first to the house of origin and then to the other house for consideration.

THE EXECUTIVE BRANCH

The governor represents Oklahoma as its chief executive. To be elected, the governor must be at least thirty-one years of age and a qualified voter for at least ten years. An elected governor can serve two consecutive terms only. The governor's powers and responsibilities include: (1) executing and enforcing all state laws; (2) appointing people to government jobs; (3) calling special sessions of the Legislature; (4) approving or vetoing laws passed by the Legislature; and (5) carrying out other duties such as issuing executive orders, calling out the National Guard, and granting pardons and reprieves to criminals.

The governor is assisted by a number of officials in the executive branch. The lieutenant governor is president of the state senate and the acting governor when the governor is absent. If, for any reason, the governor leaves office, the lieutenant governor becomes governor for the remainder of the term. Like the governor, the lieutenant governor must be at least thirty-one years of age and a qualified voter for at least ten years.

The state auditor/inspector makes sure that state funds are spent according to state regulations. The attorney general serves as the state's lawyer. The state treasurer receives state revenues and pays the state's bills. The superintendent of public instruction oversees the state's public school system. The insurance commissioner is responsible for enforcing any laws related to insurance. The secretary of state is in charge of all official state papers and records, including the laws passed by the Legislature. (The secretary of state is appointed by the governor, not elected.) Three corporation commissioners regulate all corporations including public service corporations (utilities).

THE JUDICIAL BRANCH

The third branch of state government is the judicial branch. The Oklahoma state supreme court is the highest court in the state and reviews civil cases appealed to it from the lower courts. (To *appeal* means to take a case to a higher court for rehearing.) There are nine justices on the court. The governor, with the assistance of a judicial nominating commission, appoints those justices. After serving one year, the justices must be elected to six-year terms at the next general election.

Oklahoma has another court of last resort--the court of criminal appeals, which has exclusive appellate jurisdiction in criminal cases. There are five appeals court districts and one judge is elected from each district. The judges review cases as a panel.

The court of appeals is an intermediate court. It has twelve judges (two judges from each of six districts) and decides civil appeals assigned to it by the state supreme court.

The court of general jurisdiction in Oklahoma is the district court. It has unlimited original jurisdiction over all matters. Oklahoma is divided into twenty-six district court districts and over two hundred judges serve in the district courts. Statewide, the district court caseload is very large.

There are other courts with limited jurisdictions (areas of responsibility): the workers' compensation court, the court of tax review, and the municipal courts. Workers' compensation court hears claims brought by employees against employers for work-related injuries. The court on tax review hears protests concerning tax levies. Municipal courts handle only violations of municipal ordinances and regulations. A court on the judiciary was created by a constitutional amendment in 1966 and has exclusive jurisdiction to remove or force the retirement of judges.

GLOSSARY

A

abolitionist (8) one who wished to end slavery

absentee owner (13) a property owner who does not live on or actively manage property

academy (10) an educational institution beyond a neighborhood school; similar to a high school of today

affirmative action (17) programs designed to increase the number of women and other minorities hired and promoted in the workplace

agriculture (2) farming

allotment (7) a specified portion, as of land

American Indian Movement (17) founded in 1968, a militant organization of Native Americans from tribes throughout the country that demanded "red power," freedom from BIA domination, and a return to traditional Native American culture

ancestors (2) people from whom one is descended

ancestral lands (5) lands that had belonged to the families, tribes, or ancestors of the Indians

annuity (8) an annual payment of dividends or an allowance

arbitration (9) a method of settling disputes where both parties agree to abide by the decision made by an impartial third person

Arbuckle Mountains (1) a geographical region of the state south of the Sandstone Hills and north of the Red River Plains

archaeologist (2) a scientist who studies what is left behind by ancient peoples

aristocracy (3) the ruling class

armistice (13) a temporary stop to fighting

arsonist (10) one who sets fires

artifacts (2) pieces of stone, bone, pottery, and tools left behind by ancient peoples

atlatl (2) a simple shaft or handle with weights used to throw spears or darts with more force

autonomy (17) self-government

B

barter (2) to trade one item for another

bicameral (12) two-house, as a legislature

boarding house (10) a business that provides a room and meals for lodgers

boll weevil (12) an insect that attacks the boll of the cotton plant where the fibers are formed

boomer (11) one who took part in the land "booms" of the late 1800s, when western land was opened to settlers

boycott (4) to refuse to buy something

butte (7) a hill that rises unexpectedly above the surrounding area; has sloping sides and a flat top

C

cede (4) to surrender

charter (12) official permission to operate, given to a corporation by the state

charter school (18) an independent public school that operates under a charter with a sponsoring school district and generally does not have to deal with bureaucratic and regulatory red tape other public schools do

civil rights (17) the personal liberties guaranteed to the citizens of the United States by the U.S. Constitution

Civil Rights Act of 1964 (17) federal legislation that required businesses involved in interstate commerce to open their doors to people of all races

climate (1) the average weather of a region over a period of time

coalition (13) an alliance

colony (3) a group of people who settle in a distant land but who are still under the rule of their native land

communism (16) a political system in which the community (as represented by the Communist party) owns and controls all property and means of production

commute (17) to go to and come from the workplace

Compromise of 1850 (8) a proposal introduced in Congress by Henry Clay of Kentucky by which California was admitted as a free state, part of Texas was given to New Mexico, the slave trade was banned in the District of Columbia, the fugitive slave law was strengthened, and the issue of whether slavery would be permitted in New Mexico and Utah would be determined by popular sovereignty

computer (16) a machine that can receive, store, and process information quickly and accurately

Confederate States of America (8) the name of the government formed by the southern states that seceded from the Union in the early 1860s

confederation (4) a group united by a common cause

conquistadores (3) the Spanish conquerors of the New World

consolidated school (17) a school formed by combining several smaller schools

constitution (12) a document that sets out the rules under which a government (or some other organization) will operate

consumer goods (15) goods for family or personal use

cooperative (14) an organization owned by and operated for those using its services

corporation (12) a company formed by a group of investors that has a life of its own, apart from its founders

credit (15) the ability to buy goods now and pay for the items over a period of time

credit union (15) a cooperative that promotes savings among its members and makes loans to members at low rates of interest

curriculum (17) a specific educational program

Curtis Act (10) a federal law passed in 1897 that voided all leases of Indian land, provided for the surveying and incorporating of towns in Indian Territory, gave townspeople the right to vote, set up free public schools, regulated mineral leases, and abolished tribal governments

D

Dawes Severalty Act (10) a federal law passed in 1887 that dissolved tribal ownership of land and that gave an allotment of land to families and individuals

denomination (6) a religious group, such as Methodist, Baptist, or Presbyterian

depression (5) a severe, continued decline in the economy

deregulate (16) to remove government rules and restrictions from an industry

dictator (15) a ruler with complete control

disfranchise (13) to take the right to vote away from an individual or group

dissent (13) disagreement or opposition

distance learning (18) taking classes taught by instructors miles away

downsizing (18) Reducing the number of personnel or employees

draft (13) compulsory enrollment for military service

drought (1) a long period without rainfall

drover (9) a driver of livestock

dugout (9) a house built of stone half in the ground and half above with a dirt floor and a sod roof

E

economist (15) a specialist who studies the economy

elevation (1) the height of the land above sea level

Emancipation Proclamation (8) the 1863 proclamation by which President Abraham Lincoln freed the slaves in the Confederate states

embargo (16) an order stopping all trade with a particular country

emissary (4) an agent sent to represent or advance the interests of another

entourage (3) a group of attendants and followers

entrepreneur (11) one who assumes the risks and starts a new business

environment (1) surroundings

erosion (1) the process of wearing away the surface of Earth by wind or water

evolution (14) the theory that man evolved, or developed, from earlier, simpler life forms

expedition (3) a journey for a specific purpose, such as exploration

exports (18) products sent outside the country to sell

F

fauna (1) animals

Federal Deposit Insurance Corporation (15) FDIC: a federal government program to insure depositors' accounts in banks

ferry (6) a large boat designed to carry passengers, goods, or vehicles across a body of water such as a river

financier (3) one who provides the funds for an undertaking

Five Civilized Tribes (4) a reference to the Cherokee, Choctaw, Chickasaw, Creek, and Seminole tribes

flora (1) plants

free state (8) a state that did not permit slavery

frontier (4) a region just beyond or at the edge of settled areas

fundamentalist (14) a Christian who believes that the Bible is the source of all religious authority, that the Genesis story of creation is true, and that man was the last and highest living being created

G

genome (18) a complete collection of an organism's genetic material

governor (12) the chief executive officer of a state

grandfather clause (12) a clause that, to register to vote, required a person to prove he could read and write parts of the state constitution and was a descendant of persons who were eligible to vote on January 1, 1866; this clause virtually denied blacks the right to vote

gristmill (6) a mill to grind grains such as corn

Gypsum Hills (1) a geographical region of the state west of the Red Bed Plains

H

haberdashery (10) a store selling clothing and small goods

High Plains (1) a geographical region of the state that includes the Panhandle and the land along the western border

Homestead Act (9) a federal law passed in 1862 that enabled citizens to acquire up to 160 acres of public land by occupying it for five years and paying $1.25 an acre

I

immunity (3) natural resistance to disease

impeachment (13) the act of charging a public official with wrongdoing while that person is still in office

indentured servant (4) a person who agreed to work for someone for a period of time (usually 4-7 years) in return for passage to the New World

Indian Removal Act (5) law passed by Congress in 1830 requiring that all Native Americans living east of the Mississippi River be removed to lands west of the Mississippi River

inflation (16) an economic situation that occurs when the money supply increases rapidly and there are not enough goods and services on which to spend it; leads to higher prices

infrastructure (15) basic facilities, equipment, and services

integration (17) the process of bring different groups (races) into society as equals

international trade (15) trade between countries

interstate highway (17) a limited access highway that extends through more than one state and is therefore part of the federal highway system

interurban (12) a short railroad or electric trolley that ran within a region

J

jerky (2) dried meat

Jim Crow law (11) a law limiting the rights of black citizens

junior college (14) a school that offers the first two years of college work

K

keelboat (7) a riverboat with a keel, or strong piece of wood or metal that runs along the bottom of the boat

Ku Klux Klan (12) a secret, racist organization that sought to keep political power in the hands of whites by using violence and intimidation against blacks

L

labor union (10) an organization of workers formed to improve wages, benefits, and working conditions for the workers

latitude (1) the distance north or south of the equator

lighthorseman (4) an Indian policeman

livestock (4) cattle and hogs

longitude (1) the distance east or west of the prime meridian in Greenwich, England

lottery (11) a contest whose winner is chosen by a drawing

M

maize (2) corn

martial law (14) a temporary imposition of military rule when civilian authority breaks down

merger (12) a union of two or more businesses to form one larger, more powerful company

middleman (3) a trader who buys goods from producers and sells them to other traders or consumers

missionary (6) one who is sent to do religious or charitable work in another territory or country

Missouri Compromise (8) the 1820 agreement by Congress that Missouri would enter the Union as a slave state and Maine as a free state and slavery would not be allowed in any states formed north of a line even with Missouri's southern border

monarch (3) a king or queen

monopoly (4) exclusive control over the buying or selling of a particular product

moratorium (15) a temporary delay of any action or business

myth (14) a popular belief or tradition that has grown up around someone or something

N

nationalism (9) pride in one's country

nationalize (16) to be taken over by the government

negotiations (5) the process of coming to terms over differences

neutral (13) not taking sides in a disagreement

New Deal (15) the name given to the series of laws passed during President Franklin D. Roosevelt's terms that were intended to deal with the conditions caused by the Great Depression

nomad (2) a wanderer

normal school (11) a teacher training institution

North American Free Trade Agreement (18) NAFTA; a trade agreement among Mexico, the United States, and Canada that calls for the gradual removal of tariffs and other trade barriers on most goods produced and sold in North America

Northwest Passage (3) an all-water route to Asia explorers thought existed through the North American continent

O

ordinance (13) a law passed by a local (city or town) government

Organic Act (11) federal legislation signed into

law on May 2, 1890, creating Oklahoma Territory from western Indian Territory and the so-called Territory of Cimarron (No Man's Land)

Organization of Petroleum Exporting Countries (16) a organization of oil-exporting nations formed to stabilize and control the price of oil

Ouachita Mountains (1) a geographical region in the southeast portion of the state

Ozark Plateau (1) a geographical region in the northeast corner of the state

P

Pacific Railroad Act (9) a federal law passed in 1862 authorizing the construction of a transcontinental railroad

pack train (7) a line of animals loaded with goods or supplies

patent (4) an exclusive right to something

pemmican (2) dried meat mixed with berries and fat

pirogue (1) a hollowed-out log used as a boat

plantation (6) a large estate or farm

plateau (1) a high area with some level areas

polygamy (2) the practice of having more than one wife

popular sovereignty (8) a vote on an issue, such as slavery, by those living in the territory

Prairie Plains (1) a geographical region of the state to the west of the Ozark Plateau

prehistoric culture (2) a group or community that existed before recorded (written) history

price supports (15) guaranteed higher prices for crops

profit (7) the amount earned on a business undertaking after deducting expenses

progressive movement (12) a political and social movement whose members believed that government was best equipped to correct the ills of society and who worked to (1) fight poverty and improve the living conditions of citizens, (2) break up large corporations and regulate business, and (3) increase voters' influence in government

prohibition (12) forbidding by law the making or selling of alcoholic beverages

Q

quarantine (13) a restriction of people's movements in order to prevent the spread of a contagious disease

R

railhead (9) a town to which farmers and ranchers could bring their goods to be shipped by rail

Red Bed Plains (1) a geographical region in the middle of the state running north to south

Red River Plains (1) a geographical region of the state along the Red River below the Ouachita Mountains

referendum (12) a vote of the people on a particular law before it can be put into effect

refugee (17) one who flees her or his homeland because of war or political oppression

regimen (6) a system of procedures

renegade (9) an outlaw

repeal (4) to cancel, as a law

retail business (16) a business that sells products directly to the consumer

revitalization (18) the process of restoring the livability and economic viability of an area, particularly an inner city area

rhetoric (10) public speaking

rider (11) an addition to legislation

royalty (10) a payment for the right to exploit a natural resource

rural (1) country area

S

Sandstone Hills (1) a geographical area of the state west of the Prairie Plains

satellite (17) an artifical object that orbits Earth

secede (8) to break away or withdraw from the Union

sectionalism (1) an allegiance to local interests

segregation (11) separation of the races

shaman (2) a keeper of knowledge who passed down the history and beliefs of the Indians by spoken word; also called a medicine man or woman

sit-in (17) a demonstration whereby a group of people enter a public facility and refuse to leave until they are recognized or their demands are met

slave (4) a person bound to a lifetime of service to others

slave state (8) a state that permitted slavery

Social Security Act (15) federal legislation passed in 1935 to provide retirement benefits to covered workers and financial aid to children, the blind, widows with small children, and the elderly

sooner (11) a person who crossed the starting line of a land run before the appointed time

spa (10) a health resort

specialty school (18) a school that caters to students interested in a particular subject area, such as math, science and technology, and health and research

speculator (13) one who buys items (such as land) hoping that they will increase in value and, when sold, provide a profit

squatter (11) one who settles on unoccupied land in order to gain the title to it

states' rights (8) the principle that the rights and responsibilities of the states should take precedence over the rights and responsibilities of the federal government

stock market (15) a place where the stock (shares of ownership) of corporations is bought and sold

strip mine (12) an open mine where the top layers of soil are removed to expose the shallow veins of minerals, usually coal

suburb (16) a residential area outside city limits

suffrage (12) the right to vote

T

tariff (11) a tax on goods

technology (17) the practical use of scientific knowledge, especially in business and industry

temperance (6) the antiliquor movement

tenant farmer (10) a farmer who was responsible for clearing the land and planting crops but who did not own the land being farmed

topography (1) physical features of the land such as mountains or plateaus

tornado (1) a severe windstorm whose winds can reach speeds of up to 500 miles an hour; characterized by a funnel-shaped cloud

totem (2) an animal or bird whose spirit guided the Indians

transcontinental railroad (7) a railroad crossing the continent, connecting both coasts

treaty (4) a formal agreement between two or more nations

tribe (2) a group of people who share a common ancestry

tributary (1) a stream or river that flows into a larger river

turnpike (17) a pay-as-you-drive highway system

U

ultimatum (17) a final statement of terms offered by one party to another

underground railroad (8) a network of houses and other places used to help slaves escape to the North or to Canada

W

washout (1) a place where soft soils have been eroded

Wichita Mountains (1) a geographical region of the state in the middle of the southern portion of the Red Bed Plains

wildcatter (13) a person who drills for oil in a doubtful or untapped area

worker's compensation (13) government insurance for accidental death or injury in the workplace

writ of habeas corpus (9) a court order releasing a prisoner who is being unlawfully detained

INDEX

The purpose of the index is to help you locate information quickly. The index contains references to not only text, but also illustrations and maps. A page number with **m** before it indicates a map; a page number with a **p** before it indicates a photograph or painting.

ACKNOWLEDGMENTS

PICTURE CREDITS: The following abbreviations are used for the sources from which several illustrations were obtained.

    OHS — Oklahoma Historical Society

    NMAA/AR — National Museum of American Art/
      Art Resources

    LC — Library of Congress

FRONT MATTER: Cover Robin McDonald (statue), Bruce Roberts (sunset). Back cover inset Robin McDonald. i Bruce Roberts. ii-iii NMAA/AR. iv-v (both) Robin McDonald. vii Robin McDonald. viii (both) Robin McDonald. ix (both) Robin McDonald. **UNIT I:** x -1 Cheryl Roberts. **CHAPTER ONE:** 2 Robin McDonald. 3 Robin McDonald. 7 Robin McDonald. 8-9 Robin McDonald. 9 Robin McDonald. 10 David G. Fitzgerald. 11 David G. Fitzgerald. 12 David G. Fitzgerald. 13 David G. Fitzgerald. 14 Robin McDonald. 14-15 Robin McDonald. 16 David G. Fitzgerald. 17 David G. Fitzgerald. 18 OHS. 19 David G. Fitzgerald 21 (both) Robin McDonald. 22 Robin McDonald. 24 OHS. 25 (both) OHS. 26 Robin McDonald. 27 Robin McDonald. **CHAPTER TWO:** 30-31 NMAA/AR. 32 Patrick Brady. 33 Red Mountain Museum. 34 Oklahoma Archaeological Society. 35 (above) Oklahoma Archaeological Society, (below) Red Mountain Museum. 36 Oklahoma Archaeological Society. 37 (all) Oklahoma Archaeological Society. 38 (top left) Robin McDonald, (center left, above left, right) Oklahoma State Museum of History. 39 (both) Robin McDonald. 40-41 NMAA/AR. 42 Robin McDonald. 43 Robin McDonald. 44 Robin McDonald. 45 Robin McDonald. 46 Robin McDonald. 47 Robin McDonald. 48 NMAA/AR. 49 NMAA/AR. 50 Robin McDonald. 51 Robin McDonald. **CHAPTER THREE:** 54 (above) LC, (right) U.S. Naval Academy Museum. 55 LC. 57 (left) Robin McDonald, (below) Corbis/Bettmann. 58 LC. 59 (right) LC, (below) Corbis/Bettmann. 60 University of Alabama Special Collections. 61 University of Alabama Special Collections. 62 (above) Corbis/Bettmann, (right) LC. 63 University of Alabama Special Collections. 64 LC. 65 Joslyn Art Museum, Omaha. 66-67 NMAA/AR. 68 North Carolina Department of Archives and History. 69 OHS. 7 **UNIT II:** 72-73

NMAA/AR **CHAPTER FOUR:** 74 Corbis/Bettmann. 75 LC. 77 North Carolina Department of Archives and History. 78 (both) LC. 79 Corbis/Bettmann. 80 LC. 81 OHS. 82 LC. 83 U.S. Capitol. 84 LC. 85 LC. 86 OHS. 87 OHS. 88 OHS. 89 (all) Robin McDonald. 90 Robin McDonald. 91 Robin McDonald. 92 OHS. 92-93 93 (above) Birmingham Public Library, . 94 OHS. 95 Birmingham Public Library. **CHAPTER FIVE:** 98-99 Oklahoma State Museum of History. 101 (both) Robin McDonald. 102 Fort Smith National Historic Park. 103 National Portrait Gallery. 104 Georgia State Archives. 105 Alabama Department of Archives and History. 106 Woolaroc Museum, Bartlesville. 108 Brooks Art Gallery, Memphis. 109 Philbrook Museum of Art, Tulsa. 110 OHS. 111 LC. 112 OHS. 113 Robin McDonald. 114 OHS. 115 (above left) Charleston Museum, Charleston, S.C., (above left) OHS. 116 OHS. 117 OHS. **CHAPTER SIX:** 120-121 NMAA/AR. 123 (both) OHS. 124 (both) Robin McDonald. 125 OHS. 126 (both) Robin McDonald. 127 Robin McDonald. 128 (both) OHS. 129 (above left) Robin McDonald, (above) OHS. 130 (both) OHS. 131 (both) OHS. 132 OHS. 133 OHS. 134 OHS. 135 Robin McDonald. 136 (both) OHS. 137 OHS. 138 OHS. 139 OHS. 140 OHS. **UNIT III:** 142-143 NMAA/AR. **CHAPTER SEVEN:** 144-145 Public Domain. 146 Missouri Historical Society. 147 (top) OHS, (above) Robin McDonald. 148 Filson Club, Louisville, KY. 149 Public Domain. 150 *The Prairie Traveler.* 151 (both) *The Prairie Traveler.* 152 LC. 153 LC. 154 (both) OHS. 155 (all) OHS. 156 Harper's. 157 Robin McDonald. **CHAPTER EIGHT:** 160-161 Kurz and Allison. 163 Corbis/Bettmann. 164 LC. 165 Harper's. 166 (both) OHS. 167 OHS. 168 (both) Harper's. 169 *Battles and Leaders of the Civil War.* 170 OHS. 171 Harper's. 173 OHS. 174 OHS. 175 OHS. **UNIT IV:** 178-179 OHS. **CHAPTER NINE:** 180-181 Thomas Gilcrease Museum of American Art and History, Tulsa. 182 Smithsonian Institution. 183 LC. 184 National Archives. 185 OHS. 186 Smithsonian Institution. 187 Robin McDonald. 188 (both) OHS. 189 OHS. 190 National Archives. 191 National Portrait Gallery. 192 OHS. 193 LC. 194 (both) LC. 194-195 LC. 196 OHS. 197 OHS. 198 OHS. 199 OHS. 200 OHS. 201 OHS. **CHAPTER TEN:** 204-205 Robin McDonald. 207 OHS. 208 OHS.

209 (below) OHS, (bottom) Henry E. Huntington Library and Gallery. 210 OHS. 211 (left) Robin McDonald, (above) OHS. 212 OHS. 213 OHS. 214 OHS. 215 OHS. 216 (both) OHS. 217 (top) Robin McDonald, (above) OHS. 218 Robin McDonald. 219 Robin McDonald. 220 OHS. 221 (both) OHS. 222 (both) OHS. 223 OHS. **CHAPTER ELEVEN:** 226-227 OHS. 228 OHS 229 (both) OHS. 230 OHS. 231 OHS. 232 OHS. 232-233 OHS 233 OHS. 234 (both) OHS. 234-235 OHS. 236 (both) OHS. 237 (both) OHS. 238 OHS. 239 OHS. 240 (both) OHS. 241 (both) OHS. 242 (top) OHS, (above) Currie Ballard 243 (top) Currie Ballard , (above) OHS. 244 (both) OHS 245 OHS **CHAPTER TWELVE:** 248-249 OHS. 250 OHS. 251 OHS. 252 OHS. 253 OHS. 254 OHS. 255 OHS. 256 OHS. 257 (both) OHS. 258 (both) OHS 259 (both) OHS. 260- 261 OHS. 262 LC. 263 OHS. 264 OHS. 265 OHS. 266 Robin McDonald. 266-267 OHS. 268 OHS. 269 OHS. 270 OHS. 271 (both) OHS. **UNIT V:** 274-275 OHS. **CHAPTER THIRTEEN:** 276-277 OHS. 279 (both) OHS. 280 OHS. 281 OHS. 282 OHS. 283 Currie Ballard. 284 Currie Ballard. 285 OHS. 286 OHS. 287 (top) OHS, (above) LC. 288 (both) OHS. 289 OHS 290 (both) National Archives. 291 (top) Robin McDonald, (above) OHS. **CHAPTER FOURTEEN:** 294-295 OHS. 297 (both) OHS. 298 OHS. 299 OHS. 300 OHS. 301 OHS. 302 OHS. 303 OHS. 304 OHS. 305 OHS. 306 (above) Corbis/ Bettmann, (right) OHS. 307 (top) LC, (above) Currie Ballard. 308 OHS. 309 OHS. 310 (both) OHS. 311 (both) OHS. **CHAPTER FIFTEEN:** 314-315 OHS. 317 LC. 318 OHS. 319 OHS. 320 Atlanta Historical Society. 321 LC. 322 (both) Oklahoma State Museum of History. 323 Oklahoma State Museum of History. 324 (both) LC. 325 (both) LC. 326 Corbis/Bettmann 326-327 OHS. 327 OHS. 328 (both) OHS. 329 Currie Ballard. 330 (above) LC, (right) National Archives. 331 National Archives. 332 (top) National Archives, (above) LC. 333 (both) OHS. 334 (both) LC. 335 (top) National Archives, (above) USAF Museum. **UNIT VI:** 338-339 Robin McDonald. **CHAPTER SIXTEEN:** 340-341 OHS. 342 LC. 343 Corbis/Bettmann. 344 LC. 345 OHS. 346 Robin McDonald. 347 Robin McDonald. 348 Corbis/Bettmann. 349 Corbis/Bettmann. 350 Robin McDonald. 351 Robin McDonald. 352 Robin McDonald. 353 (both) Cheryl Roberts. 354 Robin McDonald. 355 Robin McDonald. 356 Corbis/Bettmann. 357 Reuters/Corbis/ Bettmann. **CHAPTER SEVENTEEN:** 360-361 Currie Ballard. 362 OHS. 363 OHS. 364 (both) Currie Ballard. 365 Currie Ballard. 366 (both) Currie Ballard. 367 (both) Currie Ballard. 368 Corbis/Bettmann. 369 Corbis/Bettmann. 370 Robin McDonald. 371 OHS. 372 Billy Barnes. 373 Corbis/ Bettmann. 374 (both) OHS. 375 Robin McDonald. 376 Robin McDonald. 377 OHS. 378 (above) OHS, (left) Corbis/Bettmann. 379 (top) Corbis/Bettmann, (above) NASA. 380-381 Robin McDonald. 382 Corbis/Bettmann. 383 OHS. **CHAPTER EIGHTEEN:** 386-387 Don Sibley/ Metropolitan Tulsa Chamber of Commerce. 389 Duncan Convention and Tourism. 390 Robin McDonald. 391 Robin McDonald. 392 Robin McDonald. 393 Robin McDonald. 394 Corbis/Bettmann. 395 (top) Oklahoma Medical Research Foundation, (above) The Cooper Aerobics Center, Dallas, Texas. 396 Robin McDonald. 397 Robin McDonald. 398 Robin McDonald. 399 David G. Fitzgerald. **CHAPTER NINETEEN:** 402-403 Corbis/Bettmann. 404 Corbis/ Bettmann. 405 Corbis/Bettmann. 406 Corbis/Bettmann. 407 OHS. 408 Corbis/Bettmann. 409 Chester R. Cowan/OHS. 410 Corbis/Bettmann. 411 (left and below right) Corbis/ Bettmann, (above right) OHS. 412 Corbis/Bettmann. 413 Corbis/Bettmann. 414 (both) Corbis/Bettmann. 415 (all) Corbis/Bettmann. 416 Robin McDonald. 417 OHS. 418 Corbis/Bettmann. 419 OHS. 420 (above) OHS, (below) Corbis/Bettmann. 421 Corbis/Bettmann.